Legal Reelism

EDITED BY JOHN DENVIR

Legal Reelism

MOVIES AS LEGAL TEXTS

UNIVERSITY OF ILLINOIS PRESS · URBANA AND CHICAGO

This book is printed on acid-free paper.

Library of Congress Cataloging-in-Publication Data
Legal reelism : movies as legal texts / edited by John Denvir.
p.   cm.
Includes bibliographical references and index.
ISBN 0-252-02231-9 (cloth : acid-free paper). —
ISBN 0-252-06535-2 (pbk. : acid-free paper)
1. Justice, Administration of, in motion pictures. 2. Motion pictures—
Moral and ethical aspects. 3. Motion pictures—Social aspects.
I. Denvir, John, 1942– .
PN1995.9.J8L45   1996
791.43'655—dc20   95-32511
CIP

For Maxine

Contents

Acknowledgments

I would like to thank David Papke, who gave support to the idea for this book when it was only that, an idea. I would also like to thank my friend and colleague, Peter Honigsberg, who provided practical help at a time when such help was essential. And I would like to thank my wife, Maxine Auerbach, who was always enthusiastic about the project, even when she had more pressing matters on her mind.

Thanks also to the word processing staff at the University of San Francisco School of Law, especially Diane Marchesi, Karen Chaney, Kathleen Allenbach, and Helen Sigua for their competent work on the manuscript.

—J.D.

Introduction

JOHN DENVIR

I believe we can learn a great deal about law from watching movies. This insight came to me as a by-product of my stint as a volunteer film reviewer for our law school newspaper. Writing those reviews profoundly changed my perspective on film *and* law. I discovered that serious viewing of a commercial film often challenged my views on legal questions that until then I had found routine. For instance, I had always been a rather doctrinaire defender of freedom of the press, quite intolerant of Supreme Court decisions cutting back on First Amendment immunity for newspapers against defamation actions by private individuals.[1] This cavalier libertarianism received quite a jolt when I watched Fred Schepisi's *A Cry in the Dark;* Meryl Streep's portrayal of a mother falsely accused of murdering her child gave flesh and blood content to the abstract proposition that false statements can do harm to an individual's reputation. The concreteness and immediacy of the film's portrayal of the human suffering caused by predatory journalistic practices engaged my emotions in a way legal analysis of the issue had not. And yet I had to admit that the emotions provoked had not clouded my reason; they had deepened my understanding of how a difficult clash of constitutional values involves people as well as principles.

Since I found my own reactions to theoretical issues deepened by the study of film, I decided to experiment by incorporating film into my seminar on legal theory. In addition to viewing films, the class read novels and plays as well as more traditional jurisprudential texts. Once again I was surprised by the results; time and again the most stimulating class discussions came after viewing films. I clearly remember my astonishment when, during a class discussion of John Ford's *The Man Who Shot Liberty Valance* (the subject matter of Cheyney Ryan's essay in this volume), several students confessed that John Wayne's incarnation of righteous violence was the first inspiring symbol of justice they had encountered in law school. I suddenly recognized that movies reflect powerful myths that influence our reactions to issues we meet in real life, including legal issues; perhaps the "rule of law" is best viewed as one more myth competing for audience acceptance.

I noted another interesting fact; a democratic ethos enveloped the room when we discussed movies. Students who would mutely accept my conclusions about the value of works by traditional scholars, such as John Rawls or Ronald Dworkin, showed no such deference to my views on *A Touch of Evil* or *Adam's Rib.* Viewing a film seemed to level the intellectual playing field. In fact, it did more than merely level it; the students were more visually adept in absorbing a film than their professor, a relic from the print era.

The book's title argues that we can study movies as "legal texts." How can films be "legal texts"? Of course films are dissimilar from the normal legal trilogy of constitutions, codes, and cases in that they are not primarily produced with an eye to the resolution of legal disputes; but there are also similarities between films and the traditional legal canon. For instance, like other more traditional legal sources, they are cultural artifacts open to warring interpretations both on the descriptive and normative level. Just as a street map of Los Angeles, a David Hockney painting, and a Beach Boys song all are "texts" that can teach us something, different things, about Southern California, law reports and *The Godfather* (the topic of David Papke's essay in this volume) both tell us something, different things, about the "rule of law." Just as no one would claim that the street map told the whole story, neither should we think that worthwhile insights on law are all contained in law libraries. For instance, my own contribution to the volume, "Capra's Constitution," argues that Frank Capra's film, *It's a Wonderful Life,* provides an important complement, or perhaps antidote, to Chief Justice William Rehnquist's legal discussion of the reciprocal duties we owe each other as citizens. Not only do both "texts" treat the difficult legal issue of the claims of community, Capra's treatment brings out an emotional ambivalence toward community that Rehnquist's legal prose ignores.

In this respect, it is important to note that the essays that follow do not pretend to be "film criticism" in any technical sense; they are essays by nonspecialists in film that use film as a tool to get better purchase on their study of how law operates in the larger culture.

I admit that I am drawn by the irony of the fact that these disposable artifacts intended for the momentary entertainment of the masses have an important role to play in serious academic study of law and justice. But I think there is more than irony involved here; this situation also illustrates that the category "legal" is increasingly porous, signifying a symbiosis between law and popular culture that students of law can no longer afford to ignore. "Law" is no longer a concept limited to the law reports; it is a consciousness that permeates American culture.

The fourteen essays included cover a wide variety of film genres; westerns, gangster films, foreign classics, contemporary comedies, and sex thrillers are all represented. In fact, the one type of film that might be considered underrepresented is the "courtroom drama." One might expect a book on law and film to concentrate on movies like *Twelve Angry Men* or *Judgment at Nuremberg,* but actually only the essays by Mark Tushnet and Norman Rosenberg discuss movies that might be considered of the "courtroom" genre, and even then, Rosenberg's essay is more concerned with cinematic technique and Tushnet's with sexual politics than courtroom histrionics. This, I think, is additional evidence of the pluralism that has broken law from its narrow institutional bindings, allowing it to spill out into the larger culture, reflecting and creating that culture.

I believe the volume's variety of subject matter coexists with a larger commonality of political perspective toward law, legal institutions, and questions of justice. These essays echo concerns about law and legal institutions first raised by the "Legal Realist" school of jurisprudence in the 1920s and 1930s. The "realist" approach to law was deepened by the Critical Legal Studies Movement (CLS) of the 1980s and stretches forward to include current feminist and minority critiques of law.

This Realist tradition includes both a "critical" and a "utopian" orientation. In its purely critical mode, the Realist tradition attempts to show that the "rule of law" rhetoric of orthodox legal discourse often operates to mask the arbitrary political power wielded by judges and other state legal actors.[2] Alongside this "deconstructive" side of the Realist tradition is a less well-known utopian enterprise in which Realist writers have attempted to reimagine law, to adumbrate a vision of what legal institutions might look like in a just society.[3] The present essays also exhibit both critical and utopian orientations; some of the essays combine the two approaches.

David Ray Papke's essay on Francis Ford Coppola's Godfather trilogy exposes a hidden aspect of one of the 1970s' most popular films. He shows that Coppola actually had a jurisprudential purpose in making this mafia melodrama; he wished to undermine the platitude that America is a "nation of laws, not of men" by showing that in a microcosm of American society the charismatic authority of the mafia "Don" silences any appeal to legality. But, Papke points out, Coppola's attempt to demystify the "rule of law" fed his audience's appetite for another powerful American myth, the myth of regenerative violence. The audience was not so outraged by the Mafia's disregard for democratic legal process as enthralled by a community that was able to combine social solidarity with an efficient brutality. In so doing, Papke allows the film (and its reception) to show us aspects of the relationship between law and justice that traditional legal materials ignore.

Cheyney Ryan's essay on John Ford's *The Man Who Shot Liberty Valance* complements Papke's analysis of the relationship between law and violence. *Liberty Valance* depicts the interplay between Lee Marvin as a violent outlaw, Jimmy Stewart as a neophyte lawyer, and John Wayne as a laconic, but deadly, Western hero. Stewart, the representative of the emerging legal order, finds himself powerless before Marvin's malevolent violence; he only vanquishes Marvin with the covert help of Wayne's heroic violence. Thus, law itself is the product of violence, but a violence that the myth of the rule of law refuses to recognize. This "misrecognition," Ryan argues, not only erases the heroic presence of Wayne's natural aristocrat, but also compromises the legitimacy of the legal order so created and the moral integrity of its representative, the lawyer.

Francis Nevins's contribution makes clear that film meditations on the relationship between law and violence are not limited to "classic" Westerns made by famous directors like Ford. Nevins takes as his "text" three "sixty-minute westerns" made in the 1930s, films he describes as made by people with little money for viewers with even less. Nevins uses these films to tease out the popular image of lawyers and law during the Depression, and his discussion reinforces Cheyney Ryan's conclusions about *The Man Who Shot Liberty Valance*—legal rules are an empty shell unless backed up by righteous violence. In fact, in one of these almost forgotten films, *King of the Pecos* (1936), a young John Wayne creates the classic role he reprised twenty-five years later in *Liberty Valance*.

The essays by Ryan and Nevins undermine the "rule of law" by emphasizing the role of violence in legal dealings. Richard Sherwin attacks from another direction, putting in issue law's claim to rationality. Sherwin uses three contemporary films involving the common theme of homicide to question the very concepts of rational motivation and causality that underpin the criminal law. For instance, he argues that Bobby Gold, the protagonist of David Mamet's *Homicide,* is just one more victim of fate. Bobby is a good man and a smart cop; yet his virtue and intelligence lead him to betray everything in which he believes. What future, Sherwin asks, awaits a system of criminal law based on concepts of rational motivation, objective causation, and personal responsibility when it enters into a postmodern world ruled by random chance?

Tom Conley grants a rationality to law, but a perverse rationality that has little to do with traditional concepts of justice. Conley contends that Jean Renoir's *Rules of the Game* (*La Règle du jeu*) illustrates Michel Foucault's thesis that law is best viewed as a discursive practice that organizes social experience to fabricate the categories of legal and illegal. The operative code defines the same physical activity as privilege for one class and as punishable offense for another. For instance, shooting rabbits is aristocratic sport for the rich in *Rules of the Game,* but criminal poaching for the poor. Conley then argues that Renoir's film makes a parallel point about cinema; just as the law creates the criminal, cinema technique creates its audience by organizing our perceptions of sight and sound into a seemingly timeless narrative.

Imagining utopian alternatives to the status quo is a more difficult task than criticism of what already exists. For this reason, we perhaps should not be surprised that most theoretical prescriptions for the future turn out to be either tepid small-scale reforms of the status quo or maddeningly abstract blueprints for utopias with little connection to reality. Hollywood's attempts at depicting utopia suffer from similar weaknesses. Either we have the "band-aid" solution of films like *Sullivan's Travels,* which seems to argue that watching a good Hollywood comedy is the best answer to the social ills facing humanity, or the presentation of a prepackaged utopia that only replicates existing social institutions in an allegedly more exotic setting; Frank Capra's Buddhist lamasery in *Lost Horizons* bears a painful resemblance to a Southern California retirement home. The same ability to deliver concrete "reality" that so aids film in its attempts at critique subverts its ventures at envisioning utopias. Still, many feel that movies can play an important part in attempts to create a more just society by showing "traces" of the just world we long for.

For instance, my essay "Capra's Constitution" attempts to show how study of a film, *It's a Wonderful Life,* can generate insights important to the consideration of a vexing constitutional issue: whether or not the Constitution imposes an affirmative duty on the state to take affirmative action to aid its least fortunate citizens. I contend that Capra's film can dramatically alter our approach to what heretofore has been considered a bloodless legal issue. Simply stated, comparing Capra's movie with a Supreme Court opinion shows us that constitutional law can be more than a rule book to be applied, but rather an opportunity to confront on a concrete level how American democracy will respond to human suffering.

Anthony Chase's essay shows film's capacity to open up our discussions of legal issues to alternative conceptions of justice. Chase examines how "popular justice" is presented in Jean Renoir's *The Crime of Monsieur Lange* (*Le Crime de M. Lange*). He shows how Renoir uses both traditional narrative and unusual cinematic devices to argue that informal democratic legal procedures are morally superior to conventional images of due process of law.

Judith Grant's essay on Woody Allen's *Crimes and Misdemeanors* raises what might be the ultimate jurisprudential issue: Is there some moral vision supporting contemporary legal systems that differentiates them from regimes of brute force? Allen's film addresses the question of whether morality (and therefore justice) is possible in an godless world. Grant finds that Allen's film refuses to give a satisfactory answer to this question, but his reticence provokes her own reflections on the possibility of constructing an existentialist democratic political morality.

Movies often uncover aspects of law that traditional legal sources deny; but film not only "reveals" law, it often creates the social reality to which legal institutions adapt. Therefore, film must be more than a tool of critique; sometimes it must also be its object.

Margaret Russell opens this "interrogation" by pointing out all the ways in which Hollywood myths about race shape our public discourse and, ultimately, our images of ourselves. Russell argues that this hegemonic potential requires that the viewer never passively absorb a film, but must "talk back" to the screen, both exposing its unarticulated assumptions and questioning their validity. Russell "talks back" to the iconoclastic African-American director, Spike Lee. Russell praises Lee's portrayal of racial polarities in *Do the Right Thing*, but questions the film's thin depiction of gender relations.

Terry Wilson's essay extends Russell's critique by "talking back" to Hollywood images of the Native American. Wilson's essay demonstrates how John Ford's *Drums along the Mohawk* "constructs" the "uncivilized red savage," a popular distortion of historical fact that has been used to justify so much white savagery toward Native Americans.

Andrew McKenna continues the critique of film ideologies in his discussion of the "sex thriller." McKenna argues that films like *The Silence of the Lambs* project the audience's attraction to sex and violence onto outsiders like transsexuals who are then destroyed in the final scene, thus purging the audience's violent fantasies and reinforcing traditional sexual mores.

Mark Tushnet's essay continues McKenna's examination of Hollywood's sexual politics. Tushnet uses *Class Action* as a vehicle to expose Hollywood's covert advocacy of patriarchal sexual roles. Tushnet argues that what on the surface appears to be "liberal" courtroom drama in which a father and daughter lawyer team vanquish a greedy corporate malefactor actually transmits a more traditional message: "father knows best."

Russell, Wilson, McKenna, and Tushnet all speak of the cinematic construction of "conservative" or "reactionary" identities for minority groups, but film can also offer images of minorities that undermine the status quo. Elizabeth Spelman and Martha Minow argue that the female "buddy" movie, *Thelma and Louise*, illustrates this anti-hegemonic function in showing how a fatal encounter at a bar transforms two working-class women into noble outlaws worthy of a tragic fate.

Up to this point the essays have focused on the substance of ideologies advocated by Hollywood films. In his essay, Norman Rosenberg changes terms of critical inquiry. Rosenberg analyzes "how" film works as opposed to the ideological conclusions a specific film may support. He proceeds by analyzing two examples of what he calls the *law noir* genre, films that revolve around the issue of the justice system's capacity to actually deliver justice to its citizenry. One such film, *Call Northside 777,* endorses a negative answer; it is only the heroic efforts of a newspaper reporter that prevent the legal process from punishing an innocent man. In *Knock on Any Door,* an opposite conclusion is reached that supports the thesis that traditional legal procedures are our surest means of achieving justice. But, for Rosenberg, the key point is how a filmmaker, much like a lawyer marshaling precedents, uses lighting, camera angles, mise-en-scène, and other cinematic devices to create what might be called a "visual brief" to support his or her chosen ideological position.

While I hope the foregoing summary gives the reader some sense of the overall shape of the volume, emphasizing the presence of common concerns and themes in essays that cover a startling diversity of films and approaches to law, I believe that the greatest strength of the book lies in the individual essays themselves. I urge the reader to engage each essay in its full particularity.

One good norm by which to judge the worth of a book is whether it changes how you think. It is my firm hope and sincere belief that the reader of these essays will never again view law, or "movies," quite the same.

Notes

1. *Gertz v. Robert Welch, Inc.,* 418 U.S. 323 (1974).
2. See Gary Peller, "The Metaphysics of American Law," *California Law Review* 73 (July 1985): 1226–40.
3. William Singer, "Legal Realism Now" (book review), *California Law Review* 76 (Mar. 1985): 539.

ONE

Myth and Meaning

Francis Ford Coppola and Popular Response
to the Godfather Trilogy

DAVID RAY PAPKE

■

I always wanted to use the Mafia as a metaphor for America.

FRANCIS FORD COPPOLA

Playing alongside and behind the fascinating stories of the Godfather trilogy is another story of director Francis Ford Coppola and his audience. In this latter story Coppola, despite making three highly acclaimed films over ten hours in combined length, experienced frustration. Coppola's audience, it seemed to him, did not share his sense of the Godfather films' messages, sentiments, and intimations. Viewers did not respond to the films the way he thought they should.

A product of a film school background, Coppola fancied himself a cinematic demythologizer. He appreciated the tendency of the Hollywood films to reinforce reigning myths,[1] but he did not place himself among the likes of Frank Capra, Michael Curtiz, John Ford, Howard Hawks, and Raoul Walsh, directors inclined to dramatize positively the nation's history, ideology, and consciousness. He looked instead to directors such as Orson Welles and to a smaller counter-tradition determined to expose societal falsehoods.[2] In particular, Coppola was determined to challenge the mythic understanding of the United States as a pluralistic society living by a rule of law and serving as a model for the rest of the world. He proffered as a symbol for America the lawless and criminal Corleones, a family headed first by the father Vito and then by his son Michael.

However, Coppola's viewers were themselves not necessarily demythologizers. Many enjoyed and interpreted the Godfather films with reference rather than in opposition to American myths. Strengthened by decades of persistent retelling and complexly interwoven, American myths provided a context in which viewers could find meaning in the films. When Coppola realized these meanings did not coincide with what he understood as the critical message of *The Godfather* (1972), he refined and accentuated his message in *The Godfather, Part II* (1974) and then melded it with his own trials and tribulations in *The Godfather, Part III* (1990). Viewers, meanwhile, continued to find in the films more than the demythologizing messages Coppola so doggedly promoted.

This essay critically explores the symbolic story of the lawless Corleones as prototypically American, but also emphasizes the related story of Francis Ford Coppola and the popular response to his work. This latter story illustrates the reception or response theory initially developed in literary studies and in recent years widely employed in mass cultural studies.[3] Writers and directors cannot simply dictate the ways in which their works are to be received. Coppola, in the end, was unable through the Godfather films to expose the falsehood of American legalism and to tear the mythic fabric with his critical messages. Within this story of a director and his audience lurks a lesson for anyone inclined to use film as sociolegal criticism or, more generally, to pursue the interdisciplinary study of law and film.

■

While this account of Coppola and the Godfather films will on occasion treat the director as what one scholar has called the "Hollywood auteur,"[4] creative work on the extended project began not with Coppola but rather with the novelist Mario Puzo. While Coppola subsequently struggled to create a serious, artistic work, Puzo admittedly had crasser goals: profit and fame. Disappointed by the lack of respect accorded his earlier works, Puzo consciously attempted to write a bestseller. He crafted tabloid-style peeks at the ways of the Mafia, thinly veiled portrayals of actual celebrities such as Frank Sinatra, and healthy doses of ribald and illicit sex. Puzo succeeded in his efforts, and *The Godfather* sat prominently at the top of best-seller lists during the final months of 1969 and the first months of 1970.[5]

As one reviewer noted, the novel had "instant celluloid currency."[6] Paramount Pictures won the active bidding war for film rights but did not think first of Coppola as the director. Paramount offered the film to Peter Yates, Constantin Costa-Gavras, and Richard Brooks, all of whom declined. Coppola then surfaced as a possibility. His screenplays for *Is Paris Burning?* (1966), *This Property Is Condemned* (1966), and *Patton* (1970) had won praise, and he had competently directed *You're a Big Boy Now* (1967), *Finian's Rainbow* (1968), and *The Rain People* (1969). Equally important to the Paramount bosses who offered Coppola *The Godfather* was his heritage. An Italian novelist had made the book a success; perhaps an Italian director would bring the film to life.[7]

Coppola was quite respectful of Puzo, but he also set out to reshape the core story. He fashioned it as a period piece taking place in the decade following World War II rather than as a tale of the present. He gave greater depth to the Corleone brothers and removed some of the novel's trashier elements, not the least of which was a subplot concerning Sonny Corleone's monstrously large genitals.[8] Coppola also cut a sardonic line from Don Corleone that, although minor, has over the years been frequently quoted in law school corridors: "A lawyer with his briefcase can steal more than a hundred men with guns."[9] Most importantly, Coppola determined to alter the overall theme of the work, to use the Corleones to symbolize the essence and decline of America. In interviews Coppola repeatedly called attention to his intended symbolism, seeming at times almost desperate to legitimize what he feared others would regard a cheap and sensationalist film.[10] As a result of the film's success, Coppola would acquire even greater creative control of subsequent films, but even with *The Godfather* his efforts as screenwriter/director made him the film's primary imaginative force. In the opinion of Robert Duvall, who played Tom Hagen, the Corleone's adopted son and "consigliore," Coppola deserved full credit for the film, and the film would have been even better if he had possessed truly complete control.[11]

Coppola presents his extended metaphor for the ruthless and predatory aspects of capitalist America in what might be thought of as four cinematic "acts." The first begins with a twenty-six-minute sequence at the marriage of Don Corleone's only daughter Connie to Carlo Rizzi. While the excessive celebration sprawls about an outdoor garden, the Don himself is ensconced in a shadowy study entertaining well wishers and granting requests for favors. Michael Corleone, the youngest son, an Ivy League student and newly returned World War II veteran, appears at the wedding with Kay Adams, his Waspy girlfriend from New

Hampshire, but he does not participate in the darker, interior world of Corleone business. "That's my family, Kay," Michael says soberly. "It's not me." The act concludes with a more detailed portrayal of how the fictive Mafia operates. Tom Hagen journeys to Hollywood in hopes of convincing Jack Woltz, a studio head, to give a prime role in a film to Johnny Fontaine, the Don's godson. When Woltz initially refuses, he finds a surprise under his morning sheets: the severed and bloody head of his $600,000 racehorse. A change of heart presumably follows.

The second act begins with a Corleone family strategy meeting and explores in subsequent scenes the conflict over the drug business between the Corleones and their allies on the one side and Barzini, the Tattaglias, and Virgil Salozzo on the other. The latter seem at first the aggressors, given the strangling of Corleone hit man Luca Brazzi, the kidnapping of Tom Hagen, and—most significantly—an attempt to assassinate Don Corleone. However, at the end of the act Michael Corleone, having been drawn hesitantly and painfully into the Corleone business, shoots Salozzo and a corrupt policeman named McCluskey in the head over dinner in a small family restaurant. Horrifying as Michael's murders might be, they register as an example of the tolerable revenge slayings that Andrew McKenna notes have been part of Western drama since at least the Renaissance.[12]

In the third act, largely a transitional one carrying the viewer from the brutality of act two to that of act four, Michael Corleone is sent to Sicily while Sonny Corleone, the oldest son, temporarily assumes leadership of the Corleone family and its business. In Sicily Michael courts and marries a beautiful girl-woman, only to see her killed by a bomb that had been intended for him. In New York, Sonny attempts to protect his sister Connie from Carlo's beatings, efforts that prove even more violent than the precipitating domestic violence. When the Tattaglias realize the irrational recklessness of Sonny's determination to brutalize Carlo, they resourcefully use Carlo to set up and kill Sonny.[13]

In the final act the reins of the Corleone family pass from the Don to Michael. The Don arranges a gangland peace that allows Michael to return safely from Sicily, Michael marries Kay, the Corleones become involved in Las Vegas gambling, and the Don dies and is buried. In the film's climactic violence, Michael simultaneously becomes the literal Godfather at the baptism of Connie and Carlo's son and the figurative Godfather by killing the family's five chief enemies. The baptismal ritual in this amazing cinematic montage masks the violent brutality of the slayings.[14] The film then ends with Michael lying to Kay about his role in Carlo's murder and receiving recognition from various henchmen as the new "Don Corleone."

In all four acts Coppola featured the Corleone family in at least three ways, the second and third of which were increasingly symbolic and suggestive of the ultimate message he hoped to convey regarding the lawlessness of America. On the most literal and least interesting level there are the Corleones themselves, an Italian-American family that has pulled itself up by its bootstraps and maintains an intense connectedness among family members. Gender roles are traditional, sibling loyalties and rivalries are manifest, and elaborate weddings, baptisms, and funerals preserve family solidarity. On a second level, the Corleones are a Mafia family, an underworld syndicate whose "business" is criminal—extortion, loan-sharking, gambling, manipulation of the unions, and, ultimately, what Don Corleone refers distastefully to as "narcotics." Due to complaints from the Italian-American Civil Rights League and threatened boycotts and walkouts, Coppola, at Paramount's urging, left any formal reference to the Mafia or Cosa Nostra out of the screenplay,[15] but there was no ambiguity about the Corleone family's criminal activity and profit-making illegality.[16] On a third level, at least in Coppola's mind, the story of the Corleones symbolized the demythologized story of America. Young Vito Corleone may have dreamed of a special America, of a city on the hill where happiness and prosperity reign, but he made his fortune instead through aggressive business practices, strong-armed bullying, and—when push came to shove—fierce violence.[17] The Don hoped at least to free Michael for a better, more legitimate life—perhaps as a senator or governor—but Michael, as the true American native son, stumbled eventually into the family business. In the end, like the country he is intended to symbolize, Michael's criminality and his bullying dishonesty are increasingly cold, efficient, and corporate.

The third level of meaning, Coppola announced for those willing to listen, was the level that interested him most. In the two years immediately before the filming of *The Godfather*, Coppola had struggled desperately to develop a production center for younger filmmakers who wanted to work outside of the Hollywood mainstream. Warner Brothers had agreed to supply financial backing and distribution assistance, but when Coppola's *The Rain People* and other youth movies failed at the box office, backing disappeared. Coppola's San Francisco-based American Zoetrope wallowed in a pool of debt, and Coppola felt denied, restricted, and manipulated by the American corporate structure.

The Corleones were his symbol. Violent, criminal lawbreakers, they symbolized the nation's wayward ways and lack of moral vision. In Coppola's own words:

> It became clear to me that there was a wonderful parallel to be drawn, that the career of Michael Corleone was the perfect metaphor for the new land. Like America, Michael began as a clean, brilliant young man endowed with incredible resources and believing in a humanistic idealism. Like America, Michael was a child of an older system, a child of Europe. Like America, Michael was an innocent who had tried to correct the ills and injustices of his progenitors. But then he got blood on his hands. He lied to himself and others about what he was doing and why. And so he became not only the mirror image of what he'd come from but worse.[18]

When the film was released in March 1972 its commercial success was immense. Ticket sales totaled over $26 million nationwide during the first month alone.[19] On Oscar night in 1973 Marlon Brando won the Academy Award for Best Actor, and *The Godfather* itself won the Award for Best Picture. Indeed, even the Mafia liked the film. According to anonymous reports, the old-fashioned and largely abandoned custom of kissing the hands of powerful Mafia leaders revived because of its portrayal in the film.[20]

What explained the tremendous popularity of the film? Admitting that film audiences are opaque and that different sectors of the audience find different aspects of a film engaging, it seems safe at least to assume that Coppola's favored theme was not the key. Little discussion was heard of the theme, and one of the few critics who even picked up on the corporate capitalism symbolism dismissed it as "high-school" analogizing.[21] Coppola may have attempted to present the Mafia and Michael as symbols of America and thereby indict the latter for its violent, increasingly corporate criminality, but this theme seems to have gone virtually unrecognized in the nation's movie houses.

The would-be demythologizer had instead made a film coordinated with American myths adjacent to those involving lawfulness and commitment to a rule of law. *The Godfather,* in this regard, valorized the mythic family and the legend of the self-made man. The Corleones in their walled compound may for Coppola have been distastefully similar to the Kennedys at Hyannisport,[22] but for many viewers the portrayal of the Corleones was a celebration of family. The images of family rituals,

Francis Ford Coppola intended *The Godfather* to show that Michael Corleone
(Al Pacino) acts more like a corporate criminal than a democratic citizen,
but audiences received a different message. (Courtesy of
the Academy of Motion Picture Arts and Sciences.)

meals, and connectedness suggested a refuge from the cold and indifferent modern society. The Corleones were a symbolic American mini-community in a rootless, isolating epoch, and the film allegedly contributed to the surge of interest during the 1970s in family genealogy.[23]

As for the self-made man—the Horatio Alger myth that has long been powerful in American life and thought—Vito Corleone registered as a wonderful example. To be sure, the nature of his enterprise was illicit, but his life story illustrated the success possible in the United States for a man of drive and diligence. Poor, orphaned, and lacking a formal education, Vito Corleone had nevertheless fought his way to the top. Subsequent blockbusters such as *Rocky* (1976) and *Saturday Night Fever* (1977) also tapped into the American thirst for sagas of upward mobility.

Beyond a valorization of the family and the self-made man, *The Godfather* also appealed to audiences with its endorsement of authoritarian power as an alternative to legalism. The legal historian Lawrence Friedman has correctly noted the ways traditional forms of authority are in decline in American society while law is emerging and expanding as a kind of replacement;[24] invoking the much repeated phrase of Jürgen Habermas, Friedman has pointed to the "colonization" of American life by law.[25] However, many Americans are highly skeptical of this trend and the slow, unreliable, and burgeoning legal system. *The Godfather* speaks to and for this skepticism by presenting law and legal institutions as hopelessly biased: police are on the take, judges are in the Mafia's pocket, and family lawyers make offers that cannot be refused. More appealing is the face-to-face authority of Don Corleone. He relieves disappointment, reestablishes social order, and provides justice of a kind.

The fact that deception and violence are often the Don's essential handmaidens need not abrogate his appeal. Indeed, there is a long tradition in American life and popular culture of violence taking on a "moral necessity."[26] In another essay in this volume, Cheyney Ryan points out the ways "honorable violence" is especially prevalent, albeit with varying degrees of problematization, in the western as film genre (see chap. 2). *The Godfather,* still others have observed, echoes the western in this regard.[27]

The film's violence has troubled some. Nicholas Gage noted that, "The only interruptions to the scenes of carnage are scenes of eating and family festivities." Gage also described screenings at which viewers murmured with satisfaction at the various killings and praised the aesthetics of bloody murders.[28] Distinguished critics Pauline Kael and Leslie Fiedler addressed the meeting of the Modern Language Association in December 1972 and expressed uneasiness about what the popularity of *The Godfather* suggested about American society. Kael, in particular, noted the authoritarian violence of the film and argued that in the context of the Vietnam experience Americans had become willing to recognize and cheer on their own brutality.[29]

Kael's attempt to link the popularity of *The Godfather* to the Vietnam debacle might be challenged, but the popular success of the film cannot be doubted. Within two years of its release the film had earned more money than any film in the history of the cinema.[30] Inspired by the film's success, Hollywood launched a whole flotilla of comparable "blockbusters," each lengthy, placed in a period setting, full of stars, and backed by extraordinary budgets.[31] But ironically, at least vis-à-vis Coppola's professed goals, the popularity and film industry ramifications of *The Godfather* were more conservative than critical in character. While professedly imbued by a demythologizing ethic, Coppola found success with *The Godfather* because of the film's resonance with American myths.

■

When the idea that he direct a sequel to *The Godfather* first surfaced, Francis Ford Coppola expressed disdain. "I used to joke that the only way I'd do it was if they'd let me film *Abbott and Costello Meet the Godfather*," he said.[32] But as the magnitude and the nature of the public's response to *The Godfather* became clear, he changed his mind. "I was disturbed that people thought I had romanticized Michael," Coppola said, "when I felt I had presented him as a monster at the end of *The Godfather*."[33] The sequel seemed an opportunity to refine and underscore his demythologizing message about the fundamental lawlessness of America.

Another type of auteur might have been less attracted to this type of undertaking. The Spanish director Luis Buñuel, for example, whose thirty-two films gave him as much claim to auteur status as anyone, felt no need to rivet the meaning of his work. He appreciated the variable ways a film might be interpreted and enjoyed the open-ended adventure of popular response: "I make a film and then set it free. . . . If you see the film differently from how I made it, that's all right. I would even accept that your vision is better."[34] Coppola, by contrast, was disappointed when viewers took from his work a meaning other than the one he intended. "I felt that *The Godfather* had never been finished; morally, I believed that the Family would be destroyed, and it would be a kind of *Götterdämmerung*," he said. "I thought it would be interesting to juxtapose the decline of the Family with the ascension of the Family; to show that as the young Vito Corleone is building this thing out of America, his son is presiding over its destruction."[35]

Paramount, of course, hardly had to be convinced that a sequel was desirable or that Coppola was the person to direct it. The company owned rights to all of Mario Puzo's *The Godfather* and wanted to film huge sections of the novel that had not been used in the first film. Even before releasing *The Godfather* to the general public, the company had hired Puzo to begin work on a second screenplay. When the film then reset the standards for commercial success,[36] tentative plans for a second film quickly transformed themselves into casting decisions and filming dates.

While Coppola had to struggle for control of the first film, he had things firmly in hand the second time around. On paper, Mario Puzo served as co-screenwriter, and hoping to draw on Puzo's continuing public recognition, Paramount formally titled the film *Mario Puzo's The Godfather, Part II*.[37] However, Puzo's involvement ended when he delivered a first draft of the screenplay. Coppola then worked on the screenplay for well over a year, deleting all of the Marlon Brando scenes when, after a tiff between Brando and Paramount head Frank Yablans, Brando refused to participate in the second movie.[38] Coppola also rewrote and restructured the screenplay extensively after Al Pacino announced before shooting that he hated the script. In addition, Coppola put off many of the important storytelling decisions until the editing stage, actually assembling the story only shortly before its release. This brinkmanship caused the studio, the actors, and even members of Coppola's family great anxiety, but for better or worse, Coppola, the Hollywood auteur, was to have a film he could call his own.

Coppola's overarching plan was to shape his material into two narratives that would ultimately interact with one another. One narrative concerned the young Vito Corleone, his Sicilian youth, and his success as a sort of Robin Hood/Horatio Alger figure on New York's Lower East Side in the early twentieth century. The second concerned Vito's son Michael and his criminal activities and family difficulties in the present. Both stories were to end with the two major characters at roughly the same age violently addressing earlier betrayals. In one case Vito, played by Robert DeNiro, returns to Italy to kill the village chieftain who had murdered his family, while in the other Michael, again played by Al Pacino, has henchmen murder his rivals and disloyal brother Fredo. Coppola even settled on visual and aural devices that would distinguish the intercut narratives. Vito's narrative was filmed in warm, sepia tones, and often used English subtitles for the musical Sicilian dialogue; Michael's narrative was shot in cold, crisper tones with the characters largely speaking proper English.

Coppola's close friend George Lucas viewed a preliminary version of the movie, concluded that the double narrative approach did not work, and urged Coppola to abandon one narrative or the other.[39] Coppola declined and remained committed to his vision, even predicting correctly that the double narrative would prove the film's greatest strength.[40] The two narratives gave the film a grander historical sweep, with the first constituting something of a prologue to *The Godfather* and the second being the true sequel. Given the cross-cutting between the two narratives, individual scenes in one narrative could be used to underscore or contrast with scenes in the other. More importantly for purposes of Coppola's professed assault on American myth and contentment, the double narrative afforded a way to capture what he took to be the nation's disastrous devolution; he could accentuate his symbolic message through the shifting tones of the two narratives.

Both narratives are rife with images of lawbreaking, many of which are violent, but Coppola presented Vito Corleone more sympathetically than his son Michael. In the initial scenes introducing the young Vito Corleone, for example, audience sympathy for the character is blatantly solicited. In 1901 a Sicilian Mafia chieftain murders Vito's father because of an insult and then also murders Vito's older brother on the very day of the father's funeral. When Vito's mother goes to the chieftain to plead for Vito's life, the chieftain kills Vito's mother as well. Having witnessed at least the second and third killings, Vito is dispensed to America at the still tender age of nine. The Statue of Liberty looms tall and impressive over the ships of immigrants steaming into the New York harbor, but poor Vito spends his first three months in America in cell-like quarantine for smallpox. Eventually Vito settles in New York's Little Italy, marries, works diligently as a grocery store clerk, and starts his family.

When relatively early in the narrative Vito befriends Clemenza, another young Italian immigrant, he begins to engage in criminal activity. The two profit from minor burglaries, the only example of which viewers see is the comical theft of a carpet from a palatial home. More distressing and violent is Vito's killing of Don Fanucci, an extortionist and local "Black Hand" boss, but even here the lawbreaking seems almost justified. Fanucci was himself brutish, and several scenes had shown him arrogantly exploiting humble Italian immigrants. A pattern of Corleone lawbreaking has been established, but the viewer is invited through most of Vito's narrative to stand on Vito's side. After the Fanucci murder, a warm and lyrical shot shows Vito sitting with his wife on a stoop, talking in Sicilian dialect, and playing with his new baby, Michael. Only in the conclusion of Vito's narrative does sympathy break down. Vito, now a man in his mid-twenties, returns to Sicily to kill the Mafia chieftain who had killed his parents and brother. The murder, some might feel, was the type of justifiable revenge killing seen earlier in *The Godfather,* but for viewers the revenge is less sweet than it is sudden and graphic, amounting to a virtual evisceration.

The major reason for the sympathetic presentation of young Vito Corleone, as suggested, is a hoped for contrast with his more distressingly criminal son Michael, a contrast central in Coppola's tale of symbolic America gone astray. While most of Vito's crime seems benign and almost natural for an ambitious immigrant on the economic make, Michael's crime is another matter. It seems truly greedy and corrupt, and it blends fully into the ways and means of a greedy and corrupt nation. Michael's Mafia, we are invited to understand, *is* America.

Michael's narrative begins and ends at the Lake Tahoe estate to which he has moved the family after taking control of several Nevada casinos. At the opening communion celebration for his son Anthony in 1956— the type of family gathering for which Coppola invariably shows a special delight—Michael contributes a hefty check to the University of Nevada, only to be told privately by Senator Geary that he finds Michael repulsive. "Senator," Michael responds, "we're both part of the same hypocrisy." The scene then shifts to Miami and to Havanna, where Michael and the mobster Hyman Roth are planning to take control of Cuban casinos and gambling. Their partners include not only the Cuban government but also the Teamsters, United Fruit, United Telephone and Telegraph, and Pan-American Mining—the symbolic representatives of a corrupt America. At a party celebrating his sixty-seventh birthday, Roth announces with glee that the business partnership is "bigger than the U.S. Steel." Flunkies serve a cake with a lit sparkler and the map of Cuba on it, and the hungry manipulators carve into the island nation.[41]

Unfortunately for the Mafioso and their corporate friends, Batista's government falls to Castro's revolutionary forces, and Michael finds himself before a Senate committee. Michael declares his love for the country, denies he is a criminal, and deftly silences a hostile witness by fetching the latter's brother from Sicily and displaying him menacingly. Back at Lake Tahoe, where Michael's henchmen look more like generic MBAs than Italian-American hustlers, Michael learns from Kay that her miscarriage had in fact been an abortion and slaps her cruelly. At the funeral for his mother, Michael entertains a request from his sister Connie to forgive their brother Fredo for his betrayals and goes so far as to feign a reconciliation. However, Fredo shortly becomes the victim of fratricide, as other enemies of Michael also simultaneously meet their maker. The Lake Tahoe scenes end with a chilling image of Michael—alone, evil, and staring both across the Lake and, presumably, into his internal abyss.

Overall, *The Godfather, Part II* has a more imaginative form and a more overt demythologizing thrust than the preceding film. Michael Corleone, in particular, was a type of demon haunting Coppola, the specter perhaps of the unthinking, powerful corporate executive who had destroyed his own hopes for a new kind of filmmaking.[42] "The career of Michael Corleone," Coppola said, "was the perfect metaphor for the new land."[43] Despite his father's illegal activities, Michael was initially innocent and idealistic, but his fall was Coppola's symbolic warning about America's direction and possible fate.[44]

The form and critical message contributed to *The Godfather, Part II*'s acclaim. Reviews in the most serious publications praised Coppola for his artistic success and seriousness of purpose, and the film's acting, cinematography, editing, and music also registered as exemplary accomplishments of their kind.[45] The film became the first sequel to join its cinematic progenitor in winning the Academy Award for Best Picture and Coppola received the Academy Award for Best Director. However, the popular appeal of the film was relatively limited. *The Godfather, Part II* was successful at the box office, but despite its appreciably larger budget, it earned only one-third as much as *The Godfather.*

If the film's box office success was less than anticipated, Coppola was not admittedly troubled. More so than in *The Godfather,* he had at least partially succeeded in his effort to underscore America's fundamental lawlessness. What did trouble Coppola was the way the stories and characters in the film apparently continued to appeal to viewers. Coppola wanted to indict, to speak critically and symbolically. However, American myths about family and upward mobility and the American taste for authoritarian action qua violence continued to trump a tale of lawlessness with an increasingly corporate face. *The Godfather, Part II* had refined and accentuated the critical message of its predecessor, but the vicissitudes of controlling popular reception remained. "If you were taken inside Adolf Hitler's home, went to his parties and heard his stories," a resigned Coppola said after he realized what had happened, "you'd probably have liked him."[46] Even a second try at demythologizing did not necessarily produce the effects Coppola desired.

■

Although Coppola deliberately left Michael Corleone a "living corpse" at the end of *The Godfather, Part II*,[47] the production of a third Godfather film was not really surprising. Paramount Pictures, of course, continued to view the Godfather as an extremely valuable property and was eager for a third installment. Coppola himself also seemed to realize it would eventually be done. When after the release of *The Godfather, Part II* Coppola was asked if the story of Michael Corleone was truly over, he responded: "Nine times out of ten, people who say they're never going to do something wind up doing it. Right now, I don't want to make another sequel. But maybe thirty years from now, when I and all the actors have gotten really old, then it might be fun to take another look."[48]

In reality, only sixteen years had to pass before the release of *The Godfather, Part III* in 1990. As the film begins, Michael is in his early sixties and still giving immense gifts to public and benevolent institutions, amounts that now total not in the millions but in the hundreds of millions. His daughter Mary, played by Coppola's daughter Sofia, is able somehow to overlook her father's past deeds and heads a foundation he has established. His son Anthony is more estranged but partially reconciles with his father when the latter allows him to abandon his legal education in favor of a career in opera. Much of the film is set in Sicily as Anthony prepares for his singing debut, and as if a travelogue embedded in the film is not enough, Michael at one point disguises himself as a chauffeur in order to treat his ex-wife Kay to a literal tour of the island, complete with a stop at the humble home in which Vito Corleone was born.

In a more narratival and less lyrical vein, Michael schemes and is schemed against in a multinational financial affair involving the Vatican Bank, a conglomerate named Immobiliare, and assorted gangsters and corrupt clerics. At points the plotting becomes hopelessly convoluted, but at least the denouement in a Sicilian opera house is clear. As Anthony succeeds in his debut, Corleone enemies are duly eliminated. But alas, Corleone enemies are also at work. Bullets intended for Michael kill his daughter on the steps of the opera house. Michael, again played by Al Pacino, reacts with an agonized silent scream that would do Edvard Munch proud.[49]

Reviews of the film were for the most part unkind. Many ridiculed Coppola for casting his daughter Sofia in the role of Michael's daughter Mary. One called the film "lumbering,"[50] and the nastiest described it as "a tedious effort to flag an old hippopotamus into action."[51] The most intriguing aspect of the journalism concerning the film was an attempt to link the film to the classical genre of tragedy. In particular, commentators kindled images of Shakespeare's Lear.[52] Michael seemed tragic and tormented, with his largest dreams eluding him. And there was even a bastard character, Vincent Mancini, the illegitimate son of the deceased Sonny Corleone. Vincent stands in the shoes of Anthony, the unwilling heir.

As overdone as this interpretation might seem at first glance, Coppola himself endorsed it and linked Michael's tragic plight to his own. Coppola's private film company had gone bankrupt, and just as the shooting for *The Godfather, Part III* began, Coppola himself declared personal bankruptcy, citing debts of six million dollars. Coppola's ego had also taken a beating. The press had ridiculed his immense spending and poor management for *Apocalypse Now* (1979) and *The Cotton Club* (1984), and Coppola himself insisted on baring his errors and failings in the media. "After each new film," Pauline Kael wrote in the *New Yorker,* "he was so nakedly hurt and upset that you couldn't help becoming involved in his pain."[53] In a 1990 interview in the *New York Times,* Coppola said: "I'm very embarrassed about my career over the last ten years. You know, an Italian family puts a lot of stock on not losing face, not making what we call 'una brutta figura,' or a bad showing. When you have people writing about you in a mocking way and making fun of your ideas and calling you a crackpot, that's a real 'brutta figura.' I want to be considered a vital American filmmaker and have the country be proud of me, but I am aware that my career has been very troubled and controversial."[54] Michael Corleone, the Hollywood auteur announced without embarrassment, was like himself in being forced to contemplate a tragic fate. Michael had gone through on the screen what Coppola himself had experienced in real life.[55]

Critics and reviewers might also have correctly seen *The Godfather, Part III* as an extension of the demythologizing lawlessness theme central in the first two films. Throughout the film everyone seems to realize that the Corleone money is dirty, that it has been acquired through illegal activities. However, Michael is determined to cleanse himself and his family. His charitable gifts are attempts to buy legitimacy, and when the heads of American Mafia families urge Michael to remain active in his old pursuits, he tells them he now wants to travel a higher road. He sells illegitimate businesses at a loss, curries favor with legitimate businessmen, and arranges to have himself inducted into the prestigious Papal Order of St. Sebastian. To be sure, things do not always go smoothly. "Just when I thought I was out," Michael rages at one point, "they pull me back in." But still, we have the theme of a criminal bully who wants to be seen in a better light.

This same tale, symbolically understood, is in Coppola's mind the story of America. Hungry and corrupt and mean, the nation has prospered and become the richest and most powerful nation in the world. Given its clout, the nation now asks for one more thing: respect. Indeed, reviving old ways, it makes offers for respect that can't be refused. Michael as the Mafia as America is a corrupt bully who now wants to be granted dignity and honor.

Neither the notion of mirror-image tragic heroes—one a fictional character and the other its director—nor the symbolic tale of the Mafia as America had much impact on the viewing public, and indeed *The Godfather, Part III* is a less impressive work than the first two films. Nevertheless, the film can be a treat for some viewers. Al Pacino's acting is again superb and rightfully showcased. Beyond the previously mentioned silent scream, Pacino has opportunities to offer his confession to a cardinal, to agonize through diabetic strokes, and even to display a certain laconic wryness. Sofia Coppola's acting, by contrast, is amateurish, but it is intriguing that Coppola, already identifying with Michael, both casts his actual daughter as Michael's daughter and then kills her off!

Most importantly, the film recalls the *The Godfather* and *The Godfather, Part II*. One sees not only Al Pacino's Michael but also characters such as Diane Keaton's Kay Adams age and mature over time. One catches glimpses of minor characters from the earlier films such as Sonny's mistress, who had appeared briefly in *The Godfather*. And one even meets the fictive off-spring of fictive characters; in addition to Michael's children and Vincent Mancini there is Andrew Hagen, a priest and the son of Tom Hagen. A viewer coming cold to *The Godfather, Part III* might not enjoy or admire it, but anyone familiar and enamored with the films that preceded it cannot resist this completion of a cinematic epic.[56] More so than its portrayal of Michael's tragedy or its symbolic presentation of a lawless America, the film's reflexiveness—its references to the whole Corleone epic—make *The Godfather, Part III* delightful in its own way.

■

Coppola's three Godfather films merit watching and rewatching. In and of themselves they constitute a remarkable American saga, spanning three generations and the entire twentieth century and exploring the largest of American themes—family, personal achievement, immigration, and capitalism. In the history of American cinema the Godfather trilogy stands as an especially extended and intriguing exploration of what it means to be American, and Coppola ranks as one of the nation's best film directors. In addition, the story of Coppola's fussing and torment over how the public understood and interpreted the films offers lessons for those anxious to demythologize through the popular arts or simply to undertake legal-cultural studies.

As noted at the outset, the story of Coppola and his audience nicely illustrates that the insights of reception or response theory are as applicable to film as they are to literature.[57] Cultural artifacts are not simply containers into which writers, composers, and directors pour meanings that will later be drained by readers, listeners, and viewers. A director such as Francis Ford Coppola may have understood and also announced what his goals were in the Godfather films, but these goals neither exhaust what the films might say nor fully restrict what viewers might find interesting and appealing. The images, performances, and symbolic systems of a feature film are too complex for any director, Coppola and all his hubris included, to dictate and impose their meanings. Viewers bring their own tastes, values, and histories to the films, and meanings emerge from the interaction of the film and the viewers' responses to it.

That having been said, meanings available to viewers of the Godfather films and to consumers of other mass culture artifacts are not infinite and completely open-ended. While some reception theorists might emphasize the aesthetics or cognitive psychology of reception or reader response, mass culture and its reception also reside in historical epochs and in the normative relations of those epochs. These epochs and their norms set boundaries for meaning.[58]

With works such as Coppola's Godfather films, which wrestle with American images and directions, the national mythology becomes especially important. Understood not as falsehood but as symbolic stories, the nation's myths explore problems that arise in the course of historical experience.[59] They also contribute mightily to the historical bases of the viewer's appreciation and interpretation of the films.

As a would-be demythologizer, Coppola understandably chose in his Godfather films to turn the American nation's professed commitment to a rule of law on its head by casting the Corleones as *the* symbolic Americans, but Coppola failed to appreciate how mythic strands intertwine and even wind their ways in contradictory directions. To wit, a tale of lawlessness may easily become a tale of family cohesion or Horatio Algerism. The gangster tale itself, rife with images of violence and wrong-doing, might speak to Americans in both a cautionary *and* an attractive voice. As anthropologists have long recognized, mythology, be it that of a tribal group or an industrialized society, is not a simple pronouncement but rather a complex dialogue or a range of arguments. Response to the Godfather trilogy took place with this mythic range, and the customarily winning arguments within the range prevailed.

Coppola himself may never have appreciated why the production of the Godfather films was simultaneously so accomplished and so frustrating, but scholars exploring legal themes in film might extract from Coppola's story the lessons of reception theory and mythic contextualization. It may not suffice simply to speak of what one filmmaker or film "says" about law, legal processes, or legal institutions. Filmmakers and studios cannot control meaning. Viewers reside in history and myth, and they find meaning with reference to the norms and preferences of their social situations. In short, the law-related messages in films derive from a richly complex, contested, and contextualized process, and this process in turn makes the study of law-related films all the more engaging and challenging.

Notes

1. The tendency of the Hollywood film to reinforce myths has been frequently noted. See, for example, Andrew Bergman, *We're in the Money: Depression America and Its Films* (New York: Harper & Row, 1971), xvi–xvii. Robert B. Ray discusses the "voraciously assimilative power" of the American cinema in *A Certain Tendency of the Hollywood Cinema* (Princeton: Princeton University Press, 1985), 423.

2. Perhaps Coppola's most pronounced attempt to demythologize occurs in *Apocalypse Now* (1979). John Hellman, "Vietnam and the Hollywood Genre Film: Inversions of American Mythology in *The Deer Hunter* and *Apocalypse Now*," *American Quarterly* 34:4 (Fall 1982): 418–39. Other contemporary directors who stand largely in the demythologizing counter-tradition include Robert Altman and Milos Forman.

3. The most prominent, but hardly the only, response or reception theorist is Wolfgang Iser. Useful introductions to Iser's work include his essays, "The Reading Process," in Ralph Cohen, ed., *New Directions in Literary History* (Baltimore: Johns Hopkins University Press, 1974), 124–45, and "Interaction between Text and Reader," in Susan R. Suleiman and Inge Crosman, eds., *The Reader in the Text: Essays on Audience and Interpretation* (Princeton: Princeton University Press, 1980), 106–19. For a recent application and critique of response theory in mass cultural studies, see "*AHR* Forum," *American Historical Review* 97:5 (Dec. 1992): 1369–1430.

4. Jeffrey Chown, *Hollywood Auteur: Francis Coppola* (New York: Praeger, 1988), 8–15.

5. Puzo's *The Godfather* stood first on the *New York Times* best-seller list from September 21, 1969, through February 1, 1970.

6. Roger Jellinek, "Books of the Times: Just Business, Not Personal," *New York Times*, March 4, 1969, p. 41.

7. Joel S. Zuker, *Francis Ford Coppola: A Guide to References and Resources* (Boston: G. K. Hall & Co., 1984), 7.

8. Coppola also longed to remove the whole Hollywood part of the novel, but the scene in which a Hollywood director's prized horse is beheaded by the Corleones had been firmly implanted in the public's mind. As Coppola put it, "I had to cut off that stupid horse's head." Michael Goodwin and Naomi Wise, *On the Edge: The Life and Times of Francis Coppola* (New York: William Morrow and Company, 1989), 117.

9. Coppola was not himself hostile to the line, but Marlon Brando allegedly refused to deliver it. Chown, *Hollywood Auteur*, 70.

10. "I was desperate to give the film a kind of class," Coppola said. "I felt the book was cheap and sensational." Quoted in Ray, *A Certain Tendency*, 340.

11. Chris Chase, "Quick—What's This Man's Name?" *New York Times*, April 23, 1972, sec. 2, pp. 11 and 16.

12. See Andrew McKenna's essay in this volume.

13. In a fuller treatment of the structure of the film's four acts, William Simon notes that the cross-cutting between Michael's scenes in Sicily and Sonny's scenes in New York comes not from "the unimaginative linearity of the novel" but rather from Coppola's more cinematic imagination. "An Analysis of the Structure of *The Godfather, Part I,*" *Studies in the Literary Imagination* 16:1 (Spring 1983): 84.

14. Andrew McKenna notes that sacrifice not only masks violence, but also enlists a scapegoat. See his essay in this volume. Might Carlo be a candidate?

15. Zuker, *Francis Ford Coppola,* 8.

16. Coppola in fact used research on the Mafia. Debbie Fine, who worked as Coppola's research coordinator on *The Godfather, Part II,* remarked, "Many filmmakers want research done merely to verify or contradict something they've already decided. Or, they ignore what you give them. Francis Coppola, on the other hand, has a way of absorbing everything that comes his way. He has a great sense of history and respect for detail." Quoted in Chown, *Hollywood Auteur,* 108.

17. Some of the violence, the popular culture scholar John G. Cawelti argues, may be rationalized by the vigilante myth; the Corleones took law into their own hands because the system was corrupt and inefficient. "Myths of Violence in American Popular Culture," *Critical Inquiry* 1:3 (Mar. 1975): 533–34.

18. Murray, William, "*Playboy* Interview: Francis Ford Coppola," *Playboy,* July 1975, 60.

19. Zuker, *Francis Ford Coppola,* 8.

20. Goodwin and Wise, *On the Edge,* 139.

21. Stanley Kauffmann, "Stanley Kauffmann on Films," *New Republic* 166:14 (Apr. 1, 1972): 26.

22. Murray, "*Playboy* Interview," 60.

23. Chown, *Hollywood Auteur,* 65. The Corleone family might be seen, in the words of critic Fredric Jameson, as "an optical illusion of social harmony." *Signatures of the Visible* (New York: Routledge, 1990), 26.

24. Lawrence M. Friedman, *The Republic of Choice: Law, Authority, and Choice* (Cambridge: Harvard University Press, 1990), 11–17.

25. Ibid., 15.

26. Cawelti, "Myths of Violence," 525. Richard Slotkin, *Gunfighter Nation: The Myth of the Frontier in Twentieth-Century America* (New York: Atheneum, 1992).

27. John G. Cawelti, *Adventure, Mystery, and Romance: Formula Studies as Art and Popular Culture* (Chicago: University of Chicago Press, 1976), 256.

28. Goodwin and Wise, *On the Edge,* 139.

29. The Kael and Fiedler responses are reported in Jonathan P. Latimer, "The Godfather: Metaphor and Microcosm," *Journal of Popular Film* 2:2 (1973): 204–8.

30. One might take this purported achievement with a grain of salt. For one thing, if you correct for inflation, earlier films such as *Gone with the Wind* (1939) actually outperformed *The Godfather* at the box office. Goodwin and Wise, *On the Edge,* 139. In addition, *The Godfather*'s earnings have been topped in more recent years, and by 1984 it was only the eighth highest earning film. Ray, *A Certain Tendency,* 386n.3.

31. Robert B. Ray counts among these conservative blockbusters *The Way We Were* (1973), *The Sting* (1973), and *Jaws* (1972), and he also goes on to deplore the way the blockbuster complex continues to limit the creativity and flexibility of the American film industry. *A Certain Tendency,* 343.

32. Quoted in Goodwin and Wise, *On the Edge,* 162.

33. Quoted in John Hess, "*The Godfather II*: A Deal Coppola Couldn't Refuse," in Bill Nichols, ed., *Movies and Methods: An Anthology* (Berkeley: University of California Press, 1976), 83.

34. Quoted in Michael Anderson, "Review of *Objects of Desire*," *New York Times Book Review,* May 9, 1993, p. 18.

35. Quoted in Goodwin and Wise, *On the Edge,* 162.

36. The film not only had a huge box office success but also in many parts of the country asked the previously unheard of admission charge of four dollars. Goodwin and Wise, *On the Edge,* 138.

37. The actual title screened at the beginning of all three films began with "*Mario Puzo's.*" However, the print for Puzo's name was appropriately smaller than the words that followed.

38. The tiff began with Yablans's public irritation over Brando's protest on behalf of Native Americans at the 1973 Oscar ceremonies. Goodwin and Wise, *On the Edge,* 164.

39. Lucas announced bluntly, "You have two movies. Throw one away. It doesn't work." Quoted in Goodwin and Wise, *On the Edge,* 181.

40. Ibid.

41. Coppola only hints at the way the corporate "invasion" of Cuba prompted resistance and led to revolution. For a careful study of the Cuban response to one American corporate venture, see Thomas F. O'Brien, "The Revolutionary Mission: American Enterprise in Cuba," *American Historical Review* 98:2 (June 1993): 765–85.

42. Chown, *Hollywood Auteur,* 61.

43. Murray, "*Playboy* Interview," 60.

44. "I thought it was healthy to make this horror-story statement as a warning, if you like," Coppola said, "but as a nation, we don't have to go down the same road, and I don't think we will." Ibid.

45. Chown, *Hollywood Auteur,* 104. For capsule summaries of major reviews of *The Godfather, Part II*, see Zuker, *Francis Ford Coppola,* 117–50. John Hess describes the film as "the greatest Hollywood film since *Citizen Kane* and one of the three or four best Hollywood films ever made." "*Godfather II*," 82.

46. Murray, "*Playboy* Interview," 60.

47. Quoted in Simon, "Analysis of the Structure," 88.

48. Murray, "*Playboy* Interview," 185.

49. The film should have ended here, but the final scene is actually an epilogue in which a still older Michael sits alone in a Sicilian garden, takes his last breath, and topples out of his chair.

50. Pauline Kael, "The Current Cinema: Vanity, Vanities," *New Yorker* 66:48 (Jan. 14, 1991): 77.

51. John Simon, "Film: The Mob and the Family," *National Review* 43:1 (Jan. 28, 1991): 63.

52. Kael, "Current Cinema," 76; Larry Rohter, "Coppola: It Was an Offer He Couldn't Refuse," *New York Times,* Dec. 23, 1990, sec. 2, pp. 1, 26–27.

53. Kael, "Current Cinema," 76.

54. Rohter, "Coppola," 26.

55. Kael, "Current Cinema," 76.

56. Is the epic truly finished? Might there be a fourth installment? When asked about this, Coppola admitted that, "It looks as though as long as there is anyone left alive at all, there is always that possibility." Rohter, "Coppola," 27.

57. A work intelligently applying a variety of reception or response theories to film is Janet Staiger's *Interpreting Films: Studies in the Historical Reception of American Cinema* (Princeton: Princeton University Press, 1992).

58. Staiger, *Interpreting Films,* xi–xii, 48.

59. Richard Slotkin, one of the most sophisticated scholars of myths and symbols in American culture, defines myths as "stories drawn from a society's history that have acquired through persistent usage the power of symbolizing that society's ideology and dramatizing its moral consciousness—with all the complexities and contradictions that consciousness may contain." Slotkin, *Gunfighter Nation,* 5.

Print the Legend

Violence and Recognition in
The Man Who Shot Liberty Valance

CHEYNEY RYAN

■

It is fitting that John Ford's *The Man Who Shot Liberty Valance*[1] (1962; hereafter, *MSLV*) is now best remembered for the 1960s Gene Pitney song, which, though it shares the film's title, has no formal connection to it (the song is not performed in the film, nor does it or its tune accompany the opening titles or closing credits). For at the heart of *MSLV* is the problem of *misrecognition:* what we learn, as the film draws to its close, is that the man who is universally regarded as having shot the outlaw Liberty Valance, and whose political career has been built on that alleged achievement, is not the man who really shot Liberty Valance. That man, we discover, has died drunk and forgotten, ruined in fact by the act that propelled another to fame. Thus the film describes how, in the public realm, figures and events that possess a defining importance for a community can be infused with fabrication. But the film does not moralize about this fact, or preach against it. Rather, its tone is consistently ironic in suggesting that the false identifications that pervade the public order are somehow integral to that order. It is thus a film about ideology, but "ideology" in the sense that Louis Althusser used the term—a structure of misrecognition that necessarily animates the interactions and unfolding of an ordered community.[2]

It is also a film about the necessity of *violence*. But the violence that it explores is of two distinct sorts.

First, there is the overt physical violence of bloodshed and killing, the sort of violence exemplified in the life and fate of Liberty Valance himself (exuberantly played by Lee Marvin). Violence's necessity here has something to do with the conditions of effective speech, for the message of Valance's demise is something like: words, specifically the words that would constitute an ordered community, mean nothing if they are not backed up by force—specifically a gun. A second and more covert form of violence is exemplified in the fate of Tom Doniphon (John Wayne), the man who really shot Liberty Valance. Doniphon's fate has multiple meanings, but insofar as he falls victim to the legend of the man who (everyone wrongly thinks) shot Liberty Valance, the message of his demise is something like: words can involve their own *kind* of violence when they function, as they do here, as agents of erasure. So if Valance's fate involves an unrecognized violence, Doniphon's fate involves the violence of unrecognition; the fate of both involves a kind of blindness that (as I explore in the third section of this essay) has tragic dimensions. The chief beneficiary of this blindness, but also the principal bearer of its burdens, is the man most responsible for the deaths of both Liberty Valance and Tom Doniphon—Ransom ("Ranse") Stoddard, played by James Stewart.

From the very start, Ranse is the representative of legal order. As that order's champion and exemplar, Ranse's ultimate triumph represents the two-fold victory of that order over both that which stands *opposed* to law, because it champions sheer lawlessness (Liberty Valance), and that which stands *outside* society's law, because it abides by a more "natural" law (Tom Doniphon). What we learn as the story unfolds, though, is how deeply troubling Ranse's triumph has been. For the film reveals the full extent to which that triumph has implicated Ranse in both unrecognized violence and the violence of unrecognition—in ways that apparently compromise that triumph. In so doing, *MSLV* raises a troubling question for legal theory in general: To what extent does the legal order *necessarily* find its origins in kinds of violence that compromise its very legitimacy?

The question is an important one, to be sure. Yet what most recommends *MSLV* to legal theory is the *depth* with which it pursues that question. Some initial sense of that depth is provided by considering the two other figures whose relationship to Ranse marks the drift of his character over the course of the film.

I have identified Ranse as the representative of legal order, but he is not the only representative of "the law" in the town of "Shinbone," where most of the action occurs. The other is the bumbling, child-like Sheriff Link Appleyard, played by Andy Devine in a role that echoes at every turn his television show of the 1950s (in which, you may remember, he was relentlessly traumatized by an elusive frog). Appleyard, as signifier of the law and its authority, presents them both as an infantile and comical affair. Ranse too, particularly in the earlier stages of the film, presents the law as something less than serious: as an idealistic and newly minted attorney, he initially strikes us as both hopelessly naive and something of a wimp (think of George Bush when you watch the film again). As the story proceeds, then, Ranse's problem is to *distinguish* himself from Appleyard (and his own earlier self), and thus distinguish his kind of law from Appleyard's—to prove that the law per se need not be a laughing matter. Proving this, we assume from the start, will ultimately require killing Liberty Valance. For if the law is to be taken seriously it must demonstrate that it "means what it says"; and this means demonstrating (against Valance and what he represents) a capacity to meet violence with violence.

The other figure that Ranse must distinguish himself from in championing the legal order is Major Cassius Starbuckle—the mouthpiece of the cattle interests and Ranse's adversary in the election for territorial representative.[3] Starbuckle (played by a scenery-chewing John Carradine) is the film's other truly comic character along with Appleyard. While the humor of Appleyard involves his ineffectiveness—the fact that his words are totally divorced from action—the humor of Starbuckle involves the fact that his words are pure rhetoric, they are *only* a form of action—or performance. He is introduced as, among other things, a "Statesman," but he is really just a blow-hard whose verbal flights and bombastic vaporings evidence not the slightest concern for the truth. If Appleyard represents a law that does not mean what it says, Starbuckle seems to represent a law that does not say what it means. He represents the rule of political fraudulence in league with Valance's rule of personal violence.

Now at first glance it would seem that Ranse *does* succeed in distancing himself from Appleyard, but in ways that eventually blur the distance between him and Starbuckle—and him and Valance as well. To begin with, the Ranse that we see at the beginning and end of the film, the Ranse who has himself become a "Statesman," both speaks and looks like Starbuckle. There is the same pomposity and phoniness, even the same formal dress, all of which seems to suggest the same lack of substance; harkening back to the fact that Ranse's defeat of Starbuckle at the territorial convention (and the political career that followed) was due to a myth of Ranse's achievements that is every bit as fraudulent as his opponent's rhetoric. And, of course, there is the suggestion that (as he feared from the start) the methods Ranse has used to establish the law's credibility, through the use of gun-play, have only likened his law to Valance's law.

All of this seems to suggest that in establishing a certain authority for the law, Ranse has at the same time undermined its legitimacy. Yet further reflection reveals that matters are more complex, because Ranse's situation is more ambiguous. Yes, there is a certain phoniness to the older Ranse, but he is not all phoniness. After all, he does not initiate the myth that drives his political fortunes; quite the contrary: he is initially its dupe, and later (I shall suggest) even its victim. Has Ranse likened himself to Valance by adopting the latter's methods? Again, the matter must be more complex for the simple reason that Ranse (remember) doesn't kill Liberty Valance—Tom Doniphon does! Ranse is certainly *implicated* in this violence; but what follows from this fact for the appraisal of Ranse's triumph? What follows (that is) for the legal order's legitimacy from the fact that the legal order's triumph over lawlessness is due to a violence that is not opposed to the law but outside the law? Does this render that order illegitimate? Or does it compel us to reflect further on the *meaning* of "legitimacy" in such matters?[4]

What endows *MSLV* with its special depth is that in speaking to the legal order's legitimacy, it raises such questions about the meaning of "legitimacy" itself by consistently *problematizing* the distinction between the "legitimate" and "illegitimate." It is this fact that gives the film a certain *deconstructive* dimension (which explains its absence of moralizing or preaching). And it is this fact that will be my special focus in the first two sections of this essay. In the last section I reflect on how the film's concern with violence and (mis)recognition contributes to its tragic dimensions.

■

I begin this section by placing *MSLV* in relation to other westerns, paying particular attention to its similarities with *High Noon* (1952). This will provide a basis for discussing the notions of "boundary," "representation," and the "written"—notions that are important to the distinction between "legitimate" and "illegitimate" and that are consistently problematized by this film.

As a film about "civilization's" emergence, *MSLV* is concerned with both the birth of the legal order, which it identifies with being a state rather than a territory, and the conditions of "progress," specifically economic progress, which it identifies with railroads rather than stage coaches. As such, there are two general ways to place the film. One is through its relation to other *films* that speak to the same concerns— "Town Tamer" and "Outlaw" westerns. Another is through its relation to the traditions of social and political *theory* that reflect on "civilization's" character by exploring the conditions of emergence. I am thinking in particular of "state of nature theory" and its two principal variants, "social contract theory" and "invisible hand theory." I shall say one or two words in regard to *MSLV*'s relation to theories such as these, but my primary concern is with its relation to other films of its genre.

The terms "Town Tamer" and "Outlaw" are taken from Richard Slotkin's *Gunfighter Nation,* which I have relied on heavily in this discussion and which I recommend heartily to anyone interested in these matters.[5] As Slotkin describes them, Town Tamer and Outlaw westerns are concerned with matters of law, order, and social justice. But in the Town Tamer western the injustice is typically imposed by powerful criminals whom the hero must defeat—thus empowering "decent folk" to bring "progress," while in the Outlaw western, the source of injustice is typically a powerful institution, like the railroad, which is itself the agent of "progress"—and which is typically opposed by an "outlaw"/"outsider"-type figure, a sage-brush Robin Hood (hence Slotkin's term for it). The Outlaw western thus contains a more skeptical view of "progress" than the Town Tamer, which is why Slotkin regards the one as providing a critique of the other. In the 1950s, both genres experienced important modifications, most notably in their increasingly ironic tone. Some of these changes reflected the internal logic of genre development, but others reflected changes in political context brought on by the cold war. This was, after all, a time in which problems of "development" and "nation state building," both of them conceived under the rubric "modernization," were very much on the American mind—given the perceived contest between the United States and the Soviet Union in the Third World. Slotkin discusses, in persuasive detail, how the Hollywood western responded to and reflected on these problems by employing the West as a sort of surrogate Third World.

MSLV contains elements of both genres, and thus it blurs their distinction, insofar as the villain, Liberty Valance, alternates between being a free-lance criminal a la Town Tamer and an agent of the powerful, specifically the cattlemen, a la Outlaw.[6] As an Outlaw western, *MSLV* may be likened to a classic of that genre, *Shane:* like Valance, its villain, played by Jack Palance, represents the cattlemen, and he has the same sadism as Liberty (though with none of the *joi de vivre*); and there are parallels between Shane himself and our hero Ranse in their common rootlessness and absence of any past. But it is *MSLV*'s status as a Town Tamer that I want to focus on, by exploring its parallels with a classic of that genre, *High Noon*.

At the heart of both films is the contrast between a state of nature and the "civilization" made possible by a centralized legal order. Both films are more Hobbesian than Lockean in their portrayal of the state of nature as essentially a state of war or uncontrolled banditry. Indeed, one can almost imagine Valance and his side-kicks (played by Lee Van Cleef and Strother Martin) going by the nicknames "Nasty, Brutish, and Short." ("Solitary" could be a nickname for Ranse; Who then is "Poor"? Doniphon after his demise?) But where *MSLV*'s concern is how to create the legal order, *High Noon*'s concern is more how to *sustain* it, how to prevent that relapse into the state of war that Hobbes said was always possible. That relapse is threatened by Frank Miller, whose intent to wreak havoc involves, like Liberty Valance's, both self interest—he too wants a free hand in the town—and personal revenge—he too wants to "get back" at the agent of law. In *High Noon,* that agent is Marshal Will Kane, played by Gary Cooper. In certain respects, Kane's personality evokes qualities of Tom Doniphon; there is the same stoic bearing, the same reticence to speak. But his *predicament* is obviously closer to that of Ranse Stoddard.

Both Kane and Ranse, for example, are figures of detachment, indeed, isolation. They are "in" but not "of" the communities they inhabit. In Ranse's case, this reflects his status as a parvenu; thus he is always being told "how we do things around here," and he is constantly given diminutive nicknames ("Dude," "Professor"), like a new kid who has just arrived in school. Though the film twice depicts him arriving in Shinbone (once in present time, once in flashback), he never really arrives, and no sooner does he gain the trust of the townspeople than they send him, as their representative, to Washington and points East— from which, we discern at the end, he has seldom returned. (No wonder then that when he does return to Shinbone to bury Tom Doniphon he knows hardly anyone, and those whom he does remember he treats like strangers.) Marshal Will Kane's problem would *seem* to be just the opposite—for he is a man who cannot leave, something keeps pulling him back. Indeed, on the surface his predicament seems rather like George Bailey's in Frank Capra's *It's a Wonderful Life*, but only on the surface; for the pull on George Bailey has something to do with family and home, whereas Will Kane has no home, and his refusal to leave is at the same time a refusal to consummate his marriage and have a family. What pulls Kane back to town is the same thing that ultimately propels Ranse out of it: a commitment to law and a conception of duty that both men discover have little to do with their town's conception of itself.[7] Whatever their geographical location, then, both embody a deep alienation from their fellow citizens.

In both films this alienation animates a deep skepticism about democracy and its workings. On one level this skepticism is expressed in the attitudes of the central characters. Kane comes to regard his fellow townspeople as a bunch of self-involved cowards, too stupid to see that refusing to face Frank Miller and his gang is only putting off the inevitable, so that at the film's end he contemptuously throws his badge at the Mayor's feet—marking the fact that the people he saved were probably not worth saving.[8] The perspective of MSLV is only a bit less antidemocratic: Ranse, in his role as champion of legal order, does attend dutifully to such populist institutions as town assemblies and public education, but the people who participate in and sustain these institutions are consistently perceived as (except for Tom Doniphon) a flock of timid short-sighted eccentrics, whose wish to exercise their franchise (in the town meeting scene) is just slightly stronger than their craving to hit the bar for another drink. And though he professes democratic sentiments for most of the film, Ranse evidences little interest in what the townspeople actually think. Most of the time he just lectures them on what their interests are and how they can be secured.

But there is a further, even deeper level at which democracy is problematized by these films, specifically by the ambivalent status of Ranse and Kane as figures neither inside nor outside their communities. And it is a level that engages the basic distinction between "legitimate" and "illegitimate," in some important respects.

For its institutions to claim legitimacy, a liberal democracy must be able to distinguish who is a member of the community and who is not—who is "inside" and who is "outside." For example, such an order must have ways of determining who can and cannot vote, who is and who is not within the reach of its laws, and so on. In these and other respects, the legitimacy of such an order seems intimately linked with the existence of secure and clearly defined boundaries. Questions of boundary are never far from MSLV's concerns: in the town-meeting scene, the film twice raises the question of who is and is not a proper citizen; in the opening sections of the flashback (when Ranse debates with Appleyard over the Sheriff's right to arrest Valance), the film addresses the distinction between who is a legal subject and who is not. Moreover, the need for clear boundaries is implicit in the central economic conflict that drives all the other political and legal issues—the conflict between the cattlemen and ranchers over the right to build fences. The side of the ranchers, the side of goodness, is identified with the side that would establish boundaries and keep them in good repair; just as the side of manly virtue, and of resisting the threat of tyranny, is identified with "drawing the line somewhere."

How significant it is, then, that those most concerned with securing boundaries—Ranse Stoddard and Marshal Will Kane—are those whose very status as "in" but not "of" their communities seems to problematize those boundaries. Indeed, their very acts of creating boundaries seem to problematize them at the same time: Kane defends the law through means of questionable legality, and the more Ranse works to define who belongs inside and outside the community, the more he removes himself from it, as its representative. The double-edged logic here, of defining/ defending while at the same time problematizing a boundary, is one that Jacques Derrida has termed the logic of the *pharmakon*.[9] (A *pharmakon* is, among other things, a scapegoat figure. I shall have more to say about the scapegoat status of Ranse near the end of this essay.) Derrida's identification of that logic with *writing,* linked with Ranse's persistent championing of the written word, will provide another clue to Ranse's status as a *pharmakon* figure.

More so than *High Noon, MSLV* connects the problem of the legal order and its democratic context to the problem of *representation*. But it does so in a manner that deeply problematizes the notion of "representation," and with it the related notion of "legitimacy."

With his entry into politics, what Ranse eventually becomes in his quest to bring the law to Shinbone is a representative of the people—to be one who speaks for the people with legitimacy. But the impulse to represent has been present in Ranse from the start. After all, his initial desire to be a lawyer was nothing else but a desire to represent the law, in two senses: he wanted to represent the law *to* others by interpreting it through his words, and he wanted to represent the law *for* others by enacting it through his deeds. (And these projects too are intimately involved with legitimacy.) It seems that the film invites us to regard Ranse as the representative of representation—and in this respect, it invites us to regard him as rather like Don Quixote. For like Quixote, Ranse's quest is animated by the desire to live a life that he has only read about in books. This desire endows both quests with an element of the imaginary, and the comic—Ranse imagines that he kills Valance, as Quixote imagines he tilts with giants. And both, after their initial conquests, are confronted with the task of reading about themselves, in a manner that will radically destabalize any distinctions between realism and romance.

But if Ranse represents representation, what are the changes that his character undergoes supposed to teach us about representation and its logic?

For much of the film the notion of representation that Ranse both champions and embodies is a rather innocent one, if not naive. For example, both his words and his actions express the assumption that interpreting and enacting the law are relatively simple matters. Hence his unadorned veneration for the written word, specifically law books: he assumes that one need only read law books to understand what they mean, and one need only understand what they mean to act on them. This is why he equates the task of bringing law to Shinbone with the task of bringing literacy to it, and why his response to those who do not represent the law as he does is characteristically one of exasperation. By the end of the film, though, Ranse's naiveté is gone. He is now someone for whom, and in whom, the project of representation has been problematized. This problematization is enacted in Ranse's very status as "esteemed politician." Neither he, nor we, can believe that he "represents" the "people" in any meaningful sense—again, his isolation is such that he has no connection with them; when he returns to Shinbone he is not even recognized at first.

But the changed perspective on representation is dramatized even more in Ranse's changed attitude toward the written word. Earlier in the film, Ranse's respect for law books is rivaled only by his respect for *newspapers*—or those newspapers, like the *Shinbone Star* and its editor, Dutton Peabody (played by Edmond O'Brien), that print the truth regardless of the consequences. By the end of the film, though, Ranse will accept without protest the refusal of the *Shinbone Star*'s current editor to print the story of the man who *really* shot Liberty Valance. What does Ranse's acquiescence mean here? I would argue that the issue involves a more sophisticated, rather than a more cynical, concept of representation because I do not think that Ranse takes himself to be endorsing *mis*representation of the facts—anymore than he understands his political services as ones that misrepresent the "people." Ranse's transformations in the film suggest the more complex point, that the "people" as a political entity are only constituted through the representation of them, just as the facts are only constituted through the representation of them.

This is, it seems to me, the thought expressed in the editor's concluding explanation of why he will not print the story. What he says is: "This is the West, sir. When the legend becomes fact, print the legend." He does *not* say that the facts should be ignored or forgotten. What he says is that the legend has "become" fact, presumably its own kind of fact. In suggesting that the facts are constituted through the stories we tell about them, the editor's remark undermines the more naive picture of representation by blurring the distinction between the representation and what it represents—in this case, what is written and what is written about. Post-structuralists will insist that this does not undermine the truth so much as *pluralize* it. They will insist, that is, that what *MSLV* presents us with is not a true story set against a false one, but two different kinds of truthfulness. One certainly constitutes a criticism of the other, revealing its elements of what I have termed misrecognition, but it does not follow that we must, or even can, choose between them.[10]

There is a further thought expressed, or rather enacted, in the editor's remark that bears on Ranse's particular veneration for the written word. Ranse identifies with books, with writing, because he adopts wholeheartedly the association of the writing/(mere) speech distinction with the civilized/primitive distinction. And he identifies with *law* books because law books, in his view, determine the identity of the law. It is in them that we find what legal philosophers have called the "rule of recognition"—the rule that distinguishes legal norms from other sorts of norms, to determine thereby which of the sovereign's commands are legitimate. And Ranse's "rule of recognition" is quite simple: if it is in writing, it's the law. (All of this is dramatized in the opening sequence, already noted, where Ranse seeks to determine whether Appleyard has jurisdiction to arrest Liberty Valance.) One way to question this rather literalistic "rule of recognition," and the boundary between legitimate and illegitimate that it defines, is to question whether what is written down is enough or whether it must be supplemented in some way. The general thrust of *MSLV* is certainly to suggest that law books are never enough. But another way to question it is to question the whole distinction between the written and the nonwritten—question, that is, whether such a distinction can ever be intelligibly drawn.

I introduced the theme of Ranse's identification with the written word in alluding to Derrida's notion of the logic of the *pharmakon*.

Because Derrida is known for challenging what he regards as a traditional privileging of speech over writing, he is often read as reversing this hierarchy—privileging writing over speech. But (rightly understood) writing, qua *pharmakon,* problematizes the very distinction between "writing" and "speech" as much as it assumes it—and in the process, problematizes a whole set of distinctions that revolve around the writing/speech distinction. It seems to me that there is an implicit problematizing of the writing/speech distinction in the editor's concluding remark—"print the legend." For a legend, as a kind of myth, is naturally identified with the realm of speech.[11] To suggest, as the editor does, that "the West" is a culture where legends must be printed is to suggest that it is a culture where the line between the spoken and the written is blurred. If this seems like a stretch, consider the scene in which Ranse and Starbuckle compete with each other at the territorial convention, where Ranse's legend must confront Starbuckle's oratory. Starbuckle begins by saying that he had come with a prepared speech, which is presumably inscribed on the piece of paper he first holds aloft, and then discards—proclaiming, "But this is no time for speeches!" Starbuckle then proceeds to give a speech, and we quickly discover that the paper he threw away is blank. Is Starbuckle's oration "spoken" or "written"? It seems to me that is both, and neither. It is, like the legend with which it competes, something that transgresses these distinctions. There is a lesson here about politics, since Starbuckle seems to be the quintessential politician. But, given the importance of the distinction between the written and the nonwritten for Ranse's picture of law, there is also a lesson about the legal order: that any "rule of recognition" might be a rule of *mis*recognition. Starbuckle, it should be noted, is also the only character in the film who is identified as a *judge.*

∎

In the Town Tamer, the achievement or reaffirmation of the legal order is often associated with a certain clarification of gender identities and roles—a clarification that is essentially connected with the willingness to commit violence. In *High Noon* there seems to be little doubt as to what Will Kane is, or at least what he has been up until now. As Helen Ramirez (Katy Jurado) says to Kane's hapless deputy Harvey (Lloyd Bridges), "You're a nice boy, with big broad shoulders. But Kane is a *man.*" Kane, though, appears to be in danger of becoming something else, and less, because the Quaker religion of his new wife (Grace

Kelly) would compel him to give up both his badge and his gun. In the end he does give up his badge, but he is able to hold on to his "manhood" and his wife—because the conflict has so transformed her that she now recognizes the necessity of violence and the limits of what a wife can ask.

In *MSLV* the question of manhood is placed at the center of Ranse's initiation into the ways of the frontier when the stage that he is riding is ambushed outside of Shinbone and he first encounters Liberty Valance. When Valance moves to violate one of the female passengers, Ranse cannot help but object by asking, "What kind of men are you?" to which Valance retorts, "What kind of man are *you,* dude?"—and proceeds to beat him senseless. Valance's question to Ranse marks the connection, sustained throughout this picture (and others of its genre), between be(com)ing a real—that is, a legitimate—man and the capacity to engage in violence. Prior to his face-off with Valance, Ranse is consistently portrayed as both *adolescent* (he is constantly filmed looking *up* to other people, often from the floor, and, as I have noted, he is constantly identified by a string of nicknames) and *womanly* (his washing dishes, for example, and wearing an apron—even when he goes out to confront Liberty Valance). After the final shoot-out, Ranse finally gets the respect and clothes befitting a man, and he gets the girl too when Hallie reveals her love and devotion to him. Should we conclude then that Ranse has become a "true man"? The matter, as one might expect, is not this simple—as attention to his relation with Hallie reveals.

Next to the offensive and cartoon-like character Pompey, played by the great actor Woody Strode, Hallie is the least satisfying character in the film, but at least there are reasons in her case. For Hallie is meant to be a blank slate: like Mrs. Kane in *High Noon,* she is virginal—which partly marks her femininity, but also marks the fact that she has not yet assumed her designated identity as wife. But unlike Mrs. Kane, and more importantly, she is *illiterate*—for some inexplicable reason, she alone of the major characters in the film cannot read (in contrast even to Liberty Valance and his grungy sidekicks). I remarked above on how the writing/speech distinction can be identified with the primitive/civilized distinction. What we see here is the connection of both of these distinctions to the man/woman distinction. As the Pilgrims brought civilization to the virgin land, Ranse, nicknamed "Pilgrim" by Doniphon, brings law to the land and literacy to the virgin (and he identifies teaching her how to write with teaching her how to speak properly: like

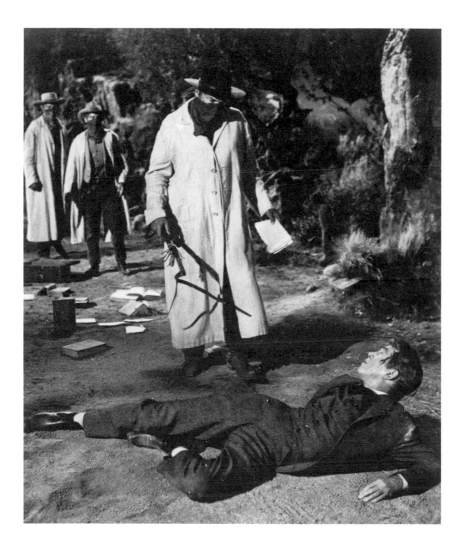

Lawyer Ranse Stoddard (James Stewart) lies supine at the mercy
of the malevolent violence of gunman Liberty Valance (Lee Marvin)
in John Ford's *The Man Who Shot Liberty Valance.* (Courtesy of the
Academy of Motion Picture Arts and Sciences.)

Henry Higgins, he is constantly correcting her grammar, paying particular attention, like Higgins, to her proclivity for saying "ain't"!). Ranse's act of bringing writing *to* her is portrayed as an act of writing *on* her. Ranse inscribes himself upon her, as Doniphon—the more patently sexist male—never does, for, unlike Doniphon, Ranse wants her to be something that she is not. In her gloom at the end there is the sense that Hallie recognizes this, that she recognizes the violence that Ranse's incessant tutoring may have involved.[12]

One expression of this, certainly, is the barrenness that their joylessness seems to signify. In the end, as they ride on the train into the sunset, they seem to be without children—and we are not surprised. For as the film progresses, their relationship has become if anything less erotic. I shall return to this ending, as it bears on the matter of parenthood. What it suggests here is that the status as "real" man that Ranse achieved at the end is a rather sexless one; and as such, it is one that seems to problematize the very distinction that it presumes.

Let us consider now Ranse's initial question to Valance and his men ("What kind of men are you?"), which is if anything even more telling than the question that they directed at him. What Ranse is questioning is not *whether* Valance is a man (as opposed to a woman), but what *kind* of man he is—whether he is "civilized" or "savage." In his *Politics,* it will be remembered, Aristotle ascribes to the "barbarian" the inability to recognize certain crucial distinctions, like that between male and female and the responses appropriate to each.[13] Ranse's question means to suggest that Liberty Valance is something of a "barbarian" insofar as his violence does not recognize any distinction between men and women, and thereby transgresses the most minimal boundaries of legitimacy in the realm of violence. (The same point is made in *High Noon,* when Frank Miller captures Mrs. Kane and holds her as a shield.) Aristotle speaks of "barbarians"; in the western the "barbarian" is identified with the "savage," specifically the Indian, and in this film, the qualities of Liberty Valance and his men are in fact those that are typically ascribed to Indians: they are violent, noisy, and drunk, and they inhabit some dark locale beyond the boundaries of the town, from which they periodically appear to disrupt the orderly workings of society.

Valance's behavior evidences a kind of lawlessness, but it is important to be clear regarding the kind of law that it violates. The law that requires that the differences between men and women be recognized is presumably not a civil law but a *natural* law. That is why Stoddard can object to its being broken even out in the countryside, a location that announces itself as outside the civil order. At the deepest level, what opposes Valance's law, the rule of "anything goes," is what might be termed the natural law of honorable violence—the law that the film identifies with the beliefs and actions of Tom Doniphon. This is the law of the *fair fight,* the law that says: don't hurt women, don't shoot people in the back, don't gang up on people, and so on. To some extent, these rules of natural law are appropriated into the civil order, but to some extent they are transformed. In particular, the personal dimension of this law gives way to the impersonal mechanisms of the legal order. "Out here we fight our own fights," Doniphon proclaims, but with the arrival of "civilization" the state is empowered to respond for the injuries done to us, which is why Tom Doniphon can never survive in such a state.

I have said that Liberty Valance plays the savage in this film. He actually plays the *ignoble* savage to Doniphon's *noble* savage. (But both, significantly, end up drunk and dead). Where does this leave Stoddard and "civilization"?

The most striking fact about this tale is that the killing of Valance and the expelling of his kind of lawlessness—a lawlessness that presumably must be expelled because it fundamentally violates the natural law of honorable violence—involves an action that itself violates that natural law. For the fight with Valance is anything but a fair fight: it is a fight of two against one, three against one if you count Pompey, and even then Doniphon shoots Valance from his blind side. The guy never had a chance. The savage, in the end, is defeated by employing savage tactics: Doniphon is quick to acknowledge this, but says that he can live with the dishonor because Hallie will be happy. He is wrong on both counts. Doniphon does not live with it very well, for the simple reason that he is now a spiritual exile: he cannot abide by the laws of civilization and he has violated the laws of nature. And Hallie, who becomes ever more buttoned up as the film progresses, does not end up very happy.

On one level, Ranse *can* live with what was done to Liberty Valance, because there was no dishonor in how he acted. On another level, though, Ranse clearly exemplifies a refusal of recognition—so it is important that we identify what it is that he has trouble living with. It seems to me that what he has trouble recognizing, and what the film suggests invariably goes unrecognized, is a more general claim about violence: that "civilization" defeats the "savage" by becoming like the "savage," which is to say that the violence that founds "civilization" (and the legal order at its heart) is one that at the same time problematizes the whole distinction

between "civilization" and its Other, and problematizes the whole justification for its existence. "Civilization" cannot recognize this, for to do so
would mean no longer recognizing itself. The self-undermining logic here
is akin to that which Derrida has more generally termed the logic of *supplementarity*—with Ranse Stoddard as the "supplement," that is, that
(somewhat external) element whose role in completing an identity at the
same time problematizes identity.[14]

What does all this suggest about the status of "civilization" and its
legal order, once they are *founded?*

MSLV does not speak to this issue directly. Its central story concludes
with the election of Stoddard by the territorial convention, anticipat-
ing its transition from territory to state. But *High Noon* certainly does.
Will Kane is the only man serious about preserving the legal order in
Hadleyville, yet his intentions clearly contradict the expressed wishes
of the people who inhabit that order, and when he carries them out he
is no longer even a marshal—having resigned the position earlier that
morning! He is, in effect, a vigilante. But the felt rightness of his actions
clearly suggests that the legal order, like "civilization" as a whole, can
only sustain itself through means that transgress its boundaries. All of
this contributes to the complexity of Kane's final act of casting down
his badge at the mayor's feet. It is natural, I think, to read this act as
Kane's renouncing his job as marshal. But Kane has already done that—
and nothing has licensed his taking it back. The badge that he rejects is
one that he no longer possesses legitimately, a badge that has endowed
him with only the appearance of legal authority.

It is, in that regard, like the false badge of honor that Ranse has worn
throughout his life (as "the man who shot Liberty Valance"), a badge
that Ranse too makes motions to reject. But the conclusion in both cases
seems to be that the arrangements of legitimacy are invariably created
and sustained by those whose badges are false.

■

The requirement to "print the legend" assumes that any community
qua community must share something like a common story, something
like a myth, if it is to be cohesive, and that the functional role of this
story/myth does not necessitate that the story/myth have much to do
with what "really" happened. This general view, I would note, is one
we find in some of the more sophisticated social contract theorists.

Rousseau, for example, begins his *Second Discourse* where *MSLV* ends—by suggesting that to understand the conditions of community we must put the facts aside as unimportant.[15] But the film does not just insist that societies require legends. It suggests that in "modern" societies, that is, societies with stable legal orders and progressive economic institutions, the myths must be *printed*—they must assume the form of historical record, a form that obviously risks obscuring their basic character as myths. The framing events of *MSLV* in fact transpire at a time, the late nineteenth century, when the relation between history and myth was very much on people's minds, particularly the minds of professional historians. It was felt by many that the society's deep crises in part reflected the waning of the country's traditional myths, but that if new myths were to be forthcoming they had to assume the guise of "objective fact" (Warren Susman has argued that Frederick Jackson Turner's influential writings on the closing of the frontier must be understood in these terms).[16] If *MSLV* presents us with a rather ironic comment on this blurring of the myth/history distinction, it does so from the perspective of the dominant mythmaking medium of our time, film—a medium that has rendered the distinction between history and myth ever more problematic.

To appreciate the power of *MSLV*'s myth, let us return to the parallel between this film and works like *Oedipus* and *King Lear*—and their epic misrecognitions between parents and children. I have spoken of Ranse and Hallie's barrenness, that at the film's end it appears that they are without any children, and it appears that this is Ranse's doing—insofar as the closer he gets to Hallie throughout the film the drier and more enclosed she becomes. Ranse and Hallie may talk of how, because of his efforts, the "desert has bloomed." As the desert has bloomed, they have withered. But Ranse is not only childless, he is also parentless in a way. In his alienated status he is something of a lost boy: the ease with which he assumes new nicknames throughout the film might lead one to conclude that he has no real name of his own. Indeed, this fluidity of identity, as distinct from the blankness of identity that Tom Doniphon suffers in death, can be associated with a condition of bastardy—that is, the condition of not being fully recognized as the child by the parent.[17] Ranse's condition seems that of a genealogical isolate; he has no one and is no one's. Again, he stands in direct contrast to George Bailey in *It's a Wonderful Life*—to whom everyone belongs and who belongs to everyone (a fact marked by the multitude of times his name is repeated in that film). George's recognition of this, and of all that he has given birth to, is a condition of his being born again. Ranse, the self-made man, cannot give birth, hence cannot be born again.

If Ranse relates to anything in a paternal manner, it is surely Shinbone itself and its democratic legal order. Just like any parents, Ranse and Hallie dote on how the town has grown, while being suitably uncomfortable in dealing with a child that has apparently gone its own way. I suggested at the outset that the film dramatizes a certain blindness of society to the conditions of its own birth, and that Ranse bears the burden of this fact. But how should we understand that burden? Ranse may relate to Shinbone as his offspring, but if (as we are led to believe) the town's birth into civilization is due to the killing of Liberty Valance, then Ranse is really not the father—Tom Doniphon is. Thus conceived, Ranse has not only assumed the paternal mantle properly due another, he has done so through an act of violence that involved stealing the true father's woman, an apparent act of cuckoldry. There are clear connections with *Oedipus* here, but also with *Hamlet* (like *Hamlet,* for example, *MSLV* reveals the truths of usurpation and cuckoldry through devices of dramatic flashback). Might Ranse's barrenness be understood then as a kind of retribution for his actions and their outcome?

But clearly Ranse did not intend any of this. Hence, if Ranse's fate is to be understood in such terms, he must properly be likened to Oedipus—one whose sufferings have a meaning for the political (and natural?) order that transcends any moral judgments of right and wrong. Clues to such a connection can be found in René Girard's interesting but also very controversial work, *Violence and the Sacred.*[18]

Girard discusses Oedipus while advancing some very interesting views about the basis of society in a founding act of violence. In Girard's account, a founding act of violence is necessary because society's general proclivity for violence cannot be contained by the sort of rational agreements dear to the heart of social contract theorists. Rather, that proclivity can only be contained by everyone's *focusing* their violence on a particular figure, or group of figures. Since it does not matter whether the object of violence in any sense "deserves" it, Girard regards the recipient of the community's violence as a *scapegoat* figure—one who, in virtue of their foundational role in the community, invariably assumes superhuman status. I have already mentioned the notion of scapegoat in connection with that of the *pharmakon;* a scapegoat serves as a *pharmakon* insofar as their expulsion both secures the boundaries of the community while problematizing them—by inscribing, into the heart of the community, what is identified as an essential threat to that community.

In *MSLV,* one sacrificial victim is clearly Liberty Valance himself, whose superhuman status is marked by the fact that it is entirely through him that the others are remembered and celebrated. It is his name, after all, that appears in the title! (On Girard's account, remember, it does not matter for their social function whether scapegoats "deserve" their fate.) One might think that Tom Doniphon is another sacrificial victim, whose fate particularly evokes Girard's claim that a community's violence will sometimes settle on its own king. But though I have spoken of Doniphon as a victim of the violence of misrecognition, the fact that he is so *un*recognized must disqualify him as a candidate for scapegoat. No, the other scapegoat can only be Ranse Stoddard himself—who experiences no physical violence, but who must suffer the fact that his community's recognition (which has little to do with who he is and what he has done) has committed him, in the name of honoring him, to a life of permanent exile. As I read it, Ranse's genealogical isolation is just the mirror of his social isolation, except that the one allows the other to be understood as a kind of condemnation, a kind of fate.

I have wondered whether society has any alternative but to originate in an ambivalent kind of violence. We might wonder whether, according to the film, Ranse's fate can be avoided. I think not: not personal failing, not bad luck, but the logic of community and its legal order require that there be individuals like Ranse who create its institutions of justice, defend its better values—and are cast out for it, perhaps because they appreciate the ambivalences that such creation and defense involve. They must suffer the violence of un- or misrecognition, so that the legal order as we know it need not give recognition to its own origins in violence. What renders Ranse an ultimately heroic figure in the film—surprisingly heroic, I think, given his unpromising beginnings—is that he seems to understand this by the end. All of Ranse's pain and alienation are focused in the film's final scene, as he departs once again from Shinbone. It is then that he speaks to Hallie of returning to Shinbone, of "setting up a little law practice," of fulfilling the desires that he believes he once had. But he doesn't believe it, and neither do we. I said the film was a tragedy.

Notes

1. My account of this film has been influenced by Tag Gallagher's discussion of it in his *John Ford: The Man and His Films* (Berkeley: University of California Press, 1986), 385–413. After completing this essay I was directed to William Luhr and Peter Lehman, *Authorship and Narrative in the Cinema* (New York: Capricorn Books, 1977), whose discussion of this film (pp. 45–84) makes many points that I did not see.

2. See Louis Althusser, "Ideology and Ideological State Apparatuses," in *Lenin and Philosophy* (New York: Monthly Review Press, 1971), 127–88.

3. Ranse participates in the destruction of Tom Doniphon (along with Doniphon himself, one might add), but Ranse does not "defeat" him—they are not adversaries in that sense.

4. Finally, one might wonder whether Ranse has truly distanced himself from Appleyard. For immediately after Valance is killed, Appleyard tries to claim false credit for the act—suggesting that he only aspires to a notoriety that Ranse in fact achieves.

5. Richard Slotkin, *Gunfighter Nation: The Myth of the Frontier in Twentieth-Century America* (New York: Atheneum, 1992), in particular 379–404.

6. The film also has an ambivalent view of "progress": while there are constant allusions to how "progress" has "made the desert bloom," the film notes that such "progress" has also thrown all the original inhabitants of Shinbone out of work.

7. The status of Kane and Ranse as barren, childless figures is connected with my sense of them as radically "disencumbered selves" in Michael Sandel's sense—akin to the abstract choosers that Sandel sees lurking behind John Rawls's "Veil of Ignorance." See Micheal J. Sandel, *Liberalism and the Limits of Justice* (Cambridge: Cambridge University Press, 1982), especially 1–65. George Bailey, by contrast, is a self that is too encumbered.

8. I am not sure what to make of the fact that the town is called "Hadleyville," and its denizens, like those in the Mark Twain story, are paragons of weakness and vanity. Reluctant Citizen (Will) Kane is the man who would not be corrupted in Hadleyville.

9. Jacques Derrida, "Plato's Pharmacy," in *Dissemination* (Chicago: University of Chicago Press, 1981), 65–171.

10. I should note that this pluralizing of truthfulness, with its blurring of the boundary between true and false, arises in another context. Near the start of the film Tom Doniphon, in an act of courtship, brings Hallie (Vera Miles) a "cactus rose," leading Ranse to later ask her "Have you ever seen a *real* rose?" Since the cactus rose acquires great importance as the film proceeds (it ultimately signifies the bond between Doniphon and Hallie and what was lost when that bond was lost), one might logically ask: Why is a cactus rose not a "real" rose? Why isn't it just a different kind of rose? The status of the "real" will

concern us below, and it will be equally suspect, in considering the notion of a "real" man.

11. This is why so-called primitive communities, which are constituted by legends and myths, are commonly identified as *oral* cultures, whereas so-called civilized communities, that are constituted by laws, are commonly identified as *written* cultures.

12. An insightful account of the gender relations in this film that is somewhat at variance with my own is found in Virginia Wright Wexman, *Creating the Couple: Love, Marriage, and Hollywood Performance* (Princeton: Princeton University Press, 1993), 116–29.

13. See Aristotle's *Politics,* Book I.

14. On the logic of supplementarity, see ". . . That Dangerous Supplement" in Jacques Derrida, *Of Grammatology* (Baltimore: Johns Hopkins University Press, 1974), 141–64.

15. J. J. Rousseau, *The Social Contract and the Discourses* (New York: Vintage Press, 1963), 128. Rather like Rawls, Rousseau regards the unity that the social contract story creates as importantly connected with its status as a medium of recognition, for the social contract story brings to recognition, by casting in relief, certain general facts about ourselves, which once recognized can provide the conditions of mutual acceptance. *MSLV* buys this general idea but stands it on its head, for the story that binds the citizens of Shinbone together is as much a medium of misrecognition.

16. Warren I. Susman, *Culture as History* (New York: Pantheon Books, 1984), chap. 1.

17. This fits with Ranse's identification with writing, whose metaphysically suspect status, Derrida has claimed, is linked to its apparent bastardy. See again Jacques Derrida, "Plato's Pharmacy."

18. René Girard, *Violence and the Sacred* (Baltimore: Johns Hopkins University Press, 1978).

THREE

Through the Great Depression on Horseback

Legal Themes in Western Films of the 1930s

FRANCIS M. NEVINS

■

From western films we can learn precious little about the historic American West but often a great deal about the time when a particular film was made. An intimate connection between a western, or for that matter any other kind of movie, and the themes and turmoil of its period adds to the film, as it does to any work of fiction, a dimension of interest that tends to grow as the work itself ages. After a generation or two, thanks to miracles of technology like the video cassette and the video projector, we who teach can use older movies almost as a form of time travel, as an introduction for students to some of the social and emotional shape of a time when even their parents were not yet born.

When I was a small boy in the early 1950s, we East Coast kids whose parents had bought one of those primitive television sets with a 12½-inch screen could enjoy seven channels—the three network affiliates, the short-lived Dumont station, and three independents—that ran very little else but old westerns, thirty or more a week. I got hooked. To some extent, as an aging law professor, I still am today. Unlike anyone else of my generation, however, I found a way to use at least a few of those westerns to enrich the law school curriculum. Fifteen years ago I created a seminar, "Law, Lawyers, and Justice in Popular Fiction and Film," in which we would explore the presentation of those topics as refracted through various novels and stories dating back to 1896 and through selected movies and episodes of television series.[1] It turned out to be the most popular seminar in St. Louis University Law School's history and

I continue to offer it once a year. A topic I take special delight in surveying with my students is the refraction of the social and legal crises of the Great Depression in the medium of certain westerns of the 1930s.

That first decade of talking films was perennially in need of story material that was rich in both emotional conflict and dialogue. Courtroom drama for this reason became a staple item on every studio's menu.[2] A few of these pictures are still esteemed today from a cinematic perspective, notably *Fury* (MGM, 1936), the first film Fritz Lang directed after his escape from Nazi Germany and subsequent resettlement in Hollywood. Most of them, however—whether still accessible on American Movie Classics and similar cable channels or surviving only in ancient vaults and as entries in comprehensive encyclopedias[3]—have little to recommend them purely as movies and are burdened with melodramatic plots and acting styles and wildly ill-informed notions of courtroom procedure that make them laughable to the legal community today and useless in a seminar like mine.[4] The major exception to this generalization, and in my judgment the finest law-related film of the decade, is William Wyler's *Counsellor at Law* (Universal, 1933), with a screenplay by former attorney Elmer Rice based on his 1931 stage play, and starring John Barrymore as a successful, well-connected New York practitioner torn apart by several personal and professional crises at the same time. The entire film takes place in a suite of law offices, and it is precisely the absence of conventional courtroom sequences that enables Wyler to dodge the bullet that maims or kills most lawyer movies of the time and to portray the practice in a manner still vivid and compelling sixty years later. Curiously enough, the same holds true for law-related 1930s westerns: those with little or no courtroom action are precisely the ones that offer the most interesting treatments of the themes of law, lawyers, and justice.

What most decisively shaped both American life and American films during the 1930s was the Depression, which brought a bleakness, cynicism, and despair to movies of all sorts, even to some of the critically invisible sixty-minute westerns.[5] Those of us who watched such pictures by the dozens on our home television screens twenty or more years later might have been amused or puzzled by how often they dealt with a greedy banker who was about to foreclose the mortgage on some young woman's ranch; but there was nothing amusing or escapist in these films to the people who were watching them in unpretentious small-town theaters at the time the pictures were made. In the thirties, losing one's home to a bank was not an exotic menace but a credible threat and all too often a grim reality. Although many sixty-minute westerns of the decade engage the desperation of the time only in relatively simple ways of this sort, a few penetrate deeper, portraying the conflict between the simple sense of decency in a community and the legal system founded on the sanctity of property and of its own rules legitimizing economic exploitation. The most engaging such film that I have discovered is *One Man Law*.

Released by Columbia early in 1932, *One Man Law* was the fourteenth in a series of twenty-eight westerns, roughly an hour in length each, which shoot-em-up superstar Buck Jones[6] made at the studio between 1930 and 1934. Like several others in the series, this one was both written and directed by Lambert Hillyer, a top specialist in films of the sort.[7] None of his other films, however, centrally engages legal themes as *One Man Law* does. Hillyer's acid contempt for a system that employs property concepts to enforce exploitation permeates almost every aspect of this extraordinary little picture.

The film opens at a sort of field day in Grass Valley County, featuring events like a turkey shoot and a horse race. The finest marksman in the valley is Brand Thompson (Buck Jones), who wins all the turkeys offered as prizes and gives them away to neighbors as fast as he receives them. That he is the most admired and trusted man in the community is clear both to us in the audience and to entrepreneur Jonathan P. Streeter (Robert Ellis), who observes Thompson as he demonstrates his shooting skills and disarms a menacing drunk. Streeter, we soon learn, has plans for Thompson's future.

Stubb (Ernie Adams), a weasel-faced outsider in Streeter's pay, approaches Thompson and manipulates him into betting that his beloved gray stallion Silver can beat Stubb's black in the day's horse race. What Thompson does not know is that the black is not a cow pony but a trained racehorse. Hillyer uses the dialogue between the two men to introduce into the film a jaundiced view of contract.

> "There never was a gray could run a lick. All grays fold up and quit too easy."
> "This gray'll be going strong when that long-legged black of yours has folded up like an empty feed bag."
> "Are you willing to risk anything on that?"
> "Anything."
> "Outfit?"
> "Sure."

"Complete outfit?"

"Down to the shirt and pants."

"That's a deal. The winner has two complete rigs."

"That's right."

"Bridles, saddles, gunbelts, boots—and two horses!"

"I never said anything about bettin' horses."

"You said two complete outfits, didn't you?'

"Sure."

"Well, that means horses too. But if you're afraid and want to welsh. . . ." [Then, after Thompson's friends have encouraged him to take the bet] "Well, what are you going to do? Are you going to back out or are you going to take a chance on your gray goat?"

"All right. Horses too."

The race itself, one of the film's highlights and a fine demonstration of Hillyer's skill as an action director, ends as expected, with Silver losing to the black by a head. Weeping, feeling not that he has lost something he owns but that he has betrayed his partner and best friend, Thompson hands over his horse to Stubb. Watching these events from the stands is Grace Duncan (Shirley Grey).

The next day Streeter invites Thompson to his luxurious ranch house, returns everything Thompson lost in the bet, including Silver, and—although careful not to tie the gift to this proposal—asks Thompson to become Grass Valley's new sheriff. Not that he expects any special favors. "Pay me by upholding the law," he says, "the very letter of the law." An ecstatic Thompson agrees and the stage is set for the film's central conflict.

Streeter and his eastern partners own title to much of the land in the valley and Streeter has leased it out in parcels to dozens of small ranchers who have spent years improving the property but without the security of legal ownership, which Streeter has often promised but never delivered. Now his eastern associates have sold these parcels of land to people who want to resettle in the West.[8] When the newcomers arrive with their deeds, they naturally enough demand possession of the land to which they have clear title under the rules of property law. Learning of this problem, Thompson goes out to Streeter, whom he still admires and trusts.

"There's been an unfortunate misunderstanding."

"That's what I thought."

"You see, my Chicago partners took certain matters into their own hands."

"Of course you'll make it good?"

"I'm deeply sorry but there's really nothing I can do about it."

"You mean the newcomers'll take possession?"

"Yes. It's the law. An unfortunate case, but nevertheless the law."

"Why, that's robbery!"

"It may seem so. But it's legal. And it's your duty to enforce it."

"It's inhuman and I won't do it!"

"Don't do anything in haste. Consult Judge Cooper before you make a rash move."

"I'll do that. I know Judge Cooper's honest."

The wise old judge (Edward J. Le Saint) confirms Streeter's view of the situation's legal aspects.

"Judge, are those deeds real?"

"Good as gold."

"And I'm supposed to put these fellows out of their homes?"

"That's your duty."

"I'll resign first!"

"That won't help anybody."

"Do you think I'd keep a job that forces me to drive my friends, people who have trusted me, off the land they've really earned?"

"Son, if you and I are going to have any chance to save those people, you've got to do that."

"I can't!"

"You've got to! . . . With you wearin' that star, maybe we can find a way."

Just as Stubb had pressured Thompson into agreeing to do something against his better judgment, so does Judge Cooper. The reluctant law man begins the process of betraying the common sense of decency in the community, of enforcing legalized robbery. "Those deeds stand," he tells the cheated ranchers. "And after tomorrow morning the legal owners will have to be given possession." "There is a law in this country after all," one of the newcomers mutters happily. All of Thompson's deputies quit their positions in disgust as he begins to dispossess his former friends. "Grimm, these folks have a legal right to this place and it's up to me to see that they get it. . . . I'm coming in, Ed, and I don't much care whether you shoot or not."

Despised by everyone in the valley, even by Grace Duncan, with whom he has fallen in love, forced to defend Streeter against threats of lynching from outraged homeless ranchers, Thompson once again consults with Judge Cooper.

"Judge, I'm through. I'm resigning. I'm going to lead those ranchers myself, and pull on the rope that lifts Streeter into the air."

"A dead Streeter wouldn't help anybody. The deeds would hold."

"I tell you I can't stand it any more!"

"You've got to! . . . The law is his weapon and we've got to turn it back on him somehow. . . . He's got to be *forced* to give back that land *willingly!*"

If a single line in the film captures its thrust with precision, that last line of Judge Cooper's is it.

At this exact moment, the golden opportunity turns up in the person of weasel-faced Stubb who, having no idea that the man he took Silver from is now the sheriff of Grass Valley, comes to Judge Cooper's office to make a criminal complaint.

"Judge! Judge, here's the answer to our prayer! Streeter stole his horse!"

"What's he worth?"

"Nine hundred."

"Grand larceny!"

"He wanted me to sell, and when I wouldn't, he hit me over the head."

"Assault and battery!"

"He hit me over the head with a tin money box. See?"

"With a deadly weapon!"

By this time Streeter has sold his ranch and is about to leave the state. Thompson rushes out to serve the judge's warrant before Streeter can remove himself from the jurisdiction, but his former deputies seize him and lock him up in his own jail so that he cannot stop the ranchers' lynch mob forming outside of town. When Grace Duncan comes to see him in his cell, he pleads with her to help him escape, which she does. Thompson, riding Silver, reaches the ranch just as Streeter is heading for the border on the black racehorse and the mob is approaching from another direction. Hillyer has brought the film around full circle to climax with another race between the same horses that competed at the beginning. After a well-directed chase scene, Thompson bulldogs Streeter off the black horse just a few feet beyond the state line marker and, in yet another gesture of contempt for rules of law, drags him back inside the jurisdiction and serves him with the warrant.

The film's final scene takes place back in the jailhouse, with Streeter, not Thompson, now in a cell.

> "But I tell you, Thompson, I've got to get out of here! I want to post bail."
>
> "Can't find Judge Cooper. He sets the amount."
>
> [Cut to a shot of the judge, sitting in Thompson's office and silently chuckling.]
>
> "That's ridiculous!"
>
> "No, it's the law."
>
> "I'm not a criminal!"
>
> "That warrant says you broke the law."
>
> "But I'm in danger! Suppose those ranchers find out I'm here?"
>
> "They know it by now."
>
> "But you can't protect me alone!"
>
> "I'm not going to try, Streeter. I think too much of my neck. Besides, I'm resigning as soon as Judge Cooper gets here."
>
>   . . .
>
> "Thompson! Thompson! I'll give you five thousand dollars to let me out of here!"
>
> "That wouldn't be legal."

Ultimately, a deal is struck. In return for not being lynched, Streeter will give the ranchers deeds to the property that by rights should be theirs and will reimburse all the newcomers what they paid for the land plus a bonus for their time and trouble. On this note Hillyer closes the legal aspects of *One Man Law,* reserving the fade-out for a kiss between Buck Jones and Shirley Grey. Of course, if any of the newcomers had decided not to take back their money but instead to keep the land they legally owned, the stage would have been set for a sequel film, without villains, and built around a genuinely tragic situation in which right clashes with right. Such a film would seem to have been beyond Lambert Hillyer's genuine but not unlimited gifts. He continued to direct low-budget features throughout the 1930s and 1940s, then began directing thirty-minute episodes of early 1950s television series like *The Cisco Kid*—in which he occasionally recycled sequences and whole story lines from *One Man Law* and other westerns he had made with Buck Jones at Columbia more than twenty years before.

If ever there was a communitarian and populist cinema in the United States, it certainly encompassed those so-called B westerns that grappled in their own way with the desperation of the time. In *One Man Law* and countless similar films, the unscrupulous banker or businessman is typically the only member of the cast who wears a suit, while the common folk dress in farmers' and ranch hands' garb—basically the same dress code one finds in the seminal Soviet films of the 1920s. These little westerns, made *by* people without much money and *for* people with far less, were hugely popular but never taken seriously or even noticed by those who followed what was happening on the nation's theater screens. Even today most film scholars continue to believe that no talking westerns worth a moment of their attention were made until John Ford's *Stagecoach* set out across the salt flats in 1939, dismissing unseen the dozens of sixty-minute shoot-em-ups in which John Wayne starred before Ford cast him as the Ringo Kid. One of those pictures, the only one that deals centrally with legal themes, is *King of the Pecos* (1936).

Wayne played the lead in six "B" westerns for Warners (1932–33) and sixteen for Monogram (1933–35), a small studio that included a contract for his services among its assets when, in the summer of 1935, it merged with several other Poverty Row operations into the newly formed Republic Pictures. During the 1935–36 season Wayne starred in eight more "B" westerns,[9] three of them directed by Joseph Kane (1894–1975), a former film editor who had taken up this new career only a year before.[10] By far the best of Kane's trio with Wayne was *King of the Pecos*, which resembles *One Man Law* in being constructed around the conflict between law that exploits the people and law that serves the people, but breaks new ground in placing two lawyer characters at the heart of the conflict.

When Holmes in "The Path of the Law"[11] suggested that the proper definition of law was from the perspective of "the bad man" who cares nothing for morality and will do anything in his own interests unless he is constrained by the social system, he seemed to have in mind the robber barons who dominated the American landscape in the decades after the Civil War and the social Darwinian world view that sanctified their outrages. Holmes did not discuss the proper role of the lawyer in the legal order he described, but the conclusion that seems to follow from his premises is that the attorney's job is to keep his "bad man" client just this side of the arbitrary technical lines dividing legal from illegal conduct. Such a social Darwinian view of lawyers and law is at the heart of the vast majority of the scathing portrayals of the profession that we find in novels, stories, and films throughout twentieth-century American popular culture, including *King of the Pecos*.

The film opens with a close-up of a rotating wagon wheel as a band of newcomers with a cattle herd wearily cross a desert landscape. But Kane quickly shows us that these are not the heroic pioneers of western myth; they are exploiters, home-grown conquistadors, bad men in every sense of the term, including that of Holmes. They are led by three men, each one standing for something exceptionally evocative for audiences during the Depression and each one represented by an exceptionally appropriate physical object. The obese capitalist Alexander Stiles (Cy Kendall), whose symbol is reserved for later in the film; his tame lawyer Brewster (J. Frank Glendon), whose symbol is the law book; his tame killer Ash (Jack Clifford), represented of course by the gun; these are the evil trinity in *King of the Pecos*.

Two hundred miles from the river of the title, Stiles halts his party and announces: "Boys, I claim this land by right of discovery. We'll locate here." That night over the campfire he confers with his attorney.

> "Stiles, your right of discovery may not hold in the future. Being your lawyer, I suggest that you let me draw up the proper legal papers. You can buy up the land with a pile of dirt-cheap land scrip."
>
> "We won't have to do that, Brewster. All we have to do is control the water holes. You file on them, and Ash and his men will hold the land for me with their guns. . . . What do you suppose our little empire'll survey?"
>
> "Oh, about a million acres."
>
> "Not bad for a start."

Studying a map of the territory, Stiles recognizes the strategic importance of the water hole at a remote location called Sweetwater.

> "Put Sweetwater down, Brewster. When they start driving Texas cattle to the Kansas markets, that's going to be the key to our empire."

"Might be trouble about Sweetwater. Man by the name of Clayborn's already settled there."

"Oh? Well, that's all right. I'll buy him out fair and square."

"What if he refuses to sell?"

"Brewster, you learned your law from Blackstone. Ash learned his from Judge Colt's. If Blackstone loses, I'm counting on Colt's to win."

Stiles pays a visit to John Clayborn (John Beck), who is making a new home in the wilderness with his wife (Mary MacLaren) and teenage son (Bradley Metcalfe).

"I'll give you five hundred dollars for your land and your shanty just as they stand. You can take your cattle and move on to a new range."

"This place isn't for sale, Stiles."

"I'll be more than fair. A thousand."

"I'm not sellin'!"

"We're buying up this country with land scrip. You'd better take the thousand."

"I've held my homestead against Comanches. Reckon I can hold it against land thieves. Get out."

"I'm sorry, Clayborn. A thousand dollars is a heap of money when all you've got to do is call your dog and move on."

There is a cut to Stiles and his gunmen attacking the Clayborn cabin from the hills around it. Young John's parents are murdered and the boy is brutally beaten and left for dead by Ash. A split second of screen time later—no one ever accused Joe Kane of boring transitions—the boy has become a man (John Wayne), a lawyer and, as we see, a crack shot. Dialogue between the relative that raised him and another rancher tells us that ten years have passed since his parents were slaughtered.

"Well, Henry, I see the boy's still at it. What's he plannin' to be, a lawyer or a gunman?"

"Looks like both."

"Well, when you hang your shingle you'll get my business. You oughta be right smart at collectin'."

"Thanks, Bill. But there's one case I've got to take care of first. John Clayborn versus Alexander Stiles."

As luck or Kane would have it, the stagecoach on which Clayborn travels to the Texas town of Cottonwood, which is the center of Stiles's million-acre kingdom, is also carrying Eli Jackson (Edward Hearn) and his lovely daughter Belle (Muriel Evans), who have bought property from Stiles by mail. The stagecoach is also carrying a huge safe imported by Stiles from St. Louis as a secure home for his money. The head of the film's evil trinity has found his symbol. When the coach reaches Cottonwood and the safe is unloaded, Stiles describes it to his men.

"They call her a Salamander because she can go through the hottest fire and never melt."

"They got nothing on you, Stiles. I ain't never seen anything make you melt either."

This is how John Clayborn, who has shortened his name to Clay, identifies his target. He approaches Stiles and introduces himself as an attorney intending to start a practice in Cottonwood.

"I'm afraid you've come to the wrong town, Mr. Clay. We already have one lawyer here. That's plenty."

"I'll take a chance on that."

Local ranchers Hank Matthews (Arthur Aylesworth) and Josh Billings (Herbert Heywood) are passing by during this exchange and take Clayborn aside a minute or two later.

"You one of them law fellas?"

"Yes."

"Well, me and Josh here have got a case for you. . . . Come up to the shack. I want to talk to you."

At their cabin the two old codgers explain to Clayborn how Stiles has become king of the Pecos.

"Let me get this straight. Stiles buys your cattle, pays you back with these notes which he refuses to honor."

"You're dang tootin'. The only way we can get anything out of 'em is discount 'em in half and take 'em out in trade at his store."

"Why do you sell him your cattle?"

"We gotta or he won't give us no more water. He owns every drop in the country. . . ."

"Sounds like a polite form of cattle rustling to me. I'll take your case, Hank."

Meanwhile, back in Cottonwood, Ash, Brewster, and Stiles are discussing their latest victim.

> "Did you give that fella Jackson fifty head of stock?"
> "He signed our usual sales contract. He has the utmost confidence in Mr. Stiles."
> "Yeah. He's working for me now and doesn't know it."

When Clayborn comes into Stiles's office and serves him with a summons and complaint, Stiles tears them up. On the day scheduled for the hearing, with the county courthouse packed, the sheriff bulls his way in and pounds the judge's bench with his gun butt. "Court's open." He pounds again. "Court's adjourned." There is a huge belly laugh at Clayborn's expense. "Where's the judge?" he demands. "He wasn't able to get here," the sheriff chuckles. As the scene ends, Clayborn and Stiles briefly exchange pleasantries.

> "Don't be discouraged, Clay. This court may open most any time in the next twenty years."
> "This court will be open Monday morning, Stiles. You'll be here."

Having had his eyes opened to one of the film's central themes, that law is an empty shell without the armed support of the people, Clayborn calls a secret night meeting of the small ranchers under Stiles's heel.

> "Men, for years you've been paying tribute to Stiles for the use of his water holes. You let him sell your cattle for worthless notes. How long are you going to stand for it?"
> "How are you going to stop him?"
> "I'll tell you how. Stiles claims all the water rights around here. As a lawyer I'm here to tell you that those claims wouldn't be recognized by any court in the Union."
> "You mean to say that the water rights don't belong to Stiles?"
> "We can prove that they're in public domain and open for you men to file on. Now here's how we'll go about it."

On Monday morning Judge Dunlap rides into Cottonwood, surrounded by an armed escort party of ranchers. Under the aegis of their firepower he opens court and makes a speech of gratitude: "I am thankful to you citizens for offering the court the protection it has lacked in the past. You have made it possible for me to render justice impartially." Then he calls the case. Kane has no interest in legal technicalities, but the courtroom scene gives him the opportunity to contrast the oral styles of Clayborn, the servant of the people, and Brewster, the servant of power.

"Your Honor, I represent the independent cattle owners of the section. They've come here to petition the court for the right to water their herds. For years they've been paying toll to the defendant, Alexander Stiles, for the use of water which is in public domain. I wish to submit evidence proving the defendant has no ownership of these water rights."

"In rebuttal I offer these documents for the defendant, Alexander Stiles, showing that the aforesaid Alexander Stiles has filed on and is legal owner of said water rights in question before this court."

The judge orders a two-hour recess while he studies the papers. Stiles and Brewster conduct a quick conference.

"There's no chance of losing this case, is there?"
"Not a chance, Salamander, not a chance."
"You'd better be sure. I haven't lost yet and I don't intend to start now."

This is followed by an ironic exchange between Stiles and Clayborn.

"I've run this country for the past ten years fair and square, and there isn't a living soul that can say a word against me."
"That's right. Dead men tell no tales."

Ash picks up one of Brewster's law books, follows Clayborn out to the street and literally throws the book at him. Clayborn knocks Ash down—reversing the scene early in the film where he had been beaten by Ash and left for dead—but the gun duel between them that seems inevitable is postponed when Judge Dunlap returns to the bench with his decision: "And the evidence before the court proves conclusively that while the defendant Alexander Stiles has filed on all these rights, he is entitled to only one claim in accordance with the homestead laws of this nation. Therefore it becomes the duty of this court to declare the aforementioned water rights are in public domain, open for filing."

There is a mad scramble out of the courtroom as everyone goes off to file their claims, which apparently requires a long ride to a distant town. As he leaves the courtroom, Clayborn has a final word for Stiles:

Attorney John Clayborn (John Wayne) finds a six shooter more effective than a law book in establishing justice in *King of the Pecos*.

"I beat you in a civil case, Stiles, but I specialize in criminal law. Particularly murder." As soon as Clayborn is out of the room, Stiles turns to his tame killer. "Ash, this calls for your kind of law now."

Roughly thirty minutes of screen time has elapsed to this point. From here on, law is literally out of the picture as Kane concentrates on action. "I doubt if there was anybody in the business who could move people any better in action films than Joe," one of the stunt men who worked with Kane said many years later. "He might kill you in the process, but he always got the job done on time and on budget."[12] Ash and his gunmen take cover in the hills and prepare to shoot down the ranchers as they ride past, while Stiles's proxies, who are wearing white armbands, will be allowed through the gauntlet. Clayborn frustrates the plot by stealing a pile of women's underwear from Stiles's store and improvising white armbands for the ranchers. He is wounded in the gun battle between factions but escapes through a cave with two exits. Later, in Cottonwood, Stiles fires Brewster for losing the water litigation, then sends Ash out to murder his former lawyer and recover his share of their profits.

The film's climax is precipitated when the Texas Pacific Railroad reaches Abilene and the new Kansas shipping point raises the price of Texas cattle from three dollars a head to twenty. Suddenly the small ranchers' herds are worth a fortune. "Round up every head of stock on the ranches I still control," Stiles orders Ash. "If they don't want to give 'em to you, take 'em." The gunmen seize as many cattle as they can, killing Eli Jackson in the process. Clayborn calls another meeting of ranchers and organizes a massive cattle drive that, as Stiles had predicted years before, must stop on the way to Abilene at the water hole he had taken by murdering Clayborn's parents. "Load the Salamander safe on a wagon. I'm heading for Sweetwater."

Clayborn and the ranchers reach Sweetwater with their herd and, as they expected, find it occupied and fortified. There is a final exchange of dialogue between the adversaries.

> "What's on your mind, Clay?"
> "Couple of things. I want you to open this gate so our cattle can have water."
> "I'll be glad to open it—for fifty percent of the herd."
> "Stiles, you have no right to block this trail."
> "No? Well, this is one piece of property I have a legal deed for."
> "And I know where you got it."
> "What do you mean?"

"I'm John Clayborn. Stiles, I want you and Ash to surrender. You're going back to Cottonwood and stand trial for murder."

Stiles of course refuses and the final conflict breaks out as Clayborn and the ranchers take basically the same positions Stiles and his men had taken in the hills above Sweetwater ten years before and besiege the cabin with a hail of lead. The siege is broken when Clayborn uses improvised flaming arrows to set fire to the cabin containing Stiles, his men, and the Salamander so that we are reminded of the joke about nothing melting either the fat man or his safe. Many of Stiles's gunfighters are cut down while trying to escape from the burning cabin and load the safe on the wagon. Stiles, Ash, and the remnants of his gang flee across the desert with the ranchers in hot pursuit, a furious action sequence that ends with something that looks more like a horrible accident than a planned stunt. The four horses pulling Stiles's wagon stumble over one another and the wagon with Stiles and the safe goes over a cliff. As Clayborn and his men ride up, Kane gives us a powerful close-up of the fat capitalist lying dead on the dry earth and his emblematic safe lying on its side next to him. Clayborn completes his revenge by chasing Ash into the rocks and, in their long-delayed but inevitable gun duel, shooting him down.

I never met Joseph Kane, but back in the early 1970s, when I was a young professor and he was almost eighty, we had some phone conversations and a little correspondence. On one occasion, perhaps a year or two after the 1972 presidential election, he mentioned that he still kept a McGovern bumper sticker on his car. This is precisely what one would expect from the man who, almost forty years before, had directed this rich little film about the connections among economic power, brute force, and the law. How I wish he had lived long enough to address one of my seminars!

By the end of the thirties, political dictatorship and the coming war in Europe had largely taken over the roles that economic injustice and the Depression had played in American life and popular culture for most of the decade.[13] The cycle of lawyer films set in the present petered out with pictures like *The Spellbinder* (1939) and *The Man Who Talked Too Much* (1940), which were inferior remakes of *State's Attorney* and *The Mouthpiece* from 1932. The cycle of law-related westerns, however, ended on a brighter note.

Made in the last months of 1939 and released in the first week of 1940, *Legion of the Lawless* was the twelfth in a group of sixteen westerns made at RKO between 1938 and 1940 starring George O'Brien[14] and (with two exceptions) directed by David Howard.[15] All sixteen, which nowadays are periodically shown on the TNT and American Movie Classics cable networks, are well worth seeing, but *Legion of the Lawless* is the only one in which O'Brien plays a lawyer. What makes this film a distinct rarity is that it presents an overwhelmingly positive picture of what lawyers are and do.

Wearing a neat suit, Jeff Toland (George O'Brien) is riding past a sign that places him a few miles from the communities of Ivestown and East Ivestown when a peddler on a wagon (Horace Murphy) is chased by gunmen across the bridge that divides those locations. He explains to Toland that he was turned back by force while on his way to deliver supplies to Lafe Barton, the owner of East Ivestown's general store. Toland suggests that he sue the people who stopped him and identifies himself as an attorney intending to practice in the area. The peddler discourages him. "Ivestown doesn't crave strangers. East Ivestown, you'd starve to death."

Toland rides on into Ivestown anyway, and the people on the street turn their backs to him as he dismounts and enters the El Dorado saloon. The bartender (Rychard Cramer) won't talk to him, and the only customer, Doc Denton (Herbert Heywood), the town drunk, can't. A brutally beaten Lafe Barton (Eddy Waller) staggers into the saloon and falls over. While Toland plays Good Samaritan and tries to take care of the injured storekeeper, Les Harper (Norman Willis), who was responsible for the beating, comes in and tosses Barton out and back across the line into East Ivestown where he belongs. Later a sobered-up Doc Denton explains to Toland that Harper is de facto head of the masked vigilante organization originally formed by his brother-in-law Henry Ives to maintain law and order in Ivestown. Its main function at present is to keep the have-nots in their place on the east side.

Not long afterward, Toland meets Ives's daughter Ellen (Virginia Vale) and tells her he is hanging up his shingle in the community.

"But lawyers have to have courts to practice in, sheriffs, and judges. We haven't any of those in Ivestown."

"Oh, but you will. Ivestown's growing up. The railroad's coming through here. That's why I'm here. You know? Early bird catches worm?"

Doc Denton expresses the same lack of enthusiasm for Toland's law practice, telling him: "The only law here is the vigilantes."

No sooner has Toland opened his office than he is visited by Henry Ives (Hugh Sothern), a gunman named Borden (Monte Montague), and Les Harper. "We don't need any lawyers in this town, Toland," Harper snarls. "That might be a matter of opinion, Harper," Toland replies. Unlike his brother-in-law, Ives is willing to debate the question, and his dialogue with Toland is from a legal perspective the most crucial in the film.

"Let me remind you that the history of the West is a history of violence and bloodshed. Every new settlement has been overrun with the worst type of lawbreaker, outlaw, and murderer. Because I was determined that Ivestown should be a city of homes and happy prosperous families, I took steps to see that such riffraff had no chance to take root here."

"So you formed the vigilantes."

"Exactly. With the full approval of our territorial governor. I tell you, ruffians give us a wide berth. If they don't, we know how to take care of them."

"Primitive and dangerous. Every man has the right to a public trial. Supposing your vigilante committee should make a mistake? What chance has that man to get justice?"

"Every case is considered fairly. We never make a move till we're positive we're right."

"A good theory—for a small community. But Ivestown's growing up. The railroad's coming through this far. There will be a great many problems that your vigilante committee won't be able to settle."

Harper breaks into the discussion with a threat to give Toland the kind of beating Lafe Barton got. Toland has a brawl with Borden after the gunman kicks the teenage boy (William Benedict) who was sweeping the sidewalk in front of the law office. Harper is about to shoot Toland in the back during the fight when Ellen Ives stops him. Later Toland and Ellen have a talk of the same sort he had with her father, only without a violent conclusion.

"The kind of peace I hate, Miss Ellen, is the one that is forced on people by abusing and terrorizing them. And that's what you're going to have here, just as long as your so-called vigilantes keep out organized law and order."

"You don't know what you're talking about, Mr. Toland. This is the best-run town in the territory."

"I don't doubt there's some good in the committee. But with the wrong man at the head of it, it becomes a dangerous weapon. Just as it is here."

As in other series westerns of the late 1930s,[16] the masked vigilantes are intended to evoke their contemporary counterpart, the Ku Klux Klan.

As Dave Marden (Delmar Watson) and a team of railroad surveyors arrive in Ivestown, Henry Ives ponders the changes in the world around him and contemplates calling a meeting of the vigilantes to discuss whether they should disband. Meanwhile, Harper starts buying up the property in Ivestown that he thinks the railroad will want and sends his goons to ransack Toland's office and scare him out of town. Believing that his best hope of changing Ives's mind is through his daughter, Toland persuades Ellen to visit East Ivestown with him and see how the other half lives. Lafe Barton's small son throws a rock at Ellen's horse as she's crossing the bridge into the ghetto. Toland asks Lafe to make a list of the crimes committed by the vigilantes but, lacking all faith in the promise of a legal system, the storekeeper refuses to cooperate.

A week later, chief surveyor Marden asks Toland to notarize his report and reveals that the railroad is going to go through East Ivestown. "The folks in East Ivestown are finally going to get a break," Toland exults as he gets Doc Denton to sign the report as a witness. Harper and his men get the doctor so drunk that he tells them the news, then they ransack Marden's papers and read the report for themselves. Toland knows that trouble will follow.

That night he follows Harper and a group of vigilantes as they ride across the bridge into East Ivestown, force a Mexican blacksmith (Martin Garralaga) to sign over his property, then move on to Lafe Barton's store and make him the same sort of "offer he can't refuse": take fifty dollars for the property and get out of town within forty-eight hours or die. Toland breaks in, a gun battle erupts and Barton's son is seriously wounded, though not before pulling a heart-shaped ornament from the gun belt of the masked vigilante who shot him. The assailants escape but leave behind bills of sale for every piece of property in East Ivestown, with the purchaser identified simply as "bearer."

Armed with this evidence, Toland visits Ives and finally persuades him to call an immediate meeting and disband the vigilantes, but Harper and his faction kill Ives on the trail and Toland finds the body. Harper then takes over the meeting, which is being held at the El Dorado, announces that the railroad will bypass Ivestown completely and, over the objections of the responsible members of the group, organizes the vigilantes to take over East Ivestown by force. Doc Denton eavesdrops on the meeting, rides off to warn Toland, who has gone to tell Ellen Ives of her father's murder, and confesses that it was his fault that Harper learned of the railroad's plans.

That night Toland gets to East Ivestown ahead of the vigilantes and organizes the oppressed into a self-defense force. The downtrodden hold an instant plebiscite and vote to secede from Ivestown and appoint Toland their sheriff. When the vigilantes ride into the ghetto they are surprised by the defenders and Harper is unmasked. "Les Harper, I arrest you for attempted murder," Toland says. Barton and the outraged residents of East Ivestown want to lynch their prisoner on the spot. "We'll do this legally, Lafe," Toland replies, and they find a building where Harper can be locked up. Meanwhile the vigilantes regroup, set fire to East Ivestown and free their leader. The people of East Ivestown are ready to set fires of their own in retaliation but Toland resists this move on the ground that "Most of the vigilantes don't belong to Harper's gang" and bargains for thirty minutes to bring Harper back. He finds the gang barricaded in the El Dorado, shoots it out with them—the fact that Ivestown is outside his jurisdiction being conveniently overlooked by all hands—and kills Harper just as the East Ivestown people march on the saloon and complete the mopping up. The governor disbands what is left of the vigilantes and Toland prepares to marry Ellen and settle down to a peaceful law practice as the film ends.

With the movement from the anguish of the Depression to the agony of the war, legal themes both in westerns and in American movies as a whole tended to recede into the background.[17] For example, when *Legion of the Lawless* was remade less than three years later as *Pirates of the Prairie* (RKO, 1942, directed by Howard Bretherton and starring Tim Holt), the protagonist was no longer a lawyer but a gunsmith. Cinematic interest in legal motifs did not return in full force until the war was over and the McCarthy-HUAC reign of cultural terror in the early fifties had run its course.[18] The period that extends roughly from 1957 through 1965 and more or less coincides with the great years of the Warren Court is often considered the golden age of American films on the subject of law, lawyers, and justice,[19] not only because of the sheer number of excellent movies the period generated—*Twelve Angry Men* (1957), *Anatomy of a Murder* (1959), *Inherit the Wind* (1960), *Judgment at Nuremberg* (1961), *To Kill a Mockingbird* (1962), and the unsung classic *Man in the Middle* (1963), to name a few—but also because so many films of the time, not to mention television series like *Perry Mason* (1957–66) and *The Defenders* (1961–65), presented lawyers and the legal system in idealistic if not idealized terms.[20] If there is any bridge leading back from this period to the law-related westerns of the Depression, it is that unpretentious little picture *Legion of the Lawless*, where George O'Brien portrays virtually an Atticus Finch on horseback and where the lawyer's function is to overthrow injustice and exploitation by subjecting them to a regime of rules. Someday perhaps such portrayals will be credible again.

Countless westerns not only from the thirties but from every decade deal either with the struggle between frontier anarchy and emerging social order or with the struggle between an evolved but unjust social order and the felt need to set things right by taking the law into one's own hands. Some films like John Ford's *The Man Who Shot Liberty Valance* (1962), the subject of this book's previous chapter, seem to deal with both themes at once. Richard Slotkin, in *Gunfighter Nation* (1992), refers to westerns centering on the first of these motifs as "Town Tamer" stories and to those centering on the second as "Outlaw" stories.[21] If we apply these terms to the better-known and critically more respectable westerns of the thirties, films like *Law and Order* (Universal, 1932, directed by Edward L. Cahn and starring Walter Huston) and *The Arizonian* (RKO, 1935, directed by Charles Vidor and starring Richard Dix) would fall into the Town Tamer classification, while perhaps the finest examples of the Outlaw category would be William Wellman's *The Robin Hood of El Dorado* (MGM, 1936, starring Warner Baxter as Joaquin Murieta), and Henry King's *Jesse James* (Twentieth Century–Fox, 1939, starring Tyrone Power and Henry Fonda). The "B" or series westerns from the thirties would yield several more instances of both types including some with the stars of the three pictures discussed at length in this chapter. *The New Frontier* (Republic, 1935, with John Wayne) and *The Marshal of Mesa City* (RKO, 1939, with George O'Brien in a remake of *The Arizonian*) would fit comfortably within the Town Tamer rubric, and the Outlaw category would encompass *The Avenger* (Columbia, 1931, with Buck Jones as Murieta).

My reason for choosing different films and a different approach in this chapter is that such westerns as I have just listed are "about" legal themes in a predominantly abstract and philosophic way, somewhat like the *Oresteia* of Aeschylus or the political writings of Hobbes and Locke. If our search is for something more concrete, for westerns that engage more strictly legal subject matter akin to what law professors and students (not to mention practicing lawyers) grapple with every day, we find at most a handful in any decade and scarcely any from the thirties except the three discussed in the body of this chapter. But, assuming that we care for westerns at all, I believe that those of us who are both trained in law and devoted to movies are apt to find uniquely interesting the rare kind of western on which I have concentrated here.

Notes

1. For a discussion of the aims and approaches of the seminar, see Francis M. Nevins, "Law, Lawyers, and Justice in Popular Fiction and Film," *Humanities Education* 1:2 (May 1984): 3–12.

2. A cross section of such films from the thirties would include *A Free Soul* (MGM, 1931, directed by Clarence Brown and starring Lionel Barrymore in an Oscar-winning performance as an alcoholic trial lawyer); *The Mouthpiece* (Warner Brothers, 1932, directed by James Flood and Elliott Nugent, with Warren William in the title role); *State's Attorney* (RKO, 1932, directed by George Archainbaud, with Lionel's brother John Barrymore in the lawyer part this time); *Lawyer Man* (Warner Brothers, 1932, directed by William Dieterle and starring William Powell); *Evelyn Prentice* (MGM, 1934, directed by William K. Howard, with Powell again playing the attorney); *Bordertown* (Warner Brothers, 1934, directed by Archie Mayo, starring Paul Muni as a Latino lawyer); *The Witness Chair* (RKO, 1936, directed by George Nicholls Jr., with Ann Harding and, as the attorney, Walter Abel); *Criminal Lawyer* (RKO, 1937, directed by Christy Cabanne, with Lee Tracy in the title role); and *The Spellbinder* (RKO, 1939, a remake of *State's Attorney,* directed by Jack Hively and with Lee Tracy in the Barrymore part). All of these and many more, for example the six-picture Perry Mason series released by Warner Brothers between 1934 and 1937, have been shown in recent years on cable. *The Mouthpiece, Lawyer Man,* and the first of the Mason films, *The Case of the Howling Dog* (Warner Brothers, 1934, directed by Alan Crosland, with Warren William as Mason), seem to me the most rewarding of the lot.

3. Browsing through a multivolume work like *The Motion Picture Guide* (Chicago: CineBooks, 1985–87), edited by Jay Robert Nash and Stanley Ralph Ross, one finds all sorts of little-known and rarely seen films that bear on the cinematic treatment of legal themes. How many times have feminist-minded students told me that *Adam's Rib* (MGM, 1949, directed by George Cukor, starring Spencer Tracy and Katharine Hepburn) was the first movie about a woman lawyer? Much earlier pictures with a female attorney in the leading role, such as *Ann Carver's Profession* (Columbia, 1933, directed by Edward

Buzzell, starring Fay Wray) and *Portia on Trial* (Republic, 1937, directed by George Nicholls Jr., with Frieda Inescort as the Portia) have never been on video cassette or cable and therefore never existed. With the recent publication of *The American Film Institute Catalog: Feature Films, 1931–1940* (Berkeley: University of California Press, 1993), we finally have a reference work with a decent subject guide to law-related movies from the talkies' first decade. Similar films from the forties, however, remain inaccessible in reference works, leaving most law students totally ignorant of pictures like *Smart Woman* (Allied Artists, 1948, directed by Edward A. Blatt, starring Constance Bennett and Brian Aherne), which dealt with a pair of feuding lawyers married to each other: the same situation as in *Adam's Rib* but played seriously, not for laughs.

4. Powerful though it is when judged purely in cinematic terms, Lang's *Fury* would be a disaster in a law-school seminar. In the trial of twenty-two members of the lynch mob that burned down a small-town jail and (so it is charged) incinerated the innocent prisoner within (Spencer Tracy), the prosecutor never presents any evidence of a dead body—not surprising since Tracy in fact escaped alive—and opens his case by putting on the stand various townspeople who swear to alibis for various defendants and then pillorying each of his own witnesses! If Lang consulted any lawyers before making this picture they must have been admitted to the bar of Cloud Cuckoo Land.

5. Nearly a thousand such films were released between 1930 and 1939. For titles, credits, and other information, see Les Adams and Buck Rainey, *Shoot-em-Ups* (New Rochelle, N.Y.: Arlington House, 1978).

6. Jones was born Charles Gebhard at Vincennes, Indiana, in 1891 and became a headlined rodeo rider and roper in his early twenties. He found his way into the movies after World War I, starring in more than sixty features for the Fox studio, most of them westerns, between 1920 and 1927. His directors at Fox included John Ford, William Wellman, and Lambert Hillyer, about whom see note 7. During the thirties and early forties, Jones starred in western series at Columbia (1930–34), Universal (1934–37), and smaller studios. In November 1942, while on a war bond tour, he burned to death in the disastrous Cocoanut Grove fire. Half a century later he is still considered one of the foremost screen cowboys. See Buck Rainey, *The Life and Films of Buck Jones: The Silent Era* (Waynesville, N.C.: World of Yesterday Publications, 1988), and *The Life and Films of Buck Jones: The Sound Era* (Waynesville, N.C.: World of Yesterday Publications, 1991).

7. Hillyer, like Jones, was born in Indiana, sometime between 1888 and 1895, depending on which reference book one consults. He began directing westerns starring William S. Hart in 1917. The features he made during the twenties were a mixed bag but included three films with Tom Mix and five with Buck Jones, all for the Fox studio. Between 1931 and 1935 he worked exclusively at Columbia and for the first half of this stint he directed nothing but Buck Jones westerns. His best-known nonwesterns are the two horror films he

made at Universal, *The Invisible Ray* (1935) and *Dracula's Daughter* (1936). During the forties he directed dozens of sixty-minute westerns, first at Columbia, later at Monogram; then when television began displacing the quickie features that were his stock-in-trade he signed a contract with Ziv Studios and made episodes of early television series like *I Led Three Lives* and *The Cisco Kid*. He died sometime between 1960 and 1962, again depending on which reference work one consults.

8. Hillyer subtly flubs his plotting at this point in the film. When Streeter manipulates Thompson into accepting the sheriff's badge, he expects to be long gone by the time the newcomers reach Grass Valley with their deeds—and therefore he has no real reason to want in office someone who will enforce "the very letter of the law." According to the film, Streeter's eastern associates sold the land prematurely and the sale of his own ranch in Grass Valley was somehow held up so that he is still around to feel the original ranchers' wrath when the new settlers arrive. But he could not have anticipated any of this at the time he rigged the horse race.

9. Most books on Wayne give these films short shrift. For fuller discussions than usual, see Don Miller, *Hollywood Corral* (New York: Popular Library, 1976), chap. 6, and Allen Eyles, *John Wayne* (2d ed., South Brunswick, N.J.: A. S. Barnes, 1979), 31–55.

10. For a substantial essay on Kane's career, see Harry Sanford, "Joseph Kane," in *Close-Up: The Contract Director,* ed. Jon Tuska (Metuchen, N.J.: Scarecrow Press, 1976), 143–87.

11. 10 Harv. L. Rev. 457 (1897).

12. Sanford, "Joseph Kane," 143.

13. Beginning in 1938, one can find covert references to Hitler within the structure of series westerns, cliffhanger serials, and other types of popular film, as robber-baron capitalists like Streeter in *One Man Law* and Stiles in *King of the Pecos* are phased out of the villain roles and replaced by political tyrants commanding uniformed legions of killers. It was not by chance that Stanley Andrews, who played the führer of Texas in Republic's fifteen-chapter serial *The Lone Ranger* (1938), looked so much like Hitler; nor that Killer Kane, the Capone-like interplanetary gangster of the Buck Rogers science fiction comic strip, was transformed into "The Leader Kane" in Universal's twelve-chapter serial *Buck Rogers* (1939), starring Buster Crabbe and with a story line clearly reflecting contemporary events in Europe; nor that the evil Emperor Ming from earlier Flash Gordon cliffhangers lost his similarity to Dr. Fu Manchu and was given a military uniform, the motto "I am the universe," and the title The Dictator Ming in Universal's twelve-chapter *Flash Gordon Conquers the Universe* (1940), with Buster Crabbe again in the lead. Two of the best Hitler-inspired sixty-minute westerns from the same period are *The Night Riders* (1939) and *The Kansas Terrors* (1939), both entries in Republic's long-running Three Mesquiteers series. But even after the United States entered the war, an occa-

sional western still pitted the hero against a thirties-style economic exploiter. In *Texas Masquerade* (United Artists, 1943) the economic exploiter is also a lawyer, and Hopalong Cassidy (William Boyd) poses as an attorney to thwart him.

14. O'Brien was born in 1900 and became a major star at the Fox studio during the 1920s, perhaps his best known silents being John Ford's *The Iron Horse* (1924) and F. W. Murnau's *Sunrise* (1927). In the thirties he starred almost exclusively in westerns, first at Fox, later at RKO. After Pearl Harbor he joined the Navy and made it his second career, although fellow naval officer John Ford occasionally arranged for him to be released from duty for roles in Ford films such as *Fort Apache* (1948), *She Wore a Yellow Ribbon* (1949), and *Cheyenne Autumn* (1964). When I met O'Brien he was eighty years old (though looking at least thirty years younger) and seemed to have a total recall of everything that had ever happened to him. He suffered a massive stroke a year or so later and died in a nursing home in 1985.

15. Born in Philadelphia in 1896, Howard worked from 1917 until the end of the silent era as an assistant to D. W. Griffith, King Vidor, Rex Ingram, and other prominent directors. His own directorial career began with Spanish-language versions of early Fox talkies. The vast majority of his English-language features were westerns starring George O'Brien. He died in 1941, a week after Pearl Harbor.

16. In *The Mystery of the Hooded Horsemen* (1937), starring Tex Ritter, the group is simply a gang of hoodlums led by a hidden mastermind of the sort common in cliffhanger serials. In *The Fighting Texan* (1937), starring Kermit Maynard, a Klan-like group pops up for no reason at all in one sequence and then vanishes from the film. The series western most clearly inspired by the Klan is Republic's *The Purple Vigilantes* (1938), a Three Mesquiteers adventure that anticipates *Legion of the Lawless* in treating its hooded terrorist organization as originally serving a legitimate purpose but corrupted over time. Preceding all of these westerns by a few years, and perhaps in a sense inspiring them, were contemporary "social consciousness" thrillers clearly intended to conjure up thoughts of the Klan, such as Warner's *Black Legion* (1936, directed by Archie Mayo and starring Humphrey Bogart).

17. Curiously enough, the transition years between Depression and war gave birth to three of American prose fiction's enduring classics on legal themes: Walter Van Tilburg Clark's *The Ox-Bow Incident* (1940), Richard Wright's *Native Son* (1940), and James Gould Cozzens's *The Just and the Unjust* (1942).

18. The most interesting law-related works reflecting the witch-hunt are Arthur Miller's play *The Crucible* (1953) and Ellery Queen's novel *The Glass Village* (1954). One of the few movies of the time that dealt with the reign of terror in a legal perspective is *Count the Hours* (1954), directed by Don Siegel and starring Macdonald Carey as an attorney, aptly named Douglas Madison,

who is ostracized by the community after he is assigned to defend an unpopular client.

19. See Thomas J. Harris, *Courtroom's Finest Hour in American Cinema* (Metuchen, N.J.: Scarecrow Press, 1987).

20. Deeply negative takes on the system are offered in two of the period's finest law-related films: Alfred Hitchcock's *The Wrong Man* (1957) and J. Lee Thompson's *Cape Fear* (1962). However, the final minutes of the latter film cheat outrageously in order to close with an affirmation of unearned faith in the legal system's efficacy.

21. Richard Slotkin, *Gunfighter Nation: The Myth of the Frontier in Twentieth-Century America* (New York: Atheneum, 1992).

FOUR

Framed

RICHARD K. SHERWIN

■

If I were having a philosophical talk with a man I was going to have hanged (or electrocuted) I should say, I don't doubt that your act was inevitable for you but to make it more avoidable by others we propose to sacrifice you to the common good. You may regard yourself as a soldier dying for your country if you like. But the law must keep its promises.

OLIVER WENDELL HOLMES

If doings such as these receive honor, why should I join the holy dance?

OEDIPUS REX

Introduction: Signs of the Times

Sudden violent upheavals in cultural life, or slower, but similarly deep cultural transitions, lead one to re-encounter the forgotten history of order's mythic origin. During such times habits of thought and perception are shaken, accepted social arrangements grow suspect, uncertainty becomes the culture's hallmark. During such times the myth of reason and the reason of myth commingle freely, if uneasily, in the mind's musings.

Signs are that ours is such a time.

Call it postmodernism. Call it the post-Enlightenment age, an era apparently lacking the secular faith—in the free and autonomous self, in reason and reason's handmaids, science and technology—that inspired the modern break with medieval sectarianism. If the moderns loved God less and humanity more than their premodern forebears, the postmoderns fall short on both accounts. They have no more love of God than the moderns had, nor more love of reason, for all its material productions and reshapings of the natural world, than would the pre-moderns before them, had they known such control were possible. The postmoderns are in love, or perhaps it is an obsession, with desire. To-day material objects proliferate and the plastic self adjusts quickly to absorb their use. But when the product's use is up, as it inevitably will be, shapeless consuming desire remains. The experience of the post-modern subject is like that: contingent upon immediate uses, constant-ly in danger of being used up.

It is the same with meanings as it is with things. Information prolif-erates. The desire to maximize the speed and quantity of fact-consump-tion increases daily at a dizzying pace. Global information networks spread from glow-screen to glow-screen in homes and offices. We are all linked up. And everywhere talking heads are busily revealing our world: in accumulated tonnage of toxic wastes, in the number of inch-es of rainfall from coast to coast, in tragedies of death and brutality, in the latest sex scandals among politicians and Hollywood stars, in news of what's in and what's out, in the size of the deficit, in the volume of shares traded on the Big Board, in the news of rising hemlines and fall-ing expectations. Day after day. What does it mean? Never mind. It is hard enough just to keep up.

But beneath the material onslaught there flows a deepening current of cultural anxiety. Basic beliefs are unstable and the rush to distrac-tion does not wholly succeed in covering up the accompanying con-fusion. Skepticism is increasing regarding our ability to control events, to choose a particular path through life, to claim a discrete identity and bear responsibility for it. Works of our culture, in art, music, lit-erature, and film today are telling us this. As the mind gropes for meaning, new stories are being told: narrative offerings seeking to frame the elusive self, the unknowable other, the fractured reality that is our social world.

In law it is no different. Why should it be? Law is both a co-produc-er and a by-product of mainstream culture. The stamp of the latter con-tinually falls upon the meanings the law produces.

What, then, we are entitled to ask, is law's version of postmodern re-ality? What could law be like, for example, in the absence of modern belief in the free autonomous self, of modern secular faith in the predict-ability of physical causation? How might we think about crime and pun-ishment if we were to lose confidence in our ability to control external events or govern our own acts? How would the law respond if it turned out that to some significant extent it is only but for fate or accident that the criminal wrongdoer does harm and suffers or goes free?

But what is "criminal" after all? Is guilt-by-misfortune still guilt, or simply misfortune? Must the actor be able to change the consequences of his or her act before the law will condemn? How much chance will (should) the law bear before it may take away a person's freedom, or life?

Consider the story of Oedipus: made king by a lucky response to the sphinx's riddle, laid low by fate as the most lawless of men, unwitting agent of incest and parricide. What is one to make of Oedipus: criminal or tragic hero?

The ancients suffered with Oedipus. If mighty Oedipus could fall so low from so high who was secure? Is he not the tragic victim par excellence, a helpless plaything in the hands of a force mightier than he, mightier in fact than any human? Yet, the modernists—the humanists, the rationalists, the existentialists—refused to tremble. Witnessing Oedipus's fate, they would rather seek redemption in freedom and knowledge: freely choosing to pierce human deceptions, even if it meant learning the truth of one's own hidden criminality.

And in the postmodern view, what is Oedipus: tragic hero or luckless outlaw? But what is criminality, or tragedy, or fortune? Hardly unexpected questions given the recurring postmodern refrain: What is truth and what is deception? It is a refrain that plays well on film, especially when the subject is homicide.

Errol Morris's *The Thin Blue Line* (1988)

Framing the Frame-up: The Limits of Subversion

Harris: "If [Adams] would have had a place to stay, he'd never have nowhere to go, right?"

Morris: "You mean, if he would have stayed there at the motel that night, this [murder] would never have happened?"

Harris: "Good possibility. Good possibility. Heard of the proverbial scapegoat? There's probably been thousands of innocent people convicted and there will probably be thousands more. Why? Who knows?"

The film begins by accident, and weaves its way through currents of chance and fate. Filmmaker Errol Morris sets out to make a film about

Dr. James Grigson, the "killer shrink." Grigson is the state's favorite expert witness in death penalty cases: he always predicts the defendant will kill again. While interviewing convicts Grigson helped put on death row, Morris stumbles upon Randall Dale Adams. Adams has been convicted for the shooting of Dallas police officer Robert Wood. Adams insists he has been framed by the district attorney. Morris is intrigued by what Adams has to say. He becomes obsessed with the case. And the film he ends up making tells the story of the felony murder case of *Randall Dale Adams v. Texas.*

It is a story that begins by accident, and weaves its way through currents of chance and fate. It was on Thursday, November 24, 1976, that Randall Adams and his brother, on their way to the West Coast from their home in Ohio, arrived in Dallas. That Saturday, Adams ran out of gas. A sixteen-year-old driver by the name of David Harris spotted Adams walking alone on the side of the road with an empty gas can. Harris had just run away from home in nearby Vidor. Along the way he had ripped off a neighbor's car, some cash, and his dad's 12–gauge shotgun and .22–caliber nine-shot pistol. Harris invites Adams into the car. Adams gets in.

Sixteen-year-old Harris and twenty-eight-year-old Adams proceed to spend the rest of the day and a good part of the night together. They shoot some pool, smoke some dope, drink some beer, attend a soft-porn drive-in, drink some more beer, smoke some more pot. Shortly after 10:00 P.M., Harris drops Adams off at the motel where Adams and his brother were staying and drives on alone toward Inwood Road. Or perhaps it is closer to midnight and Adams, having failed to get his brother's permission for Harris to stay over at the motel, drives off together with Harris.

Shortly after midnight on Inwood Road two police officers spot a car without its headlight on. Officer Robert Wood gets out and walks toward the car. As he approaches the driver's window the driver raises a small caliber pistol and fires five or six shots into Officer Wood's body. The officer falls, and in a matter of minutes he bleeds to death on the tarmac.

A couple of months later, the police are led to Vidor and David Harris. Harris tells them that it was Adams who shot Officer Wood. Based on this information Adams is arrested in Dallas and indicted for the capital offense of felony murder.

At first the state's case seems weak. It is a matter of Adams's denial and accusation of Harris as the killer against Harris's claim that it was

Adams. Adams has no prior record. Harris was driving a stolen car that night and had stolen the pistol that had been used to kill Officer Wood. Upon his return to Vidor, Harris went on a crime spree.

The defense team was optimistic at Adams's trial. But then came the three surprise eyewitnesses: the Millers and Michael Randall. All three claimed to have seen the shooting that night, and the guy with the gun that they just happened to spot was, they told the jury, Randall Adams.

The jury convicted Adams. Then they heard from Dr. James Grigson, "the killer shrink," and his colleague, Dr. John Holbrook. According to these two psychiatrists, if Adams were released into the community he would almost certainly kill again. The jury voted for Adams's death.

For over four years Adams sat on death row, waiting for his appeals to work their way through the legal system. He lost at the state court level and entered the federal system. The case eventually reached the United States Supreme Court. There his death sentence was reversed.[1] The state could now attempt to try the case again under a new, constitutional death penalty statute, but they didn't want to. And as it turned out, they didn't have to. Adams's sentence was commuted by order of the governor from death to life in prison. Thus, with no further legal issues to raise, Adams would now have to resign himself to spending the rest of his life in prison.

And there he would have remained, but for the sudden appearance of filmmaker Errol Morris. Morris was interested in Adams's story, interested enough to conduct his own filmed interviews of Adams, Harris, the defense lawyers, the judge, the witnesses at the trial, the cops involved in the investigation of the case, and even some of Harris's friends in Vidor. Out of these interviews Morris constructed a film about the Adams case. Upon its release the film prompted renewed public attention that eventually led to further judicial review of the case. And this time a Dallas criminal court judge ordered that the charges against Adams be dismissed. At this point, it has been over twelve years since the shooting occurred. Over twelve years Adams has spent in prison. The state can now retry the case, but they decline. A free man, Adams finally makes his way back to Ohio.

That's the story. *The Thin Blue Line* documents the Dallas DA's deceptions in the state's case against Randall Adams. We learn that it was a frame-up from the get-go. Harris lied. So did the eyewitnesses. The DA knew. It's what he wanted. You can't fry a sixteen-year-old in Texas. That's the law. But Adams was old enough to be electrocuted. And when a cop is killed in Dallas an electrocution is sure to follow.

And who is Randall Dale Adams anyway? "Just a drifter," recounts the lawyer in Morris's film who heard second-hand of the judge who said so. And besides, "Why spoil a local boy's whole life?" as one police officer is heard to say in the film.

Viewers of Morris's film also see and hear from the three eyewitnesses at Adams's trial, the witnesses who clinched Adams's conviction. There's Mrs. Miller up on the screen telling us that she's a great fan of detective thrillers and that she's seen crimes happening all around her: "It's always happening to me, everywhere I go, you know. Lots of times there's killings or anything, even around my house." Her game, she says, is trying to solve the crime before the police do. Anyone would recognize her pathology. Even her husband. Turns out she's even called the cops on him. No substance to it though. "Yeah," Mr. Miller sadly intones, "Oh man, she's . . ." His voice trails off. But the film viewer sees things clearly enough to fill in the gap. "Yeah, oh man, she's . . . crazy."

And as for witness number two, Mr. Miller himself, the film viewer has a clear idea of why he lied as well: reward money, a lot of it, for anyone who could help solve the case. Mr. Miller learned about the reward while he was in police custody following a knife fight with his wife. As a neighbor of the Millers says in her own film interview: "For enough money, he would testify to what they wanted him to say." We believe it.

Just as we believe the third eyewitness, Michael Randall, also lied. The film makes that clear enough. We see and hear Randall condemn the Dallas legal system as corrupt from start to finish. "The DA will put something into [your] mouth [if he wants to]," says Randall, "that's why they call it the Hall of Justice—the scales are not balanced. The scales are in the hall, and they go up and down." So, when in Rome. . . . Sure, Randall too must have had his eye on the reward money. It's all corrupt. Why shouldn't he get his share?

These are the images with which the film persuades us. Each interviewee takes his or her turn seated alone before Morris's unmoving, unblinking camera.[2] Each tells his or her version of the events that preceded or that occurred at Adams's trial. We see and we understand how the frame-up happened. We see the judge who tried to conceal his tears as he listened to the DA's final summation before the jury, the judge who's G-man dad had taught him respect for law and order and for the cops who risk life and limb to preserve the thin blue line between order and anarchy. We see and hear young David Harris and we know why he lied. Harris himself tells us: "A scared sixteen-year-old kid. Sure wants to get out of it if he can." Just as we have seen and understood the all-too-human deficiencies that led the eyewitnesses to lie: madness, greed, cynicism.

On the strength of familiar stereotypes, the ordinary images that make up our common sense of the world we live in, Errol Morris plots out the mystery of Officer Wood's murder and solves it. Randall Dale Adams was framed.

But this is no ordinary documentary film. *The Thin Blue Line* does not rely solely on interviews or on the evidentiary clues that lead to a murder mystery's pat resolution. The film weaves into an otherwise conventional mystery plot a distinct counterplot. A counterplot that subverts the very mystery/documentary genre itself.

In addition to interviews, Morris's film presents dramatized simulations of reality. Viewers of the film see actors playing out a nightmarish police interrogation of Adams. Viewers also see the scene of the shooting being simulated again and again throughout the movie. The scene varies with the person telling the story—as in Kurosawa's *Rashomon*. But unlike *Rashomon,* here the reenactments are highly stylized, self-consciously made to lack verisimilitude. For example, there's that recurring close-up of the rotating red police light wheeling within a sealed circle of fate, its audibly swooshing revolutions mimic the hypnotically redundant chords of Philip Glass's ubiquitous score. There's the slow-motion free-fall of the chocolate malt that Officer Wood's partner allegedly tossed out the squad car window as soon as she heard the first shots being fired. We see the malt splat on the ground, oozing slowly into the dirt, like blood from a fallen body.

The film toys with reality in other ways as well: for example, those obviously fake film clips, like the Hollywood gangster film scenes that play as we hear the judge reminisce about his dad's FBI career in Chicago in the days of Capone and his mob cronies. And listening to Mrs. Miller's words, evoking a fantasy world of cops and robbers, we suddenly see on the screen classic film images of Boston Blackie, as if these images, almost too comical, were unreeling within Mrs. Miller's mind.

What are these interruptions in the linear unfolding of a documentary murder mystery doing here? I believe they are in the film to remind us that the truth of the frame-up that the film reveals is itself the product of a frame-up. This is no simple documentary. It is about a particular homicide in Dallas and, more generally, it is an exploration of the way we perceive and judge the truth. The film plays with images (stereotypes, familiar cognitive schemas, the social conventions of everyday thought and perception) that persuade us to believe in the DA's frame-up, just as it plays with counter-images that make up (that perhaps even make fun of) the way we allow film images to capture our belief in the first place. It's all being framed, the film tells us. There is no place to go for objective, unmediated truth.[3]

So speaks the subversive counterplot in Morris's film. If we were inclined to listen to it, the counterplot would have us question the mystery plot's neat narrative construction of historical truth. We would have to think about Morris's cinematic frame-up of the "frame-up." Such questioning is not out of place—not in a story that begins by accident and weaves its way through currents of chance and fate. (A man happens to meet a boy while walking along a Dallas roadway. A filmmaker happens to encounter a convict on death row and makes a film that frees him from prison.)

Nor are the "facts" of the case so clear. For example, what did Harris mean when he said it never would have happened if only Adams had a place to stay? Is that to say that Adams left the motel that night with Harris? Maybe so. After all, we know that Adams's brother had denied Harris entry. As Adams said, his brother "didn't like that sort of thing." (What sort of thing?) So are we to believe that Adams *was* in the car with Harris at the time of the shooting? But why? Why would a twenty-eight-year-old man spend the day and evening with a sixteen-year-old boy that he had just met? Might there be something more difficult here for either Adams or Harris to speak the truth about ("Yes, we were together, in the car, in the dark, that night . . .") than to lie about ("No, I was alone, but then I got scared, so I blamed him, I made Adams the scapegoat . . .")?

Yet the viewer is rather more inclined to reject (if he or she ever consciously discerned) what I have been calling the film's subversive counterplot. The factual inconsistencies can be explained. And anyway, the frame-up story is compelling. As for the counterplot, surely it goes too far. Postmodern truth-play may be all right for philosophers and literary critics. But this is a real life, and a real case of homicide to boot. Everyone knows that in real life justice does not depend upon chance encounters or upon the narrative compulsions of one kind of story (a linear detective mystery, say) rather than another kind (a postmodern fact-fiction docudrama, say). The prosecutor's frame-up was real. Morris showed us. Now we know the *history* of it. We understand why it happened and how. We know the characters involved, their motives,

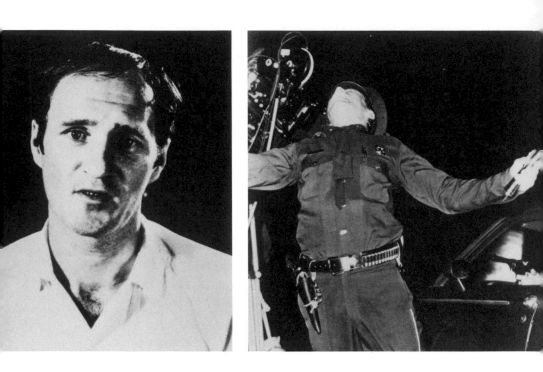

Errol Morris's *The Thin Blue Line* blends documentary techniques such as "talking heads" interviews with dramatic recreations to undermine traditional distinctions between "fact" and "fiction."

their prejudices, their cynicism and deceit. We know whom to believe and whom not to. And that is why viewers of Morris's film have no need or patience for the subversive implications of its counterplot. That at least is one of the reasons why viewers generally refuse to confront the filmic deceits that might have led them to doubt that the mystery has been solved after all.[4]

Let the matter rest. At least order has now been restored and the case has come to an end. *An* end, but perhaps not *the* end—at least not if we are willing to demask the frame-up used to demask the frame-up. But perhaps the human need for order, particularly in the face of homicide, is greater than the desire for knowledge (especially when it's taboo) and greater too than the capacity to live with uncertainty.[5]

But if viewers of Morris's film can accept the narrative necessity of a conventional detective mystery plot, insisting all the while that it is "documented" or "historical" truth that compels them, if they can deny the narrative necessity of the film's subversive counterplot, with its ceaselessly circling images of self-referential uncertainty and its disturbingly interwoven theme of fate and randomness, viewers of David Mamet's *Homicide* can enjoy no such leeway. For here there is no escaping the subversive impact of chance and necessity upon self and motivation. There is no escaping the tragic uncontrollability of human affairs.

David Mamet's *Homicide* (1991)

Subversion Unbound: The Dissolution of Character, Motive, and Causation

"If you're moved, somebody has to be doing it."

David Mamet's *Homicide* is a complex tale that unfurls with the tautness and inevitability of Greek tragedy. And in true tragedian style, the havoc it wreaks is total. By the story's end its main character, Bobby Gold, is utterly undone. What is more, the forces of his undoing, including his own complicity in the fate that he suffers, seem to be entirely beyond his control. The dissolution of the willing subject and the disjunction between a person's state of mind and the external events into which his actions flow: that is our theme.[6]

As a structural matter, the film's main plot revolves around the efforts of two cops, Bobby Gold and his partner, Tim Sullivan, to trap and take

in alive the man who killed a federal agent. Two subplots closely inter-
weave around this main one.

On his way to a meeting with the man who will serve as bait to draw
in the cop killer, Gold and his partner stumble upon a couple of police
officers responding to a shooting in a neighborhood candy story. An
elderly Jewish woman has been killed. Her guard dog is pinning down
one of the officers inside the store. Gold, responding to a rookie cop's
anxious uncertainty about how to rescue his partner, enters the store
and skillfully lures the dog away. Before he can break away from the
scene, however, Gold runs into a senior officer who tells him he's
"caught the case." It is this chance encounter with the candy store homicide that triggers the second subplot and that ultimately leads to
Gold's undoing. He is about to embark upon a shattering quest for self-
identity.

Back at the station house, Gold entreats his superiors to free him
from the candy store case so that he can work on the high profile cop
homicide. But he's stuck: the elderly Jewish woman's son is a doctor
with big connections downtown. The doctor knows Gold is Jewish and
he wants Gold on the case.

In this way, the film skillfully joins the issue of self-identity and divided loyalties. At the outset of the story, for Gold there seems to be no
question: he's a cop, first and last. The Jews? "They're not my people,
baby. . . . So much anti-Semitism the last four thousand years, we must
be doing something [to] bring it about." Trouble is he can't escape his
fate so easily. Even the cops won't let him. They too can't help but see
him as a Jew. For example, it takes only a little provocation to prompt
a superior officer to call Gold a "dumb kike." And in a later scene even
his partner, his "family," Tim, will playfully stick Gold with the same
epithet.

In any event, despite his denials, or perhaps based on them, Gold has
been acting off of his Jewish identity throughout his career as a cop. His
best credential has Jewish origins: Gold the "mouthpiece," the "bar
room lawyer," Gold, the sweet-talking hostage negotiator. The secret
of his oratorical success? As a Jew he's always felt like an outsider. And
that status has allowed him to identify with the criminal. It was his carte
d'entre. As an outsider, Gold also constantly felt the obligation to prove
himself, to prove he wasn't "a Jewish pussy." "How come you always
gotta be the first through the door? So brazen," his partner knowingly
says to Gold, their guns drawn as they stand ready to enter a suspect's
home.

With this as background perhaps it comes as no surprise when Gold gets swept into "the Jewish thing" during his investigation of the candy store case. The real surprise, however, lies in where that investigation will lead him.

The Jewish doctor calls Gold at the station house: someone's on the roof and he may have taken a shot at the doctor's wife through their kitchen window. Why would anyone do that? Gold asks. Maybe it's a conspiracy, the doctor replies. When Gold expresses his skepticism, the doctor says, "It's always a fantasy when someone wants to hurt the Jews. And when the fantasy is true, then you say 'what a coincidence, we're being paranoid and someone coincidentally wanted to hurt us.'" It's like the postmodern saw: "Paranoids are the only ones who notice things anymore." Gold checks out the roof.

On his way Gold sees a man disappearing down some stairs near a pigeon coop. Beside the coop Gold finds a crumpled slip of paper with the word "GROFAZ" written on it. He pockets the paper and then goes to take another look at the candy store where the elderly woman was shot. At the store Gold stumbles upon an old crate. Inside he finds an ordinance invoice from 1946 for Thompson machine guns and a list of Jewish names.

The ingredients of the conspiracy are now in place: Who was this elderly Jewish woman? Why was she shot? By whom? Was it the anti-Semitic group that had been distributing Jew-hating posters in the black neighborhood that surrounded the candy store? The clues suggesting that possibility are increasing.

Gold puts a trace on the tommy gun invoice and learns that the guns from the crate had been stolen. He investigates the letters "GROFAZ" and learns that it was a secret code name for Hitler during the final years of the war. Then he stumbles upon a secret Zionist organization. They know about the list of Jewish names and they want it. Gold resists; he's already tagged it, it's police property. But Gold, what are you? A Jew? The Zionists play upon his faltering sense of identity and conflicted loyalties.

Gold buckles. "Okay. I want to help you. What can I do?" "We want the list." "I can't. Anything but that." "Ach, you disgust me." But later, a member of the Zionist group allows herself to be talked into letting Gold do something for them after all. The group was planning to bomb the anti-Semitic organization that had been printing and distributing those Jew-hating leaflets. Gold implores the member: let me do this. And he does. But then the noose of events tightens around his neck.

To be a Jew, to do something for once for himself, to serve his own homeland, to be whole. Gold has been seeking himself. That search will now destroy him.

After the bombing, the Zionists and Gold meet again. "We want the list." "But I told you . . ." "Show him the pictures." And there's Gold, the cop, caught redhanded in a series of photos showing him blowing up a store. "We want the list." And as the Zionists leave him to ponder his fate, speaking together in Hebrew as they leave, double-outsider Gold knows he's been taken. His longed-for family has orphaned him already. And his "real" family is about to be killed because he dallied among strangers.

It turns out that the business with the Zionists has distracted Gold from his appointed rendezvous with partner Tim and the others who were staking out the cop killer at that moment. Gold was the lynchpin. He had sweet-talked the killer's mother into playing decoy. But without Gold she wouldn't play. And without him there, she didn't. Gold turns up late, and the trap's gone sour. His partner has been mortally wounded in the cross-fire that broke out between the cops and the killer. Gold is heartbroken and guilt-struck. Raging against his partner's killer ("I'll kill you, you fucking nigger") Gold leaps into the fray. By coincidence, the day before, a man who had been arrested for shooting his wife and two kids with a deer rifle had attacked Gold at the station house. He was after Gold's gun, to kill himself. The attempt failed, but Gold's holster strap was torn off during the struggle. Because of the missing strap, now, when Gold jumps off a ledge on his way to get the man who shot his partner, he loses his gun.

In the final encounter between Gold and the killer, Gold is shot. But he is not completely unarmed. He still has the "mouthpiece." He uses it, as revenge, on the killer: "You sorry sack of shit. Your mother turned you in." It is the one thing the killer can't accept, the last illusion he refuses to let go of. Incensed and disbelieving, the killer shoots Gold a second time. But Gold has time enough to show him proof of the trap that the killer's mother had joined. And the delay that this dallying causes is time enough for more cops to arrive on the scene and shoot the finally disillusioned killer.

Tragic threads of fate have now woven a shroud that covers everything. Gold has gotten it all wrong and it has cost him. The one insight he is left with is the one he shares with the killer: "I'm a piece of shit. It's all a piece of shit. I killed my partner and your mamma turned you in." But the last blow is yet to come.

When he has sufficiently recovered from his wounds to return to his office, Gold learns two more things: a young black kid in the neighborhood has confessed to shooting the elderly Jewish candy store owner. It seems that everyone in the neighborhood knew there was treasure in her basement, and the kid wanted it for himself. The second thing Gold learns involves the slip of paper with the word "GROFAZ" written on it. It turns out that "Grofazt" is the name of the leading manufacturer of pigeon feed.

Like Oedipus, Gold has been completely undone, an unwitting accomplice in his own tragic fate. Locked into a fortuitous chain of events, he has ended up destroying everything that is of value to him. His futile quest for identity has led to blackmail and double orphanage. His adopted family betrayed him and his real family, his partner Tim, is dead because he failed to show up on time to trap the killer. Gold has also betrayed himself by breaking his word: the promise he made to the killer's mother that he'd bring her boy in alive. That's the assurance that got her to go along with the police. But they turned out to be empty words. Gold broke his promise with different words, words spoken this time out of hate rather than empathy and compassion. And with these words Gold did more than rob the killer of his last illusion, while also giving the police the time they needed to get close enough to shoot him after all. With these words Gold also jettisoned the last shred of his self-identity. For even his status as outsider now meant nothing.

And what compelled this outcome that left Gold a "piece of shit," neither a good Jew nor a good cop, transformed from culprit-sympathizer to culprit-hater and racist killer? The force of randomness: a chance encounter with a failed candy store robbery and a mysterious anti-Jewish conspiracy that turned out to be no mystery at all: Grofazt, pigeon feed. Empty coincidence.

Gold's quest for identity has been thwarted and ends tragically; his duty has been compromised on all fronts. And Gold, like his double, that mad family killer who jumped him at the station house, or that would-be robber duped by anti-Semitic propaganda, seems all along to have been living out the wisdom in his partner's dying words: "If you're moved, somebody has to be doing it." Precisely it. Like a puppet, moved by invisible forces. Brought low, like Oedipus, by an invisible power stronger than he. Like Oedipus, the knowledge Gold gains in the end gives him insight only into his own helplessness and defeat.[7]

There is no straight line to meaning here. Even a murder mystery's resolution (the kid wanted the treasure) and a cop killer's death cannot remove the mystery of unjustifiable, uncontrollable death. Even if we can explain and condemn certain kinds of homicide, others resist easy judgment. A cornered outlaw who kills out of desperation we can blame. But do we as readily condemn the violence of a victimized people seeking political liberation and national autonomy? Those who feed on malicious myths and stereotypes and who kill out of racial hatred may be held accountable for their acts. But what about a man who kills his wife and two kids with a deer rifle? Or a cop who causes the death of a partner he loved like family?

The inexplicable homicide is tragic: as much for its inexplicability as for the pain and suffering that it causes. Perhaps it is the experience of pain and the knowledge of its inevitability (if pain is your due) that comes of our encounter with the hapless victim—the victim who does evil, the victim of fate. Perhaps here, in desperate tragedy, lies the origin of human compassion, for what it's worth.

But still we ask: On what grounds may guilt and blaming rely in the absence of human knowledge, control, or motive, in the absence even of an orchestrating sense of self? What rules for crime and punishment can come from such pervasive unruliness? To address that question, I turn now to Philip Haas's film adaptation of Paul Auster's novel, *The Music of Chance.*

Philip Haas's *The Music of Chance* (1993)

Back from Kismet: Chancing upon Order

"You tampered with the universe, my friend, and once a man does that, he's got to pay the price."

In Errol Morris's *The Thin Blue Line* we saw a straightforward detective story (who framed Randall Dale Adams?) compete unsuccessfully with a troubling counter-narrative, what I called the film's subversive anti-mystery plot. The counter-narrative suggested that truth is inescapably mediated in one narrative form or another. The question thus became: Which story is the more compelling one? To frame the issue of truth in this way leads one to confront the narrativity, one might even say the fiction (as in *"fict-io,"* the constructed aspect) of truth itself. This is hard to accept in criminal cases where so much depends upon public judgments of truth. Thus it may not be surprising that many viewers of Morris's film chose not to accept the film's counterplot, the story of how Morris framed the frame-up.[8] They would rather travel the straight line of historical truth laid down by the film's conventional mystery tale. We also saw that unlike *The Thin Blue Line*, Mamet's *Homicide* offers no room for such denial. Here there is no final resolution to fall back on once Gold's gossamer constructions of meaning are blown away by the winds of fate. In the end there is simply no comprehending the work of such an inhuman force. When the curtain falls perhaps only pity, a sense of compassion for fate's victim, remains.

In *The Music of Chance* the power of fate and accident is assumed from the outset. The question now becomes: Assuming that to be the case, how do we find order? Close on the heels of that query is the one that asks: Is law still possible?

Phillip Haas's film begins with a blind leap into the unknown. Jim Nashe, an ex-fireman, has been aimlessly driving around the country for months. He's been kept afloat on money he inherited when his father died. He drives not to arrive anywhere but for the sense of unburdened speed that driving allows. Nashe has become truly postmodern: a placeless, will-less subject in a world in which nothing lasts for longer than a moment. He simply follows the road before him.

As his cash runs out, however, Nashe realizes that things can't continue as they have. So when he spots a stranger stumbling along the roadside he doesn't hesitate. Nashe picks him up. His passenger is Pozzi, a professional card player. Pozzi tells Nashe that he was robbed and beaten during a high stakes poker game. The shame of it, Pozzi relates, is that now because he's penniless he'll have to miss the game of his life. Turns out that he was supposed to play poker with a couple of millionaires named Flower and Stone who, according to Pozzi, know nothing about the game. He stood to win a good forty, maybe fifty grand off those two, he says.

Nashe, a man without plans or prospects, is quick to leap onto the path Pozzi lays down. Nashe will use his remaining cash, ten grand, to get Pozzi into the game with Flower and Stone. In exchange Pozzi will split his winnings with Nashe fifty-fifty. And off they go.

As it turns out, Flower and Stone are no ordinary millionaires. Respectively an accountant and optometrist by trade, they won their first millions in the lottery. They chose primes: primary numbers, "numbers that refuse to cooperate, that don't change or divide, numbers that remain themselves for all eternity." Flower adds: "It was the magic combination, the key to the gates of heaven." So it would seem, for since hitting the jackpot they can't seem to stop making money. Flower describes it this way: "No matter what we do, everything seems to turn out right. . . . It's as though God has singled us out from other men. He's showered us with good fortune and lifted us to the heights of happiness. I know this might sound presumptuous to you, but at times I feel that we've become immortal."

Besides their extraordinary luck, Flower and Stone also have unusual interests. Stone is a collector. But his collection is crazy: a telephone that once belonged to Woodrow Wilson, a pearl earring worn by Sir Walter Raleigh, a half-smoked cigar filched from an ashtray in Winston Churchill's office, William Seward's Bible. Random, beside-the-point stuff. But to Stone it is something else: "Motes of dust that have slipped through the cracks." He preserves things for what they are, their purpose is irrelevant. And now Stone has branched out. He recently purchased a fifteenth-century Irish castle and had the stones, all ten thousand of them, shipped back to America. They're sitting on his property in a heap. He plans to build a wall out of them, just a straight wall.

Flower's interest is different. Rather than collect he builds. Flower is an artist. He is constructing a perfect replica, in miniature, of a city. He calls it the City of the World. There are scenes here from Flower's childhood and more recent history. Tiny figures, of Flower and Stone and others. There's the Hall of Justice, the Library, the Bank, the Prison. Everything in the city is in harmony. Even the prisoners are happy, glad they've been punished for their crimes. For now, as Stone admiringly puts it, "they're learning how to recover the goodness within them through hard work."

Surely by now we realize this is no ordinary story about people about to play a game of cards. Surely this is a mythic tale, a parable. Consider the setting: from the outset we are thrust into a world in which choice and direction have disappeared. Nashe doesn't plan, he reacts. Pozzi has made a life out of luck and instinct. And Stone and Flower have gone a step further. Propelled by luck to a mastery of the material world, they have now assumed an almost god-like status. (Perhaps they *are* immortal as Stone muses. Perhaps God *has* singled them out.) In Stone's philosophy things need no purpose. It is enough that they exist as they are. That is why he can snatch odds and ends from beneath the black veil of history and render them eternal. For Flower it has become possible to orchestrate reality itself, to shape events according to harmonious principles: law (the Hall of Justice), economy (the Bank), knowledge (the Library) and penitence (the Prison). And, stranger still, it is not only the past that is represented in his City of the World. So, too, as we shall see, is the future: Pozzi's and Nashe's.

If Nashe has relinquished all efforts to control his life, yielding instead to fate, if fate has placed beside him Pozzi, a more experienced player in the field of chance, Flower and Stone turn out to be the masters of fate's domain. It is as if they already knew Pozzi and Nashe would come, lose all their money at cards, and be forced to pay back the debt with money earned by working for Flower and Stone. What work? Why, to build the stone wall of course. And that is precisely what transpires. With one additional detail well worth noting.

When the card games begin, Pozzi's good fortune is running high. He is in gear, and can hear luck's music playing. He is sure he can't go wrong. But then something happens that stops the music cold. Some hours into playing, Nashe decides to stretch his legs. Where does he go but back to the room with Flower's City of the World. And what does Nashe do? Why he snatches up a miniature Flower and a miniature Stone and stows them in his pocket. Mementos of a strange and glorious day, he thinks. Wrong. As Pozzi would later observe: "It's like committing a sin to do a thing like that, it's like violating a fundamental law. . . . You tampered with the universe, my friend, and once a man does that, he's got to pay the price."

And, indeed, from that moment on Pozzi's luck could not have been worse. Upon Nashe's return he finds Pozzi losing without end, until finally he is in serious debt to his hosts. In a last desperate measure Nashe puts his car into the pot. But Pozzi loses that too. That's when Nashe arranges the work contract: he and Pozzi will build the wall with Stone's ten thousand stones for an hourly wage, for as long as it takes to pay off the card debt. What choice do they have? After all, Stone has threatened to use his influence to ensure trouble with the authorities if they refuse. So their work begins.

There is but one brief stretch to cover now before the story ends. Nashe and Pozzi have consigned themselves to manual labor on Stone's and Flower's property. The wall goes up. The debt goes down. But then there's a snag. Pozzi and Nashe thought that small expenses like food and entertainment would be covered by their employers. But that turns out not to be the case. It seems they'll have to work a few weeks longer than they thought.

Pozzi buckles under the idea of more forced labor. And Nashe agrees that Pozzi, fragile to begin with, probably isn't up to the task. Nashe suggests that Pozzi make a break for it while Nashe stays on to finish out the contract. They say their goodbyes and Pozzi escapes. Early the next morning, however, Nashe wakes to find Pozzi lying outside in the cold grass bruised and unconscious. He's been beaten silly.

Now comes the caretaker with his son-in-law to take Pozzi to the hospital, they say. Nashe is convinced that it was the caretaker, probably with the help of the son-in-law, who were responsible for Pozzi's beating. Retribution for the escape, Nashe figures.

The next days and weeks are hard for Nashe. Without his companion, whom he grew fond of during their time of shared labor, Nashe battles with guilt, sadness, loneliness, and thoughts of revenge. As time passes, the caretaker begins to take pity on Nashe's solitary duty. So when the wall is about completed the caretaker invites Nashe to a tavern for a friendly, celebratory drink with him and his son-in-law. Nashe agrees to go. They drive there together in Nashe's car, the one he lost in cards and that Flower and Stone apparently gave to the caretaker.

A few drinks at the tavern, some friendly talk, and a couple of low-stake games of pool with the son-in-law, with this catch. When the son-in-law loses to Nashe and Nashe waives away his winnings the son-in-law is not to be outdone. He insists on returning the favor. What'll it be Nashe? Why, how about a chance to drive the car back to the house? So be it.

Nashe takes the wheel. The old feelings of aimless freedom flood back. Just motion and distance, with a musical score courtesy of the car stereo. Gradually Nashe increases the speed. When he's past seventy the caretaker panics. He snaps off the music. The caretaker's sudden move breaks Nashe's concentration. He's going too fast. There's a headlight ahead, closing in like lightning. Nashe loses control and crashes into some bushes on the side of the road. The caretaker is dead. Injured and stumbling along the roadside, Nashe spots a passing car. It stops, Nashe gets in. The story ends.

A mythic gem. In the land of chance as it was in the beginning, so it is in the end. One injured chance passenger replaces another. And who knows what adventure is about to unfold, what Stone- and Flower-like design is waiting to be realized? For if things just happen, by fate or chance, the film tells us, there are also the chance gods who have laid up the patterns of fate. Destiny is already made out, in advance, in replica, so to speak.

And in this parable of fate we also learn there is harmony in destiny's order. The story of Pozzi and Nashe confirms it. It is as Stone said about Flower's city: the prisoners are happy in their labor, learning to recover the goodness within them, just as Nashe did. There was nothing to be found in his aimless and solitary driving. Nashe was no *easy rider*. He realized that his shielded existence on the road was an empty fantasy that could not be sustained. It was only when he began his labor with Pozzi that Nashe found what he lacked before: human companionship, a sense of sharing with and caring for another human being, the basis for community. Moreover, forced labor though it was, Nashe's work with Pozzi provided him with a sense of worth and purpose. As the wall grew, he and Pozzi took pride in their efforts and those efforts were plain to see, they were tangible, made in stone.

Fate is strange: in aimless freedom Nashe was a lonely prisoner of placeless speed and empty distance; in forced labor he found solidarity, freedom, and peace of mind. But then the order of things was disturbed again. Doing penance to pay off their card debt was in harmony with basic principles. But when Nashe, convinced that Pozzi could no longer take it, coaxed Pozzi to escape, that harmony was shattered. As in the card game before, and the car ride with the caretaker later, once the music shuts off a payment has to be made. When Nashe by his rash act stopped the music of harmonious penance he could not avoid paying the price, as would Pozzi for his own disharmonious repudiation of penance altogether.

And so it goes. From car to car on the road of chance and necessity. Yet even if human will, the ability to govern or design one's fate, is forfeited, responsibility for one's actions does not disappear. There is it seems an order deeper than human designs can go. As the ancient Greek philosopher Anaximander said: "And into that from which things arise they pass away once more, according to necessity; for they pay penalty and retribution to each other for their injustice according to the assessment of Time."[8] If we breach the natural order, our fate is sealed. It is best, then, to seek harmony; failing that, it is best to seek happiness in penance. So speaks the wisdom of the fate gods.

Let us review now the film trail we've been traveling: (1) from denial of chance and fate in deference to human designs (identifying with Adams's fate as the prosecutor's "scapegoat" in the *The Thin Blue Line* while resisting the film's anti-mystery story counterplot); (2) to acceptance of fate and chance along with tragic self-loss and incomprehensible suffering (identifying with Bobby Gold's fate in Mamet's *Homicide*); (3) to acceptance of chance, fate, and natural principles of harmony for the breach of which penance is inevitable (identifying with Nashe's fate in Haas's *The Music of Chance*). But what are the implications for the legal culture of the realities that these three films depict?

Conclusion: Law through a Postmodern Frame

> *"Bitzer," said Mr. Gradgrind, broken down, and miserably sub-*
> *missive to him, "have you a heart?" "The circulation, sir," returned*
> *Bitzer, smiling at the oddity of the question, "couldn't be carried*
> *on without one. No man, sir, acquainted with facts established by*
> *Harvey relating to the circulation of blood, can doubt that I have*
> *a heart."*
>
> CHARLES DICKENS, *Hard Times*

With increasing skepticism toward the modern ideal of technological progress and the ability rationally to control one's life, with the growing realization that much of what goes on in the world, including our own acts and desires, will never yield to human control, it may not be surprising to see a newly emerging belief in alternative, nonrational mythic forces. Forces like chance and fate. It is that development that I believe these three films by Morris, Mamet, and Haas portray.

Consider again what Errol Morris shows us through the homicide case of Randall Dale Adams. Comprehensive rational truths do not stand alone, naked and pure in the objectified space of historical documentation. If we choose to believe a truth it is because we also choose to accept the form of its mediation. Perhaps the history story or the mystery tale with its neatly rational resolution of clues *is* more compelling under one set of circumstances rather than another. The credibility of its truth, however, is inescapably the product of the narrative by which we get it. And in the process of 'getting it' much goes on at a subconscious level, hidden from view. Subconscious processes not only affect our perceptions of truth, they do so independently of the reasons we may posit for what we believe to be the case. In this sense, Morris is inviting us not to deny truth but to stop denying the mediations by which our beliefs are activated.

One of the narratives most frequently denied by legal authorities in the modern age is the one that tells of the loss of human control. In the age of reason, the loss of control was not the official story. David Mamet revives the tale. In doing so he subverts the rule of modern reason.

We cannot hope to comprehend all that befell Bobby Gold. All we can do, perhaps, is what audiences in the ancient Greek amphitheaters did when they beheld Oedipus's fate: they felt overwhelmed by horror, pity, and a sense of collective vulnerability to inhuman forces against which no one is secure.

And once we allow ourselves to see through the false armor of reason, what then? Cross our fingers and wait for the ax to fall? Phillip Haas's adaptation of Paul Auster's novel suggests otherwise. If chance and fate are forces that must be reckoned with in this life, there are also rules. Even chance has its harmonies. Stop its music and there will be a penalty to pay. Neither rational calculation nor irrational denial can avoid the retribution that must come.

In the modern era, jurists, like most people, took pride in reason and the order it could impose on natural and human events. And why not? After all, this was an age when technological advances were a marvel to behold. What would man invent next to improve the human lot? A similarly optimistic attitude shaped and informed the modernists' rational aspirations for society. For example, one influential group of modern idealists believed that individuals in state-controlled economies would find all that they needed for contentment in life by devoting themselves to the ideals propagated by the state. Other modernists believed that individuals who lived in free market societies would find similar reward if they would only emulate the ideal of the rational calculator. The free citizen who knew how to maximize in his or her rational choices the best interests of society would surely share in the wealth that those choices would help to produce.

But the modern era has gone into decline, and faith in modern reason and its rational ideals has diminished. The marvels of modern technology? Yes, of course. But what of machines of mass destruction? What of technological wreckage and waste that ravage the planet? As for the rational engineering of society by the state: the fall of Communism has attested to the fallacy of that ideal. And while free economies have fared better, their weaknesses are increasingly apparent. For example, today we see that the modern ideal of the rational agent as the best generator of social wealth is gradually being overtaken by other, far less rational images of the self.

If the invisible forces of the free market are still perceived as active in the world today, it seems increasingly likely that they are not operating alone. What names will we give in our time to other inhuman forces, among them perhaps the gods of chance and necessity? I do not know. What stories will we be telling of their dealings in human affairs? I cannot say. What I am saying is that the prospect ahead is for more such nonrational mythic tales about law and justice.

Let me close this essay with a more specific musing on law as viewed through a postmodern frame. As we increasingly come to see, along with Morris, that there are multiple narratives by which truth and justice may be constructed, it is likely that the ascendancy of modern reason in the legal culture will end. As the rhetoric of rational control begins to compete with other forms of legal discourse, different sources of knowledge, previously repressed (or delegitimized) as taboo, will enter the mainstream. Consider, for example, the rhetoric of the emotions.

No longer an outcast in the realm of truth, the emotions could bring the law back from the brink of hyper-rationality, the frenetic, obsessed quest for final causes and neat, formalistic resolutions in the face of human conflict. If the emotions render us vulnerable to the particularities of a given case, eschewing detached legal formality for a more empathic consideration of the fates of the parties concerned, this is not to be considered a vice. Rather, it is a virtue. The emotional response to the fate of the other, even when the impulse is strong to deny that we could ever suffer the other's destiny, brings life to the law.

Now it is true that such a highly contextualized approach might make the law less predictable. But the question arises: What price are we willing to pay for formal order? In any event, with increased awareness of life's tragic subversions of artificially posited rational norms the rule of law is unlikely to remain unaltered. It is plausible that over time law will be viewed as operating on a field of causation and human agency as well as accident and necessity. In this way we may see, if not an end to, at least a reduction in the law's repression of uncertainty in its quest for closure. By opening up to the separate rhetorics and respective truths of rational order (agency/causation) and the emotions as judgments of value[9] (accident/fate) the law may acquire a more compassionate and thus a more human face.

There is no closure here. I have no way of knowing whether the norms depicted in the three films that I have discussed will ever achieve cultural dominance. However, one thing is certain. If the life of the law were to imitate the art of Morris, Mamet, and Haas, the stories the law tells would be different. And the cultural balance between the yearning for order and the impulse toward mercy would surely change.

Notes

1. *Randall Dale Adams v. Texas,* 448 U.S. 38 (1980).

2. The novelty of the camera lies in its ability to present to the interviewee live video images of the interviewer. In this way, the interviewee is able to maintain constant eye contact with his or her interlocutor while staring directly into the camera. Morris calls his invention the "interrotron."

3. See John J. O'Connor, "The Film That Challenged Dr. Death," *New York Times,* May 24, 1989, 22 (quoting Morris: "What I want to do in those reenactments is to take people deeper into the ambiguities of the case, not to show what really happened"); Peter Bates, "An Interview with Errol Morris," in *Cineaste* 17:1 (1989): 17 (quoting Morris: "Truth isn't guaranteed by style or expression. It isn't guaranteed by anything"). See also Bill Nichols, "'Getting to Know You . . .': Knowledge, Power, and the Body," in *Theorizing Documentary,* ed. Michael Renov (New York: Routledge, 1993), 179–80 ("Morris creates a minor dissonance that upsets our usual assumptions about the historical authenticity of what we see. It is but a small step to realize that the conventions of documentary themselves guarantee the authenticity of that to which they refer. . . . Morris questions the reliability of evidence while still asserting that there is a reality to which memory and representation allude").

4. See Michael Renov, "Towards a Poetics of Documentary," in *Theorizing Documentary,* ed. Michael Renov, 203n.55 ("The popular attachment to truth in cinema suggests that the erosion of referentials associated with the postmodern is being resisted in some quarters with great intensity"). See generally Saul Friedlander, *Probing the Limits of Representation* (Cambridge, Mass.: Harvard University Press, 1992), and Richard K. Sherwin, "Law Frames: Historical Truth and Narrative Necessity in a Criminal Case," 47 *Stanford Law Review* 39–83 (1994). In the latter work I question Morris's tendency in *The Thin Blue Line* to suppress the film's subversive counterplot for the sake of a stronger, linear resolution to the question, Who killed police officer Wood?

5. But see Tony Hilfer, *The Crime Novel: A Deviant Genre* (Austin: University of Texas Press, 1990), 2–3. "The function of the detective hero is to guarantee the reader's absolution from guilt. This is basic to the genre's form of wish fulfillment. In contrast, the reader of the crime novel [and, one might add, the viewer of the equally subversive crime film] is maneuvered into forms of complicity."

6. See generally Martha C. Nussbaum, *The Fragility of Goodness: Luck and Ethics in Greek Tragedy and Philosophy* (Cambridge: Cambridge University Press, 1986).

7. See the *New York Observer,* October 7, 1991, quoting Mamet: "[*Homicide*] has no moral. It's not a cautionary tale. . . . It's a myth: a symbolic exploration of the unconscious—it purifies and cleanses through enabling the

auditor to respond on other than a conscious level. . . . It's the myth of the minotaur. He goes deeper and deeper into the labyrinth to out what plagues the city, only to find out it is him."

8. See, e.g., Martha Sherrill, "Errol Morris: The Auteur as Advocate," *Washington Post,* January 3, 1989, B1 (describing Morris's film as a "feature-length documentary"); Alvin Klein, "Film Dissects Murder and Justice," *New York Times,* October 23, 1988, 14 (describing the film as a "nonfiction feature film"); and Pat McGilligan and Mark Rowland, "100 Film Critics Can't Be Wrong, Can They?" *Times Mirror,* January 8, 1989, 20 (describing the film as a "crime documentary").

9. See John Burnet, *Early Greek Philosophers,* 4th ed. (New York: Meridian Books, 1969), 52; G. S. Kirk and J. E. Raven, *The Pre-Socratic Philosophers* (Cambridge: Cambridge University Press, 1957), 106. The ancient Greek philosopher Heraclitus expressed a similar thought: "The sun will not overstep his measures; if he were to do so, the Erinyes, handmaids of Justice, would seek him out." Philip Wheelwright, *Heraclitus* (New York: Atheneum Press, 1968), 102.

10. See Martha Nussbaum, "Emotions as Judgments of Value," *Yale Journal of Criticism* 5:2 (1992): 201–12; and Nussbaum, *Fragility of Goodness.*

FIVE

The Laws of the Game

Jean Renoir, *La Règle du Jeu*

TOM CONLEY

■

In a remarkable discussion of Michel Foucault's philosophical writings, Gilles Deleuze observes that in modern times, in almost every social sphere, legal practice involves various *integrations of illegalisms,* or "illegalism-laws," that manage and promote illicit behavior.[1] By illegalism is meant a transgressive activity that a law or body of laws prohibits, but that it also promotes through different institutional and strategic means. An illegalism might be considered in its broadest sense as whatever a rule of law invites, directly or indirectly, as its consequence. For nonspecialists of legal practices (such as the author of this essay), the integration or management of illegalisms might be typified in the economy of narcotics in everyday life in the western hemisphere. The illegality of use, transport, and possession of controlled substances ("drugs") is treated so stringently that prisons are stuffed to the point of collapse. Yet the drug industry is so integral to business that a punitive "war on drugs" appears to be nothing more than a sham protecting the image of the authority of law. Between actions in the courtroom, media images, and everyday life it can be said that production and consumption of drugs is carefully managed by the executive branches of our government.

A rule of law generally means that the same decree should apply to everyone without distinction; in particular, however, the same rule applies degrees of violability. Such concessions condone or encourage illegalism. We might say that with decisions involving the death penalty, convicted criminals will be condemned or rewarded according to their status. Foucault treats the issue in a broad way when he notes, in *Dis-*

cipline and Punish: The Birth of the Prison (Surveiller et punir), "In the eyes of the law, detention can be a privation of freedom."[2] He suggests that with the democratization of France, in the aftermath of the revolution of 1789, the new government construed law to be that which grants, like manna, something that the social body had never before imagined: liberty. A general rule of punishment entails a removal of a degree of liberty from the subject who has committed an infraction. Foucault goes on to show that in the nineteenth century new systems of incarceration use *spatial* and *discursive* means to mete out units of privation of liberty, but that these units in themselves promote new kinds of illegal behavior.

Illegal practices such as these may have led the French government, notes Foucault, to denounce (in the years 1820–45) the retributive system "the great failure of penal justice" (*Surveiller et punir* 269). In the celebrated instance of the panopticon, in which prisoners are deprived of liberty while being viewed in the solitary confinement of cells facing a central surveillance tower, the illegalism-law that would result might be construed as the detainees' impulse to flaunt pornographic behavior *en flagrant délit* (willfully, in misdemeanor) so as to excite, enervate, and give the prurient imagination of the law something at once to fret about and enjoy. Or it might be a mimicry of good conduct so fake and so ludicrous that it would leave strategic orders wondering if indeed the privation of liberty is subverted by the paradox of creative erotic practices of liberation taking place in forced solitude.[3] It would draw the visible form of control into the erotic discourse being forbidden, leaving thus an illegalism-law that reigns over and above the formal penal codes.

This illegalism is "directly useful" in that the privation of liberty turns into a condition fostering delinquency. The example of erotic counterpractices functioning in the midst of panoptic control begs correlation with issues concerning cinema and law. Cinema has an obviously panoptic structure in the formal conditions of its viewing in public theaters. It would be said that by offering imaginary "illegalisms" in the forms of "adult dramas," cinema extends and commits to a general sphere what Foucault detected in the post-revolutionary world of detention (for example, in Jonathan Demme's *Philadelphia* a heterosexual male spectator can feel the excitement of gay sex taking place under the seats of the "Palomino" movie theater all the while he buys into absolution from guilt by eating the film's ideological pabulum about sensitivity and contrition). Delinquencies become the stuff and substance of cinema. They are not illegal because they are illegalism-laws of the medium. They remain licit insofar as their representation cannot be held accountable for leading directly to criminal activities, but they can imply all kinds of prurience and offer models for delinquency in other areas of life.

The panoptic example has compelling cinematic virtue in its articulation of form and content. Its own architecture is what Deleuze calls a *forme de contenu* (form of content) in that anyone who *sees* the conceptual plan immediately understands how the legal and illegal aspect of the system will work. The central gaze will seek to see what it dares not to practice. It will also correlate with its visual plan of subjugation, a *forme d'expression* (form of expression) that concerns a whole "regime of language that classifies and translates infractions, that calculates its punishment; a nexus of statements, and also a threshold" (*Foucault* 39–40). It will use speech, such as loudspeakers and megaphones, to order behavior so that it will inspire prisoners to whisper and penetrate each other's eyes and ears with erotic substance.

To explore these problems I would like to study Jean Renoir's *La Règle du jeu* (*The Rules of the Game,* 1939), a feature that, roughly, owns a place in the French tradition of cinema comparable to that of *Citizen Kane* in the history of American film. Apart from their canonical status, both films are vexed by illegalism. They deal with the ugliness of patriotism and study how infractions are essential to the social orders that exploit national identity. In strictly filmic terms, just as *Citizen Kane* sums up a relation of form and style, of industry, art, and history as no other work since Griffith, *La Règle du jeu* invites analysis of many practices, histories, and institutions that percolate through it. Not only does *La Règle du jeu* crystallize the labor of most French cinema of the *entre-deux-guerres,* it also serves as line of demarcation between two eras, what Deleuze elsewhere calls "image-movement" (including the traits of classical cinema since its beginnings in the late nineteenth century) and "the time-image" (or the study of duration through self-reflection that marks films following the postwar years).[4]

Before considering Renoir, we should recall some of the tenets that bind Foucault's concepts of illegalism to Deleuze's study of their manifestations in aesthetic domains that include cinema. According to Deleuze, when Foucault's concept of power is actualized and enforced, the power of a state, would be expressed in law, law being conceived sometimes as a condition of peace imposed upon brute forces, and at others as the result of a war or struggle won by the stronger parties (but in both cases law is defined by the constrained or willing cessation of a war, it is opposed to illegality that it defines through exclusion; and revolutionaries can only reclaim another legality that passes through the conquest of power and the establishment of another state apparatus). One of the most profound themes of *Discipline and Punish* consists in replacing this unwieldy opposition of law-illegality with a delicate correlation of *illegalism-laws*. Law is always a composition of illegalisms where, formalizing them in the ways it does, also differentiates them. (*Foucault* 37)

It follows that law becomes the "management of illegalisms," such that some are permitted, invented, or made possible as a privilege of the dominant class, while others are negotiated, compensated, interdicted, or exchanged with competing powers according to immediate need or contingency. Readers familiar with *Discipline and Punish* will recall how the seemingly "decadent" activities that had been licit under Louis XVI and his forebears go underground and, as it were, assume new forms, thanks in part to what results from imposition of strict codes of conduct.[5] After the French Revolution, new institutions bear the signs of efficiency and productivity in spatial, architectural, and geographical design: the hospital, the military barracks, the factory, the educational institution, and the prison. Whereas the first four are designed to institute or "redress" masses of subjects, indeed to massify a single type of subjectivity (or, in our world, a range of human experience), the last institution acquires the utility of fabricating illegality and delinquency. Following implementation of modes that "correct" entire sectors of the French population, Jeremy Bentham's panoptic model is implemented to become a norm and a common ground plan.

According to Deleuze, in the panopticon we witness a creation whose form is its content, a *forme de contenu* or a *forme d'expression* that concerns a whole regime of language—one that classifies and translates infractions as well as calculates its punishment; one that provides a nexus of statements and also a threshold. In other words, there is born all of a sudden a system that coordinates both *discursive* and *visible* formations that will exercise power over growing masses of subjects. The prison, as a concrete manifestation of a concept, is on the side of the visible, whereas penal laws, disposed in consubstantiality with the architecture of confinement, are on the side of the discursive. Together they form a *diagrammatical* construct that "is no longer the auditive or visual archive, but the city-plan, the map, or cartography coextensive with the entire social field" (*Foucault* 42). An "abstract machine," the diagram knows no distinction between a form, a content, an expression or, we might say, its discursive and visible components.

When Deleuze studies the mechanism in detail, he could as well be describing a cinematic apparatus as an effect of the perpetual battle of law, an apparatus that is "profoundly unstable and in flux, forever mixing matters and function so as to constitute mutations," an "intersocial" form in a perpetual state of becoming, a "map of relations of force, of density, intensity, that proceeds through primary, floating linkages, and that passes simultaneously through every point" (*Foucault* 43–44), where causes are at once embroiled and actualized in their effects. When these effects do not acquire a fixed shape, we discern *law as an integration of illegalisms* (*Foucault* 45).

If cinema is built upon the divided relation of plotted images and sounds—if it is "tracked" according to relations of differences between what it presents to be visible and to be audible—it would be something of a "diagram" that at once promulgates laws and their illegalisms.[6] Cinema would resemble the panoptic plan in at least two ways. First, the historical affinity that film has for classical perspective betrays a tendency to code the frame of the shot as a perspectival field of illusion. If a depth of field is used as a vehicle for narrative, establishing shots will tend to mark vanishing points where the visible and invisible are conjoined, and where, too, the spectator is being fixed in respect to the given view that sets in place the story that is being told. The vanishing point would mark the area where the spectator harbors the illusion of being "in control" of the objects and movements defined all about the periphery of the perspectival axis.

It almost goes without saying that films that fold such conditions of viewing into their optical and discursive designs—their "diagrams"—are likely to theorize the relation of cinema to law. These films make manifest a contract that, as Deleuze noted, elsewhere has to remain "diffused" or "fluent," "virtual, potential, unstable," and so on, in order to align illegalism with the general stakes of cinema.[7] Films that bring their process of production into their diagram would tend—but not always—to call into question the illegalisms at their basis. At worst, they become elegant exercises in hyperesthesia (for this viewer, Fellini's *8½*) and at best truculent and forceful interrogations of the medium (Keaton's *Sherlock*

Jr., Lang's *Fury,* Godard's *Contempt).* In between these two extremes, certain films use their self-consciousness to yield intermediate views of illegality: they are recidivist insofar as they employ their self-consciousness to redeem the medium by simply letting go, or aligning the practice of illegalisms with the pleasure of well-wrought narratives (for example, the end of Preston Sturges's *Sullivan's Travels)* that, once all is said and done, afford good doses of entertainment.

In this scale Renoir's *La Règle du jeu* stands out as a highly problematic work. The dialogue never directly states that the film is concerned with the making of a film, nor does the visible field ever quite draw the camera into view. Yet the director commands a central role as an intermediary in the narrative ("Octave," the aptly named music critic who seems to be the rotund O, a vanishing point through which seven characters pass), and the plot literally turns upon optical mechanisms synonymous with fate or chance (the binoculars that allow Christine to view La Chesnaye and Geneviève de Marrast embracing as they depart "once and for all" in front of the bogs on which they stomp in the autumnal marshes near the Château de Solognes). At all times the film seems to be mired in the constraints of its making, but without ever spelling out the point or pronouncing any allegory about its relation as cinema with all the laws—or rules—the title promises to be its content (hence in the credits an inserted disclaimer and marvelous evidence of denial underscoring that the film is meant to be "entertainment, not social criticism"). Because it is never quite named as a film about a film, *La Règle du jeu* becomes at once a *forme de contenu* as well as a nuanced view of illegalisms in both its portrayal of a French social sector in 1939 and the attention it calls to the problems of its own making.

A prevailing story line in Renoir's films of the 1930s tells of an outsider's entry into a closed or economically determined social group. He or she brings about confusion, upsets a given (and usually closed) order, and either leaves or is brought to an untimely end. The outsider forces the members of the established order to realize that no one has any proprietary right to a given space or niche. Characters never really belong where they are. Unlike animals, "man," a species estranged from the rhythms of the world, does not really have a place in nature.[8] Like other outsiders, André Jurieu lands in a world that is not his own; crazy, mad, in love, he strives to reach a vanishing point of his desire; after turmoil and chaos, when he nears the object he seeks, he is murdered. Parallels with religious structures are almost too obvious to equate

Jurieu with a sacrificial victim or scapegoat whose demise is responsible for maintaining a social order.

Because the film sets in counterpoint outsiders both at the top of the economic world (La Chesnaye) and at the margins or the bottom (Marceau), Jurieu seems to mirror what becomes an increasingly pervasive condition of contradiction: between La Chesnaye and Marceau are Christine, who is displaced from her native land by the implied conquest of the Nazis after the 1938 appeasement policies; her maid Lisette, who is married to a man by whom she cannot abide, and who sublimates her erotic energies through boundless admiration of Christine; Lisette's husband, Schumacher, an Alsatian who finds himself in a "rigorously insipid" continuum of a country bachelor, displaced into the middle of France where he patrols the borders of the Château de Sologne (even his name seemingly floats between French and German inflection, such that, because he wears squeaky leather boots, he is both "Shoe-ma-chère" (my dear shoe) and "Shoe-macher" (shoemaker), the maker of the shoes that Marceau, his arch-enemy, is too busy to polish when he cavorts with Lisette); Geneviève de Marrast, Chesnaye's vampish mistress, often sporting the attributes of hunted animals (pheasant and leopard), who is destined to remain on the outside of her paramour's life; Octave, the music critic who loves both Christine and Lisette "in his own way" ("*à ma façon*," he avows to Jurieu), who considers himself a parasite and a piece of human rubbish who has never gained "living contact" with a real audience.

The clearest evidence of the multiple displacements may be found in what the spectator sees and hears when La Chesnaye makes the rounds of his property. The marquis meets Marceau, who has been caught *en flagrant délit* for having poached some rabbits. When asked to defend himself before the jury of the surveiling patrol, Marceau betrays the condition of the film in the grain of his voice. Gargling his syllables and drawling his words, he sounds more like an urban Parisian barkeep than a provincial bumpkin who ekes out a living in the Southern Touraine. And as he listens to Marceau, the nobleman struts about his property with a cane-chair, an emblem of the common expression, *On mène une vie de bâton de chaise* ("you lead the life of a cane-chair," meaning you approach a condition of a vagabond), which implies that with the objects he fondles the marquis acts out a desire to enjoy a vagrant or nomadic existence free of legal barriers. Such are the two polar figures when they meet each other on the property surrounding the château.

All the signs of the film indicate that a closed and absolutely hermetic order of relations is undone from within.[9]

How and why, and in what thematic and "diagrammatical" ways that pertain to illegalism-law it remains for us to discover. We quickly ascertain that the other characters swirl about the ensemble of these eight players. The others make up a chorus that proffers narrower views of legality as they draw pleasure from what the marquis bestows upon them. Perhaps for that reason Saint-Aubin and the old general are cued to be a median "point of view" at the two delicate moments—turning points that do not turn—in the narrative. When, upon Jurieu's entry out of the rain and into the château, Christine avows that her relations with the heroic pilot developed under the sign of pure friendship, the general scoffs at Saint-Aubin for snickering about the endogamy ("it's all in the 'family' . . .") of a closed world where everyone buggers everyone else.[10] And, at the end of the film, after Jurieu is killed by accident, La Chesnaye rises to the occasion (just as had Christine before) to dispel doubts about what might be construed as a murder. After Chesnaye's last words, Saint-Aubin snidely states that we have witnessed *une nouvelle définition du mot: accident* (a new definition of the word: accident). But then the old general rises to the occasion. His parting shot carries over and beyond the end of the film and blends with the last notes of Mozart on the sound track. "No, no, La Chesnaye has class. Yes, he has class, and you know, that's dying out, you know, that's dying out!" (shot 337). Whenever he is addressed, the general, a cipher of order and legality, insures that law, order, *and* transgression are being maintained as they ought to be. The old general seems to ventriloquize many of Foucault's observations about illegalisms and their shifting emphases from one political order to another.[11] The frolics, mistakes, shuffles, scuffles, and "accidents" are simply part of an Ancien Régime of aristocratic rules that are intolerably loose for the social orders that have followed 1789.

The narrative implies that the largesse and vision that La Chesnaye embodies seem to have disappeared with the bourgeois revolution. But not that a return to despotism or the royal order is possible either, for the aristocracy might indeed foment a revolution against the lower classes: when Corneille (a hero, like those who dominate the heroic drama of the playwright of his name), the majordomo, discovers that Marceau has not shined the guests' shoes before they awaken, he exclaims that "there might be a revolution in the château!" (shot 224). Will the aristocracy, pure and impure, resident and émigré alike, revolt against the masses? Will it now invert the great inversion of 1789 (that Renoir had recently chronicled in his 1937 *La Marseillaise*)? The answer to these questions probably can be found neither in the director's avowed ideology nor in what seems to be the film's covert allegory. Renoir had aligned himself with the popular front government and was staunchly anti-Fascist. Now the order of the film would tend to imply that the illegalisms practiced by the aristocracy (most obviously, adultery) amount to a waste of time when the nation would better be readying itself against armed, trigger-happy enemies stationed near the border of Alsace-Lorraine; that the week spent at the château is tantamount to the French *Sitzkrieg* at the moment when Nazi Germany was about to launch its *Blitzkrieg*.[12] As the film shows that the French were, in Renoir's words, "dancing on a volcano," one wonders why there is regress to praise of illegalism and to unproductive activities.

Just where it seems to be at once a symptom, a chronicle, and a prediction of events within and beyond its time, the film's appeal to a lax condition can be construed less as a sign of paralysis or of ironic resignation or sense of failed relations of film and history than as an adamant expression of political utopianism. We recall in fact how the film takes care to decline its paradigms of rules. "*Il y a des règles,*" insists Octave, that have to be respected, not long before he also confesses that everyone "has his or her reasons" (shot 64). One is not right to believe in something, but one is right to believe in the coextension of contradictory reasons. Reasons are paraded no less than rules. *On a ses raisons:* mere pluralization of the formula *avoir raison* destroys everything that claims to be legal or unilaterally correct. Wherever a rule is invoked, it is transgressed and licitly illegalized by being pluralized. In this light the persisting view of the Ancien Régime's loosely maintained standards seems to hold and to call into question whatever historical allegory the film might be espousing. It may be that the fake aura of collective and common bliss, the dream of the French Revolution in which every subject would own an equal status, would be *citoyen* and *citoyenne,* avers to be too close to the Fascist and Nazi ideology of unity.[13] Reinscription of hierarchies, the bane of the Revolution, now attempts to preserve conduct that will not be proscribed by totalitarian orders. There seems to exist a defense of illegalism to counter the atrocious order of exclusions that the impending regime of National Socialism sells through appeal to the myth of collective inclusion.

These defensive mechanisms are concretized everywhere in the thematic register of the film. First, the ideology of progress, that Renoir himself had spurned, is impugned insofar as it seems to belong to the others (ourselves) who spy on the antics of the nobility. And second, if there is a nobility that is praised, it runs absolutely contrary to French views of its own history. In *La Règle du jeu* the "Jewish French aristocracy" personified by La Chesnaye is as hilarious as Freud's contemporaneous concept of the "Egyptian Moses" who founds the Jewish nation.[14] For right-wing sympathizers aligned with Charles Maurras and the Action Française in the late 1930s (or today, adepts of Le Pen's Front National), placement of a Jew on a pedestal reserved for the most noble and historically valid embodiment of France is tantamount to flagrant infraction of moral and familial values.[15] With the repeated placement of the one *in* the other, of the antagonist *in* the protagonist, of waste into progress, or the impure in the pure, and so forth, Renoir seems to proclaim a general "law" about the pluralities of human nature. As many have noted, it is historically grounded, it addresses specific sympathies of the 1930s, and it revises French "tradition"—what Freud called the "incomplete and blurred memories" a nation has about its past—for political ends.[16]

The film in fact spells out some of the ways that illegalisms are managed in the post-revolutionary world. The sequence of the hunt displays a grandiose ritual—and ritual murder—reserved for the elite. The celebration takes place on the same grounds where Schumacher arraigned Marceau for stealing rabbits, meaning that the episode (shots 127–82, pp. 85–99) shows how activities proscribed for certain sectors are sanctioned for others. The paradox that has given rise to so many allegorical readings of the film (and also prompted deconstructive treatments) confuses social conflicts with the limiting properties of the frame. The poacher is caught for doing what is good for maintaining the owner's domain. Though hardly injurious to the broader order of nature about the château, his illegal actions are nonetheless emblematic of the nobility or of modes that had prevailed during the Ancien Régime that the left had had to liquidate in the name of common inclusion.

Social and visual barriers converge at the moment when La Chesnaye states that he does not want rabbits chewing up his plantation. Wire-net barriers are needed to keep the rodents out, but La Chesnaye does not want any barriers, either in his own life or on his property (shot 71, in dialogue with Schumacher). An irony smiles through the discourse. The remarks are exchanged in a world so fenced up that the frame surrounding the dialogue becomes congruent with other dilemmas in the film. La Chesnaye wants to erect a protective wall around his marriage

In Jean Renoir's *The Rules of the Game,* the same act—shooting rabbits—is sport for aristocrat de la Chesnaye (Marcel Dalio) but criminal poaching for worker Marceau (Julien Carette). (Courtesy of the Museum of Modern Art.)

at the same time he wishes to bid gentle adieu to his former ways; he would like to have a utopian, "nobiliary democracy" reign supreme at the château but is impelled to endorse a fluid play of illegalism in order to bring fresh air to the world imprisoned in La Colinière.

Here the protagonist's admiration for the poacher broaches a long-standing literary theme associated with the history of illegalism. When La Chesnaye befriends Marceau, he seems to project onto the vagrant his own desire to be rid of the constraints that he has known. With Marceau he becomes a recidivist. Marceau enters the film less as another character than an "other" irrupting in and about La Chesnaye and his world. When living under Corneille's control in the setting of the château, Marceau personifies an illegalism that the majordomo successfully "manages."

The type of illegalism that Marceau embodies seems to reach back to at least two sources. First, in André Gide's tale of a respected citizen's confession about illegal behavior, *L'Immoraliste* (1902; *The Immoralist*) we follow a report in which a well-to-do specialist of classical antiquity, reconstructing his past, tells of the ways that he learned how to poach rabbits on his own farm in Normandy. Some dubious traits of the narrator, Marcel, are revealed as he recounts how he learned from a young rustic, for whom he shared hidden erotic cravings, the art of snaring rabbits. Aroused by the rough pleasure that the bumpkin might offer him, rather than committing an overt transgression, Marcel displaces his desire into committing infractions—poaching bunnies—that go unseen in the official affairs of the narrator's domain.[17] The other type reaches back to Renoir's films. In *La Chienne* (1930), the lead, a cashier and Sunday-painter named Maurice Legrand (Michel Simon), is pauperized as a result of a sordid imbroglio that entailed an incestuous circulation of paintings and a theft of company funds. The plot eventually leads to the apparition and disappearance of the character's "self-portrait," such that Renoir himself is implied to be a thief in his own film.[18] Legrand's character resurfaces in *Boudu sauvé des eaux* (1932) and in fact crosses through the film and disappears in a sort of collective apotheosis of tramps, vagabonds, and vagrants.

Marceau seems to be born of these sources of collective and personal signature. In *Rules,* however, the character is set in a broader history of law and transgression whose current condition appears to be determined by two centuries of illegalism that have developed since the French Revolution. To obtain the breadth of the tradition that relates illegalism to post–Revolutionary France it suffices for us to recall (a) the affinity that Marceau has for the delinquent and (b) the relation that his actions hold with the structure of the sordid news item, "accident," or *fait divers*. The past of La Chesnaye's mirror-image on the other side of the social spectrum is brought back through a heated conversation that the nobleman witnesses when Schumacher, having caught the poacher "red handed" (shot 81, p. 60; in French, *en flagrant délit,* or "in misdemeanor"), begs to be rid of the knave. La Chesnaye asks Marceau if he is indeed a poacher. Marceau responds by stating that he is a chair-repairer (as La Chesnaye sports his cane-chair!). Furious and injurious, Schumacher interrupts, labeling Marceau a "rascal" (shot 85, p. 61), a coward who should have been shot during the last war.

The composite identity that is constructed in the course of the exchange likens Marceau to an established type that in fact emerged from the management of illegalism in nineteenth-century prisons. In recalling Foucault's portrait of Béasse, a historical figure who personified an illegalism that resisted all modes of correction, we discover one of the character's collective origins. When interrogated before a judge and jury, Béasse showed his inquisitors that all the illegalisms a tribunal habitually registers as infractions of the law were for him, to the contrary, "a force of life": absence of a home as the vagabond's living condition, absence of any teacher or school since he is autonomous; absence of labor since he lives in liberty; absence of any schedule as he lives day and night with indifference, and so forth (296–97). Béasse's illegal status becomes his right, his very liberty. Foucault concludes the account in noting that "across all these various indisciplines" that mark Béasse's being "it is 'civilization' in general that is being put on trail, and 'savagery' that is made manifest" (298). The description could well pertain to Boudu or to Marceau, figures of transgression and of illegalism who are more than those of an outsider, an "other," a tramp, a trickster, or a scoundrel who lives on the margins of political and historical frames. The film implies that Marceau and his admirers are consequences of a history of illegalism, dating well beyond 1789, that has evolved into a fluid relation of law and transgression during the era of the growth of the French middle classes.[19]

The presence of the *fait divers* in the world of nobiliary behavior may serve to tell why. When La Chesnaye and Jurieu apologize to each other for having engaged in fisticuffs in their skirmish over Christine, each avows that he acted like "a real peasant." As the camera tracks and pans to follow the couple as they slowly strut toward the dining room, the marquis exclaims, "Do you know what our little exhibition of 'pancratium' makes me think of? From time to time, I read in the newspapers that in a distant suburb, an Italian navvy has tried to carry off the wife of some Polish laborer and that it finished up with a stabbing. I didn't believe such things possible. They are, my dear chap, they are!" (shots 292–93, p. 148). The remark casts into the accelerating narrative a stray piece of news summing up what is about to happen just outside of the château. Not that La Chesnaye is a Polish laborer: but his fascination with the world of delinquency, reflecting his affinity for Marceau, stages the history of the emergence of the *fait divers,* like that of cinema itself, as an integrating force of illegalism within the fabric of acceptable society.[20] The sleazy "news-item" was a product of journalism spawned not long after the institution of the bourgeois monarchy of Louis-Philippe. Then (and now) newspapers took upon themselves the task of reporting crimes as events both familiar and formidable. As of 1840,

> through its daily repetition, the criminal *fait divers* provides a positive reception for the sum of controls maintained by the courts and the police that grid the society; it tells from day to day a kind of inner battle against the faceless enemy; in this work, the news item constitutes the daily bulletin of alarm or of victory. Together, the police novel and news item have produced for more than a century a stupendous mass of 'crime stories' in which delinquency especially appears as something at once very near and quite distant, as something perpetually menacing to the fabric of everyday life, but extremely removed in its origin, its designs, and in the place where it unfolds as something at once habitual and exotic. Through the importance that is accorded to it, along with its discursive festiveness, about it we see a line traced, a line which, by exalting it, also sets it apart. Coming from such a strange horizon, what illegalism could ever shine through such a redoubtable delinquency . . . ? (Foucault, *Surveiller et punir* 292)

Now if we recall the relation that Deleuze establishes between illegality and mechanisms of visibility and discourse, there remains to be seen how the film works through its *own* transgressions in respect to its composition; in other words, how the montage at once extends and calls into question the possibility of any mimesis—as farce, as tragedy, melodrama, *fait divers* (shot 292), or even historical allegory. The film suggests that any attempt to deal with it outside of its filmic rules entails transgression of a vital and necessary practice of incest. Transgression of a transgression? Because it has its own laws, its own practices, its own *règle du jeu,* the film repels any "reading" for the simple reason that the viewer discovers that he or she is before an articulation that cannot be understood through a habitual separation of lexical and visual codes. The film constantly plays on differences within its field of language and figure, thus summoning everything that would establish a law of its composition and meaning. In an urgent way, *La Règle du jeu* is "impossible" or "destructive" of practices that ground laws of visibility and discourse by virtue of its calligraphic or hieroglyphic composition that confuses lexical and cinematic orders.[21] The narrative continually verges on collapsing itself through what Deleuze might call its "diagrammatical" configuration and the relation of "illegality" that ties its form and content to the surrounding historical context.

As a prologue to what ought to be a broader analysis, two aspects of the film are illustrative. First, the film indeed folds the Marxian dynamic of recurring inversions of historical manifestations of tragedy and farce (his celebrated *18th Brumaire*) into a narrative drawing on Marivaux (*Le Jeu de l'amour et du hasard*) and Alfred de Musset (*On ne badine pas avec l'amour* and *Les Caprices de Marianne*). Negotiating literary and political sources, the film seems to play on inaction and time lost in a historical moment that portends the Fall of France within a year of its showing.[22] Self-involvement would seem to be the film's symptom and its illness to the degree that pleasure and pathos obtained from oscillation between comic and tragic modes are brought to an end with the artifice of murder. The rich parallels that can be drawn with the *Sitzkrieg* and the schizoid character of French political sympathies of the 1930s are modified when we realize that a commanding intertext is Chaplin's *The Idle Class* (1920). In that film a series of sketches about social conflict furnish material that seems to inspire much of the play in the corridors of the château, the masked ball, and the almost timeless picture of social contradiction that both directors ultimately share.

In Chaplin's film the narrative hinges on the tramp's resemblance to a nobleman who is spurned by his wife (Edna Purviance). In leaving her husband, she hopes that he might reform his penchant to drink. The film begins when the tramp emerges from the underside of a train that had carried a group of rich patrons to a station near the nobleman's estate. The tramp traverses a golf course, meets the elegant wife who spends the afternoon riding her horse, imagines a life of bliss with the beautiful lady, is chased by the police, and enters the residence in which a masked ball is taking place. His costume fits the occasion: he wins the attention of the nobleman's wife, is flattered by her charms, but bungles when he tells the father-in-law that he is not (yet) married to the daughter sporting a costume reminiscent of Marie-Antoinette. All these exchanges of identity take place as the husband finds himself trapped in a costume of medieval armor. Unable to lift either the visor or the entire headpiece, he flails in jealous rage while the tramp gains intimacy with the wife.

The picture of the "idle" class identifies that of *La Règle du jeu*. And so does the husband's plight when he is incarcerated in his armored costume: when Octave cannot remove his *sacrée peau d'ours* (damned bearskin) after the first masquerade (shot 240), he mimes Chaplin's antics so deftly that a viewer's memory of the sequence in *The Idle Class* intensifies the relation of comedy, vaudeville, and attenuated slapstick to the depiction of the French nobility. The tramp's entrance into the space of the "other" world matches that of Marceau into La Chesnaye's company; and the long take of Chaplin the decadent nobleman, preening himself before an elegant mirror over a rococo buffet, immediately recalls the exposition of the film (shot 24) that shows La Chesnaye in medium close-up, in front of a mirror, sending a telephone call to his mistress as he toys with a music box. The words exchanged (in shot 23) with his wife have just ended on a note of trust. The protagonist asked her if indeed he lies to himself, but only at the instant before he calls his paramour. The same self-deception in fact identifies Chaplin's character in relation to himself, his double, and to the act of mirroring. Whereas for Chaplin the protagonist cannot rid himself of his taste for martinis, Renoir's character cannot be done without a lingering love of adultery.

The interference of Chaplin's film points, second, to the more pervasive relation of illegalism and mechanisms of visibility. In *La Règle du jeu,* the telephone call that is represented in shot 24 picks up the theme of the broken communication passed over the radio (shot 7), in which the artificial synchrony of voice and image is called into question by the presence of the back side of the box that displays its cathode tubes in the unlikely setting that resembles an eighteenth-century *petit appartement* at the château of Versailles. When Christine ambles from background (where she was seated in front of a mirror) to foreground to turn off the radio, the shot cuts back to the Le Bourget airport, where a specialist, called to replace Jurieu, who had broken the rules of decorum that hold for interviews, describes in a metallic tone the "serial" nature of the apparatus that has just broken Lindbergh's records. Christine *cuts* the radio at the point where the shot is cut, but *we* proceed to see and hear the drivel that she has had the good sense to extinguish. The mechanism of artifice that divides and sustains the narrative is called into view at once in the framing and editing. The insertion of the cut reinforces our persisting sight of a wire unwinding from a coil to the microphone that a female radio announcer pulls as she tries to cross through a crowd pressing by the runway at the airport: "*Attention au fil!*" (shot 1). "Watch out for the wire" is addressed *off*, without any single receiver denoted. Her words could be spoken to us and to the implicit crowd both in and out of frame. The implied statement is that we ought to heed the thread (*fil*) of a narrative that is wound about and around itself and its own mechanical disposition, and that we are the masses who produce the law that acclaims and condemns the film in which we participate, as it were, before our eyes.[23]

Similar manifestations are not haphazard. One of the domestics, dining at the table adjacent to the kitchen, flatly refusing to eat anything that is not fresh, digs a fork into a jar to retrieve a pickle in brine (shot 118). When Jurieu and La Chesnaye have their last words together, the marquis admits that "something bothers me" (*il y a quelque chose qui me chiffonne*) in all this business (implied, of lady-swapping), and that it has to do with the perils of being an aviator (shot 293). The remark is made just as La Chesnaye wipes off (*chiffonne*) Jurieu's jacket with his handkerchief (shot 294). *Le chiffonné chiffonne,* that is, he who is bothered bothers: but in a way such that the iconic traits of La Chesnaye's caressing gesture, combined with the familiar French expression, are momentarily arrested—again *en flagrant délit*—as another of the miniature short-circuits or betrayals that reiterates what happens everywhere else in the film. There is little difference between the servant's gesture at the table, the marquis's dusting of the aviator's jacket, and the strange breakages in the narrative threading that are witnessed in the exposition.

These connections and collapses of meaning between the image track and sound track comprise something resembling what Deleuze calls the "refined correlation of *illegalisms-laws*." The correlations multiply almost everywhere in *La Règle du jeu* and move indiscriminately—almost transgressively—between lexical and visual registers. Perhaps one of the most memorable and grisly details of the film emblematizes the problem and can serve as a conclusion to this discussion. André Bazin and others have marveled at the way the murder of a rabbit seen in close-up over a duration of four seconds, in the hunt sequence (shot 178), either anticipates or sets into a *mise-en-abyme* the murder of André Jurieu (shot 323).[24] English subtitles translate Marceau's report of the accident (shot 329) into an allegory that relates the two events to each other. Jurieu was gunned down "like a rabbit," but in reality (or in French) Marceau remarks that Jurieu was felled *comme une bête.* The editing does not make such easy sense of the exchange if *bête* is taken in a broader sense, in the context of the crackling of nature—frogs, cicadas, crickets—in the night about the château (shot 295, etc.), or in the banter that marks this and other of Renoir's films, where *bête* is used to describe characters who tease each other ("vous êtes bête," quips Anne-Marie Chlöe to the tramp in *Boudu sauvé des eaux* and passim). Humans become *bêtes humaines,* like the title of the film adapting Zola's novel, *La Bête humaine* (1938) that preceded the making of *La Règle du jeu,* and prompt the spectator to move across and about the filmic material in a way that transgresses all laws of narrative unity or controlling limits of single films.[25] The construction that divides the image and language into a "diagrammatical" configuration not only allows historical allegories to be set in place (as if the shooting of the rabbit—it suffices only to imagine how it was "shot" by Renoir's crew—would be the blow precipitating a concatenation of murders that both summarizes and elicits the coming of the Second World War), but they also prompt the viewer to interrogate systems in cinema that produce legalities of meaning.

We can finally hypothesize that *La Règle du jeu* puts forward at every moment of its diegesis those "diagrammatical" or discursive and visual mechanisms that make illegalism a vital function of law. They pertain not only to the representation of French history past and present, or to the frame of meaning in narrative cinema, but also to the mechanisms and limits of representation in sound film. Few films fold into their form the correlation of illegalism-laws as extensively or pervasively as *La Règle du jeu.* For that reason it stands as a film that displays and impugns production of what in this body of essays John Denvir aptly calls "legal reelism," or a tension of legal and cinematic practices in Hollywood cinema. It may be, too, that a study of a French film in the context of Hollywood may comprise a practice of geographical and national illegalism within the body of a volume devoted to American cinema.

Notes

1. Gilles Deleuze, *Foucault* (Paris: Minuit, 1986), 49–52 (hereafter cited in the text).

2. Michel Foucault, *Surveiller et punir* (Paris: Gallimard, 1975), 261 (hereafter cited in the text). See also the English translation, *Discipline and Punish: The Birth of the Prison,* trans. Alan Sheridan (New York: Vintage, 1977). Here and elsewhere all translations from the French works of both Foucault and Deleuze are mine.

3. On this score, see Jane Giles, *Le Cinéma de Jean Genet* (Paris: Macula, 1993), which details how Genet, in his only finished film, *Un Chant d'amour* (1950) portrays prisoners obtaining pleasure through the illegalism-law of masturbation, voyeurism, and anal congress in a "panoptic" context that includes relegating the police to observing what inmates practice with lust and affection inside the walls of the prison.

4. The two movements are embodied in the very form of Deleuze's two studies *L'Image-mouvement* (Paris: Minuit, 1983) and *L'Image-temps* (Paris: Minuit, 1985); in English as *Cinema 1: The Movement-Image,* trans. Hugh Tomlinson and Barbara Habberjam (Minneapolis: University of Minnesota Press, 1986), and *Cinema 2: The Time-Image,* trans. Hugh Tomlinson and Robert Galeta (Minneapolis: University of Minnesota Press, 1989). The two works require some familiarity with the author's commitment to philosophy, literature, and the fine arts. Jean-Louis Leutrat's review of the two volumes, in *Kaléidoscope* (Lyon: Presses de l'Université de Lyon, 1988), explains how Deleuze articulates his distinction between the two types of film. "Image-movement" pertains to the classical years of the medium, when film explored and achieved its sense of the range of its form. "Image-time," by contrast, stands as a different moment or attitude that interprets cinema as duration and that follows, like a Baroque moment, experimental and classical phases of the medium.

5. Foucault notes that "disciplinary techniques bring forth individual series: the discovery of an evolution in terms of genesis." The two great "discoveries" of the eighteenth century, "the *progress of societies* and the birth of individuals are quite possibly correlatives of new techniques of power and, in particular, of a new way of managing time and of making it useful by means of segmentary division, seriation, synthesis, and totalization" (*Surveiller et punir* 162, emphasis added). As we shall see, Renoir's cinematic style calls into question the same idea of progress in its manifestation as "law of human nature" in his own historical context.

6. Theorists of cinema have made the divided text of film something of an axiom. Such is the position of Marie-Claire Ropars-Wuilleumier, in *Le Texte divisé* (Paris: Presses Universitaires de France, 1981) and *Ecraniques* (Lille:

Presses Universitaires de Lille, 1990). In his most recent work, *L'Énonciation impersonnelle ou le site du film* (Paris: Meridiens-Klincksieck, 1991), which studies deixis and the establishment of subject-positions in film, Christian Metz observes how the relation of sound and image tracks weakens or even erases sites that would establish identities of interlocutors (in the narrative of a film being seen) and even the viewers (in the theater or in front of a television monitor). If any study proves how law integrates illegalism in its formulations, it is Metz's: wherever we think we discern a message or a statement in our viewing of a film, the technology of its divided tracks shows that the content of the exchange is entirely fabricated, illusory, and so mobile that it can be used for anything one wants. Following a similar line of inquiry, in *Film Hieroglyphs* (Minneapolis: University of Minnesota Press, 1991), I have tried to argue that classical cinema puts forward doubled forms, "rebuses" or visible writings, that at once split and suture the viewer's activity of seeing and reading. At these points we discover how the medium advances its ideology—its law and illegalisms—on the basis of a division inherent in film form (ix–xxxv).

7. In a different but correlative register, Andrew J. McKenna calls this state of diffusion a "sham exercise of the law," where codes of genre, of spectatorial expectations (as it were), preempt what can be said or made of film: "No law is possible against imagination that would not collude with its superstitions" ("The Law's Delay: Cinema and Sacrifice," *Legal Studies Forum* 15:3 [1991]: 211).

8. The cumulative view obtained from Renoir's films, from *La Fille de l'eau* (*The Water Girl,* 1924) up to *Rules,* resembles Charles Baudelaire's observations about landscape painting in the 1859 *Salons.* In "Paysage," the critic upbraids artists who insist on inserting staffage—human elements that bring about scale and mimetic range—that reduces the difference between the order of humans and that of an environment that works better without them. See Charles Baudelaire, *Oeuvres complètes,* ed. Claude Pichois (Paris: Gallimard-Pléiade, 1978), vol. 2, pp. 660–68. Renoir's work also ratifies a prevailing ethnographic view which holds that because the world will live much longer than man, humans do not need to spoil it with their overbearing presence. In this respect, Claude Lévi-Strauss's observations in *Histoire de lynx* (Paris: Plon, 1991, pp. 218–20) appear to derive from Baudelaire and to be of a context similar to what inspires Renoir.

9. The commanding otherness from within points to a general condition of illegality in *La Règle du jeu.* If none of the characters belongs where he or she is, everyone is a stranger in society, a prima facie criminal, perhaps, because he or she does not live according to the codes of post-revolutionary economy. In its context, criminals originate in the lower echelons and are destined to live "in society like strangers" (Foucault, *Surveiller et punir,* 280).

10. Jean Renoir, *Rules of the Game,* trans. John McGrath and Maureen Teitelbaum (New York: Simon and Schuster, 1970), shot 105, p. 73. This edition is

based on the original reprinted by *L'Avant-scène du cinéma* (Paris, 1965). References to this edition are cited parenthetically in the text.

11. Foucault: "It can be stated, albeit schematically, that under the Ancien Régime, every different social stratum kept for itself its margin of tolerated illegalism: non-application of the law and failure to observe countless edicts or ordinances were a condition of the political and economic maintenance of the society" (*Surveiller et punir,* 84). He adds, as if ventriloquizing the old general's reiterated remarks about the goodness of the old ways, "this illegalism was then so deeply rooted and so necessary for the existence of every social stratum that it had in some way its own coherence and economy" (*Surveiller et punir* 85), even though the structure was not entirely "proper" to the Ancien Régime.

12. In the most thorough allegorical reading of the film to date (written under the banner of new historicism), Stephen Tifft argues that the paralysis of action in the film matches the ways that British and French statesmen responded to Adolf Hitler's invasion of the Sudentenland. Theirs was "an almost suicidal form of moral and strategic paralysis. A similar paralysis, in the form of obligingly standing pat as dangers mount to exceed one's control, haunts the *Rules of the Game*" ("Drôle de Guerre: Renoir, Farce, and the Fall of France," *Representations* 38 [Spring 1992]: 127–60, 135). Using Marx's *18th Brumaire* to guide part of his interpretation, Tifft shows that all the farce in the film tends "to play out a failure to represent one's historical moment" and that the film thus exposes the limitations of a society's sense of that moment: "One's moment and oneself fail together" ("Drôle de Guerre" 159).

13. Louis-Ferdinand Céline had smelled it in the latrines of Wall Street in *Voyage au bout de la nuit* (Paris: Gallimard, 1932). It was a *communisme joyeux du caca* (joyous communism of shit). But Céline seems also to have had a nose for the false ideals of French historical reconstructions in the 1930s. The "classical age" of French cinema after the First World War saw a growth of patriotic films that papered over the horror of 1914–18 by appealing to the founding myth of the French Revolution. In *French National Cinema* (London: Routledge, 1993, p. 97), Susan Hayward notes, "Given that the Great War devastated the rural population . . . it was vital to those in power that the deaths were seen to have a purpose because of the huge potential for anarchists and radical revolutionaries to foment unrest. Thus, at least where film was concerned, the myths and icons mobilized by historical reconstructions served the ruling bodies' purpose well."

14. Sigmund Freud, *Moses and Monotheism* (1936), in *The Standard Edition of the Complete Psychological Works of Sigmund Freud.* 24 vols. (London: Hogarth Press, 1955), vol. 23; Michel de Certeau, *L'Écriture de l'histoire* (Paris: Gallimard, 1982), 321–27, and note 15 below.

15. In his review of the film in *Action Française* (July 7, 1939), the right-wing critic François Vinneuil noted that Renoir had it "both ways" when portraying

La Chesnaye at once as an aristocrat's aristocrat and a Jew to boot. See *French Film Theory and Criticism 2, 1929–1939,* ed. Richard Abel (Princeton: Princeton University Press, 1988), 273.

16. Sigmund Freud, "Latency Period and Tradition," in *Moses and Monotheism,* 23:71.

17. "How passionately I poached!" Thus the narrator, casting himself as a neophyte trapper, sums up an adventure in which he discovered two rabbits caught in the snares he had set the day before. See André Gide, *L'Immoraliste* (1902), in *Romans, récits et soties: Oeuvres lyriques* (Paris: Gallimard-Pléiade, 1958), 448ff. So striking is the parallel that the reader is tempted to see in the name of La Chesnaye's château, La Colinière, a portmanteau combination of Gide's farm, La Morinière, with the French word for snare (*collet*): *un collet* + La Morinière = La Colinière.

18. See Jean-Louis Leutrat, "Le Portrait dans l'auto (*La Chienne* de Renoir)," *Lendemains* 68 (1992): 8–13.

19. Fluid insofar as the very style of Renoir's film matches that of its content. In *The Movement-Image* (pp. 77–80), Deleuze notes that a predilection for "liquid perception" favors both movement and sensibility that, being molecular, cross or dissolve barriers imposed by form and social orders. Stressing the value in Vigo and Grémillon, Deleuze does not entirely underscore the political dimension of this heightened state of affectivity in Renoir.

20. To the account of illegalism in nineteenth-century France can be appended Noël Burch's incisive account of the popular transgression that marks early French cinema. "People" in the films (thus also hypothetical viewers of the new medium) get away with crime and are praised for doing so. At its very origins film becomes complicitous with a penchant to live on the other side of the law. See Burch, *Life to Those Shadows,* trans. and ed. Ben Brewster (Berkeley: University of California Press, 1990), 43–79.

21. The film is close to what Foucault finds so appealing about Magritte's effraction of discourse and image in *This Is Not a Pipe* (trans. and ed. James Harkness [Berkeley: University of California Press, 1982, p. 21]), where the calligram—like Renoir's field of image and writing—"aspires playfully to efface the oldest oppositions of our alphabetical civilization: to show and to name; to shape and to say; to reproduce and to articulate; to imitate and to signify; to look and to read."

22. As convincingly shown by Tifft, "Drôle de Guerre," 158–59.

23. Marie-Claire Ropars-Wuilleumier's close and sustained analysis of the first eighteen shots of the film cannot be matched here. See "Le Linéaire et le monté, ou 'La Règle déjouée,'" in *Le Texte divisé* (Paris: Presses Universitaires de France, 1981), 75–87. But *attention au fil* harks back to Renoir's prior dissolution of unilateral narrative in Lestingois's last remark in *Boudu*. Saddened by his exit, the company pressing about Lestingois (amid fig leaves) asks about

where Boudu has vanished. He has followed *le fil de l'eau,* replies the bookseller. It is a threadless thread, a dissolving, pluralizing line. . . .

24. André Bazin, *Jean Renoir,* ed. François Truffaut, trans. W. W. Halsey II and William H. Simon (New York: Simon and Schuster, 1973), 82.

25. Transverse analytical movement of this kind resembles what Michel Foucault calls the "labor of the signifier" in *L'Ordre du discours* (Paris: Gallimard, 1971), 75ff. For Renoir the same labor turns out to be an argument for the auteur, led not at a thematic level but in areas of articulation that mimetic models do not control.

SIX

Capra's Constitution

JOHN DENVIR

■

This essay argues the unusual thesis that the study of Hollywood movies can dramatically change the way we understand constitutional theory. Readers may experience some initial resistance to my project since constitutional theory and popular film seem to have little in common; popular film is considered an escapist mass medium, while constitutional theory prides itself on being the most rigorous of intellectual pursuits. Nor will, I fear, my choice of concrete examples be very reassuring since I hope to show that Frank Capra's *It's a Wonderful Life* (1946), usually considered a sappy example of Hollywood sentimentality, can help give us new intellectual purchase on one of constitutional theory's most intractable problems: the issue of whether the state has an affirmative duty to provide care for its least fortunate citizens.

My strategy is simple. I first discuss a traditional "legal text," Chief Justice William Rehnquist's opinion in a case involving the duty of the state to a young boy who was the victim of his own father's violence; then I discuss Capra's film to see how it might enlarge our perspective on the same case. While the dissimilarities between the legal opinion and the film are evident, they also, I believe, share a common attribute; each is a "text" questioning the role of community in American life, and the obligations that community places upon us in dealing with fellow citizens.

Rehnquist's Constitution

The issue of the state's affirmative constitutional duty to provide minimum care to its citizens has bedeviled constitutional theory since the

1960s, when the Warren Court started to confront the gross inequalities between races and classes in American society. The issue, simply stated, is whether the state owes a duty to provide certain minimum protection to its citizens even in the absence of legislation providing such protection. Usually the issue revolved around protection from economic hazards; whether, for instance, the state had a duty to provide certain "just wants" to the poor without charging for them.[1] An increasingly conservative Supreme Court has answered this question in the negative in a series of cases involving providing free housing and abortions to destitute citizens.

In one sense, we might dismiss the issue of the affirmative duty to provide assistance as merely one small corner of constitutional doctrine, but I hope to show that it is the one issue that best illuminates how American citizens stand in relation to each other and their government. The affirmative duty to provide assistance also remains of immediate import for contemporary constitutional issues like the society's duty to provide shelter to the homeless and a quality education for all school children.

The question of the state's affirmative duty reappeared in a new guise before the Supreme Court in *DeShaney v. Winnebago County Dept. of Social Services*,[2] a case that even Chief Justice Rehnquist conceded involved "undeniably tragic" facts. Rather than a question of a citizen's need for protection from economic hazard, this case involved protection from a violent, abusive father. My strategy is to compare the narrative of Joshua DeShaney and the response to it by Justice Rehnquist's opinion for the Supreme Court with the narrative presented by Capra in *It's a Wonderful Life*. I ask the reader's forbearance in my detailed recitation of the facts of Joshua DeShaney's case; I believe that a detailed understanding of the concrete facts of Joshua's tragedy are necessary to an honest consideration of the appropriate constitutional response to his legal claim.

Joshua DeShaney was born in Wyoming and was brought as an infant to Wisconsin by his father, Randy, who had been awarded custody in a divorce proceeding. There were early and numerous indications that his father was mistreating Joshua. Early on, Wisconsin police noted that Randy had "hit the boy, causing marks and is a prime case for child abuse." Soon thereafter, Randy's new girlfriend brought Joshua to the emergency room covered with bruises and abrasions. Emergency room personnel suspected child abuse and notified the Winnebago County Department of Social Services, who obtained a court order placing Joshua temporarily in the hospital's custody. An "ad hoc child protection team" was formed (pediatrician, psychologist, county attorney, police detective, and welfare caseworkers) to study Joshua's case. They decided there was insufficient evidence to charge Randy with child abuse and returned Joshua to his father's custody. A month later, welfare case worker Ann Kemmeter, (a member of the "ad hoc child protection team"), received word from the emergency room that Joshua was again being treated for "suspicious injuries." After talking to emergency room personnel, Kemmeter decided that there was no evidence of child abuse.

Ms. Kemmeter visited the DeShaney home a few months later. She noted a bump on Joshua's head, but accepted Randy's explanation that Joshua had fallen off a tricycle. When Kemmeter visited again in September, she found no one home, but was told by neighbors that Randy had just brought Joshua to the emergency room to be treated for a scratched cornea.

On her next visit, Ms. Kemmeter noticed another bump on Joshua's head. During the next visit she noted bruises on his chin that looked like cigarette burns. This same month Joshua was again brought to the emergency room with a cut forehead, bloody nose, and bruises on both shoulders. Emergency room personnel notified the welfare department that they believed Joshua was the victim of child abuse. No action was taken.

About one year after her first visit, Ann Kemmeter again visited the DeShaney home, but was told she could not see Joshua, who was in bed with the flu. She did not return for several months and then she again did not see Joshua, although she was told that he had recently fainted in the bathroom. Ms. Kemmeter did not even ask to see Joshua.

Within a month of that visit, four-year-old Joshua was so brutally beaten by his father that he suffered severe and permanent brain damage. The neurosurgeon who examined Joshua at that time found evidence of previous trauma to the head and also found that Joshua's body was covered with bruises and lesions. When Ms. Kemmeter was told, she said, "I just knew the phone would ring some day and Joshua would be dead."

As a result of his father's violence, half of Joshua's brain is destroyed. He will live for the rest of his life in an institution for the profoundly retarded. His father received a two-to-four year sentence for child abuse.

Joshua and his mother filed a lawsuit against the county claiming that Joshua's injuries were the result of the state's violation of one of his due process rights. This immediately raised the issue of whether the Due Process Clause of the Fourteenth Amendment placed an affirmative duty on Wisconsin to protect Joshua from his father's violence. The case worked its way through the court system and eventually reached the U.S. Supreme Court.

In his opinion for a majority of the court, Chief Justice Rehnquist did not find Joshua's case to present a particularly difficult constitutional question. As to whether the Fourteenth Amendment's Due Process Clause obligated Wisconsin to protect Joshua from his father's violence, he answered clearly in the negative:

> The Clause is phrased as a limitation on the State's power to act, not as a guarantee of certain minimal levels of safety and security. . . .
>
> Its purpose is to protect the people from the State, not to ensure that the State protect them from each other. The framers were content to leave the extent of governmental obligation in the latter area to the political processes.[3]

Rehnquist not only held that there was "no affirmative right to government aid," but cautioned those who might be moved to sympathy by Joshua's sad tale: "Judges and lawyers, like other humans, are moved by natural sympathy in a case like this to find a way for Joshua and his mother to receive adequate compensation for the grievous harm inflicted upon them. But before yielding to that impulse, it is well to remember once again that the harm was inflicted not by the State of Wisconsin, but by Joshua's father."[4]

Justice Rehnquist's opinion in the *DeShaney* case is in complete harmony with a constitutional philosophy that sees autonomous, competitive individuals coming together to cooperate in the few areas where they believe cooperation beneficial to each. The enactment of legislation marks the limits of such cooperation.[5] To be sure, Justice Rehnquist would have no quarrel with the citizens of Wisconsin if they chose to enact legislation that would provide compensation to Joshua under the facts presented by his case: "The people of Wisconsin may prefer a system of liability which would place upon the State . . . the responsibility to act in situations such as the present one. They may want to create such a system . . . by changing the tort law of the State in accordance with the regular law-making process."[6] But the majority of the citizens of Wisconsin chose not to bestow such a legislative gift on Joshua, one more example of Joshua's bad luck. And, of course, the same holds true for the homeless and children in under-funded schools. If the legislature chooses to respond compassionately to their situation, so much the better. If not, that's fine too. Their fellow citizens owe them nothing.

We should not be surprised by Justice Rehnquist's opinion. He is a self-proclaimed apostle of "strict construction" who believes that the constitution sanctions very few individual rights against the majority other than those related to economic liberty. We should not be surprised, but perhaps we should be shocked. George Bailey sure would be.

Capra's Constitution

George Bailey is the hero of Frank Capra's *It's a Wonderful Life*. Of course, a Hollywood movie cannot articulate a constitutional theory in any technical sense. Movies only tell stories, but just as theories imply narratives,[7] narratives articulate themes. These themes revolve around the social and psychological conflicts the audience experiences in their everyday lives. By focusing our attention on the meaningful conflicts within American culture, film can reorient theory to attend to problems that its abstract categories have ignored. It is my contention that not only *It's a Wonderful Life* merits consideration as a "legal text," but that it provides a much richer discussion than Rehnquist's opinion of both the claims community places upon us and the threats to personal autonomy that such claims represent.

It may seem odd to suggest that Frank Capra's films can make an important contribution to American constitutional theory since his reputation is at best that of a skilled craftsman who made mostly sweet, sometimes saccharine, comedies. Certainly, *It's a Wonderful Life,* with its wingless angel and teary Christmas Eve reunion fits this description. And since the appearance of Joseph McBride's biography of Capra, he must be defended not only against charges of superficiality and sentimentality, but also of cynicism, since it seems that Capra, the supposed populist defender of the "little fella," was a lifelong Republican who vehemently opposed the reforms of the New Deal.

Paradoxically, it is this "dark side" of Capra that provides his greatest value to constitutional theory. McBride shows that "Capra's supposed optimism was a cover for his more fundamental pessimism";[8] it is that emotional ambivalence resonating within *It's a Wonderful Life* that makes it an important text for American constitutional law. Of all Capra's films it most deeply explores "the complex and troubled consciousness" of modern Americans.[9] And it is exactly this troubled consciousness that constitutional theory must confront and to which Justice Rehnquist is so oblivious in his *DeShaney* opinion. The title of this essay indulges in a revealing pun; there is a necessary connection between our individual constitutions and our public one.

My brief is not to present an aesthetic judgment on *It's a Wonderful Life*. It may not be a great film, perhaps not even Capra's best. I wish instead to argue its value in making constitutional theory face up to deep-rooted tensions in our images of American democracy.

It's a Wonderful Life relates the life and (almost) death of George Bailey of Bedford Falls. George (James Stewart) is an honest businessman, loving husband and father, and helpful neighbor, who, because of another's error finds himself on the brink of financial scandal. After a lifetime of labor, he suddenly realizes that an insurance policy is his only asset and that he is therefore "worth more dead than alive." Bailey contemplates/attempts suicide only to be saved by Clarence, an angel who convinces George that his life has been amply justified by all the people he has helped in his life. The final scene is a Christmas Eve neighborhood reunion where all of George's neighbors, his community, chip in to solve his financial problems, thus proving that it is indeed "a wonderful life."

The film's first image of democracy is encapsulated in a scene in which George is about to leave on his honeymoon with his bride Mary (Donna Reed). As they begin to depart, they are interrupted by a "run" on the town bank. This "run" will bankrupt George's Building and Loan Association if all his shareholders insist on redeeming their shares at the same time.

George rushes to the Building and Loan to intervene before his depositors transform themselves from a group of friendly neighbors into an unruly mob. The first depositor confronts George with the individualist demand, "I'll take mine now." George responds with an explanation that the Building and Loan is not a bank but a cooperative venture in which shareholders lend money to each other so that each can afford to build a decent home; the whole venture depends on the trust of each individual in the larger enterprise and his fellow shareholders. As George puts it: "We've got to stick to together! We've got to have faith in one another!"

This fictitious Building and Loan society is Capra's first metaphor for American democracy. It is not so much a set of rules as a network of relationships tying individuals into a community. Robert Bellah described a similar conception of democracy in his book *Habits of the Heart:* "public life is based upon the second languages and practices of commitment that shape character. These languages and practices establish a web of interconnection by creating trust, joining people to families, friends, communities, and churches, and making each individual aware of this reliance on the larger society. They form those habits of the heart that are the matrix of a moral ecology, the connecting tissue of a body politic."[10]

Citizens, like friends, must take responsibility for each other. Throughout the film George is presented as the epitome of the citizen as friend. He spends much of his time helping others. For instance, he loses hearing in one ear while diving into a frozen pool to save his younger brother's life, prevents his drunken druggist employer from accidentally poisoning a customer, informally lobbies a corporation to set up a new factory in economically depressed Bedford Falls, and during World War II (since he is 4–F due to his ear) serves as an air raid warden and leads scrap and paper drives to aid the war effort.

But George's primary community service comes from his mundane role as president of his family-run Building and Loan society, where he helps working people who "do most of the working, paying, living, and dying in this town" fulfill the American dream of owning their own home.

Capra's first image of American democracy is a mixture of Thomas Jefferson and Norman Rockwell. It is an ideal that can be attacked as having little resemblance to contemporary American society. This attack is just if we assume that ideals are meant to be descriptions of concrete reality, but of course ideals aspire to more than mere description. In any case, it is not the only image of democracy presented in *It's a Wonderful Life.*

The second image of American democracy Capra presents is the vicious capitalism espoused by George's archenemy, the wealthy banker Henry C. Potter (Lionel Barrymore). Capra illustrates his view of the consequences of unrestrained individualism in a scene where the angel Clarence shows George what Bedford Falls would look like if George had never been born. Since Bailey is Capra's symbol for community, what we really see is Capra's vision of America without community. It is a film noir industrial slum named Pottersville, replete with prostitutes and gin mills, a place where cash is the only social value. It's what happens when people stop looking out for each other.

One possible reading of *It's a Wonderful Life* holds that it presents only a maudlin contrast between George's "altruistic" Jeffersonian community and Potter's "selfish" capitalism. But upon reflection, I believe this view oversimplifies the film, which shows that the tension between duty to self and duty to community is not just between Bailey and Potter, but within Bailey himself.

For although George may be a good citizen, he is not a happy man. As Potter taunts him, George feels "trapped" by his altruism; he has paid a terrible personal price for his sense of community. Bellah speaks of culture as providing a "second language" that shapes social character; in George Bailey's case, the language of "community" is experienced as much as a prison as a haven. Time and again Capra shows us George's impulses for freedom, adventure, and romance being stifled by his community's conventions and his own sense of communal duty.

George wants to be more than good son, nephew, husband, father, and friend. He cries in desperation, "I want to do what I want to do." In a professional sense, he wants to "do something big . . . build skyscrapers one hundred stories high and bridges a mile long." For romance, he wants to walk barefoot through the grass on a moonlit night with a beautiful girl.

Yet responsibility to family forces George to forego college to run the family business. His community has little tolerance for his dreams of romance; social convention pushes him toward marriage with the safe Mary instead of the racy Violet (Gloria Grahame). And when he does burst through convention to suggest an all-night revel to Violet she thinks him quite mad. Violet's idea of sex has more to do with consumer fetishes like mascara and spiked heels than unrestrained eroticism. And it is George's socially supported loyalty to his incompetent Uncle Billy (Thomas Mitchell) that leads him to the brink of financial disaster and social scandal.

This threat of social ostracism brought on by Uncle Billy's bumbling finally causes George's long-suppressed anger and resentment to erupt. He calls Uncle Billy a "silly, stupid old fool," screams at Mary and the children, and runs from the house to get drunk. It is now that the idea of suicide occurs to him. George's final reaction to his beloved community is anger and despair.

Here is Capra's third image of American democracy, a vision in which all the impulses to freedom and self-realization are sacrificed

In Frank Capra's *It's a Wonderful Life,* George Bailey (James Stewart) incarnates the tension in American culture between the demands of community and autonomy. (Courtesy of the Museum of Modern Art.)

to the sterile replication of social convention. In this scenario George is not so much the hero of democratic culture as its victim. He no longer sees community as a group of supportive friends, but as an emotionally castrating mob. We think of Capra's nightmare vision in *Meet John Doe,* where a group of political supporters suddenly and viciously turn on the Christlike protagonist "John Doe."

It is this third image of democracy to which constitutional theory should pay the most attention. It is a powerful antidote to the pomposity that often poisons judicial and scholarly rhetoric. If we strip *It's a Wonderful Life* of its saccharine ending, we find Capra has given us a good look at a dilemma constitutional theory too often ignores, a deep continuing tension within democracy between the claims of community and autonomy. In a democracy, how do we reconcile our need for community with our fear of it? Or as Richard Rorty (following John Stuart Mill) phrases the question, how do we "optimize the balance between leaving people's private lives alone and preventing suffering?"[11] This is the crucial issue that Capra raises and that Rehnquist ignores.

CapraCon

Film critics have written volumes on "CapraCorn"; perhaps it is now time to investigate "CapraCon." How would a Capra-inspired constitutional jurisprudence differ from Justice Rehnquist's? First, it would differ as to the role of the text of the Constitution. Rehnquist purports to believe the text can relieve us of responsibility for determining the contemporary meaning of American democracy. CapraCon knows better; constitutional interpretation is more than the logical parsing of a two-hundred-year-old text. CapraCon recognizes that democracy is always in the process of reinventing itself. As citizens, we face inevitable conflicts between the claims of community and autonomy;[12] constitutional law is the process in which we try to mediate those tensions.

This emphasis on the inevitable conflicts between our yearnings for autonomy and community contrasts starkly with Chief Justice Rehnquist's constitutional jurisprudence, which supports neither community nor autonomy. Just as Rehnquist would impose no communal duty on the majority to aid Joshua DeShaney, he also would not support a family's autonomous right against state intervention if the majority so chooses. Both the child and the family are left at the mercy of the political processes.

CapraCon, on the other hand, would draw inspiration from Justice Louis Brandeis's famous comment that "those who won our independence believed that the final end of the State was to make men free to develop their faculties."[13] Brandeis recognized that, viewed from a larger perspective, the community/autonomy conflict is artificial: the individual is impotent without communal nurturing, but reciprocally the community's true raison d'etre is the flourishing of each individual.

Not only is Rehnquist wrong when he attempts to find refuge in the text from contemporary conflicts, his reading of the text itself is quite problematic. He claims that the Constitution is merely a charter of negative liberties, but history shows that the Fourteenth Amendment that he is interpreting was intended by its authors to have a remedial, not a negative, purpose.[14]

Furthermore, CapraCon would reconsider the role of emotion in constitutional method. It will be remembered that Chief Justice Rehnquist was wary of permitting emotion to enter into legal decision making; he thought it distorted rational thought. Rehnquist favors a rule-oriented jurisprudence in which the specialist judge first locates the applicable rule and then dispassionately applies it. CapraCon views emotion differently. Emotion is not the enemy of reason, but the engine that powers rational thought. Just as it is impossible to imagine George Bailey making moral decisions divorced from his emotions, our emotional response to Joshua's plight determines the amount of responsibility we choose to take as a community for his fate.

CapraCon would endorse Justice William Brennan's comment that "the internal dialogue of reason and passion . . . does not taint the judicial process, but in fact is central to its vitality."[15] This is not to deny that communal passions can lead to injustice; history teaches too many lessons of the evil that can result from an excess of communal passion. But CapraCon recognizes that theory's denial of the role of emotion in social life does not in any way curb such passions, while it does weaken theory's accuracy. Reason should attempt to refine the passions rather than ignore them.

CapraCon would also accentuate the role of concrete facts over abstract rules in constitutional method. Lawyers tend to look for "neutral principles" to decide cases; for instance, Justice Rehnquist's first step in the *DeShaney* opinion was to determine whether the state owed an abstract affirmative duty of care to its citizens. His negative answer to this self-proposed question permitted him to decide the case without confronting Joshua's pain. CapraCon would adopt a more flexible view of judging, one which centers attention on the complex, concrete reality of the particular case presented.[16] For instance, it would find that Rehnquist's articulation of the case as involving only the state's failure to act quite specious; the facts of the case clearly show that the state returned Joshua to his father's custody. And, as Professor Laurence Tribe of Harvard Law School has pointed out, Wisconsin's welfare policies had fundamentally altered the legal space in which Joshua and his father interacted, thereby making Joshua more vulnerable to this violence.[17] These are not omissions, but acts to which Rehnquist must pay attention. Of course, judges must do more than merely respond intuitively to the facts before them, but they should never allow abstract concepts to blind them from concrete reality.

The anthropologist Clifford Geertz sees law as society's attempt to mediate between quotidian reality and its larger ideals. Geertz argues that law's function is to "translate between a language of imagination and one of decision and form thereby a determinate sense of justice."[18] Law, therefore, is not (as Rehnquist assumes) a rule book to be applied, but rather the process in which we attempt to simultaneously bring concrete reality and our culture's animating ideals into focus. The ideals guide us in handling the concrete dispute and the concrete dispute forces us to rethink those ideals.

But if law is the process by which we reconcile our social practices to our cultural ideals, it is necessary for us to better understand what those ideals are. Where might a judge find evidence of these ideals? Capra-Con would make use of the imaginative resources of the entire culture. Certainly traditional legal sources should not be ignored; the text, history, and structure of the Constitution should not be ignored. So too the legal opinions of judicial giants like Brandeis and Brennan have much to teach us. But our culture provides other imaginative resources that CapraCon would not ignore. Popular art forms, like movies, can alert judges to images of justice that reflect the inarticulate yearnings of common people, who, we must not forget, are the sovereign power in a democracy.

As described above, the *DeShaney* case involves the question of community—what duties citizens owe to one another. This is a truly difficult issue in a post-industrial society where traditional forms of community are fast disappearing.[19] But if Geertz is right in defining law as the process by which we reconcile social reality with our ideals, a good starting point might be to look for images of our ideal of community.

Here *It's a Wonderful Life* proves a valuable legal resource; the scene about the "run" on George's Building and Loan Association in which he reminds his depositors of their communal bond provides what Stanley Cavell calls a "spiritual parable" about how democracy should work.[20] Bailey's cry that "we all have to stick together" puts a point on a political truth that Justice Rehnquist's opinions seems to entirely forget.

CapraCon would also disagree with Rehnquist's ruling in the *De-Shaney* case. Instead of Justice Rehnquist's scholastic distinction between affirmative and negative liberties, a CapraCon judge would ask himself or herself exactly what prevents us from coming to Joshua's aid. Certainly not the constitutional text that has been tortured to serve too many divergent purposes during the last two hundred years to definitively exclude one more. The text cannot absolve us from taking responsibility as a community for acting or not acting in Joshua's defense. Why should we not take George's diving into the frozen pond to save his brother as a metaphor for our communal aspirations? Perhaps this example may seem to overstate the case because Joshua is not our brother, but then neither are the victims of natural disasters like hurricanes and floods to whom we respond with such generosity. The issue is the same: What is our communal duty to fellow citizens in distress? It is a question that cannot be answered (as Rehnquist attempts to) by abstract principles, but by reflection on concrete facts in relation to our ideals.

The essential constitutional question is not about "original intent," but who now are "We, the People" referred to in the Constitution's Preamble, the people who symbolically come together to "establish justice" and "to promote the general welfare." Does "we" include children like Joshua? If so, what do we owe them?

I am not arguing that this question will always be easy to answer, but it does not appear to be an especially difficult one in Joshua's case.[21] Sometimes we might fear state intervention because of respect for the autonomy of the family, but that hardly seems an important consideration here. Joshua's father forfeited that autonomy with the first cigarette burn. It is also true that we have individual desires that compete for funding with our alleged communal duties. For instance, greater social services require higher taxes and higher taxes leave us with less discretionary income to spend on our own individual desires. But, on the facts of Joshua's case, the taxpayer would have saved money if there had been intervention before injuries were inflicted that made Joshua a ward of the state for life.

Justice Rehnquist will remind us that in aiding Joshua we have stepped on to that "slippery slope" law students are so often warned against. If we intervene to protect Joshua in this context, won't we also have to guarantee him a safe home and a decent education? These, of course, are much more expensive measures and do invoke questions about exactly how many potentially private resources we will expend to provide a social environment in which every child is given an opportunity to flourish.[22] I do not mean to imply that these are easy issues, or that our duty to others always trumps fulfilling our individual desires. Quite the contrary, the image of George Bailey's anguished face should remind us that unrestrained altruism is not always the correct response. But I do contend that study of Capra's film points us in the right direction, focusing on Joshua's pain and the question of our appropriate response to it.

Notes

I would like to thank Maxine Auerbach, Jeffrey Brand, Michael Davitt Denvir, Judith Grant, Peter Honigsberg, and Terry Wilson for helpful comments on earlier drafts of this essay.

1. For example, Frank Michelman, "Foreword: On Protecting the Poor through the Fourteenth Amendment," *Harvard Law Review* 83 (Nov. 1969): 7–59.

2. *DeShaney v. Winnebago County Dept. of Social Services,* 489 U.S. 189, 191 (1989).

3. Ibid., 195.

4. Ibid., 203.

5. For a more detailed discussion of Justice Rehnquist's constitutional theory, see John Denvir, "Justice Brennan, Justice Rehnquist, and Free Speech," *Northwestern Law Review* 58 (Apr. 1985): 285–320.

6. 489 U.S. at 203.

7. See generally, Robin West, "Jurisprudence as Narrative: An Aesthetic Analysis of Modern Legal Theory," *New York University Law Review* 60 (May 1985): 145–211.

8. Joseph McBride, *Frank Capra: The Catastrophe of Success* (New York: Simon and Schuster, 1992), 434.

9. Raymond Carney, *American Vision: The Films of Frank Capra* (New York: Cambridge University Press, 1986), 380.

10. Robert Bellah et al., *Habits of the Heart* (Berkeley: University of California Press, 1985), 251.

11. Richard Rorty, *Contingency, Irony, and Solidarity* (Cambridge: Cambridge University Press, 1989), 63.

12. See Roberto Mangabeira Unger, *Passion: An Essay on Personality* (New York: Free Press, 1984), 96. Unger tells us that we must confront our "unlimited mutual need" and "our unlimited mutual fear."

13. *Whitney v. California*, 274 U.S. 357, 372, at 375 (1927) (Brandeis, J., concurring).

14. See Aviam Soifer, "Protecting Civil Rights: A Critique of Raoul Berger's History," *New York University Law Review* 54 (Dec. 1979): 651–706.

15. William Brennan, "Reason, Passion, and the 'Progress of the Law,'" *Cardozo Law Review* 10 (Oct.-Nov. 1988): 3–23.

16. See Martha Nussbaum, *Love's Knowledge: Essays on Philosophy and Literature* (New York: Oxford University Press, 1990), 153.

17. Laurence Tribe, "The Curvature of Constitutional Space: What Lawyers Can Learn from Modern Physics," *Harvard Law Review* 103 (Oct. 1989): 1–39.

18. Clifford Geertz, *Local Knowledge* (New York: Basic Books, 1983), 174.

19. See Raymond Williams, *Resources of Hope: Culture, Democracy, Socialism*, ed. Robin Gable (London: Verso Press, 1989), 111–19.

20. Stanley Cavell, *Pursuits of Happiness: The Hollywood Comedy of Remarriage* (Cambridge: Harvard University Press, 1981), 7.

21. For instance, a newspapers story in San Francisco relate a tragedy brought about *by* state intervention. A Laotion refugee couple were determined to have used corporal punishment on one of their children, leaving a bruise on the child's wrist. The couple's three children were removed from the home, despite the parents' pleas that moderate corporal punishment was an acceptable form of discipline in Laotion culture. The newspapers report that one of the children died from a "mysterious" disease soon thereafter. *San Francisco Chronicle*, Feb. 12, 1994, col. 1

22. Charles Reich, "The Individual Sector," *Yale Law Journal* 100 (Mar. 1991): 1409–48.

SEVEN

Popular Culture/Popular Justice

ANTHONY CHASE

■

No one questions any longer the place of economic and legal history within the field of cultural studies. To take just one example, the industrial structure and legal relations of Hollywood film production have shaped the way American motion pictures look and the aesthetic experience shared by film audiences.[1] Can the study of popular culture, in reverse fashion, make a useful contribution to our understanding of social and economic reality? University students have long read famous novels by Dickens and Balzac as part of their nineteenth-century history classes. But what about movies and popular music, television and mass diversion as tools for better understanding the nature of history and politics?[2] It will be argued here that popular culture, specifically a motion picture directed by Jean Renoir in France during the 1930s, can open up existing academic consideration of an important legal issue, that of popular justice.

Before turning to an analysis of Renoir's film *Le Crime de M. Lange* (*The Crime of Monsieur Lange,* 1936) and its relationship to the popular front period in French history, it is essential to briefly discuss what is meant by "popular justice." However much popular justice, in practice, may belong to popular and grass roots movements (democratic or otherwise), its discourse—or at least its definition—would seem to have fallen into the hands of legal sociologists. In a recent symposium issue of *Social and Legal Studies,* an international scholarly journal devoted to the sociology of law, Sally Engle Merry describes popular justice as a "process for making decisions and compelling compliance to a set of rules which is *relatively* informal in ritual and decorum, non-professional in language and personnel, local in scope and limited in jurisdiction." For Merry, popular justice is nonbureaucratic, informal, accessible, and is "located on the boundary between state law and indigenous or local law." For Christine Harrington, the most interesting thing about popular justice "movements" is their contradictory relationship to the state. Traveling farther along lines laid down by Merry and Harrington, Peter Fitzpatrick argues that popular justice or "alternative justice" stands in opposition to official power, to the "formalized and centralized power of the state." Popular justice, in Fitzpatrick's vision, "does what the state cannot." These legal sociologists emphasize the way in which popular or community justice at least presents itself as an alternative to the formal legal process of the state and its legal apparatus.[3]

Having constructed a broad and intriguing initial model of popular justice, the sociologists nevertheless allow their definitions to come to rest on a relatively narrow group of movements and institutions. After issuing his own critique of neighborhood mediation panels, Fitzpatrick concludes that popular justice is an impossibility. What he describes as a "dissection of the informal and the popular" leads him to the conclusion that such movements have failed to "found a justice that was alternative," instead simply reinforcing official power and helping to secure "the integrity and efficacy of state law."[4] While not as decisive in their conclusions as Fitzpatrick, Merry and Harrington argue that, generally speaking, popular justice is presented as more distinct from state power than it really is.

Potentially extending the insights of legal sociology within the field of popular justice studies, popular culture provides a richer portrait of movements for alternative justice—a popular "jurisprudence" of opposition to formal state power and its legal apparatus.

From the 1936 Warner Brothers motion picture *Black Legion* to the contemporary documentary film *Blood in the Face* (1991), one of the main subjects of popular culture's focus on "alternative justice" has been the Ku Klux Klan and other movements representing the far right. Surveying the current mood of the Klan, Aryan Nation, and American Nazi Party, *Blood in the Face* provides an extraordinary scene set in picturesque rural Michigan, at a family picnic with a sinister purpose, where an older man in a plaid, flannel shirt, surrounded by friends, children, even barnyard pets, converses with a younger man, wearing a hooded sweatshirt. It seems a crisp and invigorating fall afternoon.

Older Man: But we have to take care of the Big Bankers, we have to get the Rockefellers. Those guys should be . . .

Younger Man: Talk about organized crime . . .

Older Man: That's it!

Younger Man: Government *is* organized crime.

Older Man: That's it. If we had a good government, these people would be by a citizens' court sentenced today . . .

Younger Man: That's who's running organized crime—the government.

Older Man: . . . and they would hang legally. But if you hang somebody they call you a Klansman. [Fake scream] See the difference?

Blood in the Face makes specific reference to the assassination of talk-show host Alan Berg in Denver, whose murder provided a basis for the movie *Talk Radio* (1988). From the Broadway musical and later film *Cabaret* (1972), drawn from Christopher Isherwood's popular fiction, to Costa-Gavras's thrillers *Z* (1969) and *Missing* (1982), popular culture has not shied away from showing brownshirts and hooded thugs imposing an alternative justice in the streets, threatening the existing legal system, or paving the way for a formalization of authoritarian rule under fascist auspices.

Even the pulp television series *Wiseguy* (1987–90) managed to spend weeks unraveling the drama latent in pitting government penetration agents against a Klan-like white supremacist group, the Pilgrims of Promise. Certainly the Klan's theory of justice is not "popular" with everyone. But that is not part of the *Social and Legal Studies* symposium definition of "popular justice." The point is that these right-wing groups enact a mode of justice outside formal legal channels. Even where existing government, in the United States or elsewhere, has concrete links with outlaw organizations on the right, it does not follow that these groups are the same thing as the state. The motion picture *Mississippi Burning* (1988), which casts an FBI agent as civil rights hero may have gotten the historical record wrong but that does not mean that the FBI and KKK are identical.

It is the state itself that, eventually, catches up with and eliminates Michael Douglas's character, "D-Fens," in the controversial film *Falling Down* (1993). According to critic Carol Clover, Joel Schumacher's motion picture defines D-Fens "as your average short-tempered neighbor who just happens to break one day," and proceeds to enforce a kind of savage "neighborhood justice" that deserves our attention even if it is not the conventional textbook variety of legal dispute resolution.[5]

Perhaps still unequaled, however, in the screen history of populist legality is the trial that concludes Fritz Lang's classic picture *M*. Lang's original title for the film was *Murderers among Us* but he was denied production facilities as a result of Nazi pressure—the party assumed the film must be about them! Released in 1931 (with a new title), the movie tells a story based upon the case of the Dusseldorf child murderer. Peter Lorre brilliantly plays the role of a psychotic killer whose horrifying deeds send a shudder of fear throughout the community. Early in the film, Lang presents the viewer with a crowd on the verge of executing an innocent victim, inexplicably chosen as fitting the description of the wanted man. Given Lang's later films, including *Fury* (1936), and the comments of critics like Lotte Eisner (who see in Lang's depiction of the crowd seeking vengeance a critique of the Hitler terror), one might expect from *M*'s concluding trial sequence a cut and dried representation of the makeshift jury as protofascist mob. But Lang's treatment is a good deal more nuanced than that.

The clever fugitive whom criminals (not the authorities) have managed to capture is, in fact, guilty of heinous crimes. Grief experienced by the murdered children's parents (some of whom apparently sit in the mass jury) is palpable on the screen. Peter Lorre plays the killer as sniveling and dishonest, a pathetic creature at best who admits he cannot control his own destructive urges. His jury does not manifest the jackbooted authority of those in power but is, rather, made up of crooks, con-artists, and petty thieves, while being presided over by a man who has himself taken human life illegally. At the very moment that Lang reveals this jerry-built court as reflecting all the emotional or group psychological dangers of the crowd turned lynch mob, he also has the court grant Lorre a defense attorney who stands up straight, interrupts those who would silence his appeal and who first diffidently—then passionately—presents an argument against ever imposing punishment on one who is insane and should not be held criminally responsible. Daniel McNaughten could not have been more effectively represented.

As Lorre brings the jury/audience into his nightmare world and describes the overwhelming desire and guilt that have repeatedly led him to commit irresistible acts of homicide, several hapless men among those sitting in judgment upon him shake their heads knowingly, as if they had experienced some of the same disabling mental forces. Only the unexpected arrival of the police interrupts a process that appears incapable of arriving at an acceptable conclusion—the question of justice here seems unresolvable.

Popular culture, of course, has not limited its focus to right-wing or xenophobic alternatives to official legality, though most "anti-lynching films," from *Young Mr. Lincoln* (1939) through *Johnny Guitar* (1954) and *To Kill a Mockingbird* (1962), have been moderate or liberal in their political orientation and have tended to portray the sources of informal justice as racist or populist. As early as *The Mayor of Hell* (1933), directed by Archie Mayo shortly before he made *Black Legion* (1936), we have a film that seems to *celebrate* an arguably left-wing form of popular justice. An endearing gang of young toughs, clamped down in a juvenile prison farm, manage to prosecute, convict, and execute their vicious reform school boss. Leonard Maltin calls the film "fascinating, somewhat strange," not without reason.[6] The film's only slightly qualified endorsement of radical legal shortcuts needs, perhaps, to be placed up against contemporaneous events like President Roosevelt's abortive attempt to "pack" the U.S. Supreme Court. In a different context, the interrogation, trial, and execution of a CIA agent in Uruguay, in Costa-Gavras's *State of Siege* (1973), is presented forcefully, from the point of view of left-wing terrorists who seek to overthrow the official (and authoritarian) regime in their country, a nation whose police have been trained in methods of surveillance and torture by the U.S. government. Real events and social movements, needless to say, stand behind many of popular culture's representations of left-wing popular justice, as was the case with right-wing forms of alternative legality. It is worth taking a moment to look more closely at a few of these informal justice proceedings orchestrated by the left.

■

After a seemingly endless war to liberate their country from Japanese, French, and American control, the Vietnamese people completed their historic struggle for national independence in 1975. As the Revolution (*Cach Mang*) rolled through the streets of Saigon, virtually unresisted by what remained of the U.S.-sponsored regime, some may have expected that an effort to "even the score" would be the first order of business. Nevertheless, here is what Italian journalist Tiziano Terzani actually saw: "If the liberation of Saigon, unlike that of Paris and other European cities, did not mean flowers, neither did it mean executions. In Saigon on the day of the Liberation there was no settling of accounts, no hunting down of fascists; the vanquished were not exhibited in public or humiliated. There were no naked women with shaved heads shoved back and forth between two lines of a crowd, as I saw as a boy during the Liberation of Europe." There was, however, an administration of criminal justice that certainly falls within the parameters of informal or nonbureaucratic legality suggested by the legal sociologists. Terzani reports that on the morning of May 17, 1975, the *bo doi* (soldiers of the people or "new authorities") convened a people's tribunal at the corner of Yo Tanh and Truong Tan Buu in Saigon. Two defendants (eighteen and twenty years old, respectively) were charged with having stolen a drum of gasoline from a garage in the neighborhood, and the assembled crowd of about five hundred was asked to sit as a jury. Witnesses were heard, the *bo doi* with a megaphone asked the jury for its verdict (a multitude of hands were raised in favor of execution), and "in the name of the people," the convicted thieves were shot in the head. "Traffic resumed," Terzani adds. In a similar incident, a man who "stole and sold drugs, and made young people in the area buy drugs from him," was subjected to popular justice, relatively informal in ritual and decorum, as Merry would put it. "The tribunal was made up of people who had been this fellow's victims," a twenty-three-year-old woman who worked as a typist in a commercial firm told Terzani, "and they voted for the death penalty. The *bo doi* carried it out on the spot. It was violent, but with someone like that what else can you do?" Terzani observes that during his three months in Saigon after the Liberation, about thirty such "summary executions of ordinary criminals" took place, all of which seem to fulfill the requirements of a sociological definition of community justice but still tend to be ignored in the academic literature that provides our point of departure.[7]

To take another Asian example, but this time from a country already industrially developed and economically advanced, let us consider Japan at the conclusion of the Second World War. As Joe Moore describes in his excellent account of postwar labor struggles during the U.S. occupation, miners at Mitsubishi Bibai in Hokkaido took over the mines and instituted "production control," a militant form of workers' management, effectively denying their corporate bosses a right to complete domination over the coal industry. The company refused to negotiate with the miners' union so, on February 17, 1946, the miners "put their employers before a 'people's court' (jinmin saiban), and made them answer for their past crimes." Ironically, Nishimura Takeo's first-hand account of this incident, reported in Moore's book, makes the event sound more like the trial of Dudley Digges, the malevolent reform school boss in *The Mayor of Hell,* than any of the legal proceedings before empirically studied community boards. Eventually, according to Moore, those company officials placed on trial "escaped without injury, a remarkable outcome considering the baring of the workers' emotions as they contrasted their own fight for survival to the comfortable lives the officials had lived. Assuredly, the people's court left the company officials with emotional scars, if not from the personal abuse they had to endure then from the fear they must have felt that the miners' anger would burst into violence against them." Such "punishment," imposed by this kind of highly informal, popular, virtually spontaneous, alternative tribunal, would seem to be just the sort of process that legal sociologists and anthropologists might consider bringing within their sites.[8]

Consider another illustration of left-wing popular justice, this one drawn from western Europe. In a fleeting reference, Sally Engle Merry says that subsequent to the Chinese Communist Party's rise to power, "Mao Zedong turned to the Soviet Comrades' Courts for inspiration." If the Chinese borrowed from the Soviets, others would borrow from the Chinese. "The Trimarchi affair," according to historian Robert Lumley, "is interesting as an example of the student movement's application of Chinese-style Cultural Revolution in Italy." While the Chinese peasantry had confronted landlords with their past crimes and abuses, demanding an admission of guilt, left-wing students at the State University of Milan, in 1969, "occupied the faculty, and were responsible for the kidnapping (*sequestro*) of a law professor, who was put on trial for his allegedly reactionary behaviour." Italian political culture generally, during this period, and terrorism in particular, are the subject of a left-wing film *Diavolo in corpo* (*Devil in the Flesh*), directed by Marco Bellocchio and starring Maruschka Detmers. A right-wing perspective on Italian terrorism, and the kidnapping of Aldo Moro, is provided by John Frankenheimer's motion picture *Year of the Gun*. The same events and issues were covered in the television documentary *Terror: The Decay of Democracy,* hosted by Jack Perkins and produced and directed by Tony Stark for the Arts & Entertainment cable network in 1990. The latter film, dealing with Italy's Red Brigades, shows (according to Perkins) "how left-wing revolutionaries who started as idealists became killers and were destroyed by their own violent methods." Concluding his comments on the Trimarchi Affair, Lumley observes that the students who sought to place one of their law professors on trial at the University of Milan were themselves "brought to trial in the 'normal' way." Popular culture, on one side, and political history on the other present legal sociology with a clear sense of direction if it seeks a broader empirical framework as well as genuine inclusiveness in its treatment of alternative courts, in its assessment of movements that pursue justice other than in the "normal" way.[9]

■

The demise of one "popular unity" government in Chile helped lead to the possibility of another, in Italy, in the 1970s. In the wake of a U.S.-sponsored coup against Salvador Allende, a "new grand alliance resembling that which the anti-Fascist forces had created in the period 1943–47" was what Italian Communist Party (PCI) general secretary, Enrico Berlinguer, had in mind (in the words of Paul Ginsborg) when he proposed that a "historic compromise" be struck among Italy's political parties of the left and center. Opposition from the United States to any participation in the government by Italian Communists (in spite of the fact the PCI had polled 34.4 percent in national voting in 1976) is certainly one reason why the Italian popular front of the 1970s ultimately failed. Another reason, supplied by Eric Hobsbawm, is commonly referred to as "red terrorism." Citing events that provide the basis for both the television documentary *Terror: The Decay of Democracy* and Frankenheimer's *Year of the Gun,* Hobsbawm observes that Italy's right wing was ready to overthrow any government that included the PCI and "cheer—perhaps even assist—the ultra-left assassination of the Christian-Democratic statesman most favorable to this policy" of popular unity in the face of reaction. Ginsborg suggests a further explanation for failure: the historic compromise, in context, was a historic error in strategy by the PCI. Rather than making an alliance with the conservative Christian Democrats, the PCI should have capitalized on the anger and strength of emerging popular movements from below. While acknowledging that this "left alternative" was, under the circumstances, the most dangerous strategy, Ginsborg argues that if "pressure from below for change and the mobilizations of 1968–76 were to be sustained, there had to be a convincing opposition to lead them." Such a credible opposition could not be mounted in alliance with the Christian Democrats, who had no authentic commitment to change, and thus a left-wing strategy that sought real structural reform rather than compromise was both "risky and necessary."[10]

Such debates are characteristic of the entire history of popular front political movements. Hobsbawm observes that popular front strategies were first embraced in France and Spain in the mid-1930s. Prior to that time, the left was generally suspicious of alliances with social democratic parties that usually expressed the class interest of the bourgeoisie. The unique political circumstances of the 1930s caused revolutionaries to join ranks with liberal progressives in the hope of averting the nightmare of fascism achieving hegemony across Europe. The French popular front, which actually came to power in 1936, "never overcame its internal contradictions and the half-heartedness of the socialists who led it, and faded away in 1938." Later in his analysis, Hobsbawm stresses a further contradiction, arguing that there was not a "revolutionary situation in France in 1936." Whether the rise and fall of the popular front in France between 1936 and 1938 should be ascribed to internal or external causes, inept political judgment or objective social conditions, it is sufficient for our purpose to acknowledge that it was in the initial stage of this incandescent period in French public life that Jean Renoir and his compatriots in the Groupe Octobre collaboratively created one of the great motion pictures made anywhere during the tumultuous 1930s: *The Crime of Monsieur Lange*. The issue of popular justice, forcefully raised by academic sociologists, and the additional question of popular (or cooperative) control of production, are effectively joined in this justifiably famous work of popular art.[11]

A French-Soviet accord, reached in the hope of discouraging Hitler's interest in foreign aggression, was followed in the summer of 1935 by the Communist International's embrace of the popular front policy. At the same time, the spontaneity and size of mass demonstrations and strikes *within* France compelled parties of the left to join ranks in giving voice to such dramatic popular mobilization against reaction and in behalf of radical change. Nevertheless, as Helmut Gruber points out, the new position of the Comintern "unquestionably played an important role" in the French Communist Party (PCF) shifting to a position of support for a government of popular unity. Renoir himself visited the Soviet Union in late 1935, in preparation for directing the PCF's campaign film *La Vie est à nous* (*It's Our Life*). "Before leaving for Moscow," reports Célia Bertin, "Jean Renoir had finished *Le Crime de M. Lange* . . . shot in twenty-eight days between October and November in 1935." The film opened at the Aubert Palace in January 1936, and within just a few months the popular front government had swept into office.[12]

Perhaps the first aspect of *M. Lange* that deserves mention is the extraordinary way in which the film was made. Thirty years later, French filmmaker Jean-Luc Godard would draw a distinction between making political films and making films *politically;* in the view of a militant director like Godard, genuinely radical films could only be made through a process that broke sharply with conventional film production practices. It was not enough that a film should be revolutionary in content, nor even sufficient that it be revolutionary in form. It especially should be the creation of a committed left collectivity, the product of a cooperative and egalitarian filmmaking process. The most important member of the avant-garde and "extreme-left" proletarian theater cadre, Groupe Octobre, to work on *Lange* was none other than Jacques Prévert. "I'm sure it would be impossible," Renoir remarked later, "to trace the origins of ideas in this film, to know whether it was Jacques or I who found this or that. We really found everything together." Alexander Sesonske points out that by the time the movie was finished, so many different friends of Prévert and Renoir had found a way to contribute something to its creation that some film critics "call *Le Crime de M. Lange* a film by the *groupe Octobre.*" In the 1960s, Jean-Luc Godard could have chosen the Groupe Octobre as easily as the practice of Russian revolutionary Dziga Vertov for his model of radical filmmaking. Perhaps it comes as no surprise, then, that the Arizona Jim collective in Godard's *Weekend* constitutes a direct reference to the fictional hero championed by Monsieur Lange himself.

The second characteristic of *Lange* that demands attention is precisely its unusual construction, its formal, structural, and narrative shape. It is designed using a legal or trial framework, a three-part sequence including an opening argument, presentation of evidence, and concluding verdict. François Truffaut has said that *Lange* has a "detective-story plot" but, in this case, one with a twist. This is a detective story in which the criminal's identity is revealed at the outset. Don Siegel's film *The Killers,* loosely based on an Ernest Hemingway story, is similarly structured. In the opening scene, Lee Marvin and Clu Gulager (playing hired hit men) gun down John Cassavetes and then spend the large middle section of the film trying to find out who hired them and why. The crime itself is not a mystery; what is unknown is why the victim just stood there and indifferently accepted his fate. Only in the film's concluding section do we discover that the big time criminal calling the shots, from behind the scenes, is Ronald Reagan! Conventional suspense techniques are even less relied upon in *M. Lange.* In the very first few minutes, guests at a rural inn on the French and Belgian border discover that a recent arrival, accompanied by his girlfriend, is in fact wanted for murder by the police. They are about to inform the authorities when, as André Bazin puts it, "Valentine takes it upon herself to explain the case to those who would turn him in. This improvised popular jury will decide their fate." Valentine, who is very much in love with the amiable murderer, "thinks that by explaining the circumstances to these simple people," as Renoir himself stated, "she can convince them to change their minds and close their eyes to Lange's escape."[13]

The second, broad middle section of the film is told in flashback and is, in essence, defense counsel Valentine's argument to the jury. It is a magnificently rendered story of how the corrupt and abusive manager of a printing concern is, apparently, killed in a railway accident and his former employees take over the print shop and run it as a cooperative. It turns out, however, that once the business has become a booming success under popular rather than elite management, cooperative rather than hierarchical control of production, the former boss (who escaped the rail mishap, after all) returns and demands the right to resume his dictatorial powers. Having "played dead" to avoid his angry creditors, he now wishes to seize what is no longer his, if it ever was. Amédée Lange, the effervescent creator of the cooperative's greatest commercial success, the cliff hanger serial featuring wild west hero, Arizona Jim, promptly shoots and kills the boss, Batala, played by the peerless Jules Berry. There is a considerable literature, in English as well as French, on the single camera shot employed by Renoir to reveal the crime of Monsieur Lange. At the time of the film's initial release, critic Roger Leenhardt referred to Renoir's disorderly "zigzagging pans." More self-consciously attuned to Renoir's intent, André Bazin would later describe the "stunning turn of the camera" that was only "apparently contrary to all logic." Christopher Faulkner goes beyond Bazin's attempt to explain this camera movement in terms of its "spatial expression" of the motion picture's general visual organization. Faulkner suggests that the reverse, 360-degree pan that culminates in Batala's elimination but abandons Lange himself in the process, a shot that runs contrary to conventional narrative psychology, is really a key to the defense being mounted in Lange's behalf: "So the discontinuity of the shot, its displacement from the otherwise seamless linear narrative flow, depersonalizes it and should direct attention away from questions of moral-psychological value and towards a cognitive awareness that Lange's action encompasses a political will, the real political will of the entire community within the film and the potential will of the audience." Thus, not only is the plot of *The Crime of Monsieur Lange* structured in the form of a legal proceeding but the formal visual properties of the film as well reflect an overriding concern with securing a popular or alternative conception of what justice might actually entail.[14]

The defense rests its case. Lange walks in on the proceeding and is told, simply, that a guide will be provided to assist the couple in leaving France. "The decision of this improvised jury having been stated," observed Renoir and Jean Castanier at the end of their initial outline of *M. Lange*, "the scene jumps to the little caravan preparing to climb the majestic peaks beyond the border." The last frame of the film, according to Célia Bertin, "pregnant with optimism and good humor," was shot on the beach at Berck, on the North Sea, a beautiful beach "that seemed to go on forever." Faulkner expresses the view that "the film's consciousness is confirmed more by the action of shooting Batala than by setting up the cooperative." But he also acknowledges that "Valentine's defense of Lange to a sort of jury made up of his working-class peers" is a key aspect of the film's politics and is designed to justify the killing of Batala in the name of the cooperative. Not surprisingly, concludes Faulkner, "by its framing device the film raises the issue of a social justice in conflict with the letter of the law, since it is on that distinction that the group at the cafe is asked to make its decision." Thus the crime of Monsieur Lange itself is framed by the opening sequence of the film, in which Lange's de facto counsel makes an opening statement to the jury, and by a closing sequence that culminates in the jury's verdict of not guilty (or "justifiable homicide"?) and the subsequent escape to freedom, authorized by a community parallel to the one from which Valentine and Amédée have come. Goffredo Fofi, Jonathan Buchsbaum, Allen Thiher, and Alexander Sesonske, among others, have demonstrated the close links between the films of Renoir and French politics in the 1930s, particularly those of the popular front and its heady optimism about real change. Faulkner is not alone in reading *The Crime of Monsieur Lange* against the background of "specific historical circumstances." According to Sesonske, not only are the time and place within which *Lange* is situated "very much the Paris of the Front Populaire," but, in fact, "success within the film entails the realization of the goals of the popular front." Fofi states unequivocally that *The Crime of Monsieur Lange* was the initial motion picture to communicate to a mass audience all the excitement of those popular movements which, at that moment, gripped the national political imagination: "It is permeated with all the enthusiasm and hope that enlivened

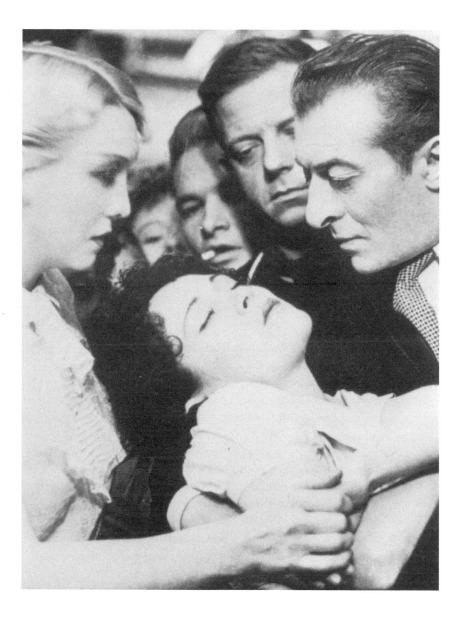

Beau monde of the exploiting class, Batala (Jules Berry) here feigns concern for an employee, only to become a target of "popular justice" in *The Crime of Monsieur Lange*. (Courtesy of Interama, Inc.)

the people of France during those years. The same joy that the men in the factories were to feel when they again saw themselves on the screen during those magnificent days in 1936, is recognizable and reflected in it." Without stretching too far, one recalls the years between 1968 and 1970 in the United States, when student radicals would demonstrate against the Vietnam War, often clashing with police during the day, but making sure to return by dinner time to apartment or student union in order to watch themselves on the evening news, in the company of friends and comrades. Perhaps the fugitive relationship between popular visual culture and the "not so peaceful road" to social change needs its own historian. The radicals of the 1960s, however, strained to find in Hollywood movies of the period the reflection of themselves and their movements that French workers so readily identified, in Fofi's view, in *M. Lange*.[15]

■

What Peter Fitzpatrick calls "the informal and the popular" certainly seems to enjoy a variegated convergence around *M. Lange*. The film is a work of popular culture, by a popular figure in French cinema, who recalls that *M. Lange* had a good reception and "was certainly a solid undertaking." The film itself delights in popular culture, selecting as its hero an author of popular westerns that are sponsored by Ranimax pills! One of the central subjects of the film is the considerable advantages to be derived from workers' control of production and, indeed, *M. Lange* is the product of a popular or cooperative approach to filmmaking. The *Oxford Companion to Film* describes how the Groupe Octobre "took their works to factories, shops, and strike meetings" and had a "marked effect on French cinema of the thirties," preeminently through *The Crime of Monsieur Lange*. Richard Stourac and Kathleen McCreery, in their research on the history of workers' theater, describe the left-wing popular theater movement as an alternative to formal conventions and institutions of bourgeois culture. The informal and popular were redefined, in these movements, "as that which made complex problems easy to understand and handle and made learning enjoyable." On this evidence, a juxtaposition of popular justice movements with popular trends within progressive dramatic performance and filmmaking seems inescapable.

If *M. Lange* is, as Sesonske quotes in *L'Encyclopédie du cinéma*, "the *only French film* in which a cooperative organization has been seen taking into its own hands a production enterprise and making it prosper," it is also one of the most remarkable films ever made in which a makeshift jury has been seen taking into its own hands a complex question of legal responsibility and arriving at its own independent judgment, based upon the facts.[16]

How does the rough and ready verdict entered in Lange's case stack up against those reached in the historical examples of popular justice cited earlier? Street corner juries in Saigon authorized the death penalty and an informal jury in *M. Lange* found another "execution" (Lange's killing of Batala) justifiable. Nevertheless, these two cases differ in that the print shop boss was no common criminal, and, further, he was eliminated as much to prevent future conduct as punishment for past deeds. As Renoir and Castanier explain in their original treatment, *M. Lange* "is based on the idea that any man who has carved out a place for himself in society and is worthy of his position has the right to keep his place and to defend it against one who would take it from him, even if this thief bases his action on legal principles." Raymond Durgnat describes *M. Lange* as "first and foremost a political comedy," and (echoing Renoir and Castanier) characterizes its theme in terms of "the spirit of initiative which the working class and its allies ought to adopt towards certain problems; notably, how to avoid being swindled out of the just rewards for one's labour." Where theft has been written into law, such conduct can only be adequately rectified by an alternative legality. It was just such a notion of community justice embraced first by Lange, then by those who sat in judgment listening to Valentine's account, within which homicide could be regarded as excusable. In a sense, Lange stood for the right of the working class to defend itself against the owners and managers it sought to displace, just as Batala had himself been made redundant by the Arizona Jim cooperative.

Kidnapping and public trials such as those staged by left-wing students in Italy, which they copied form the Tupamaros in Uruguay, were designed primarily as educational or "consciousness raising" political actions. But Christian Democrat Aldo Moro, like United States security official Dan Mitrione in Latin America, was killed rather than "educated," and such grim acts of terror may have won few converts to radical opposition. If Hobsbawm is right, the execution of Moro was actually done to sabotage the popular front movement in Italy and, to that extent, could be seen as contradicting the politics of *M. Lange*. From a different left-wing perspective, however, Moro and the Groupe Octobre's Batala could be more closely identified, certainly in terms of their class position. The Red Brigades regarded Aldo Moro as Lange did Batala: a thief and class enemy. Describing the "jury deliberation" in Renoir's film, Christopher Faulkner states, "we arrive at our particular judgment because we recognize our common cause with Lange against the unremitting selfishness of capital interests: 'maybe he killed a rat,' someone says." According to Ginsborg's thumbnail sketch of Red Brigade terrorism, shop floor industrial workers were not always as hostile to violent tactics, including terrorism, as their union leaders and the PCI sometimes suggested.[17]

There is also an interesting parallel between *The Crime of Monsieur Lange* and the events that took place at the Mitsubishi coal mine in Hokkaido during the American occupation of Japan. The justification for Lange's conduct, the reason he is allowed to escape, is inextricably tied up with the legitimacy of workers' control and the survival of the cooperative enterprise led by an unassuming creator of wild west tales. And the regime of popular justice deployed by miners at Mitsubishi Bibai is equally bound up with their efforts to run the coal fields for themselves. Just as *jinmin saiban* and tactics of public confrontation continued to play a role in postwar Japanese politics, so did the strategy of production control. The veteran Japanese labor leader, Higuchi Tokuzo, discussing a widely publicized factory occupation at Petri Camera in 1977, reminds us that participants "learned by experience that workers can produce useful things for themselves—without the capitalists. That is the most important lesson."[18]

We would, however, be seriously remiss in failing to point out the similarity between the politics of *M. Lange* and those of the Maquis, the rural resistance to fascism based in southern France in the period after 1941. Indeed, here we have a social movement that not only developed within the same national political culture as the Groupe Octobre (and within a decade of Renoir's popular front cinema) but, further, constitutes perhaps the preeminent illustration of mass popular justice in modern history, a system of alternative legality so thorough that it constituted something akin to a popular administration of social reality.

The historian H. R. Kedward, in his landmark study of Maquis organization and structure, repeatedly returns to the theme of "outlaw culture" in an effort to come to terms with the alternative legal system established by France's rural resistance forces. "Previously law-abiding citizens, and increasing numbers of officials and gendarmes," asserts Kedward, "found themselves taking the first steps towards what must be recognized as an outlaw culture: the belief that natural justice and moral rectitude can no longer be equated with the official process of the law and can only be found outside it." This closely mirrors at least the intentions of some of those orchestrating alternative justice institutions charted by empirical sociology.

It began with civil disobedience in the face of governmental requirements that the population actively participate in attempts to hunt down *refractaires,* French citizens refusing compulsory labor in Germany, as well as other fugitives from Vichy justice. Thwarting conventional arrest procedures or attending funerals for youthful maquisard heroes became increasingly common. German food requisitions and market controls imposed upon the peasant economy led to massive resistance. Vichy policy in the countryside managed to keep the peasantry "in a state of defiance, illegality, and nervousness, which organizers of *refractaires* and maquisards were able to use to their advantage."

Gradually, the Maquis came to replace entirely the Vichy machinery of regulation with its own system of equipment distribution and price controls, crop requisition and sabotage, which was effectively, however informally, enforced. Even the popular culture of the maquisards served the purpose of radical resistance: rumors spread that handbills announcing Maquis policy had been posted overnight in the Haute-Correze by a dozen or more heavily armed maquisards. In fact, Lucien Seince and two comrades, one pistol between them, had done the job. This taste of real alternative power would not fade quickly—Kedward observes that there were many among the Maquis "who demanded military recognition but as the irregular armed forces of the Resistance with a positive outlaw history and a role to play in deciding the social and political changes at the Liberation." Renoir's Arizona Jim cooperative would certainly have found itself at home in a maquisard stronghold as the war's conclusion approached and hopes turned to a new world along the horizon.[19]

Perhaps the most valuable lesson that can be drawn from viewing *The Crime of Monsieur Lange,* even today, is that in law as well as the economy, popular alternatives do exist. Make no mistake: Valentine's defense of Lange (and, obviously, the perspective on his culpability advanced by the Groupe Octobre in its popular front militancy) is not the only possible point of view. What *M. Lange* does accomplish, however, is that it removes this case from the world of conventional courts and codes, rules of criminal procedure, and places it instead in the more popularly accessible context of cooperative decision making and alternative legality. Popular culture, like the real history of cooperative production and popular justice, indicates that *it is possible* to get outside the system. How we get there and what it will be like represent, precisely, the question mark hanging from the blustery and enigmatic clouds of gray above Valentine and Amédée Lange as they wave goodbye in the concluding sequence of *M. Lange* and then cross over to the other side.

Notes

1. See, for example, David Bordwell, Janet Staiger, and Kristin Thompson, *The Classical Hollywood Cinema: Film Style and Mode of Production to 1960* (New York: Columbia University Press, 1985); *For Fun and Profit: The Transformation of Leisure into Consumption,* ed. Richard Butsch (Philadelphia: Temple University Press, 1990); Douglas Gomery, *The Hollywood Studio System* (New York: St. Martin's Press, 1986); *The Hollywood Film Industry,* ed. Paul Kerr (New York: Routledge & Kegan Paul, 1986); *Resisting Images: Essays on Cinema and History,* ed. Robert Sklar and Charles Musser (Philadelphia: Temple University Press, 1990).

2. For a general overview of contemporary popular culture theory that emphasizes "the new politics of difference," see *Cultural Studies,* ed. Lawrence Grossberg, Cary Nelson, and Paula Treichler (New York: Routledge, 1992). For more conventional historical approaches to the study of popular culture, see Neil Harris, *Cultural Excursions: Marketing Appetites and Cultural Tastes in Modern America* (Chicago: University of Chicago Press, 1990); Steven L. Kaplan, *Farewell, Revolution* (Ithaca: Cornell University Press, 1995); *Popular Culture in America,* ed. Paul Buhle (Minneapolis: University of Minnesota Press, 1987); Warren I. Susman, *Culture as History: The Transformation of American Society in the Twentieth Century* (New York: Pantheon Books, 1984).

3. Sally Engle Merry, "Popular Justice and the Ideology of Social Transformation," *Social and Legal Studies* 1 (June 1992): 161–76, 162, 163; Christine Harrington, "Popular Justice, Populist Politics: Law in Community Organizing," *Social and Legal Studies* 1 (June 1992): 177–98; Peter Fitzpatrick, "The Impossibility of Popular Justice," *Social and Legal Studies* 1 (June 1992): 199–215, 200.

4. Fitzpatrick, "Impossibility," 213.

5. Carol Clover, "White Noise," *Sight and Sound* (May 1993): 6–9, 8. Since *Falling Down* was released in 1993, events have overtaken my analysis and made the point, in spades, that far right "popular justice" organizations with-

in the United States can, indeed, come into violent conflict with established legal institutions. Waco, the Oklahoma City bombing, and the shootout at Ruby Ridge are now part of popular culture as well as political history. See, for example, Daniel Junas, "The Rise of Citizen Militias: Angry White Guys with Guns," *CovertAction Quarterly* (Spring 1995): 20; James Corcoran, *Bitter Harvest: The Birth of Paramilitary Terrorism in the Heartland* (New York: Penguin Books, 1995); James Coates, *Armed and Dangerous: The Rise of the Survivalist Right* (New York: Hill and Wang, 1995); *Requiem for the Heartland: The Oklahoma City Bombing* (San Francisco: HarperCollins, 1995).

During the Reagan/Bush era, the American public was effectively mystified about the nature of terrorism by a host of bestselling authors whose works represented no serious research and little familiarity with political reality. While the Soviet empire was disintegrating, Claire Sterling's *The Terror Network* (New York: Readers Digest Press, 1981) nevertheless imagined that the KGB was behind every terrorist plot in the world, something even Ian Fleming could not have dreamed up. Reviewer Susan Brownmiller described Doris Lessing's *The Good Terrorist* (New York: Vintage Books, 1986) as the crowning achievement of Lessing's literary career. Yet while Lessing conjured up alienated liberal intellectuals who eat at exotic Indian restaurants, see films like *Diva* (1981), quote Lenin page after page, ad nauseam, and then blow up a fashionable downtown hotel, tearing their randomly selected victims to pieces, real terrorists in the American heartland (who do not see foreign films or study Marxist classics) were learning how to use fertilizer to make a bomb. Even the pulp fiction of John Grisham reveals a more intimate understanding of the politics and psychology of terrorism than the "high art" of writers like Doris Lessing.

6. *Leonard Maltin's Movie and Video Guide, 1994,* ed. Leonard Maltin (New York: Penguin Books, 1993), 815.

7. Gabriel Kolko, *Anatomy of a War: Vietnam, the United States, and the Modern Historical Experience* (New York: Pantheon Books, 1985); Tiziano Terzani, *Giai Phong!* (London: Angus & Robertson Publishers, 1976), 105, 132–33.

8. Joe Moore, *Japanese Workers and the Struggle for Power* (Madison: University of Wisconsin Press, 1983), 126, 132.

9. Merry, "Popular Justice," 161; Robert Lumley, *States of Emergency: Cultures of Revolt in Italy from 1968 to 1978* (London: Verso, 1990), 136, 142. Consider also, in this regard, William Blum's comments on the Tupamaros in Uruguay, whose kidnapping of Dan Mitrione provided the basis for Costa-Gavras's film *State of Siege,* mentioned above; see William Blum, *The CIA: A Forgotten History* (London: Zed Books, 1986), 226: "A favorite tactic was to raid the files of a private corporation to expose corruption and deceit in high places, or kidnap a prominent figure and try him before a 'People's Court.' It was heady stuff to choose a public villain whose acts went uncensored by the legislature, the courts and the press, subject him to an informed

and uncompromising interrogation, and then publicize the results of the intriguing dialogue."

10. Paul Ginsborg, *A History of Contemporary Italy: Society and Politics, 1943–1988* (New York: Penguin Books, 1990), 355, 374–75, 377; Eric Hobsbawm, "Fifty Years of Peoples' Fronts (1985)," in Eric Hobsbawm, *Politics for a Rational Left: Political Writing, 1977–1988* (London: Verso, 1989), 103–17, 117.

11. Hobsbawm, "Peoples' Fronts," 103. "In short," wrote François Truffaut, *M. Lange* "is a film touched by divine grace." François Truffaut, "Filmography," in André Bazin, *Jean Renoir* (New York: Da Capo Press, 1992), 242.

12. Helmut Gruber, *Léon Blum, French Socialism, and the Popular Front* (Ithaca: Cornell University Center for International Studies, 1986), 8; Célia Bertin, *Jean Renoir: A Life in Pictures* (Baltimore: Johns Hopkins University Press, 1991), 112. Alan Williams regards Renoir's "(justifiably) celebrated but (unjustly) little seen" PCF campaign film as the "fullest cinematic expression of [the] sensibility and methods" of the Groupe Octobre; see Alan Williams, *Republic of Images: A History of French Filmmaking* (Cambridge: Harvard University Press, 1992), 224. See also Larry Ceplair, *Under the Shadow of War* (New York: Columbia University Press, 1987), 123–53; George Ross, *Workers and Communists in France: From Popular Front to Eurocommunism* (Berkeley: University of California Press, 1982), 8–13.

13. Colin MacCabe, *Godard: Images, Sounds, Politics* (Bloomington: Indiana University Press, 1980); Alexander Sesonske, *Jean Renoir: The French Films, 1924–1939* (Cambridge: Harvard University Press, 1980), 189; Jean Renoir, *Renoir on Renoir: Interviews, Essays, and Remarks* (New York: Cambridge University Press, 1989), 86; François Truffaut, "Introduction to the First Version of *The Crime of M. Lange*," in Bazin, *Renoir*, 159; Bazin, *Renoir*, 41; Jean Renoir and Jean Castanier, "First Version of *The Crime of M. Lange*," in Bazin, *Renoir*, 161.

14. Roger Leenhardt, "Le Cinéma: *Le Crime de M. Lange*," *Esprit* 4:42 (Mar. 1, 1936): 977, quoted in Christopher Faulkner, *The Social Cinema of Jean Renoir* (Princeton: Princeton University Press, 1986), 67; Bazin, *Renoir*, 46; Faulkner, *Social Cinema*, 69.

15. Renoir and Castanier, "First Version," 171; Bertin, *Renoir: A Life*, 83–84; Faulkner, *Social Cinema*, 62–63, 70; Sesonske, *French Films*, 192–93; Goffredo Fofi, "The Cinema of the Popular Front in France (1934–1938)," in *Screen Reader 1: Cinema/Ideology/Politics* (London: Society of Education in Film and Television, 1977), 172–224, 181; see also Roy Armes, *French Cinema* (New York: Oxford University Press, 1985); Ronald Bergan, *Jean Renoir* (Woodstock, N.Y.: Overlook Press, 1995), 147–50; Jonathan Buchsbaum, "Left Political Filmmaking in the West: The Interwar Years," in *Resisting Images*, ed. Sklar and Musser, 126–48; Jonathan Buchsbaum, *Cinema Engagé: Film in the Popular Front* (Urbana: University of Illinois Press, 1988); Allen

Thiher, *The Cinematic Muse: Critical Studies in the History of French Cinema* (Columbia: University of Missouri Press, 1979).

16. Renoir, *Renoir,* 87; *The Oxford Companion to Film,* ed. Liz-Anne Bawden (London: Oxford University Press, 1976), 311; Richard Stourac and Kathleen McCreery, *Theatre as a Weapon* (New York: Routledge & Kegan Paul, 1986), 174; *Encyclopédie du cinéma,* ed. Roger Boussinot (Paris: Bordas, 1967), 1268, quoted in Sesonske, *French Films,* 220.

17. Renoir and Castanier, "First Version," 160; Raymond Durgnat, *Jean Renoir* (Berkeley: University of California Press, 1974), 114; Hobsbawm, "Peoples' Fronts," 117; Ginsborg, *Contemporary Italy,* 384–85; Faulkner, *Social Cinema,* 64.

18. Joe Moore, *Japanese Workers,* 126–32; Frank Upham, *Law and Social Change in Postwar Japan* (Cambridge: Harvard University Press, 1987); "Workers Production Control and the New Militancy: An Interview with Higuchi Tokuzo," *AMPO: Japan-Asia Quarterly Review* 10 (Oct.-Dec. 1978): 28–33, 29; "Autonomous Production: An Interview with Tsuzuku Ken," *AMPO: Japan-Asia Quarterly Review* 24:2 (1993): 2–3.

19. H. R. Kedward, *In Search of the Maquis: Rural Resistance in Southern France, 1942–1944* (Oxford: Oxford University Press, 1993), 55–57, 88–89, 95–102, 201–3.

Morality and Liberal Legal Culture

Woody Allen's *Crimes and Misdemeanors*

JUDITH GRANT

■

Writing about morality in the United States in the late twentieth century may seem about as urgent as decrying the dangers of the Bolshevik menace. The issue seems at once old, repugnant, and unfit for contemporary social theory. Yet the problems of morality and politics, or of morality and the law, remain stubbornly and irksomely present. All legitimate legal systems maintain their authority through an appeal to some shared moral vision. The alternatives are on the one hand, a legal system that makes decisions on a completely ad hoc basis, or one that maintains itself solely via the exercise of force.

And yet, having said that legal systems rest on an assumed set of shared moral values or principles does little in terms of characterizing the precise nature of such a vision. The problem was exemplified when Oliver North raised the issue at the Senate hearings on Iran-Contra by claiming that he followed a higher law in disobeying the express orders of Congress. The entire notion of morality has most often been associated with conservative politics, and it is sometimes forgotten that even classical liberal thinkers, the founders of the American system among them, assumed a common moral code. Paradoxically, it was the presence of a common moral vision that allowed them to argue for individual freedoms. That is, most liberals believed that there were some broad parameters of belief and behavior that could be assumed among all rational people. It was within those parameters that freedom must be protected. This is not an assumption that is shared by contemporary liberals or radicals, however. Indeed, the idea of a shared morality is, generally speaking, anathema to the ideological left. Consequently, discussions of morality and law have mostly been left to those on the right.

The conceptualization of progressive politics as a moral issue has been articulated in a spate of articles by Michael Lerner that appeared in 1992 in the progressive Jewish magazine, *Tikkun*. In advocating a "politics of meaning" Lerner rejected moral relativism and took the position that, "A politics of meaning *is* committed to tolerance, but only as one of a set of values that includes love, caring, cooperation, responsibility, justice, peace and moral and spiritual sensitivity."[1] In calling for a language of shared ideals and suggesting that the Democratic party develop a party platform based on a politics of meaning, Lerner contended that, "Liberals have not succeeded in keeping values out of public life, they've only succeeded in keeping their values out, and have left the terrain open for right-wing values."[2] Hillary Clinton invoked the rhetoric of the politics of meaning in her advocacy of a national health care plan. In April 1993, the first lady delivered a speech in which she said, "We lack at some core level meaning in our individual lives and meaning collectively, that sense that our lives are part of some greater effort, that we are connected to one another."[3] Thus, talk of morality seems to strike a chord, and has even crept onto the liberal policy agenda. It is worth reviewing some of the debate that has taken place regarding liberalism and morality.

Today, legal systems are practically speaking the places where public issues of right and wrong get decided. Unlike early liberals who conceptualized individual freedom as taking place inside a shared moral context (most often religious), the idea of a shared moral vision has slipped away from our legal culture and has been increasingly supplanted by the idea that freedom is in and of itself a moral value.

Historically, morality has had an ambiguous relationship to legal systems, and the secularization of the state in western capitalist countries during the modern period has only compounded this issue. Law in western liberal states is continually confronted with a crucial dilemma: Is it possible to devise and sustain a legitimate system of rules that is not rooted in any particular moral vision? If there are not transcendent values or eternal truths, but only a person's individual and virtually unfettered freedom, what is the basis for law, judicial interpretation, and the just resolution of disputes? Indeed, on what grounds can we speak of justice at all? Can secular legal systems ever have the same force as they once had before they were torn from their religious and natural law foundations? This is really to ask, as one of the other contributors to this volume has done, "Is law possible?"[4]

Some have argued that even liberal states and legal systems are ultimately dependent upon some grounding notion of God even when they claim they are purely secular. This argument was made, in fact, by liberalism's preeminent theorist, John Locke. In the course of making the case for religious pluralism, Locke disallowed the need to tolerate atheists as, "Promises, covenants, and oaths, which are the bonds of human society, can have no hold upon an atheist. The taking away of God, though but even in thought, dissolves all."[5] In Locke's view, without an omnipotent judge or God-eye, we cannot know the difference between right and wrong, and moral action becomes impossible. It is, then, probably no accident that the concerns of one of the major architects of liberalism remain with us in liberal legal systems today.

The problem that Locke raises lurks beneath many very lively legal debates among social theorists, legal positivists, critical legal studies advocates, and rights theorists.[6] If the individual is by nature greedy and appetitive, as the predominant liberal capitalist ideology holds, without laws to restrain us we would surely follow our most base instincts. By extension, positive laws without transcendent foundations are merely arbitrary rules.

This contemporary problem regarding the nature of justice in a godless world is illustrated nicely in Woody Allen's film, *Crimes and Misdemeanors* (1989). The film is useful as a concrete example of a moral dilemma, and seeing it that way can serve to sharpen our analysis. The use of popular culture to illustrate debates in so-called high theory also shows the extent to which the stuff of theory exists as part of the practice of everyday life. This essay is not intended to deepen anyone's understanding of film theory. It is no more than a meditation on the issue of morality as it exists in contemporary liberal legal culture.

Though it can be said that moral dilemmas are a kind of personal obsession for Allen, it is in *Crimes and Misdemeanors* that morality is most starkly counterposed to nihilism. I use Allen's film as a way to discuss the problem underlying liberal legal systems; the possibility of morality and justice in a world where God is dead. Allen's film can be used to illustrate the dilemma and to provide a coherent discussion of the issues raised by it. Ultimately, the film reflects the view that justice is not possible because there is no redeemer, and that, therefore, the key is to sustain the hope that happiness and goodness are possible even in the face of amorality. On its most basic level, *Crimes and Misdemeanors* is a film about the perfect crime, which asks where one can draw the line between good and evil if one has no externally valid moral principles.

The Film

Crimes and Misdemeanors opens at a testimonial dinner for one Judah Rosenthal (Martin Landau). Rosenthal, a cultured ophthalmologist and philanthropist, is being lauded for raising the money to build an ophthalmology wing at a local hospital. He looks modest and pensive. Yet, in a flashback we learn that earlier that day a letter had been delivered to his home. The letter was from his very distraught mistress of two years, Delores Paley (Anjelica Huston). In the letter, addressed to Judah's wife, Delores had confessed her two-year love affair with Judah and requested a meeting with his wife, Miriam (Claire Bloom).

When we return to the testimonial dinner, Judah has risen to speak. Even though he has always been a man of science and a skeptic, he explains, he must admit that the hospital wing is the result of "answered prayers." He then proceeds to tell a story about his father. It is a story that frames the rest of the film. A religious Jew, his father had told the young Judah that, "the eyes of God are on us always." Judah tells the testimonial dinner audience that he had wondered as a boy: "What were God's eyes like? Unimaginably penetrating, intense eyes, I assumed." By his own admission, it is no coincidence that he chose a specialty in ophthalmology, and by extension, no coincidence that the main character in this film is an ophthalmologist. For this is a film precisely about seeing, not seeing, and the nature of God's eyes.

At this point in the film we are allowed to see through Judah's eyes, that is, we are told a story from his perspective. As he sees it, the problem is Delores. Angrily, Judah confronts Delores with the letter she sent to Miriam. She, in turn, hysterical, accuses him of breaking his promise to leave his wife. "You've been my whole life for two years," she cries, telling him she's given up "other men" and "business opportunities" for him. Judah claims in turn that he made no promises. He charges that she gave up nothing, and begs her to understand that he cannot walk out on twenty-five years of marriage.

The Judah/Delores relationship is juxtaposed to a seemingly lighter drama. This second major story line concerns Cliff (Woody Allen). We are introduced to it in a scene in which Cliff is at the movies with his young adolescent niece, Jenny. He shares with Jenny a love of 1940s movies, and confides in her (far too much) about his failing marriage, his faltering career as a documentary filmmaker, and his rivalry with his brother-in-law, a narcissistic but well-respected television producer, Lester (Alan Alda).[7]

The subtext of all of the major relationships in this film is the problem of moral decision making. Questions of morality are posed here as a series of conversations between several rival authorities. In particular, the religious and existentialist views are featured as personified by Judah's wife's second brother, Ben (Sam Waterston), a rabbi who has trouble with his eyes, and a philosopher named Louis Levy.[8] The third view, a nihilistic "might makes right" perspective, is articulated later by Judah's Aunt May. Allen's film can be read as a study of these three positions.

Cliff is utterly taken with the old professor Levy and is making a documentary film about him. As we watch Cliff's film, Professor Levy speaks directly into the camera, and we too are confronted with him as he seems to speak to us: "The unique thing that happened to the early Israelites was that they could see a God that cared. He cares, but at the same time, he also demands that you behave morally. But here comes the paradox: What's one of the first things that that God asks? That God asks Abraham to sacrifice his only son; his beloved son to him. In other words, in spite of millennia of efforts, we have not succeeded to create a really and entirely loving image of God. This was beyond our capacity to imagine."

In contrast to Levy, Ben, the rabbi, believes that it is precisely God's love and forgiveness that can offer redemption for the minor indiscretions one invariably commits in life. While examining Ben's eyes and looking deeply at the Rabbi, eye to eye, Judah breaks down. "I'm in such trouble, Ben. . . . May I confide in you?" He proceeds to tell Ben of his affair with Delores. He tells Ben he cannot remember if "promises were made," as Delores accuses, but that he feels the affair was a foolish adventure undertaken only for pleasure and lust. Ben tells Judah to confess the "small infidelity" to Miriam, to ask her forgiveness, and to go on to a richer life.

"Our entire adult lives you and I have been having this same conversation," Judah responds in frustration. "I know," shrugs Ben, "It's a fundamental difference in the way we view the world. You see it as harsh and empty of values and pitiless; and I couldn't go on living if I didn't feel with all my heart, a moral structure with real meaning and forgiveness and some kind of higher power; otherwise there's no basis to know how to live." In this dialogue with Judah, Ben very clearly states the religious position.

The stakes are raised for Judah when it is disclosed that he took a temporary "loan" from the money he raised for the hospital wing in order to cover his losses in the stock market. Though the money was returned, Judah is made aware by Delores's threat to disclose the "loan" that he is actually technically guilty of embezzlement. The morality of Judah's whole life is called into question by Delores's deconstructing gaze, which forces him to face his several "indiscretions" from another point of view; that of a judgmental other.

At this point it is useful to remember Judah's earlier story about the ever-watchful "eyes of God," which construct us as moral subjects. Absent those eyes, is universal moral subjectivity possible? And what of Delores's gaze? What is Judah to make of *her* judgments against him? Thus, the question posed to Judah is whether to accept the perspective of the other (whether God or Delores) and to confess his wrong, or to ignore all impulses save for his own selfish ones and to continue leading what he now discovers has been a rather immoral life.

Meanwhile, Cliff has been hired by his nemesis, Lester, to do a documentary about the latter's life. The film will be for a television program called "Creative Minds." The producer of the documentary, Halley Reed (Mia Farrow), describes Lester as "an American phenomenon." Cliff, in contrast, despises Lester and is wildly jealous of his success. Lester fancies himself something of a philosopher, though, unlike Levy, Lester's thoughts take the form of shallow maxims like, "comedy is tragedy plus time," or "if it *bends* it's funny, if it *breaks,* it's not." Lester carries with him a hand-held tape recorder into which he says things like, "Idea for TV farce: A poor loser agrees to do the story of a great man's life and in the process comes to learn deep values." In the end, Cliff is fired by Lester for inter-cutting scenes of Lester with footage of a ranting Mussolini. "God," Cliff complains to Halley, "you'd think nobody was ever compared to Mussolini before!" Besides providing some very funny moments, Lester's character raises the issue of perspective once again, since everyone else in the film greatly admires Lester, not the least of whom is Cliff's aloof wife, Wendy. Wendy shows this by continually making unfavorable comparisons between her husband, Cliff, and her much adored brother, Lester.

As the film progresses, Judah's situation becomes more desperate. Eventually, he is led to call his sleazy and financially insecure brother, Jack. Jack symbolizes Judah's darker side as indicated by the alliterative effect of their two names. Jack tells Judah (a name too unusual and too similar to "Judas" to be overlooked) that Delores "can be gotten rid of." When Judah reacts incredulously to the hint of murder, Jack rebukes him: "you called me because you needed some dirty work done. That's all you ever call for." Complaining that Judah doesn't live in the "real world," and that he, "never liked to get his hands dirty," Jack claims that his own poverty has forced him to "face reality." The contrasts between "reality and romanticism," "reality and privilege," and "reality and morality" provide running motifs in this film. The implication is that the "real" world is unromantic, amoral, and impoverished. It is, of course, Judah whose entire life has been based on the illusion that he is a moral person and who is now thrust into complete confusion by the specter of his own amorality, and by his relationship with his brother.

Time passes. It is Judah's birthday. The birthday gift from his family, a treadmill, serves as an apt metaphor for his own indecision and frustration. Delores is calling his home. He walks the floors at night. He thinks endlessly about Ben, about Delores, about the ever-increasing urgency of his dilemma. The Ben in his dreams cautions, "It's a human life! Don't you think God sees!?" Finally reaching his decision, Judah responds to the dream-Ben, "God is a luxury I can't afford. . . . Jack lives in the real world. You live in the kingdom of heaven. . . . I will not be destroyed by this neurotic woman." Ben is appalled, "But the law, Judah! Without the law it's all darkness!" To which Judah asks in response, "What good is the law if it prevents me from receiving justice? Is this what I deserve?"

In this key scene, Judah turns away from "the luxury" of religious foundations to what he perceives as the "reality" of moral relativism and nihilistic individualism. Oddly, it is God's law that stands between him and his own definition of justice, which, it turns out, is no definition at all. Judah's notion that his own selfishness is a standard for justice would appear ironic were it not for the fact that individualism and individual judgments about moral questions are precisely the hallmarks of liberal societies. We are confronted here with the view that without a belief in something other than oneself, only the fear of punishment prevents us from doing wrong. Absent that fear, all is possible. The deeper issue is, of course, how are laws to be formulated and enforced without some implicit or explicit moral structure?

Again, time passes. One night while Judah and his family sit around the living room making plans for his daughter's wedding, Jack calls to inform Judah that, "it's over and done with so you can forget about

In Woody Allen's *Crimes and Misdemeanors,* Dr. Rosenthal (Martin Landau) faces the issue of whether or not morality is possible in a world that has abandoned God. (Courtesy of the Academy of Motion Picture Arts and Sciences.)

it. . . . It's like the whole thing never happened." Judah flees to the bathroom to wash his hands, evoking the familiar religious metaphor. Jean-Paul Sartre, too, has used the notion of "dirty hands" to suggest that man alone has responsibility for his actions, and that having that responsibility, he alone bears the guilt for evil in the world.

Indeed, at this point Judah does collapse into guilt. Memories of the warm times he once had with Delores come rushing back to him. He leaves the dinner party on a pretext about forgetting papers at his office and goes to Delores's apartment. He sees her lying dead; the camera pans to her eyes, which are open and focused directly on him. Still, Delores's gaze continues to accuse him. Here we are presented with another possibility. If the eyes of God are absent, perhaps the eyes of other people can create some moral structure. This is, in fact, the position of humanist existential philosophy, but it too is rejected by Judah.

Judah leaves the apartment in a rush, racked with guilt, and lies awake all night. Significantly, though he had at first interpreted Delores's eyes as accusing, he now begins to redescribe them to himself and to Jack in other terms. This redescription is the beginning of Judah's escape from guilt and responsibility. He describes Delores's dead eyes to Jack; "there was nothing behind her eyes if you looked into them. A black void." There is no soul behind the eyes, and there is no life behind them. Put in the terms of existentialism, Judah confronted nothingness, and the implications of this are considerable. In a flashback, we see Delores and Judah early in their relationship. He is giving her an eye examination. She asks, "do you agree the eyes are the windows of the soul. . . . My mother taught me that I have a soul that will live on after me when I'm gone." The film asks who is correct, Judah, who says that nothing is behind the eyes, or Delores, for whom the eyes are windows to an eternal soul.

In search of some kind of answer, Judah embarks on a journey into the past. He goes to the house where he grew up. When the woman who now owns the house allows him to have some time alone in the dining room, he reminisces about the seders of his childhood. He remembers, in particular, a debate among his adult relatives about the existence of God. For his Aunt May, a teacher, the fact of the Holocaust proves that "might makes right" and that there are no external standards. History is written by the winners, she argues, and if the Germans had won the war, everyone would understand that period of history very differently. "For those who want morality," she contends loudly, "there's morality; nothing's handed down in stone." Judah's father, in contrast, has no doubt but that evil people will be punished. What if all religion is "mumbo jumbo," another relative asks him? "Then I'll still have a better life than all of those that doubt," he responds defiantly. And what if it could be shown logically that God does not exist, they demand? "I will always choose God over truth," he answers. And here is the new dilemma Judah faces—on the one hand, a religious tradition that demands faith in God even in the face of rationalist proofs to the contrary; and on the other, the possibility as articulated by Judah's Aunt May, that might makes right. For Aunt May, the "might makes right" view is merely the realist one. The acknowledgment that there is no God is a type of freedom enabling man to take charge of his own destiny. While for Judah's father, May's position can only lead to spiritual desolation and decadence.

For Cliff, whose very name suggests a man poised on the precipice of evil, the ethical dilemma is, at this stage, a more innocent one. Yet it is the same one Judah once faced earlier in his life; namely, whether or not to cheat on his wife. In the context of the film, the actions of Cliff and Judah are on a continuum. Cliff desperately wants to have an affair with Halley (the TV producer), but is aware that irrational sexual desires may be leading him astray. "It's very hard to get your heart and head together," he quips to his niece, "In my case they're not even friendly."[9]

Up to this point, Cliff had been comforted by the theories of Louis Levy. But Cliff is thrown into a crisis when Levy commits suicide, leaving behind an unlikely and amusing suicide note that says simply, "I've gone out the window." As told by the note, Levy's philosophy has also been metaphorically thrown out the window. "The world is a cold place," Levy had said in an earlier interview, "it's we who invest it with our feelings." What does it mean, then, for Levy to commit suicide? Cliff laments, exasperated, "for seventy years he says 'yes' to life, now all of a sudden today he says 'no.'"

Some resolution to these questions comes during the final scenes of the movie, which take place at a wedding. By this point, Ben has gone completely blind from the illness Judah had diagnosed many months before. Cliff and Wendy are divorcing. But Judah; Judah is very happy and relaxed. Cliff, still in a crisis over the death of Levy and his own divorce, wanders about the wedding party lonely and unhappy. Across the room Cliff sees Halley enter with Lester, to whom, as it turns out, she is now engaged to be married. Further devastated by this news, Cliff slips into an empty room away from the main party. Symbolically, it is a room into which Judah also happens to stray. The subsequent scene provides the final discussion on the issue of moral decision making.

Judah remarks, "You look very deep in thought." And Cliff responds, playing to the knowing movie audience, "I was plotting the perfect murder." Judah asks whether it is for a movie plot, then says thoughtfully, "I have a great murder story; great plot. . . . My murder story has a very strange twist. . . . Let's say there's man who is very successful. He has everything . . ." And with that Judah proceeds to tell Cliff his own story.

> "He finds that after the awful deed is done he's plagued by deep-rooted guilt—little sparks of his religious background which he'd rejected are suddenly stirred up. He hears his father's voice, he imagines that God is watching his every move. Suddenly, it's not an empty universe at all, but a just and moral one, and he's violated it. He's panic stricken. He's on the verge of a mental collapse; an inch away from confessing the whole thing to the police. And then, one morning he awakens. The sun is shining and his family is around him, and mysteriously—the crisis has lifted. He takes his family on a vacation to Europe and as the months pass he finds—he's *not* punished. In fact, he prospers. The killing gets attributed to another person—a drifter who has a number of other murders to his credit, so, what the hell, one more doesn't even matter. Now he's scott free. His life is completely back to normal, back to his protected world of wealth and privilege."

"Yes," Cliff breaks in, "but can he ever really go back? . . . His worst beliefs are realized. It would be tough to live with that."

"What do you expect him to do; turn himself in!? This is reality! In reality, we rationalize, we deny or we don't go on living," says Judah.

But Cliff doesn't like Judah's story. If it were going to be his movie, he says, he would have the protagonist turn himself in, "because then your story assumes tragic proportions. In the absence of a God, people are forced to assume that responsibility for themselves." Here, Cliff articulates the existentialist position.

"That's fiction!" Judah bellows. "That's movies! I'm talking about *reality*. If you want a happy ending, you should go see a Hollywood movie." Thus, Judah's transformation has been one in which both God and the possibility of morality have been rejected. For Cliff, though God is dead, moral decisions are still possible, but only if humans are willing to take on those formerly God-like responsibilities themselves.

The irony cannot possibly be lost on the audience; the scene concludes with a long shot on Judah walking out of the room in a classic Hollywood ending. Judah's wife, Miriam, gazes up at him lovingly and says, "You look very handsome tonight." "And you look beautiful," he replies, just before they kiss and walk around a corner arm in arm. The happy Hollywood ending is ironic, of course, since great evil has been done and gone unpunished, and there is no redemption. Meanwhile, Lester gets Halley, Levy is dead, and Cliff's wife is divorcing him. On these levels, the ending is not happy at all.

The closing scene of the film is a shot of the blind rabbi dancing with his daughter, a lovely and happy bride. As the music comes up, the old World War II standard "I'll Be Seeing You," we are again reminded of the importance of the gaze of an other. The voice-over is of Professor Levy: "We're all faced with agonizing moral choices. On a grand scale, most of these choices are on lesser points—*but*—we define ourselves by the choices we have made. We are, in fact, the sum total of our choices. . . . It is only we with our capacity to love that give meaning to the indifferent universe. . . . Most human beings seem to have the ability to keep trying. And even to find joy from simple things—like the family, their work, and from the hope that future generations might understand more." At that moment, the dance between the rabbi and his daughter ends to applause. Black out.

A Context for Analysis: The Problem of Morality in Legal and Social Theory

Woody Allen's *Crimes and Misdemeanors* can be read as a text that serves to illustrate a problem in late twentieth-century social theory and jurisprudence: The privileging of individual freedom in liberal societies, and the concomitant rejection of universal morality traditionally associated with religious or natural law systems, seems to leave no basis for moral decision making whether on an individual or systemic level. The worst case scenario is presented in *Crimes*. In the film we see a hypothesis presented in the form of a story. The hypothesis is that individuals (that is, Judah and his brother) who realize there is no punishment either in this life or the next will make decisions based only on naked self interest. The same issue recurs in legal theory in the form of the argument that the absence of absolute and universal rules about right and wrong, and the contention that all rules are human-made, means that the rules in legal systems are arbitrary and meaningless. In a sense, then, Allen's film reflects the view that a universal standard must be in place in constitutional interpretation lest the legitimacy of the court be damaged for the simple reason that its judgments are arbitrary, biased, politically motivated, or rest on force.[10]

In addition to the point about moral relativism, *Crimes* restates important issues regarding perspective and interpretation. In the film, competing individual interpretations call into question the very possibility of one *single* and *true* reality. This has been articulated in recent social theory as the condition of postmodernity.[11] If individual humans are the only true judges of their own behavior, we will be left with irresolvable, adversarial perspectives about everything. For example, in *Crimes* we are shown several perspectives about many events for which no one true answer is provided—did Judah make promises to Delores as she contends, or is she merely a neurotic woman; a case of "fatal attraction"? Is Lester really the insufferable boor that Cliff presents or is he the "creative mind" that Halley sees? Is Cliff a tortured genius, as he seems to think, or the "poor loser" that Lester sees?

The two problems illustrated in *Crimes*—the lack of a universal moral foundation and the postmodern problem of competing truths—are among the most significant issues in contemporary social theory and jurisprudence. It would seem that the problem of morality remains present even in an age of radically social-constructionist social theory. In evaluating some recent debates, it is worth considering how much recent social and legal theory has been able to move us beyond the choice faced by Judah—between religious determinism and nihilistic moral relativism.

One view that the film seems to portray seriously is a kind of existentialist viewpoint (a perspective half-heartedly represented in *Crimes* by Levy). In Jean-Paul Sartre's version of existentialism, the death of God is transformed into a liberating force. In explaining his philosophy, Sartre wrote, "God does not exist," and "it is necessary to draw the consequences of his absence right to the end." For Sartre, the existentialist "finds it extremely embarrassing that God does not exist, for there disappears with Him all possibility of finding values in an intelligible heaven. There can no longer be any good *a priori*, since there is no infinite and perfect consciousness to think it. . . . Dostoyevsky once wrote, 'If God did not exist, everything would be permitted'; and that, for existentialism, is the starting point. Everything is indeed permitted if God does not exist, and man is in consequence forlorn for he cannot find anything to depend upon either within or outside himself."[12]

For Sartre, the recognition of the death of God, which first appears to us as loneliness, can be reinterpreted by us as a most profound freedom. Although life is meaningless in and of itself and there is no human essence that precedes existence, this can be interpreted by us to mean that the main project of each human being must be to create meaning from the nothingness of life. For Sartre, all there *is* is human freedom and choice, and we are obligated to derive from them the meaning of our lives. Sartre's view, while compelling on many levels, does not relate directly to the problem as it pertains to states and legal systems. His is an individualist solution. One of the failures of *Crimes* then, is its inability to present a moral vision that is not tied either to God or to the individual. That is, the film presents no social or political vision of morality.

We might look to the Marxist tradition to find a way to conceptualize morality that is neither religious nor liberal nihilism. In that search we would be disappointed, however. Though Marxists have addressed moral questions, they have done so mostly obliquely.[13] The Marxist left has had a difficult time with moral questions, as the very language of "morality" has seemed to smack of religiosity, essentialism, and transcendentalism—all things the left has vigorously opposed as anathema to the ideas of historical change and the power of human agency.

Still, the problem of morality has begun to surface even in radical and social democratic circles. Steven Lukes has written convincingly about the paradox in Marx and Marxism regarding morality. On the one hand, Marx dismissed concepts like "justice" and "morality" as mere bourgeois ideology, but on the other, much of the Marxist critique of capitalist social relations has been offered in moral terms.[14] As Engels wrote, "According to the laws of bourgeois economics, the greatest part of the product does *not* belong to the workers who have produced it. . . . We are merely saying that this economic fact is in contradiction to our sense of morality."[15] Lukes concludes that the paradox regarding morality in Marxism can be resolved by realizing that Marx was critical of *bourgeois* and *idealist* concepts of morality, but not of liberatory ones rooted in concrete democracy.[16]

Perhaps the most interesting discussion of morality from a progressive perspective came in the work of the contemporary legal philosopher, Roberto Unger (who is credited with having later founded the

Critical Legal Studies Movement).[17] In his early work, Unger specifically addressed the problem later posed in Allen's film, terming it a problem of the liberal "privatization of ideals." The problem for individual
judicial interpretation is related and no less formidable. Since meaning
is not given and obvious, and there is no transcendent truth for jurists
to find, doctrine appears arbitrary, ideological, and biased. Indeed, this
is exactly what Unger and the Critical Legal Studies Movement subsequently argued that legal doctrines are. Unger writes,

> If we admit that words lack self-evident reference, that meaning
> must ultimately be determined by purpose and context, and that
> the intent of prior lawmakers is always more or less incomplete, it
> becomes doubtful whether a truly impartial method of judging
> could ever be fashioned within the conditions of liberal society.
> The sense of the precariousness and of the illegitimacy of consen-
> sus makes it difficult for the judge to find a stable authoritative set
> of shared understandings and values upon which to base his inter-
> pretations of the law. Hence, every case forces him to decide, at
> least implicitly, which of the competing sets of belief in a given
> society should be given priority. And it requires him to rely on an
> accepted morality that, even if it can be identified, is increasingly
> revealed as the product of a social situation itself lacking in sanc-
> tity. To this extent adjudication aggravates, rather than resolves,
> the problem of unjustifiable power.[18]

Unger's unusual solution suggests that universal values must be re-
tained, but they must not be conceptualized as transhistorical. He sees
this as a return to some notion of human nature, albeit one that is never fixed but always attuned to the shifting particularities of various
cultures, time periods, and individual desires. For Unger, human life will
always be a struggle between a human's individualistic, desiring self and
his or her aspirations toward the ideal, the good, and community.

Unfortunately, Unger believes that this ideal can never be fully
achieved in history except by God. Thus, he ends *Knowledge and Politics* with a prayer, "But our days pass, and still we do not know you
fully. Why then do you remain silent? Speak, God."[19] This, of course,
is a profoundly disturbing conclusion as it, in effect, offers the return
to a pre-bourgeois past as the solution to the contradictions in liberalism. As Stanley Fish has pointed out, Unger's solution is no solution at
all, as it leaves us with the initial question it sought to resolve.[20]

Unger's claim is that we are often in tremendous agony about the decisions we make and that the conflict we feel can be conceptualized as an internal conflict that is figured in a liberal context as one between individualistic desire, on the one hand, and an impulse toward community, on the other. Despite its ultimate religiosity, Unger's early view has some advantages. It allows for confusion (in the best possible sense), for a wavering between possibilities, for "negativity" and for what has been called in some Marxist circles, a "subjective moment." That is, people are not *wholly* determined by their circumstances. They retain the ability to speculate and to choose among competing possibilities that are presumably neither wholly determined by their contexts, nor fixed a priori (a la religion). This moment of choice can be described as the moral potential of humankind—a potential that exists, to be sure, within a given social context. But it is a context we have created, and one that is changeable. As Marx wrote,

> The production of ideas, of conceptions, of consciousness, is at first directly interwoven with the material activity and the material intercourse of men, the language of real life. Conceiving, thinking, the mental intercourse of men, appear at this stage as the direct efflux of their material behavior. The same applies to mental production as expressed in the language of politics, laws, morality, religion, metaphysics, etc., of a people. Men are the producers of their conceptions, ideas, etc.—real, active men, *as they are conditioned by a definite development of their productive forces and of the intercourse corresponding to these, up to its furthest forms.* (emphasis added)[21]

In this moment of indecision we are, in effect, not completely contextualized, not completely committed to any one particular identity, yet we remain partly contextualized within the larger liberal context. The character of Judah illustrates the way in which we redescribe reality and change our own identities in the course of moral decision making. The question remains, can we conceive of an interpretive guide that is not deterministic and transcendental (like religion), not nihilistic (like liberalism), not apolitical (like existentialism), and not evasive (like most of Marxism)? Is it possible that there is a need for some kind of an ethic rooted in a critique of liberalism and based on a democratic, multicultural, humane ideal?

Notes

Thanks to John Denvir, Bill Halthom, Melissa Wye, and the audience and my co-panelists for the panel, "Law and Popular Culture" at the 1994 Western Political Science Association meetings for comments on this essay.

1. Michael Lerner, "Politics of Meaning," *Tikkun* (July-Aug. 1992): 10.

2. Ibid.

3. Quoted in Kathryn Robinson, "Hillary Gets Religion," *Seattle Weekly*, June 9, 1993, p. 7.

4. Richard Sherwin, *Framed*, in this volume.

5. John Locke, *A Letter concerning Toleration*, with an introduction by Patrick Romanell (Indianapolis: Bobbs-Merrill, 1955), 52.

6. The debate between H. L. A. Hart and Ronald Dworkin, for instance, was at bottom a debate about why we should obey laws and which kinds of rules should govern interpretation and obedience. The positivist position, that laws are things passed by legislators, contrasts with the Dworkin position that "rights" are privileged. Critical Legal Studies, of course, disputes both of these positions in holding that law is basically reflective of the ideology of the dominant culture, and that its foundation is power. My point is that these debates are only possible (and necessary) in the context of secular legal systems. See H. L. A. Hart, *The Concept of Law*, (Oxford: Oxford University Press, 1981); Ronald Dworkin, *Taking Rights Seriously*, (Cambridge: Harvard University Press, 1978); Dworkin, ed., *Philosophy of Law* (Oxford: Oxford University Press, 1979); and Roberto Mangabeira Unger, *The Critical Legal Studies Movement* (Cambridge: Harvard University Press, 1986).

7. After the Woody Allen/Mia Farrow break-up and custody debacle, one cannot help but notice the parallels between the incestuous overtones of the Jenny/Cliff relationship and Allen's real-life indulgences with his stepdaughter/lover, Soon-Yi Farrow Previn. Allen's real-life moral drama is undoubtedly all too related to his preoccupation with the same in this film. Thus, the central question of the film—is betrayal on a moral slippery slope with murder?—achieves a kind of personal immediacy. Note also the covert references to incest, both in Wendy's relationship to her brother Lester, and again in Cliff's relationship to his niece, Jenny.

8. Apparently, this character is based on the psychoanalyst/writer Martin S. Bergmann. See his book, *In the Shadow of Moloch: The Sacrifice of Children and Its Impact on Western Religions* (New York: Columbia University Press, 1992), and the review of it by Wendy Doniger, "Why God Changed His Mind about Isaac," *New York Times Book Review*, August 1, 1993, p. 17. Interestingly, the book is about the transition from religions in which children are sacrificed to the nonsacrificing religions of Judaism and Christianity. Bergmann interprets this as a move toward the creation of a loving God.

9. Again, we might be reminded of Woody Allen's oft-quoted remarks to the press after the disclosure of his affair with his ersatz stepdaughter Soon-Yi Farrow Previn to the effect that, "the heart doesn't know from logic." We might wonder whether he pondered his own indiscretions in terms of the competing viewpoints we see in this film.

10. See, for example, Robert H. Bork, *The Tempting of America: The Political Seduction of the Law* (New York: Free Press, 1990).

11. See David Harvey, *The Condition of Postmodernity* (Oxford: Basil Blackwell, 1989).

12. Jean-Paul Sartre, *Existentialism and Humanism* (New York: Methuen, 1965), 32–34.

13. Marxism is often misunderstood as an amoral or even an anti-moral philosophy. In fact, the dream of creating and sustaining moral men in a moral society is one of the major underlying problematics of Marxism. Moreover, explicit attempts to link Marx and religion are found also, of course, in "liberation theology." See Alfred T. Hennelly, ed., *Liberation Theology: A Documentary History* (Mary Knoll, N.Y.: Orbis Books, 1990).

14. Steven Lukes, *Marxism and Morality* (Oxford: Oxford University Press, 1987), 3.

15. Quoted in Lukes, *Marxism and Morality*, 13.

16. Ibid., 59.

17. See Unger, *Critical Legal Studies Movement*.

18. Roberto Mangabeira Unger, *Law in Modern Society* (New York: Free Press, 1976), 180.

19. Note also that Unger is saying not only that we have abandoned God, but that God seems to have abandoned us. Thus, the situation he points to is not unlike that lamented by Heidegger as a withdrawal of Being. Roberto Unger, *Knowledge and Politics* (New York: Free Press, 1975), 295.

20. For an interesting critique of Unger's argument, see Stanley Fish, "Unger and Milton," in *Doing What Comes Naturally* (Durham: Duke University Press, 1989), 399–436.

21. Karl Marx, *The German Ideology*, ed. and with an introduction by C. J. Arthur (New York: International Publishers, 1947), 47.

NINE

Rewriting History with Lightning

Race, Myth, and Hollywood in the Legal Pantheon

MARGARET M. RUSSELL

■

According to an oft-told tale from the early days of Hollywood film, the debut of D. W. Griffith's *The Birth of a Nation* in 1915 was greeted with acclaim by no less prominent a figure than the president of the United States; after a private White House screening, Woodrow Wilson reportedly exclaimed, "It is like writing history with lightning." When *The Birth of a Nation* met with widespread controversy because of its racially inflammatory views, Wilson qualified his earlier effusiveness by explaining that he respected the film for its technical brilliance rather than its message.[1] Nevertheless, Wilson's vivid metaphor is a revealing illustration not only of his own (and countless others') apparent willingness to succumb to Griffith's distorted silver screen visions as "history," but also of the tremendously forceful and visceral impact of film itself as a medium.

In another sense, however, Wilson was right in ways that he doubtless did not intend. Hollywood movies *do* "write history with lightning," particularly in their embodiment of myriad racial stereotypes that are deeply inscribed throughout American culture, including this nation's legal system. As a teacher of constitutional law, employment discrimination law, and race discrimination law, I find it important and helpful for students to understand that the roots of American racial hierarchy lie not at the level of cases and statutes, but rather at the deeper and more painful levels of racial history and myth. The historian Gerald Horne has observed, "Myths are not necessarily lies, but explications. . . . They help to explain the world."[2] In attempting to explain the legal historical world of "Jim Crow laws" as well as its continuing influence today, it is essential to place American law within the cultural context of the racial myths to which it is partially a response.[3]

Hollywood racial myths in particular are subtly but firmly ensconced in our national culture. Racialized images, stereotypes, plots, and metaphors have long comprised a major component of this country's cinematic and legal histories; these tropes, in turn, infuse our vocabularies and our visions with preconceived notions about what race signifies in our interpretations of social relations and of laws. Hollywood films exert influences both large and small in the continuation of such notions. Racial degradation permeates Hollywood extravaganzas such as *Gone with the Wind* (1939) and lurks quietly in the corners of the most trivial of "throwaway" scenes.[4] Seamlessly woven into the imagery and language of Americana, Hollywood racial myths and stereotypes do indeed write "with lightning" the history of race relations in this country.[5].

In this essay I explore several ways in which Hollywood racial myths might be used to foster a critical understanding of the role of race and racism in American law. My central points are twofold. First, in recognizing popular film as a potentially rich source of insights about racism in the law, it is important to be alert to ways in which legal and popular discourses about race have been and continue to be shaped by images and perspectives from Hollywood racial mythology. Recent and increased attention in the legal academy to the role of interdisciplinary studies is premised in part upon the realization that law is itself in many ways a derivative discipline, drawing its normative foundations from other aspects of knowledge and culture; the medium of film, with its facility in affording access to multiple perspectives and experiences, can serve as a striking prism of historical attitudes about race. A second and related point concerns the usefulness of film as a legal pedagogical tool in eliciting and enhancing the critical reading of legal texts involving issues of race. The process of challenging the insidious distortions of Hollywood racial images, even while acknowledging and responding to their emotive and aesthetic force, can be an instructive experience for the reader of traditional legal texts. Learning to "talk back" to the deceptions and omissions of legal texts, in a manner that both apprehends and resists their power, is a critical skill fundamental to understanding how racism operates in the American legal system.[6]

In the next section, I discuss several ways in which Hollywood racial myths have affected legal and popular discourse about race, and consider how a critical understanding of these myths might help undo their more troublesome influences in the law. In the third and final part of this essay, I examine these themes in the context of Spike Lee's *Do the Right Thing* (1989), a significant recent film that is comprised of both Hollywood myths and anti-myths about race and the possibilities for legal justice.

Sapphires, Sambos, and the Violence of the Word: The Role of Racial Imagery in Legal and Cinematic Contexts

The rational, linear verbalism of conventional legal discourse often obscures its more subtle visceral, visual, and aural dimensions. The legal scholar Robert Cover described the phenomenological and ideological implications of this tendency as law's "violence":

> Legal interpretation takes place in a field of pain and death. This is true in several senses. Legal interpretive acts signal and occasion the imposition of violence upon others: A judge articulates her understanding of a text, and as a result, somebody loses his freedom, his property, his children, even his life. Interpretations in law also constitute justifications for violence which has already occurred or which is about to occur. When interpreters have finished their work, they frequently leave behind victims whose lives have been torn apart by these organized, social practices of violence. Neither legal interpretation nor the violence it occasions may be properly understood apart from one another.[7]

In cinema studies, a different kind of textual "violence" has been discussed in terms of the pervasive influence of electronic popular cultural imagery on individual and collective notions of social identity; for example, Teresa de Lauretis has characterized this as the power of mass media discourses to inflict psychic harms that are nonetheless real, even though their traumas are bloodless.[8] Although literal rather than metaphorical comparisons between the corrosive natures of language/image discourses and the violence of actual "deeds" raise complex philosophical and jurisprudential implications beyond the scope of this essay,[9] the above perspectives reflect a core concern of both postmodern legal scholarship and postmodern cultural studies—that is, the centrality of the only seemingly mundane "text" as a source of power and domination in everyday life.

One of the most compelling examples of such text-based power and domination lies in the function of racial stereotype in both legal and popular discourse. Inscribed upon the nation's consciousness, racial imagery is deeply embedded in both legal and cinematic representations. To extend Cover's point, neither racist texts (whether legal or cinematic) nor the harm that they occasion can be properly understood apart from one another; detection and dissection of racial legal themes cannot be accomplished without a fuller understanding of the resonance of racial images themselves in the public imagination.

A watershed event in recent American legal and popular history may serve to illustrate this point: the prime-time television coverage of the October 1991 confirmation hearings of then U.S. Supreme Court nominee Clarence Thomas. Although it is perhaps not surprising that this "real-life" historical event was largely a construct of the "reel" dimensions of film and television, the Thomas hearings are nevertheless a stark contemporary reminder of the power of historical and Hollywood racial myths to shape popular judgments and perceptions of a legal event. Both the image and the reality of the legal event were derived from long-standing racial stereotypes in American law and culture, thus effectively blurring the distinction between myth and fact in the minds of many observers and participants. Consequently, in addition to—and in fact regardless of—the "actual" events in question, the proceedings became a battle between racial images and myths rather than a debate about judicial qualifications and legal issues. Through the intersection of legal and visual contexts, the hearings presented simultaneous opportunities for the exploration of law's effect on racial stereotype, and racial stereotype's effect on law.

For example, when Thomas appeared before the Senate Judiciary Committee to refute Professor Anita Hill's allegations of workplace sexual harassment, his fiercest vitriol was expressed through conscious invocation of—and in response to—degrading racial images.[10] Angrily denying Hill's allegations that he had harassed her with tales of his sexual prowess and with bestial pornographic fantasies, Thomas accused the Senate Judiciary Committee of indulging racist assumptions about black male sexuality in evaluating Hill's charges. Worst of all, Thomas asserted, was the ineradicable violence inflicted upon his name; he contended that regardless of anything that might be said or done to exculpate him, the vicious stereotypes invoked by such accusations would simply never "wash off." Thus, in responding to Hill's specific claims, Thomas dramatically brought to the surface, acknowledged, and then combatively used the power of the brutal "Buck" stereotype to reconfigure the underlying debate.[11]

From an advocate's standpoint, Thomas's deployment of this strategy was both ingenious and ultimately effective: by explicitly confronting members of the Senate Judiciary Committee (as well as the public) with the charge that they were all too ready to believe racist stereotypes about him as an African-American male, he in effect enabled them to "disprove" his hypothesis by succumbing to equally pernicious stereotypes about African-American women. Once Thomas had carved such a space in legal, political, and public discourse for the expression of hostility against Hill, it was readily filled with "Sapphire"-like depictions of Hill as a cold-hearted careerist,[12] and "Jezebel"-like characterizations of her as a delusional erotomaniac.[13]

Moreover, Thomas employed a second corrosive racial metaphor to bolster the legitimacy of his legal position. Thomas assailed his confirmation process as a "high-tech lynching" inflicted because he was an "uppity black" who refused to comply with liberal orthodoxy on issues of race and social policy.[14] The choice of "image" weaponry in the terms "high-tech lynching" and "uppity black" was a highly persuasive piece of legal advocacy on several levels: first, it allowed him a temporary (albeit manipulated) moral high ground from which to obscure the concrete issue of his fitness for the Court by conflating real allegations of sexual harassment with the "reel" (and easily vilified) glare of the media's scrutiny; second, it enabled him to reconstruct and valorize his conservatism—denounced by many in the progressive black community as stereotypical "Uncle Tom"-ism and "Sambo"-ism—as heroically "uppity" because of its iconoclastic departure from mainstream civil rights ideology; and finally, it accorded him another opportunity to supplant any emergent sympathy for Anita Hill as the female victim of sexual harassment with the perhaps more palatable image of Thomas as the male victim of feminist, "politically correct" harpies. Again, perhaps most striking of all was Thomas's tacit acknowledgment throughout the hearings of the enormous potential of the racial image itself as a defining, legitimating, and destabilizing influence in the realms of racial and legal discourse.

Given the ready recognition and assimilation of such hoary stereotypes—"Buck," "Sapphire," "Jezebel," "Uncle Tom," "Sambo"—into the public debate involving Anita Hill and Clarence Thomas, it is beneficial for those interested in the intersection of racism and the law to accord thoughtful attention to the strands of racial mythology woven throughout the history of these and other Hollywood-driven images. Examples of the persistence of such racial themes abound. D. W.

Griffith's *The Birth of a Nation* and Spike Lee's *Jungle Fever* (1991), for example, provide radically diverse yet unsettlingly interconnected commentaries on the roots of anti-miscegenationist phobia in white supremacist attitudes. In comparing the 1950s serial "Amos 'n' Andy" with the current Fox television variety show "In Living Color," we witness the "evolution" of the vaudeville buffoon to the pop hero, "Homey the Clown."[15] Fantasies of Indian identity cycle from the savages of *Incendiary Indians* (1911) to the noble warriors of *Dances with Wolves* (1990).[16] The "Yellow Peril" continues to spring from and fuel xenophobic fervor, from *Patria* (1919) to *Rising Sun* (1993). And, of course, Ricky Ricardo lives on forever, through the power of syndicated reruns.

Given that we seem to be a nation enmeshed in and perhaps ultimately enslaved by racial myths and symbols, what (beyond enlightened knowledge) does careful study of popular stereotypes offer the critic of Hollywood movies as legal texts? As more than one cynic has observed, complaining about stereotypes in Hollywood movies is like complaining about sand at the beach. In a recent law review article critiquing the limitations of First Amendment jurisprudence in addressing the harms of racist expression, Richard Delgado and Jean Stefancic express pessimism that even the well-intentioned reader of verbal and visual texts can escape the malevolent influence of racist imagery.[17] Rather, they contend, the cumulative effect of this torrent of stereotypes is the irreparable distortion and diminution of our ability to identify and respond to contemporary instances of racism in legal and other settings. After surveying the history of popular cultural stereotypes of four "outsider" groups—African Americans, Native Americans, Asian Americans, and Mexican Americans—Delgado and Stefancic posit that the American constitutional commitment to free expression is incapable of combating the racial inequalities institutionalized by such imagery. They assert:

> Racism is woven into the warp and woof of the way we see and organize the world—it is one of the many preconceptions we bring to experience and use to construct and make sense of our social world. Racism forms part of the dominant narrative, the group of received understandings and basic principles that form the baseline from which we reason. How could these be in question? Recent scholarship shows that the dominant narrative changes very slowly and resists alteration. We interpret new stories in light of

the old. Ones that deviate too markedly from our pre-existing stock are dismissed as extreme, coercive, political, and wrong.[18]

Because of the pervasiveness and tyranny of ethnic imagery in the law, Delgado and Stefancic conclude, transcendence is a naive hope and effective resistance is unlikely.

The bleakness of the legal and cultural landscapes limned by Delgado and Stefancic is indeed difficult to ignore; yet, I believe that the very process of critical awareness, interrogation, and engagement (an effort laudably furthered in their essay) *does* present promising prospects for legal and social progress. Challenging the power of the text—in whatever realm or discipline in which it may occur—fosters a creative kind of rebellion against the truths which that text holds to be self-evident.

The Role of Hollywood Racial Myths in Teaching about Legal Perspective: Questions of Viewpoint and Response

In viewing Hollywood movies as texts about race and the law, one might productively start with questions about origin and perspective. Whether one draws upon *Gone with the Wind* or *Glory* (1989) for insights about the Civil War and Reconstruction, the issue of authorial control of the narrative is as essential in gleaning a full understanding of this "legal" text as it is with regard to more traditional legal materials such as cases and statutes. Whose story is being told? From whose perspective? Whose experiences are being excluded or distorted, and why? These questions might also serve to highlight the subjectivity of judicial constructions of racial issues in cases often read as objective, doctrinal analyses.

Certainly, a large number of Hollywood movies are characterized by the "dominant gaze" of racism—that is, the unspoken and usually unquestioned assumption that the experiences of whites are central and that those of people of color are peripheral in any given Hollywood story.[19] One need not look far to find examples: the "darkie" sidekicks from Shirley Temple musicals and the "Tonto" character from Lone Ranger adventures provide vintage illustrations, while the skewed focus on white heroism (and concomitant marginalization of blacks' roles) in the civil rights movement in *Mississippi Burning* (1988) offers a more recent demonstration. This perspective tends to flatten and trivialize the real-life experiences of people of color by contriving cinematic images of members of these groups to fit particular racial stereotypes: the grinning pickaninny; the lazy, shuffling Negro; the inscrutable Charlie Chan; the tempestuous Latin lover. The enduring resonance and cyclical resurrection of these images in the popular imagination can be more fully explained by reference to the enormity and breadth of the repository of cultural artifacts from which they have sprung. In this regard, two tremendously useful compendia from a legal pedagogical standpoint are the Marlon T. Riggs documentaries *Ethnic Notions* (1986), which provides a partial chronicle of the history of racial stereotypes in American popular culture, and *Color Adjustment* (1988), which traces the evolution of portrayals of blacks on prime-time television from the 1950s through the 1980s. While these films are not exhaustive in their coverage of the history of such images (perhaps an impossible task?), they are outstanding examples of the power of the "dominant gaze" to define the contours and content of the American legal stories about race.

Linked to the aesthetic question of authorial perspective are legal and political issues of access to the production and consumption of culture. For example, the well-documented exclusion of women and racial minorities—and particularly, women of color—from the creation, production, and direction of Hollywood films further underscores the significance of identifying narrative position and privilege in deciding whose racial stories have been and will continue to be told.[20] What legal and cultural myths (for example, the "welfare queens," "quota queens," "wetbacks," and "Willie Hortons" of recent so-called "policy" debates) have unfolded from the proliferation of "Mammy," "Sapphire," "greaser," and "Buck" images, and what real histories have disappeared from lack of attention?

Finally, issues of narrative authority assume even more complex dimensions with the recent emergence of a trickle of people of color, mostly male, as writers, producers, and directors of Hollywood projects of their own design. The work of these new Hollywood "myth-makers"—directors such as Spike Lee, Mario Van Peebles, and John Singleton—provide additional fertile ground in their efforts to provide counter-narratives about race, law, and justice. These filmmakers ask questions in their work parallel to those of legal scholars seeking to elicit counter-narratives in American legal history: Whose story is this? Whose perspective or narrative has been distorted or excluded, and why?

"Talking Back" to Racial Myths in Film and Law

In commenting upon the relativistic nature of interpretation, literary/ legal scholar Stanley Fish has observed that different ways of reading a text connote different understandings of what it means to be human.[21] Similarly, varying modes of "reading" a film as legal text can be transformed profoundly by the agency of the spectator. The question of "who is watching," and indeed how one watches, therefore emerges as a strategically important one in terms of examining the Hollywood film as a text about race and the law. As cinema studies scholar Manthia Diawara has observed, "Every narration places the spectator in a position of agency; and race, class, and sexual relations influence the way in which this subjecthood is filled by the spectator."[22]

In this regard, there are a number of similarities between the objectives of critical legal theory (including feminist and critical race studies) and critical film theory in questioning the power of the text to shape racial realities, attitudes, and perceptions. bell hooks identifies this cinematic power as a distinctly political one, and describes her own "interrogating gazes" as a spectator's form of civil disobedience:

> Black viewers of mainstream cinema and television could chart the progress of political movements for racial equality *via* the construction of images, and did so. . . . Black looks, as they were constituted in the context of social movements for racial uplift, were interrogating gazes. We laughed at television shows like "Our Gang" and "Amos 'n' Andy," at these white representations of blackness, but we also looked at them critically. Before racial integration, black viewers of movies and television experienced visual pleasure in a context where looking was also about contestation and confrontation.[23]

hooks asserts that critical spectators may combat their quiescent consumption of racial images by looking back at—and "talking back" to—degrading visual texts. In this light, "talking back" to the silver screen becomes an act of rebellion, creativity, and survival.

Jacqueline Bobo, in an essay on the complexity of black women's reactions to *The Color Purple* (1985), suggests that the difficult and sometimes contradictory nature of cinematic back talk echoes the complexity of blacks' lives in the "real" world: "For Black audiences the struggle to resist the pull of certain works is the same struggle waged against domination and oppression in everyday life. Their work of resistance involves acknowledging that mainstream works will at some point present caricatures of Black people's lives and balancing that knowledge with their more personal responses to the parts of the films that resonate with other elements of their lives."[24]

Both hooks's and Bobo's provocative descriptions of this ambivalent dynamic of repudiation and acceptance suggest another reason why the critical spectator may benefit from and even take pleasure in an "oppositional gaze"—namely, that such a gaze enables at least temporary reconciliation of the contradictions involved in both embracing and despising the history of dehumanizing stereotypes through which one's racial identity has been represented.

Similar notions of "talking back" to texts containing racial myths can be applied to the study of law as well as to the spectatorship of films. As Elizabeth Fajans and Mary Falk have noted, the reading of judicial opinions can be illuminated considerably by challenging the underlying assumptions and stereotypes that judges may bring to their analyses of the facts of record. Consider, for example, the role of such myths in the case of *Korematsu v. United States,* 323 U.S. 214 (1944), in which the Court upheld the conviction of Fred Korematsu, a United States citizen of Japanese ancestry, for violating a World War II military order excluding all persons of Japanese ancestry from designated West Coast areas. In concluding that military authorities had adequately established that the orders of curfew and exclusion were justified by "pressing public necessity," the Court explained that Korematsu had been excluded not because of racial animus, but because

> we are at war with the Japanese Empire, because the properly constituted military authorities feared an invasion of our West Coast and felt constrained to take proper security measures, because they decided that the military urgency of the situation demanded that *all citizens of Japanese ancestry* be segregated from the West Coast temporarily, and finally, because Congress, reposing its confidence in this time of war in our military leaders—as inevitably it must—determined that they should have the power to do just this. There was evidence of disloyalty on the part of *some,* the military authorities considered that the need for action was great, and time was short. (emphasis added)

Without knowledge of or reference to the pervasive anti-Japanese hostility of this era, it would be difficult to comprehend the degree of fear that led the government to permit and the Court to uphold such wide-ranging restrictions on the individual liberties of West Coast citizens of Japanese ancestry. Moreover, without "talking back" to the majority's pronouncements that racial antagonism had nothing to do with these governmental actions, both teachers and students of constitutional law miss a valuable opportunity to explore the ways in which judicial decision making can result from the fusion of historical memory and myth. In his dissenting opinion in *Korematsu,* Justice Frank Murphy alluded to such an interconnection between racial myth and racial reality in terming the exclusion orders "an accumulation of much of the misinformation, half-truths and insinuations that for years have been directed against Japanese Americans by people with racial and economic prejudices—the same people who have been among the foremost advocates of the evacuation. A military judgment based upon such racial and sociological considerations is not entitled to the great weight ordinarily given the judgments based upon strictly military considerations." In *Korematsu,* the "Yellow Peril" of Hollywood mythology had found its way into judicial reasoning in a manner that would take decades to uncover.[25]

Do the Right Thing: A Contemporary Hollywood-ization of Law and Racial Conflict

Released by Universal Pictures in 1989, Spike Lee's *Do the Right Thing* in many ways illustrates the contradictory nature of contemporary Hollywood marketing and racial ideologies. A serious and artistically impressive effort to address the subject of urban racial tensions in the wake of Howard Beach and Bensonhurst, the film initially faced resistance from major studio heads who feared that its controversial themes and somber climax would somehow in and of themselves provoke violence.[26] Stylized, polished, and consciously arty in presentation, *Do the Right Thing* was nevertheless somehow viewed by studio heads as too "real," inflammatory, and threatening in its depiction of racial hatred to be unleashed on the moviegoing public without advance warning and increased police presence.[27]

Yet, once the film had passed with flying colors the litmus tests of commercial viability and critical acclaim, both *Do the Right Thing* and its iconoclastic creator were embraced (at least for the time being) by the Hollywood establishment as brave and honest prognosticators of America's imminent class warfare. Perhaps unsurprisingly, the film's success was also accompanied by the quick assimilation of several of the film's catchier phrases (for example, "Fight the Power" and, of course, "Do the Right Thing") into the contemporary vernacular, as well as by enhanced marketing possibilities for Air Jordan sneakers, Rayban sunglasses, and other products prominently featured in the film.

In a classic twist of irony so typical of the process of "Hollywoodization," the resounding audience acceptance of *Do the Right Thing* was attributable in part to the latter phenomenon of its commercial attractiveness, rather than to the American public's receptiveness to Lee's underlying political statement. Certainly, Lee's continuing uphill struggles to finance subsequent efforts—for example, *Malcolm X* (1992)—illustrate that despite his tentative and conditional acceptance as a Hollywood "insider" after the commercial and critical success of *Do the Right Thing*, he is still very much an outsider as well. This contradictory, "insider/outsider" space occupied by Lee and other emerging, commercially successful filmmakers of color (for example, John Singleton and Mario Van Peebles) makes their works particularly interesting examples of the effect of the "dominant gaze" on films that try to "talk back" to earlier generations of Hollywood racial mythology.[28] In the remainder of this essay, I discuss Lee's use of racial (and race-gender) myths in *Do the Right Thing* to address two law-related themes—the tension between violence and nonviolence as responses to legal and social injustice, and the role of stereotypes and slurs in the eruption of lawlessness and interracial conflict.

Racial Reelism, Part 1: "America's Biggest Problem"

In extensive journal notes prefacing the published screenplay of *Do the Right Thing*, Spike Lee chronicles the evolution of the film from impressionistic concept to nearly completed production. In his first journal entry on December 25, 1987, Lee sets forth his central theme: a hot summer day in the life of a black neighborhood in Brooklyn.

> This block is in a Black neighborhood in Brooklyn. On one corner is a pizza parlor run by an Italian family who have refused to leave the neighborhood. One of the young Black characters will have a job at the pizzeria.
>
> Although the Black and Puerto Rican block residents seem to get along with the Italian family, there is still an undercurrent of hostility. Of course this tension explodes in the finale. There should

be a full-scale riot—all hell should break loose. Something provocative must set it off, like a cop shoots a kid and brothers go off.²⁹

The film proceeds to unfold exactly in this manner, using the simple
structure of a day in the life of a block in Bedford-Stuyvesant as a microcosm of American interracial conflict; at the dramatic center lies the
racial/legal conflict between a young African-American man and the
police. Mookie, the pragmatic protagonist (played by Lee), ekes out a
meager living working as a delivery man at Sal's Famous Pizzeria, a
neighborhood Italian restaurant operated by Sal (Danny Aiello) and his
sons Vito and Pino. Whereas Sal, the middle-aged businessman committed to maintaining a "respectable" business, and Vito (the younger
son) express at least a conditional willingness to deal with their black
customers and employees in a civil manner, Pino is an outspoken racist
who despises the neighborhood and regards all people of color, especially blacks, as subhuman. Mookie, in turn, maintains emotional distance from all three, choosing to divide his time among his deliveries,
an erratic romance with his teenage girlfriend Tina and their baby, and
a crankily affectionate relationship with his older and more mature sister Jade.

Other distinctive characters populate the scene as well. Community
"elders" of a sort are represented by the quirkily griotic Da Mayor
(Ossie Davis) and Mother Sister (Ruby Dee); three comically philosophical "corner men" offer running commentary on the entire neighborhood. Rebellious youth of the community are represented by Radio
Raheem, whose omnipresent and gigantic music-blaring stereo dominates every space he enters; Buggin' Out, who badgers Sal for failing to
include portraits of blacks on the pizzeria's "Wall of Fame"; and Smiley, a quietly persistent peddler of "Martin Luther King/Malcolm X"
photographs that depict the two leaders smiling joyously in a moment
of collaboration. Finally, the whole community is surveyed from a
storefront window/radio station by Mister Señor Love Daddy, the popular, sage, and seemingly omniscient disc jockey of WE LOVE radio,
108 FM, who periodically reminds the community to "chill out" and
live together in peace.

The pivotal events around which this fragile neighborhood tableau
disintegrates begin with a boycott of Sal's Famous Pizzeria initiated by
Buggin' Out, who condemns as racist the sole focus of Sal's "Wall of
Fame" on Italian-American celebrities such as Sylvester Stallone, Liza
Minnelli, Frank Sinatra, and Perry Como. Buggin' Out demands that

Sal acknowledge his debt to his black customers by adding portraits of blacks to the wall: "Put some brothers up on this Wall of Fame. We want Malcolm X, Angela Davis, Michael Jordan tomorrow."[30] Sal's position is straightforward: "You want brothers up on the Wall of Fame, you open up your own business, then you can do what you wanna do. My pizzeria, Italian Americans up on the wall."[31]

Later, Buggin' Out returns to the restaurant with Radio Raheem and his music. Sal warns Radio Raheem, "Turn that JUNGLE MUSIC off. We ain't in Africa"; Radio Raheem replies, "This is music. My music";[32] Sal picks up a baseball bat and smashes Radio Raheem's box; and a fight ensues, ending with the arrival of the police, who beat and choke Radio Raheem into unconsciousness and apparently to death. The film then climaxes with the "full-scale riot" originally envisioned by Lee and catalyzed in the movie by Mookie's tossing of a garbage can through the window of Sal's Famous Pizzeria. The restaurant burns to the ground, including in its wreckage Radio Raheem's melted stereo and Smiley's last-minute addition to the torched "Wall of Fame"—a photograph of the smiling and triumphant Martin Luther King and Malcolm X. As the camera pans over the charred remains, the rap record heard emanating from Radio Raheem's box so frequently throughout the movie is heard yet again: Public Enemy's "Fight the Power."[33]

Early in his screenplay notes, Lee observes that his film was gradually and seemingly inexorably turning into a story about race relations: "This is America's biggest problem, always has been (since we got off the boat), always will be."[34] Lee attempts to probe the complex dimensions of "America's biggest problem" through the juxtaposition of two legal themes: the question of whether the rule of law can ever adequately address systemic social injustices such as racism, police brutality, and the devaluation of human lives in black communities; and the related question of whether people of different races and ethnicities can transcend the burdens of stereotype and prejudice in their perceptions of and interactions with one another.

The first legal theme—and indeed the film's primary structural framework—concerns the tension between two philosophical responses to racial and social injustice, both epitomized in the photograph distributed by Smiley throughout the movie: the rule of nonviolence as espoused by King, and the rationale of aggressive (and, if necessary, violent) self-defense as articulated by Malcolm X. Lee's concern with these legal, political, and moral choices pervades the film and frames its beginning and concluding scenes. Lee consciously and jarringly contrasts

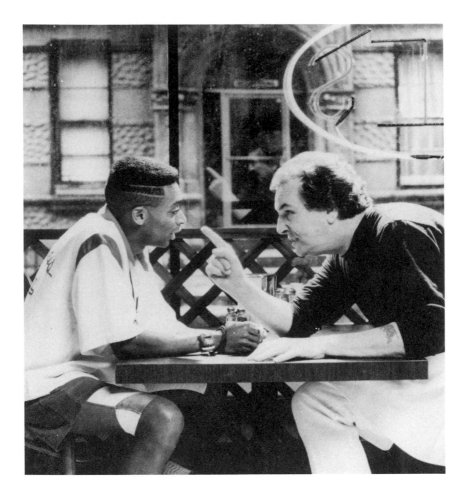

Spike Lee's *Do the Right Thing* talks back to the Hollywood myth of "law and order" by showing police misconduct against African Americans. (Courtesy of the Academy of Motion Picture Arts and Sciences.)

the two approaches by beginning his opening credit sequence with the peaceful, melodic strains of "Lift Every Voice and Sing,"[35] the black national anthem of racial pride and uplift; these strains quickly give way to the bold, MTV-style image of an athletic female, dance-boxing to Public Enemy's "Fight the Power." In the final scene, Lee explicitly maps this dichotomy to two quotations that, along with the Martin/Malcolm photograph, end the film:

> Violence as a way of achieving racial justice is both impractical and immoral. It is impractical because it is a descending spiral ending in destruction for all. The old law of an eye for an eye leaves everybody blind. It is immoral because it seeks to humiliate the opponent rather than to convert. Violence is immoral because it thrives on hatred rather than love. It destroys community and makes brotherhood impossible. It leaves society in monologue rather than dialogue. Violence ends by defeating itself. It creates bitterness in the survivors and brutality in the destroyers.—Rev. Dr. Martin Luther King, Jr.

> I think there are plenty of good people in America, but there are also plenty of bad people in America and the bad ones are the ones who seem to have all the power and be in these positions to block things that you and I need. Because this is the situation, you and I have to preserve the right to do what is necessary to bring an end to that situation, and it doesn't mean that I advocate violence, but at the same time I am not against using violence in self-defense. I don't even call it violence when it's self-defense, I call it intelligence.—Malcolm X

By identifying King's and Malcolm X's visions as representing the range of reasonable options for African Americans suffering from persistent racial and legal injustices, *Do the Right Thing* is an attempt to "talk back" to the predominant Hollywood racial myth of black subordination. The legal theme of the film thus is developed not as a question of the rule of law versus the reign of violent disorder, but rather as a reflection upon what the "rule of law" means to contemporary black America. Lee further explores this tension by teasing out its ramifications in postmodern legal terms. For example, in Lee's bleak vision of a consumption-oriented, nihilistic America, racial conflict emerges not simply as a series of conventional struggles over rights and entitlements, but also in episodes of psychic and potentially violent contest over cultural, physical, and symbolic space. So profound are the depths of contemporary despair, Lee suggests, that battles can be fought and lives lost over such seemingly evanescent yet essential symbols as the images on a "Wall of Fame," or the freedom (and volume) of one's musical preferences. In another striking scene about the significance of space in urban neighborhoods, Clifton, a white "yuppie" who has recently "gentrified" the community, accidentally steps on Buggin' Out's new Air Jordans:

> Buggin' Out: Who told you to step on my sneakers? Who told you to walk on my side of the block? Who told you to be in my neighborhood?
> Clifton: I own a brownstone on this block.
> Buggin' Out: Who told you to buy a brownstone on my block, in my neighborhood on my side of the street? . . . What do you want to live in a Black neighborhood for? Motherfuck gentrification.
> Clifton: I'm under the assumption that this is a free country and one can live where he pleases.
> Buggin' Out: A free country? . . . I should fuck you up for that stupid shit alone.[36]

Through these vividly drawn strokes—the Martin/Malcolm debate, the bitter street-level struggles over sneakers and gentrification, the barbarism of police brutality and the nihilism of community-destroying retaliation—Spike Lee seeks to use the highly accessible medium of film as a springboard for reflection about law's violence. As discussed above, the exploration of racial imagery can illuminate the effort to understand law's violence in the area of race relations; in a similar vein, Lee's second law-related theme in *Do the Right Thing* concerns the extent to which we may all be enslaved by vicious stereotypes that prevent us from truly seeing and communicating with each other across racial and ethnic boundaries.

Racial Reelism, Part 2: The Racial Slur Montage

Whereas the assault of Radio Raheem and the burning of Sal's Famous Pizzeria comprise the physically violent climax of *Do the Right Thing*, the verbally corrosive climax is the "racial slur montage," Lee's term for a jump-cut sequence in which individual characters take turns addressing the camera directly with a barrage of racial and ethnic slurs. Jump-cut sequences are featured in two of Lee's earlier films, *She's Gotta Have It* and *School Daze*; however, as Lee observes in the production notes to *Do the Right Thing,* the technique was expanded in the racial slur montage to have the camera zoom in quickly rather than remain static while the character was speaking. Accordingly, in five staccato jump-cuts, the spectator sees first an African American (Mookie); then an Italian American (Pino); then a Latino American (Stevie); then another Italian American (Officer Long); and finally a Korean American (Sonny). Mookie slurs Italian Americans; Pino slurs African Americans; Stevie slurs Korean Americans; Officer Long slurs Puerto Ricans; and Sonny slurs Jews.[37] Each character, using the second-person mode to address the camera, spews a series of vile epithets, stereotypes, and ethnic mimicries. Although each character speaks for no longer than ten seconds or so, the overall effect is powerful and unsettling. The anger and revulsion evoked by these five characters is scarcely mitigated by the sixth and final jump-cut, a zooming close-up of disc jockey Mister Señor Love Daddy, who cautions the viewing and listening public: "Yo! Hold up! Time out! Time out! Y'all take a chill. Ya need to cool that shit out . . . and that's the truth, Ruth."[38]

Lee's decision to juxtapose issues of law's violence and the lingering onus of racial stereotypes is a telling one. In the context of one Bedford-Stuyvesant neighborhood, Lee attempts to illustrate that despite close physical proximity and even intermittently friendly personal relationships, the pall of decades-old and indeed centuries-old ethnic notions prevents us from seeing one another, very simply, as human beings. Instead, Lee posits, the American dream of rich diversity—or even of a more traditionally assimilative "melting pot"—is mired in mistrust and animosity, economic crisis and political paralysis. The cities of America are not parts of Clifton's "free country," but instead a snarling tangle of bigots who are all too ready to see each other as "pizza-slinging," "gold-chain-wearing," "kickboxing," "Goya-bean-eating," "chocolate-egg-cream-drinking" enemies.

In pointing out the compelling connections among the persistence of racial stereotypes, the pervasive disaffection in urban communities, and the legal system that remains inadequate to address these problems, Lee's racial slur montage and related scenes underscore Cornel West's diagnosis of the underlying causes of despair in black communities: "black existential angst derives from the lived experience of ontological wounds and emotional scars inflicted by white supremacist beliefs and images permeating U.S. society and culture. These beliefs and images attack black intelligence, black ability, black beauty, and black character daily in subtle and not-so-subtle ways."[39]

As one prominent Hollywood director's exploration of both his own angst and anger at the destruction of his community, *Do the Right Thing* is in my view a well-crafted and innovative effort to raise issues of racial injustice in a provocative and accessible manner. For that reason alone, it can serve as a tremendously useful text for the examination of racial themes in the law. However, as suggested above, all Hollywood racial myths—including nontraditional and postmodern myths in the films of Spike Lee, John Singleton, Mario Van Peebles, and others—deserve serious attention and critique for what they omit and distort as well as what they include. Accordingly, in concluding this essay, I briefly discuss what I consider to be *Do the Right Thing*'s major flaw as a text about race and the law: its ultimately acquiescent and in many ways traditional approach to its central themes of racial hatred and conflict. In these respects, *Do the Right Thing* does not follow through on its enormous potential, perhaps leaving to the promise of critical spectatorship a response to its unsatisfactory resolution.

Racial Reelism, Part 3: Rewriting Racial Myths?

In her thought-provoking essay, "Counter-Hegemonic Art: Do the Right Thing,"[40] bell hooks forcefully challenges *Do the Right Thing*'s avowedly radical intentions and asserts that in fact the film reinforces the "scary, conservative idea . . . that everybody is safest in their 'own' neighborhood, that it is best if we remain with people like ourselves."[41] While I do not share the depth of dissatisfaction expressed by hooks in her evaluation of the film—and in fact find *Do the Right Thing* to be overall a significant step forward (if not considerably far away) from the predominant Hollywood racial myths of previous generations—I do agree that Lee's attempt to make a serious statement about "America's biggest problem" is marred by the ambivalence and at times opaqueness of his vision.

Certainly, Spike Lee—even with his larger-than-life persona in the Hollywood pantheon—is only one person with one person's perspectives on the black experience. In my view, his work has made significant contributions in "talking back" to both Hollywood power and to the "Hollywood-ization" of racial myths; yet, it is important to keep in mind that visions of the black experience are plural rather than singular and eclectic rather than uniform. Thus, successive "readings" and discussions of the racial themes raised in *Do the Right Thing* can reveal additional opportunities for analysis. Examples of such issues might include: whether and to what extent Lee accurately characterizes the Martin/Malcolm dichotomy in terms of the material conditions facing the characters in the movie; the degree to which individual characters might be viewed as verifying rather than transcending the stereotypes that Lee aims to excoriate; the efficacy of the moving-camera jump-cut sequence in eliciting broad-based and cross-cultural recognition of the ugliness of racial and ethnic slurs. Lee's goal may very well have been to foster a deliberate open-endedness to these questions in order to render the movie more effective as a whole. However, in several significant respects, the structural framework of the movie and its development of major characters belie the ostensible rebelliousness of the director's gaze.

Two examples may serve to illustrate this point. First, although the film's beginning and closing scenes strongly urge the spectator to ponder the story as a sociolegal parable about the Martin/Malcolm dichotomy, in my view the intervening scenes surprisingly emphasize the destruction of Sal's Famous Pizzeria—rather than the brutality inflicted against Radio Raheem—as the core violent event. Whatever Lee *hoped* to achieve by according such strong force to this scene, the reality is that the burning down of white-owned property—and not the murder of a young black man—emerges clearly as the film's most dramatic, tragic, and drawn-out sequence; therefore, it is hardly surprising to me that it was the most talked-about portion of the movie. In fact, because the character of Sal himself is by far the more complexly developed character of the two, this viewer was given a fuller sense of the injury inflicted upon Sal than upon Radio Raheem—an ironic consequence given the devaluation of black life, community, and culture obviously intended to be symbolized by Radio Raheem's fate. Despite its courageous intentions, *Do the Right Thing* fails to use the drama of its own racial imagery to "talk back" explicitly to a common racial myth: that center stage treatment is to be given to the plight of characters such as Sal, while the Radio Raheems occupy a marginal role.

A second flaw of *Do the Right Thing* lies in the area of gender stereotype and gender relations. Observers of Spike Lee's work (not to mention Lee himself) have noted the one-dimensionality of female characters in most of his films; in *She's Gotta Have It* and *School Daze,* the two full-length films preceding *Do the Right Thing,* Lee presents black female characters little better than the stock "Sapphire" and "Jezebel" myths of old. Ironically, in the journal notes for *Do the Right Thing,* Lee concedes this deficiency and vows to do better; yet, shortly there-after, he fantasizes: "As usual I gotta have a vicious sex scene. For this one it's gonna be a naked female body with ice cubes. We should shoot it similar to the scenes in *She's Gotta Have It,* with extreme closeups."[42] As it turns out, the ice cube-covered body will belong to Tina, Mook-ie's girlfriend, who is described by Lee in the journal notes as follows: "Mookie's girlfriend Tina is one of the thousands of teenage Black girls who has a child, but is still a child herself. Mookie is the father. I want an unknown young woman, maybe someone who's not an actress, to play Tina. I need a real live Ghetto Babe."[43]

Lee's infamous acerbic humor (and Rosie Perez's dramatic talents) aside, Tina does indeed emerge in the final work as a creature of Lee's "Ghetto Babe" mentality about women of color. Certainly, the other female characters in *Do the Right Thing* do not fare much better. Whether responsible yet ineffectual and somewhat naive (Jade), or enig-matic yet clearly removed from temporal concerns (Mother Sister), these women form at best an appealing backdrop to the "real men" (that is, Mookie, Sal, Pino, Buggin' Out, Radio Raheem) whose strug-gles, passions, and conflicts form the heart of the film. In this respect, Lee reveals a disappointingly partial vision of "America's biggest prob-lem"; by portraying the theme of law's violence almost exclusively as it affects and is conceptualized by males, he misses a promising opportu-nity to engage feminist spectators in a shared gaze critical of racial su-premacy.

Conclusion

As we approach the end of Hollywood's first century, it is important to recognize in its annals of exclusion a stark and depressing parallel with the history of racial discrimination in this nation's legal system. This parallel will doubtless continue, given the lingering effects of such ex-clusion in legal and popular discourse about race. Therefore, American popular film may serve as a particularly accessible medium for the ex-amination and critique of both older, more conventional stereotypes and subtler, newer ones. Certainly, film is not literally capable of rewrit-ing this nation's legal history with lightning, but I must admit that I find the possibilities for change intriguing. Perhaps like Spike Lee's efforts in *Do the Right Thing,* many of us struggle to achieve new racial visions, only to reveal how tethered we remain to the myths of our past. But in seeking to shed the "bondage of myths"[44]—or at least to understand it—we can only benefit from learning to talk back to the silver screen, even while in its thrall.

Notes

1. David A. Cook, *A History of Narrative Film* (New York: W. W. Norton and Company, 1981), 77–78.

2. Gerald Horne, "'Myth' and the Making of *Malcolm X,*" *American Historical Review* 98 (Apr. 1993): 440.

3. For example, the term "Jim Crow"—which is used to describe the system of laws used to perpetuate racial segregation—is derived from a song popularized in the early nineteenth century by Thomas D. Rice's blackface minstrel "Jump Jim Crow," who in turn was based on an elderly black slave of that era. Jannette L. Dates and William Barlow, eds., *Split Image: African Americans in the Mass Media* (Washington, D.C.: Howard University Press, 1990), 7.

4. In "Do He Have Your Number, Mr. Jeffrey?," writer Gayle Pemberton recalls with resentment how her memories of a much-beloved Alfred Hitchcock film are marred by a racially demeaning, "insignificant" one-liner. She notes with even greater revulsion the ostensibly casual, off-handed manipulation of race in old Shirley Temple movies: "In *The Little Colonel,* young Shirley has just been given a birthday party; there are hats and horns and all sorts of scrubbed white children celebrating with her. At some moment—I refuse to watch the film again to be precise—she gets up and takes part of her cake to a group of dusty and dusky children who are waiting outside in the backyard of the house. The only reason for their existence is to be grateful for the crumbs and to sing a song. There can be no other motivation, no reason to exist at all, except to show the dear little Colonel's largesse and liberal-mindedness, befitting someone not quite to the manor born but clearly on her way to the manor life." Gayle Pemberton, *The Hottest Water in Chicago: On Family, Race, Time, and American Culture* (Boston: Faber and Faber, 1992), 42–43. bell hooks notes a parallel marginalization and appropriation of black culture in Madonna's breezy use of black religious symbols and dancing "sidekicks" in her MTV video for the hit record "Like a Prayer": "Made to serve as supportive backdrop for Madonna's drama, black characters in 'Like a Prayer' remind one of those early Hollywood depictions of singing black slaves in the great plantation movies or those Shirley Temple films where Bojangles was trotted out to dance with Miss Shirley and spice up her act. Audiences were not supposed to be enamored of Bojangles, they were supposed to see just what a special little old white girl Shirley really was. In her own way Madonna is a modern day

Shirley Temple. Certainly her expressed affinity with black culture enhances her value." bell hooks, "Madonna: Plantation Mistress or Soul Sister?," in *Black Looks: Race and Representation* (Boston: South End Press, 1992), 162.

5. For thoughtful historical analyses of the durability of such myths and stereotypes, see generally John Hope Franklin, *"Birth of a Nation*—Propaganda as History," *Massachusetts Review* 20 (1979): 417–34. George M. Fredrickson, *The Black Image in the White Mind: The Debate on Afro-American Character and Destiny, 1817–1914* (Middletown, Conn.: Wesleyan University Press, 1971); Patricia Nelson Limerick, *The Legacy of Conquest: The Unbroken Past of the American West* (New York: Norton, 1987); Ronald T. Takaki, *Iron Cages: Race and Culture in Nineteenth-Century America,* 2d ed. (New York: Oxford University Press, 1990).

6. In "Against the Tyranny of Paraphrase: Talking Back to Texts," *Cornell Law Review* 78 (Jan. 1993): 163–205, Elizabeth Fajans and Mary R. Falk decry the predominantly narrow, uncritical and anti-intellectual manner in which law students and lawyers learn to approach the reading of judicial opinions. As possible antidotes, they offer pedagogical insights drawn from their efforts to teach students in their legal writing seminar to "talk back" to the power of legal texts: "there are at least three good reasons to talk back to power, to resist the tyranny of paraphrase. First, ours is explicitly a 'text-oriented' democracy—from the Declaration of Independence to the Constitution to the written opinions of courts—and unexamined authority is incompatible with democracy. Second, the close examination of legal rhetoric is fun of a particularly edifying sort; there is a healthy zaniness to searching for all of a text's texts, intended and hidden. Third, cognitive psychology teaches that all readers of legal texts, judges as well as law students, subconsciously supply multiple contexts when they read, whether they believe they do or not. When judges interpret precedent, they respond 'personally' to the text, and bring their subjective readings into their decisions, even while claiming in good faith that they merely 'find' the law in the first case and 'apply' it to the second. Thus, close reading not only helps readers to understand and make use of their own reading response, but also illuminates the judicial decision-making process" (165; footnotes omitted). In "Talking Back," in *Talking Back: Thinking Feminist, Thinking Black* (Boston: South End Press, 1989), bell hooks describes "back talk" as a step toward liberation—"speaking as an equal to an authority figure" (5).

7. Robert M. Cover, "Violence and the Word," *Yale Law Journal* 95 (1986): 1601. For other interesting dimensions of the debate regarding textual authority, see Martha Minow, Michael Ryan, and Austin Sarat, eds., *Narrative, Violence, and the Law: The Essays of Robert Cover* (Ann Arbor: University of Michigan Press, 1993); Robin L. West, *Narrative, Authority, and Law* (Ann Arbor: University of Michigan Press, 1993).

8. Teresa de Lauretis, "The Technology of Gender," in *Technologies of Gender: Essays on Theory, Film, and Fiction* (Bloomington: Indiana University Press, 1987).

9. The continuing vitality and importance of the "speech/image as violence" debate in First Amendment theory is reflected in such recent and diverse works and projects as Richard Delgado, Charles R. Lawrence, Mari J. Matsuda, eds. *Words That Wound: Critical Race Theory, Assaultive Speech, and the First Amendment* (New York: New Press, 1993); Franklyn Haiman, *"Speech Acts" and the First Amendment* (Carbondale: Southern Illinois University Press, 1993); and "Speech, Equality, and Harm," March 1993 Conference Proceedings, University of Chicago.

10. Recent works on the legal, social, and political significance of the Thomas-Hill event for gender and race relations include: Robert Allen and Robert Chrisman, eds., *Court of Appeal: The Black Community Speaks Out on the Racial and Sexual Politics of Clarence Thomas vs. Anita Hill* (New York: Ballantine Books, 1992); Toni Morrison, ed., *Race-ing Justice, En-gendering Power: Essays on Anita Hill, Clarence Thomas, and the Construction of Social Reality* (New York: Pantheon, 1992).

11. The heinous stereotype of black men as bestial, sexually depraved "Bucks" who pursued and attacked white women, was promoted with particular intensity during the Reconstruction era as a "justification" for the thousands of lynchings that took place during that time. Catherine Silk and John Silk, *Racism and Anti-Racism in American Popular Culture: Portrayals of African-Americans in Fiction and Film* (New York: St. Martin's Press, 1990): 39.

12. On the significance of the "Sapphire" image in discourses about African-American women, see generally Hortense Spillers, "Mama's Baby, Papa's Maybe: An American Grammar Book," *Diacritics* 17 (Summer 1987): 65–81; Wahneema Lubiano, "Black Ladies, Welfare Queens, and State Minstrels: Ideological War by Narrative Means," in Morrison, ed., *Race-ing Justice, En-gendering Power,* 323–63; Regina Austin, "Sapphire Bound!" *Wisconsin Law Review* (1989): 539–78.

13. In assessing the subtle resilience of the "Jezebel" stereotype in popular culture, historian Nell Irvin Painter observes: "The depiction of the oversexed-black-Jezebel is not as salient in American culture as that of the black-beast-rapist/lynch victim, but she has sufficient visibility to haunt black women to this day. . . . Overdetermined by class and by race, the black-woman-as-whore appears nearly as often as black women are to be found in representations of American culture. Mary Chesnut, in her Civil War diary, pities the virtuous plantation mistress surrounded by black prostitutes anxious to seduce white men and boys. . . . The figure of the oversexed-black-Jezebel has had amazing longevity. She is to be found in movies made in the 1980s and 1990s—*She's*

Gotta Have It, Jungle Fever, City of Hope—in which black female characters are still likely to be shown unclothed, in bed, and in the midst of coitus." Nell Irvin Painter, "Hill, Thomas, and the Use of Racial Stereotype," in Morrison, ed., *Race-ing Justice, En-gendering Power,* 209–10.

14. For insightful analyses of some of the patent and latent contradictions of both the "uppity black" image and the lynching metaphor, see Painter, "Hill, Thomas, and the Use of Racial Stereotype," 200–214; and Kendall Thomas, "Strange Fruit," in Morrison, ed., *Race-ing Justice, En-gendering Power,* 364–89.

15. For an exploration of the significance of African-American humor in popular culture, see Mel Watkins, *On the Real Side: Laughing, Lying, and Signifying: The Underground Tradition of African-American Humor That Transformed American Culture, from Slavery to Richard Pryor* (New York: Simon & Schuster, 1994).

16. In "Lawrence of South Dakota: *Dances with Wolves* and the Maintenance of the American Empire," in *Fantasies of the Master Race: Literature, Cinema, and the Colonization of American Indians,* ed. M. Annette Jaimes (Monroe, Maine: Common Courage Press, 1992), American Indian Studies scholar Ward Churchill takes issue with the widespread acclaim accorded Kevin Costner's revisionist epic: "Stripped of its pretty pictures and progressive flourishes in directions and affirmative action hiring, *Dances with Wolves* is by no means a movie about Indians. Instead, it is at base an elaboration of movieland's Great White Hunter theme, albeit one with a decidedly different ('better') personality than the usual example of the genre, and much more elegantly done" (245).

17. Richard Delgado and Jean Stefancic, "Images of the Outsider in American Law and Culture: Can Free Expression Remedy Systemic Social Ills?" *Cornell Law Review* 77 (Sept. 1992): 1258–97.

18. Ibid., 1278–79 (footnotes omitted).

19. Margaret M. Russell, "Race and the Dominant Gaze: Narratives of Law and Inequality in Popular Film," *Legal Studies Forum* 15 (Spring 1991): 243–54.

20. Works chronicling the exclusion of women and people of color from the film industry include: Donald Bogle, *Toms, Coons, Mulattoes, Mammies, and Bucks: An Interpretive History of Blacks in American Films,* 2d ed. (New York: Continuum, 1992); Julie Burchill, *Girls on Film* (New York: Pantheon, 1986); Lorraine Gamman and Margaret Marshment, *The Female Gaze: Women as Viewers of Popular Culture* (Seattle: Real Comet Press, 1989). With the scant exception of Euzhan Palcy's *A Dry White Season* (1989), Julie Dash's *Daughters in the Dust* (1992) and a few others, the works of female filmmakers of color have received even less attention and visibility in Hollywood.

21. Stanley Fish, *Is There a Text in This Class? The Authority of Interpretive Communities* (Cambridge: Harvard University Press, 1980).

22. Manthia Diawara, "Black British Cinema: Spectatorship and Identity Formation in Territories," *Public Culture* 1 (Summer 1989).

23. hooks, "The Oppositional Gaze," in *Black Looks,* 117.

24. Jacqueline Bobo, "The Politics of Interpretation: Black Critics, Filmmakers, Audiences," in *Black Popular Culture,* ed. Gina Dent (Seattle: Bay Press, 1993): 70.

25. In 1984, Fred Korematsu's conviction was vacated after extensive investigation and legal work established that the government had submitted false information to the Supreme Court in the 1940s regarding the threat of invasion. *Korematsu v. United States,* 584 F. Supp. 1406 (N.D. Cal. 1984).

26. Despite the overwrought hue and cry that have generally preceded the opening of films by young black directors such as Lee, John Singleton (*Boyz N the Hood* and *Poetic Justice*), and Mario Van Peebles (*New Jack City*), these works have not fomented the widespread violence and class rebellion prophesied and feared by studio heads and media pundits.

27. In contrast, note the riotous reception to *The Birth of a Nation* over seven decades earlier, the lasting historical legacy of which was the modern rebirth of the Ku Klux Klan. According to Klan leaders, the film was used as a recruitment and training film of sorts well into the 1960s. David A. Cook, *History of Narrative Film,* 90.

28. For example, in *Posse* (1993), Mario Van Peebles uses the resources of black cowboy history both to "talk back" to the dominant Hollywood racial mythology of cowboys as white, "John Wayne" types, and to reclaim the quintessentially American genre of the "western" as his own.

29. Spike Lee with Lisa Jones, *Do the Right Thing* (New York: Simon and Schuster/Fireside Books, 1989): 24.

30. Ibid., 142.

31. Ibid., 141.

32. Ibid., 242–43.

33. "Fight the Power" (1989), music and lyrics by Carlton Ridenhour, Hank Shocklee, Eric Sadler, and Keith Shocklee.

34. Lee, *Do the Right Thing,* 33.

35. "Lift Every Voice and Sing," music and lyrics by James Weldon Johnson and John Rosemond Johnson.

36. Lee, *Do the Right Thing,* 167–68.

37. Ibid., 186–87. Building up to the montage is a lengthier scene at the restaurant with Mookie, Pino, and Vito, in which Pino attempts to "explain" to Mookie why his favorite celebrities (all African Americans—Eddie Murphy, Prince, and Magic Johnson) are ". . . not really Black. They're more than Black. It's different" (183–85).

38. Ibid., 188.

39. Cornel West, *Race Matters* (Boston: Beacon Press, 1993), 17–18.

40. bell hooks, *Yearning: Race, Gender, and Cultural Politics* (Boston: South End Press, 1990), 173–84.

41. Ibid., 175.

42. Ibid., 26–27.

43. Ibid., 73.

44. The phrase is from Martin Luther King Jr.'s "Letter from Birmingham Jail," reprinted in King's *Why We Can't Wait* (New York: Harper and Row, 1963), 76–95, in which he draws a parallel between critical intellectual tension and civil disobedience: "Just as Socrates felt that it was necessary to create a tension in the mind so that individuals could rise from the bondage of myths and half-truths to the unfettered realm of creative analysis and objective appraisal, so must we see the need for nonviolent gadflies to create the kind of tension in society that will help men rise from the dark depths of prejudice and racism to the heights of understanding and brotherhood" (79–80).

TEN

Celluloid Sovereignty

Hollywood's "History" of Native Americans

TERRY WILSON

■

They from the beginning announced that they wanted to maintain their way of life. . . . And we set up those reservations so they could, and have a Bureau of Indian Affairs to help take care of them. . . . Maybe we should not have humored them in wanting to stay in that kind of primitive life-style. Maybe we should have said, "No, come join us. Be citizens along with the rest of us. . . ." You'd be surprised. Some of them became very wealthy, because some of these reservations were overlaying great pools of oil. And you can get rich pumping oil. And so I don't know what their complaint might be.

RONALD REAGAN

Responses by Native Americans to President Ronald Reagan's answer to repeated requests for a policy statement addressing Indian concerns in 1988 were surprisingly temperate, given the rage they must have felt. Their chief executive could not imagine that Indians had a problem? The nation's most disadvantaged people by virtually any measure—health, education, economics, political power—had witnessed his administration's halving of federal appropriations for Indian programs and Reagan was bewildered at their protest? Only native peoples, long accustomed to governmental hyperextensions of illogic and misinformation, could eschew invective in favor of weary sighs and renewed attempts at further dialogue with the Great Communicator.

Perhaps Indian America should have anticipated Reagan's presidential stance. While campaigning along the political trail to the White

House, he was asked during an interview to name those persons whose lives he would have enjoyed living. Among those he listed were Vasco Nunez de Balboa, Hernando Cortez, Father Junipero Serra, Meriwether Lewis, and William Clark. Cortez and Balboa explored and invaded parts of native America and Father Serra oversaw the establishment of California Indian missions that exploited native labor and coerced religious conversion. The selection of Lewis and Clark, President Thomas Jefferson's explorers of the Louisiana Purchase, was explained in Reagan's final listing: "And any number of those men who first crossed the Plains in the opening of the West. In other words," he added, "I'm fascinated by those who saw this new world when it was virtually untouched by man."[1]

Apparently Reagan regarded the native presence in America as scant or of relative insignificance, and had no qualms about subsequent Euro-American colonization. Where did the president get his notions about Indians and Indian/white relations? He was a college student in the 1930s, and any history textbook of that period would have utilized the paradigm of the frontier to characterize United States history. Historians invariably described the course of nation-building in terms of the inexorable march of frontiersmen across the continent, bringing civilization to previously savage lands. Native Americans were posited as an obstacle, not unlike deserts and mountains, to be overcome and tamed. Then again, recalling the presidential penchant for fond remembrance of his Hollywood years, maybe Reagan simply acquired his understanding of history and the role of Indians in the national past through an osmotic celluloid process.

Generations of Americans, native and non-native alike, have been vastly influenced by the movie-made Indian. Not a few citizens have received their basic understanding of Native Americans almost exclusively from images cast by Hollywood. Without the threat of Indian attack, the frontier drama would not resonate. Indians were occasionally noble, always savage, and inevitably defeated by the last reel. Variations on this theme occurred, notably during the last forty years, but the lasting impressions on moviegoers have changed less than the makers of films such as *Dances with Wolves* (1990) and *Thunderheart* (1992) hoped. People act toward one another according to their perceptions, not realities. If, as I believe, the majority of the non-Indian population's attitudes, and consequently policies, toward Native Americans are based to a significant degree on notions gained from the movies, a clearer understanding of the Hollywood Indian is crucial for all those interested in the cultural survivals of the nation's smallest racial minority.

From the days of the nickelodeon through the decade of the 1960s, Native American images were prominent on movie screens. Immigrant viewers with little or no English appreciated action sequences during the silent film era that provided easily discernible heroes and villains. Feather-bedecked, bow and arrow-wielding Indians attacking wagon trains and forts, settlers and cavalrymen, filled the bad guy roles admirably. Occasionally a director would fashion a film that peered behind the war-painted faces of the savages to reveal indigenous people protecting their homelands, but until the 1950s few moviemakers questioned the validity of the Indian as a constant threat to pillage, rape, burn, and kill.

That for decades Hollywood's Indians generally represented a menace to the majority white culture is scarcely surprising. The nature of relations between Native Americans and Euro-Americans virtually demands such an interpretation of the past by non-Indians. Every nation state was created at the expense of some to promote the welfare of others. This truism rarely figures prominently in the historical and cultural memories that make up the collective national consciousness. Moviemakers have both reflected U.S. society's mythology about Indians and reinforced and refined its images of native peoples.

Regardless of how historians have presented the frontier process, there is an inescapable unpleasantness associated with the formation of the United States: nation building necessitated the dispossession of indigenous Americans. The New World offered those who made the Atlantic crossing something that was in short supply in Europe—available land. Native peoples occupying the land constituted an obstacle to colonial America's primary goal of asserting control over territory that would yield a living and, ultimately, a way of life.

Colonial leaders understood the problems of dispossession. There were more Indians than Euro-Americans for several generations after 1607, which meant that a purely military solution would not suffice. Superiority of technology and utter ruthlessness of strategy aided conquest; however, the invaders' most effective weapon of dispossession lay with the law, or at least quasi-legal means. Although even a cursory reading of colonial literature—sermons, histories, diaries, letters, captivity narratives—reveals contempt, fear, and hatred of Native Americans, relations with the various tribes were carried out on the premise that they were nation states.

This meant that negotiations and agreements between the colonists, and later the United States, with the tribes replicated the practice of international law. Treaties were signed that invariably included the transfer of Indian land to non-Indian governments and peoples. The negotiations were marked by bad faith and misdirection if not outright fraud and deception. Promises were made that in exchange for land, friendship, alliance, and trade would be forthcoming. Intertribal ill feelings and warfare were exploited by the colonials, whose military technology could prove decisive in native conflicts. It is noteworthy that treaties were generally negotiated after the capacity of the tribes for armed resistance was severely limited from the attritions of war, disease, and destruction of food supplies. The documents of land transfer were written in English, rarely explained to tribal leaders accurately, often accompanied by bribes and blandishments, and finally interpreted according to the majority culture's system of law. Native governance was largely ignored as colonial and U.S. envoys arbitrarily chose the weakest tribal representatives with whom to deal, bypassing legitimate leaders and later insisting that the entire tribe was bound by the treaty.[2]

Why were the colonists and their succeeding generations so punctilious about spreading a veneer of legality over their dealings with tribal peoples? Euro-American thought endowed Native Americans with a noble savagery until Indians were at close proximity, then they were rendered ignoble by the infiltration of Western values and mores. Admired from afar, the Indian was contemned when he stood in the path of progress. Justifications for displacing him were plentiful but the niceties of human conduct and international protocol had to be observed. No group desires the calumny of conquerors; people want to believe that they are in the right. Through the treaty system, however unequally instituted and practiced, the colonies and later the United States could claim possession of the American continent *legally*.

There was a price attached to positing the tribes as fit partners for treaty making: recognition of their status as sovereign entities, self-governing peoples exerting control over themselves and their lands. To establish this concept in law required some tricky legal finessing. Fortunately for the young United States, a jurist, equal to the challenge, sat on the nation's Supreme Court. Chief Justice John Marshall in a series of three decisions resolved the issue of Native American sovereignty and U.S. trust responsibility and along the way reflected the political, cultural, and psychological rationale for the dispossession of the Indian, the healing balm for a troubled national conscience.

In 1823 Marshall wrote the majority decision for *Johnson v. McIntosh*. The issue of the case was whether Indian tribes held title to lands on which they lived. If they did not, all land transactions through the treaty process were invalid. Marshall's opinion reflected the court's view that the tribes held title as a result of original occupancy, "but their rights to complete sovereignty, as independent nations, were necessarily diminished" by the claims of European powers' right of discovery. Thus England, and later the U.S. as a consequence of successful declaration of independence, possessed "the sole right of acquiring the soil from the natives . . . either by purchase or by conquest."[3]

The chief justice admitted that "the title by conquest is acquired and maintained by force. The conqueror prescribes its limits." This was certainly an accurate assessment of historical fact, but was unpalatable for those men leading a new nation that prided itself on providing liberty and justice for all. Marshall noted that "Humanity . . . has established as a general rule, that the conquered shall not be wantonly oppressed . . . that the new subjects [Indians] should be governed as equitably as the old." He went on to describe how it was unavoidable that Euro-Americans displace the Indians because they "were fierce savages, whose occupation was war. . . . To leave them in possession of their country, was to leave the country a wilderness."[4] This was the argument made by politicians, including presidents like Andrew Jackson, newspaper editors, ministers, and all other proponents of manifest destiny and mission who held that God intended Euro-Americans to uproot savage and pagan native hunters so that Christian agriculturalists could establish civilization in the wilderness, whatever the cost to America's original inhabitants.

Further refinements of the relationship between the federal government and Indian tribes were enunciated by Marshall in *Cherokee Nation v. Georgia* (1831) and *Worcester v. Georgia* (1832). These cases are especially interesting given the chief justice's characterization of Native Americans as savage hunters, as they involved the Cherokees, a tribal people designated as "civilized" in the 1830s due to their farming activities, intermarriage with Euro-Americans, and constitutional governance patterned after the U.S. constitution. At issue in the cases was a conflict between the federal government and Georgia over jurisdiction regarding the Cherokee Nation residing inside the state. Although the decisions declared emphatically for the primacy of the United States in Indian relations, the Cherokees were eventually removed from Georgia by political chicanery and military force, a course desired by the state.

More important, Native American sovereignty was defined in the decisions. Marshall had to uphold the principle that past acts of the U.S. government "plainly recognize the Cherokee nation as a state," but not a "foreign nation," else all treaties acquiring legal title to the national domain would be invalid. Because of their savagery, however, the tribes could not be "foreign nations," rather they should be "denominated domestic dependent nations . . . in a state of pupilage. Their relation to the United States resembles that of a ward to his guardian."[5] Thus the federal government settled on a degree of sovereignty for Indian tribes, partial and limited. It also assumed a trust relationship with the tribes that dozens of later court decisions expanded upon, requiring the United States to look after the best interests of the Indians, including the disposition and use of their natural resources on reservations.[6]

All of the questionable political and legal tactics used to try to legitimize the conquest of Native Americans rested on a decidedly slanted interpretation of U.S. history. Hollywood has played a significant role in perpetuating images of Indians that support the majority culture's self-mythologizing "history." The first movie I discuss noticeably follows the Indian-as-savage-and-thus-undeserving theme as it glorifies the progress of the frontier's advance. The second film, avowedly sympathetic to Native Americans, nonetheless furthers the notion of legal dispossession. The last two films are plainly revisionist, focusing on the failures of the federal government's trust responsibility in safeguarding present-day reservation resources and the internal governance of tribes exercising their limited sovereignty. The four movies' content and messages reflect the times in which they were made and together offer an ever changing commentary on relations between native and non–Native Americans, legal and otherwise.

In 1939 Twentieth Century–Fox released *Drums along the Mohawk,* one of several popular historical dramas produced by Hollywood for the 1939–40 movie season. It was based on Walter Edmonds's 1936 best-selling novel about the New York frontier during the American Revolution. Henry Fonda and Claudette Colbert played Gil and Lana Martin, the newly married couple whose struggle to survive the rigors of war include several Mohawk raiding forays and a climactic assault on a fort. Producer Darryl F. Zanuck chose John Ford to direct from a script rewritten several times to simplify the novel's historically detailed complexity and the initial story treatment's perfervid patriotism, and to emphasize the personal drama of frontier people balancing individual effort and group interdependence to achieve a rural paradise.[7]

The film celebrates traditional frontier virtues: rugged individualism, ambition, hard work, democratic society, rough good humor, bravery, and helping one's neighbors. It also features one good Indian and a large number of bad natives. Zanuck's studio publicity department bally-hooed *Drums along the Mohawk* as historically accurate, including the choice of an authentic Iroquois, septuagenarian Chief Big Tree, to assume the role of Blue Back, a kind of Everyman's Tonto. He provides marital advice to Gil Martin, a warning of impending Indian attack to the frontier community, and intermittent comic relief. A cultural mixed blood, Blue Back speaks broken but emphatic English, attends church services enthusiastically, and aids in the defense of the fort.

His age, eagerness to please, and dull-wittedness render Blue Back's contribution to the advancement of the frontier seemingly ideal. His sudden appearance at the Martins's cabin initially startles Lana, who screams her fright and requires comforting from Gil, who explains that the old Indian is harmless, indeed he has gifted them with a deer haunch. Blue Back repays Gil's reassurance that this Indian's friendship is appreciated by offering the new husband a stout stick with which to beat his wife to ensure docility. To show Gil's enlightenment as opposed to this savage custom, actor Fonda forebears using the gift on Lana, although he underscores his rugged manhood by looking at the stick, then meaningfully at his wife, before deliberately hanging it above the fireplace for possible future use.

A little later in the film narrative, after discountenancing fellow church worshipers with overly loud hallelujahs, Blue Back interrupts a neighborly land-clearing get-together at the Martins to sound the alarm of approaching hostiles. He accompanies the fleeing settlers to the safety of the community's stockade and then virtually disappears for the remainder of the movie. In the last moments, after the climatic battle scene when the viewers are, presumably, emotionally exhausted from tension, Blue Back reappears as the victorious colonials look for the evil loyalist and leader of the Iroquois horde, Caldwell, among the dead or survivors of the conflict. The camera pans to a close-up as Blue Back rises, slowly pulls Caldwell's trademark eye patch over one of his own eyes and grins broadly if vacantly at this triumph. The last glimpse of the old chief catches him offering an open-palmed "Indian" salute to the new American flag just hoisted over the fort's ramparts.

No one who saw *Drums along the Mohawk* could doubt that Blue Back was the movie's only good Indian. All the others, save two drunken warriors, are bent solely on mayhem. During the raids and in the final assault on the fort they are uniformly menacing. With identical roached hairstyles—later known widely as Mohawks—they glide through the forest until the moment of attack, then frenziedly whoop, loose arrows, and pursue the fleeing colonists or later storm the fort. None of their number appear to be in charge; they move on the orders of Caldwell and other loyalist officers.

The only time individuals arise from the swarming raiding parties occurs when a curmudgeonly wealthy widow, Mrs. McKlennar, is awakened from a nap by the intrusion of two obviously inebriated Iroquois. Her character as a no-nonsense frontier matriarch has already been established before this sequence and it is immediately clear that she will not be intimidated by mere Indians. Audiences were delighted as Mrs. McKlennar slaps away the inquiring hands of one warrior who fingers the hem of her dress and laughed appreciatively when she successfully commandeers the hulking intruders' help in rescuing her bed from the upstairs bedroom of the house that they themselves had put to torch.

The Indian images projected in *Drums along the Mohawk* are unambiguous. The faceless masses of warriors are mindlessly intent on murder and destruction as aroused predators. They are a primitive force of nature made malevolent through the sinister machinations of the opponents of frontier democracy, the loyalists. As individuals they can be managed when confronted by civilization. Mrs. McKlennar treats them like misguided children when they are rendered somewhat malleable by alcohol, and Blue Back is looked upon fondly as a faithful tamed Indian become virtuous through Christianization and continuous interaction with the colonial community.

The film mirrors colonial attitudes and the new American nation's Indian policy perfectly. When resisting the spread of civilization, native peoples' savagery must be curtailed with force. Only those Indians who ally themselves with the white man can be counted good—good enough to fill the role of not overly bright but faithful retainers. Pacification and eventual acceptance of a new order of life, regulated by a benevolently firm majority culture, is their inevitable fate. *Drums along the Mohawk* permits no feelings of regret by audiences over this unwanted upending of traditional life by giving individual characterization to one Indian only, Blue Back. The director consciously or unconsciously avoided any sentimentality over the passing of the native world through the device of massing the Indians as a group menace. Most effective, however, in the dehumanization process was what the filmmakers left out

Top: John Ford uses scenes like these marching colonial troops
to show stalwart Americans opposing the oppression of the British and
the lawless savagery of their Indian allies. *Bottom:* Ford depicts Indians
as near childlike in their glee over the destruction of a colonist's
log cabin. (Courtesy of the Museum of Modern Art.)

of the movie: there is not even a suggestion of native women and children, no Iroquois families, no tribal culture, nothing to be lost that would distress the film's viewers. The cost of nation building is couched solely in terms of the colonial dead.

A decade passed before Hollywood produced a western that deviated much from the formulaic pattern of Zanuck's and Ford's vision of Native Americans. In 1950, however, the mold was broken when Delmar Daves directed James Stewart, Jeff Chandler, and Debra Paget in *Broken Arrow,* adapted for the screen from Elliot Arnold's 1947 novel, *Blood Brothers.* Purposely revisionist in its depiction of Indian-white relations, the movie earned critical and commercial success, inspiring a popular television series of the same name starring Michael Ansara as the Chiricahua Apache chief, Cochise.

The plot of this ninety-minute film is easily summarized. Tom Jeffords, an ex-army scout played by Stewart, while prospecting for gold in Indian country succors a wounded Apache boy. Grateful to Jeffords for saving his life, the boy convinces his adult male relatives, who appear suddenly and threateningly, to spare the white man's life. Later, in town, Jeffords confounds old friends and skeptical listeners with his story of Apache fair play. Angered at their disbelief, he hires an acculturated Chiricahua to make him fluent in the Apache language and tribal customs. He then sets out to find the secret stronghold of Cochise, acted by Chandler.

Apache lookouts allow Jeffords to enter the camp where he convinces a wary Cochise that he is sincerely interested in seeking an end to the enmity between whites and Indians. The chief invites him to stay a few days and attend a ceremony featuring Sonseeahray, Debra Paget in brown face. Mutually attracted, the young Apache woman and the older white visitor put their feelings on hold while Jeffords returns to town with Cochise's offer to let the U.S. mail deliveries go through his territory unmolested. The townsfolk are angry over a recent Apache raid and nearly lynch the peace-talking Jeffords, who is saved at the last moment by General Oliver O. Howard. The army officer asks Jeffords to return to Cochise and arrange a meeting to discuss a treaty of peace.

Returning to the stronghold, Jeffords is temporarily sidetracked; wooing, wedding, and honeymooning with Sonseeahray. He convinces Cochise that Howard is someone to be trusted, then fetches the one-armed, Bible-toting general to the stronghold. After several days of negotiation, most of the Apache leaders Cochise had summoned to the peace talks agree to try a preliminary truce as the first step toward a permanent agreement. The most vocal among the dissenters is Geronimo, whose bellicosity leads Cochise to banish him and his followers from Chiricahua territory. The truce is an uneasy one, but both sides appear willing to tolerate if not embrace each other.

Geronimo leads an attack on a stagecoach, breaking the peace, but Jeffords manages to reach Cochise, who personally effects a rescue of the passengers. A few days later, just as all parties are breathing easier, an Indian-baiting enemy of Jeffords springs a trap, attempting to kill Cochise and make it look as if the Apaches dishonored the truce. Jeffords is wounded and Sonseeahray killed as the plot is foiled. The movie ends with General Howard and the townspeople coming to the stronghold to pay their respects to Sonseeahray and inform Jeffords and Cochise that the killers have been arrested and will be punished.

Broken Arrow had much to offer early 1950s audiences, and its appeal has been lasting: students in my Native American and Cinema course at the University of California at Berkeley between 1977 and 1993, have responded enthusiastically to the film's positive qualities. Their approval has been partially based on having previously viewed several movies that are variations on the Indian-as-savage theme. *Broken Arrow*'s Native Americans are portrayed as three-dimensional humans who are capable of self control, sustaining a worthy system of governance and spiritual life, romance and good humor.

Jeff Chandler's Cochise is no treacherous redskin bent on destruction. Physically imposing, the Chiricahua chief is a true man of the people, courageously rallying his warriors to defend the Apache homeland. Although suspicious, he perceives in Jeffords an integrity that matches his own. Cochise becomes his new acquaintance's guide to tribal culture, leavening his teachings with a notable wit. He volunteers his services as matchmaker after Jeffords expresses a desire to marry Sonseeahray. When Cochise returns from a meeting with her parents he greets the anxious white man dolefully, saying, "You have no luck, her mother and father refuse your suit." Just as a chagrined Jeffords exclaims that he'll take Sonseeahray without permission, Cochise slyly reveals that he was merely making a joke at his friend's expense. Throughout the movie, the chief displays a noble but very human character, a clearly wrought role reversal from most westerns' imaging of Indian leaders; he even maintains his higher purpose, preventing Jeffords from exacting revenge on Sonseeahray's murders so that the truce will remain intact.

Jeffords's developing friendship with Cochise is very convincing, much more so than his romance with Sonseeahray. Debra Paget's Indian maiden not only looks like Hollywood's notion of native beauty—Caucasian features darkened for verisimilitude's sake—but she is unbelievably naive and overly girlish. Nonetheless, she is a fleshed-out character, a humanizing advance over the dull-countenanced "squaws" that comprised part of the background figures in numberless westerns.

Perhaps most revisionist in director Daves's conceptualization of Apache life is his rendering of the internal cultural life of an American native people. Drawing from the authentic ethnographic detail in Elliot Arnold's novel, Daves does a decent job of highlighting the White Painted Lady ceremony, and the traditional wedding ritual's simplicity is only partially marred by the hoary nonsense of pricking the principles' hands to mingle their blood and the use of impossibly anachronistic pastel-colored feathers to decorate costumes. And many moviemakers could learn something about Indian gender relations and mating customs from the film's several references to an orderly courtship procedure strongly suggesting that sexual license was not the norm.

Especially commendable is Daves's depiction of Apache governance. That the Chiricahuas were but one division of those Native Americans called Apache is made refreshingly clear. When General Howard and Jeffords come to Cochise's camp to negotiate the peace, they are obliged to wait four days while a large number of Apache headmen and chiefs deliberate the matter. Finally they are allowed to attend the final council at which Cochise announces his intention of signing a treaty, giving up the warrior's life, and accepting a reservation existence. The majority of the council support his position but Geronimo and a few others refuse. With the kind of consensus decision making used by the Apaches and most other Native American groups, the result is logical: unable to abide the majority's view, the dissenters, in the film's language, "walk away."

Utilizing the voice-over narration that introduced the film, Jimmy Stewart's comfortingly reassuring voice also provides a "feel-good" ending. He notes that the treaty he helped facilitate lasted, due in part to the seal of interracial harmony and cooperation that the general sorrow and dismay over Sonseeahray's death had elicited. The tenor of Broken Arrow makes it obvious that superficial differences of skin color and cultural variances had obscured a basic common humanity that spans the racial divide. Once again, given the past record of Hollywood, this was no small contribution and merits positing Broken Arrow as a watershed in the history of filmic portrayals of native and non-native relations.

Unfortunately, as much of an improvement as *Broken Arrow* was, its final form and message fell far short of readily attainable possibilities. And by giving an impression of historical reality, since the movie *was* based on actual people and events, the impact on audiences was dangerously illusory and convincing in ways that less subtle predecessors like *Drums along the Mohawk* could not achieve. To understand the veracity of these assertions, one must examine the historical milieu in which the filmmaking occurred and weigh the filmmaker's decisions about the movie's message by comparing and contrasting the cinematic product with its literary and historical sources.

During the late 1940s and continuing through the early 1950s, there was in the United States a detectable urge toward homogeneity. The wonderful exhilaration of having emerged victorious from a second world conflict all too quickly faded in the postwar realities of major economic and social adjustments at home coupled with the unforeseen international division and polarization of the globe between Communist and anti-Communist powers led by the Soviet Union and the United States. Voices in the federal government, the news media, churches, and schools expressed concerns about the threat of Communism's spread and the potential for internal subversion. Paranoia shaped the style of many pundits and politicians, one of whom, Senator Joseph McCarthy of Wisconsin, gave his name to an era that witnessed the House Committee on Un-American Activities investigating groups as diverse as the Boy Scouts and Campfire Girls, the U.S. State Department, and the film industry for evidence of subversive activities.

President Harry Truman sent massive economic and military aid to shore up democratic nations abroad and at home expressed support for a growing movement to effect a change in federal Indian policy. The acculturationist and assimilationist thrust of the pre-1933 period's governmental stance was renewed with vigor. Between 1933 and 1945, under the auspices of the Indian Reorganization Act (IRA), the previous emphasis on "civilizing" native peoples gave way to efforts aimed at preserving tribal cultures and instituting constitutionally based tribal governments. Controversial for myriad reasons, the IRA programs were attacked by some, within and outside the Indian community, as "socialistic" since they sustained the continuance of communal land holdings (reservations) and group (tribal) societal and political interdependence. These objections seemed especially timely to some in the postwar years and the result was an aggregate of executive and collective decisions known collectively as "termination policy."

Prevalent social scientific thinking embodied in the melting pot theory that emphasized the ways in which America's disparate groups' distinctive traits had largely disappeared over time, appeared to support the renewal of assimilationist policy. Termination of the special relationship between Indians and the United States that recognized Native Americans as discrete cultural and political entities was widely endorsed as a further homogenization of the national population. While certain tribes were listed as ready for termination, Congress instituted a relocation program whereby Indian families or individuals were encouraged and financed to move from reservations to urban areas. Thus "detribalized," it was hoped they would soon become indistinguishable from the American mainstream.

Broken Arrow's cinematic message replicated terminationist thinking by celebrating the friendship of Jeffords and Cochise, an actual historical event, while retaining older majority culture notions about Indians. In the process the moviemakers took interesting liberties with Arnold's *Blood Brothers* and the historical record. The film opens with Jeffords's voice-over and all subsequent action is narrated in the same fashion. He explains that the story is historically based and that the only departure is that when the Apaches speak their own language their words will be translated into English. The audience then, can reasonably expect verisimilitude.

Having Cochise and the other Chiricahuas carrying on conversations in this fashion represents a giant step forward from the grunts, exclamations, signs, and fierce glares that constituted Indian speech in most movies. Cochise's humor and Sonseeahray's astonishment at white ways would not have been possible without this expedient. Yet the filmmakers were not willing to leave old conventions behind entirely. Cochise and the others presumably would speak fluent Apache, but in the movie translation all articles are left out of their utterances; the speech pattern is understandable, scarcely eloquent. Jeffords's Apache speeches, however, are grammatical, if couched in simple declaratives for the benefit of his "primitive" Indian listeners.

Arnold's Apaches speak idiomatically: the decision to stress the "uncivilized" nature of the Chiricahuas was made by the moviemakers. Actually, they had already established a framework significantly different than the novel before any Apache appeared on the screen. Arnold, wanting to penetrate the internal culture of the Chiricahua and offer a native perspective, begins his narrative with Cochise and his band. When he does introduce a white presence in the book's second chapter, the novelist has already begun the process of making his readers see the world through tribal eyes, thus emphasizing the fact that the white man was the intruder on the Chiricahua homeland. In *Broken Arrow* the viewers know that they are going to catch a glimpse of the exotic and they are enjoined by the ensuing drama to sympathize with the Apaches, but always through the vision of Jeffords. It is he who initiates peace talks with the Apache chief, a demonstration of American good will and desire to treat the Indian fairly.

When Jeffords brings General Howard to Cochise to talk peace, the Chiricahua chief spends four days consulting other headmen and leaders in private. Finally he is ready to hear Howard's offer. The general produces a map with a 50,000 square-mile reservation demarcated for a permanent Apache homeland. Additionally he promises a skeptical Cochise that white men will be barred from the area, cattle and farming implements issued, and punishment meted out to any transgressors of tribal sanctity. For his part Cochise is expected to cease all raiding activities, including those against the Apaches' centuries-old Mexican enemies, and to take up farming and ranching as a new way of life. Jeffords assures his Apache friend that Howard can be trusted and the general explains that the treaty will be honored and guaranteed by the president of the United States.

In a dramatic scene, Cochise leaves the two white men, taking the map and written agreement, and presents the terms to a group of about twenty-five Apache leaders sitting on an open expanse of rock. He convincingly parries all unbelieving questions until one headman challenges him over the dictum against raiding Mexicans and foregoing that tradition for an agrarian life. Cochise declares that those who cannot accept the white man's road must "walk away" from the council. If a majority do so, he will relinquish his leadership. Eight or ten stand up, one at a time, announce, "I walk away!" and group behind the most vehement dissenter. He angrily tells Cochise that henceforth he will be known as "Geronimo," the name given him by his Mexican enemies. Coldly, Cochise orders Geronimo and his followers to leave Chiricahua territory forever.

There is not much serious difference in this sequence and Arnold's novelistic description of the negotiation; however, the film does considerable damage to the historical record. Although much more dignified and powerful, Cochise in embracing the proffered peace begins to resemble Blue Back in *Drums along the Mohawk*. The only way to be a good Indian, even in the liberal-oriented *Broken Arrow*, is to accept the inevitability of Anglo-American dominance and cooperate in the acculturation of one's people. This is not to suggest that Cochise's decision was dishonorable or mistaken, rather that neither was Geronimo's. Certainly his decision to dissent from a treaty that would result in irrevocable and unwanted change from the old Apache life was a legitimate one. The film portrays him as maddened with hatred, a real savage whose blood lust will not allow good sense to prevail over base instinct. Undepicted in the film, the Chiricahuas under Cochise settled down to a reservation existence, but it was three years before raiding across the border in Sonora ceased. Cochise led no marauders personally, keeping his word, but his son, Taza, and others were quite active with his knowledge.[8]

Every Native American leader like Cochise and Geronimo, confronted by the overwhelming military and demographic advantage of the American nation, was forced to choose among unpalatable choices. Continued resistance might well lead to annihilation while submission meant forsaking tradition and struggling with accommodations to a changed status of dependency. Generally the movies have not recognized the moral ambiguity of Indian decision making, positing as "good" those leaders who made the treaties and characterizing as "renegade" those who rejected forced acculturation. Filmmakers should not be unduly criticized; they only mirrored governmental attitude and public sentiment.

In studying the ways in which Indians are cinematically rendered, the scenes left unfilmed are often the most telling. I have theorized that *Broken Arrow* reflected the era of its making as far as glossing over differences between natives and non-natives: expanding and extending the film's narrative further illustrates that point. Oddly enough, General O. O. Howard's known historical personage varies little from the fictionalized portraits in Arnold's novel and Delmar Daves's movie. He was notably pious to the point of naiveté, and as dedicated to seeking justice for Native Americans in 1872 as he had been for African Americans right after the Civil War, when he served as head of the Freedmen's Bureau. Nonetheless, Howard's simplistic trust in his fellow man would not have extended to the lengths indicated in *Broken Arrow*.

The cinematic Jeffords and Howard reassure Cochise that any agreement he makes with the general will be binding on the United States. Both men, historically, knew this to be a falsehood. As the treaty-making era had been ended by Congress in 1871, a two-thirds vote of the Senate was not necessary for Howard's truce to be observed, only executive approval was required. In the movie, however, this point is not forthcoming and viewers are led to believe a *treaty* is being negotiated. Formal treaty or executive action both require final approval in Washington. Fully authorized representatives of the U.S. government on numerous occasions made promises to tribes during negotiations that were later drastically altered or repudiated outright later in Washington. *Broken Arrow* broaches no such possibility, nor of the many instances of unfulfilled pledges contained in treaties and executive agreements.

The movie's denouement underscores the notion of good faith and mutual brotherhood toward the Indian. Comforting Jeffords on the loss of Sonseeahray, General Howard commiserates, "Your very loss has brought our people together and the will to peace; without that will *treaties* won't work." The final voice-over by Jeffords reflects on the general's statement and its truth as the screen fades to blankness. The lasting impression is one of enduring peace. *Broken Arrow* was a short movie, why not add a few minutes to the running time and complete the story of the blood brothers, Jeffords and Cochise? Arnold required fewer than sixty pages of his 453–page novel to cover the ensuing reservation years, Cochise's death in 1874, and Jeffords's demise in 1914.

Tacking on the highlights of the reservation days would have violated the film's message of the wisdom of acculturation and assimilation, not the theme of brotherhood. Jeffords was appointed Indian agent for Cochise's Chiricahuas and strove mightily to gain an equitable peace according to the 1871 truce agreement for his charges. Historians and novelist Arnold have provided accounts of promised supplies undelivered to Cochise's people and the forced removal of the Apaches away from the originally agreed-upon agency site to a new location over tribal protests. They also wrote about the aging chief's despair over the white man's way and ever-lengthier and more debilitating drinking binges. After his death most of his people followed his sons to the barren San Carlos reservation along the Gila River, where the government had decided all Apaches from several small agencies in Arizona should be gathered. A few Chiricahuas such as Geronimo defied U.S. authority until 1886 when they were captured and imprisoned in Florida. A fitting end for a "bad" Indian and a downbeat finish for an unbeat film like *Broken Arrow*—no wonder director Daves and screenwriter Michael Blankfort opted for an early conclusion to their tale.

Western heroes battling Indians eventually gave way to detectives chasing criminals, spies chasing one another, and later commanders of spacecraft confronting diabolic aliens as America contemplated the new frontiers of the 1960s, 1970s, and 1980s. All other minority groups were shunted to the side as the nation's race issues increasingly revolved around a black/white dichotomy. Native Americans intermittently made headlines by way of Alcatraz, Wounded Knee, and the Trail of Broken Treaties to Washington. Vine Deloria Jr.'s polemical *Custer Died for Your Sins: An Indian Manifesto* (1969), N. Scott Momaday's Pulitzer Prize-winning *House Made of Dawn* (1969), and Dee Brown's popularly historical *Bury My Heart at Wounded Knee: An Indian History of the American West* (1970) ensured that readers could find information and insight about Indians beyond television and newspaper accounts. In 1970 Hollywood released "revisionist" westerns like *Little Big Man, Soldier Blue,* and *A Man Called Horse* in which Indians were ennobled anew.

Seven years later at Berkeley the new Native American and the Cinema course far exceeded my expectations by drawing 350 students. My elation soon edged toward a degree of cynicism as it became apparent that many in the class were seeking entertainment via cowboys-and-Indians movies more than scholarly deconstructions of film portrayals of Native Americans. A larger concern for me, however, was a paucity of movies with prominent native content whose plots were set in the twentieth century. With the exception of a few, such as *Flap, Billy Jack,* and *One Flew Over the Cuckoo's Nest* it seemed that Hollywood's revisionist imaging of Indians did not include placing them, cinematically, in the recent past. Apparently the romance of cultural reparations dimmed when the Native American present was contemplated.

The extraordinary critical and popular success of *Dances with Wolves* proved that the American public could still be enthralled by the exoticism of a vanishing native lifestyle. It is tempting to analyze the film and its impact fully, but that would not allow space to consider two other recent films that focus on Indians in the present, *Powwow Highway* and *Thunderheart.* In many ways not much more than a better acted and photographed remake of *A Man Called Horse, Dances with Wolves* also bears comparison to *Broken Arrow* in its filmic usage of a white male protagonist providing an identifying lens through which largely non-Indian audiences could glimpse *real* Indians and sigh over injustices comfortably distant in time. Unfortunately Kevin Costner's epic adds little that is new to discussion about Indians and the intersections of law, justice, and cinema.

Director Jonathan Wacks's *Powwow Highway,* released in 1989, had only a brief stay at theaters before enjoying fair success in video cassette sales and rentals. Although garnering a first place award in the feature film category at San Francisco's American Indian Film Festival, the movie was not the recipient of a large publicity campaign from its producers. It had no big-name stars and its subject matter dealt with the gritty realities of modern reservation life. This male-bonding road show lacked the romanticism of a period piece like *Dances with Wolves* to draw crowds, but its good humor, pointed commentary on mineral exploitation, and scenes of the interior of tribal and intertribal life has elicited favorable responses from Native American viewers. *Powwow Highway,* despite some obvious faults, did offer characters immediately recognizable to most Indians. Most importantly, the film depicts Indians, individually and tribally, taking effectual charge of their own destinies. Too often the idea of tribes making rational decisions in an organized fashion is foreign to Hollywood "historians."

Buddy Red Bow and Philbert Bono had grown up on the Northern Cheyenne reservation located in Montana near Billings. The athletic Buddy mostly ignored the hugely overweight Philbert and the two rarely crossed paths when they became adults. Philbert stayed on the reservation, pursuing no distinguishable goals while Buddy served in Vietnam, joined the Indian occupation at Wounded Knee in 1973, and when the film begins is working as his tribe's agricultural purchasing agent. Philbert's constant preoccupation with food is momentarily interrupted when he watches a television commercial in which the pitchman refers to his used cars as Indian ponies. He trades a bottle of whiskey, a small quantity of marijuana, and a few dollars for a rusty 1964 Buick LeSabre, promptly dubbed "Protector," the war pony. Before driving far in search of tokens to achieve warrior status and a warrior's name, Whirlwind Dreamer, Philbert is stopped by Buddy, who asks assistance. Buddy's sister, Bonnie, has been framed on a narcotics possession charge in Santa Fe, New Mexico, and her two small children placed in a state institution. Buddy has no car, but he has $2,000 given to him by the tribal chairman to buy livestock, and he entices Philbert to join forces to rescue the incarcerated Cheyennes.

The remainder of the film is taken up in adventures along the way. Philbert sees the journey as a modern version of the search for legitimacy as a warrior while Buddy continually derides his companion's quest for spiritual and cultural renewal. He gradually softens as Philbert's determination to "gather power" noticeably transforms the previously undirected and inept fellow tribesman. That the underlying plot involves an unconvincing scheme by federal government and corporate interests to keep Buddy away from the reservation to facilitate a coal resource grab is unimportant. The movie moves along entertainingly, if episodically, as Philbert's neo-traditionalism merges with Buddy's activist pragmatism to effect the rescue of Bonnie and her children. More damaging to the film's integrity is the heavy-handed typing of nearly all the non-Indian characters as ethnically insensitive or rabidly racist. This simplistic dichotomization of good Indian and bad white person weakens the movie's revisionist message, a fault *Powwow Highway* shares with *Dances with Wolves.*

David Seals, who wrote the novel *The Powwow Highway* (1979), was also employed to write the screenplay. As might be expected there is a close correlation between novel and screenplay; however, there are some significant differences. Probably following instructions from the film's makers to simplify, conflate, and bowdlerize, Seals made his Indian protagonists into near caricatures. Buddy's last name in the novel is Red Bird; the change to the cinematic Red Bow could be dismissed as minor if it was not a signifier of something important. The novelist Seals takes pains to emphasize the individuality of Indians and tribal differentiations. Buddy is first, last, and always Cheyenne, regardless of his AIM (American Indian Movement) affiliations and pan-Indian radical activities. In the movie he is Red Bow—a stronger, more militant warrior-like name than Red Bird—with Sioux friends who he is slightly embarrassed to have meet Philbert. In the novel Buddy is less contemptuous of Philbert, readier to accept his friend's growing spirituality; he is a prototypical 1980s Indian, anxious to observe the old tribal traditions, if he could figure out how. Apparently the filmmakers lacked faith in audiences' ability to recognize multidimensional native characters.

Powwow Highway does present several correctives about modern tribal governance, especially in the area of reservation resource management. One of the opening sequences features a Cheyenne tribal council meeting at which Sandy Youngblood, a Ute from Colorado, representing a multinational energy corporation, is pitching a coal contract. After listening to Youngblood's unctuous presentation the tribal chairman asks for questions. Several hands go up from the seated council members but Buddy Red Bow, leaning casually against a wall, queries Youngblood about his fancy new Chrysler LeBaron parked outside. The council members snicker appreciatively, then listen seriously as Buddy notes that the tribe's unemployment rate has risen since the last contract. He exclaims bitterly that the Cheyennes are not living the American dream; "this here's the third world."

The use of pointed humor to illustrate an issue and gain an advantage is common in tribal and intertribal politics. For cultures who traditionally reared their children without physical coercion and lived out small group interactive lives without the socially soothing benefits of western diplomacy's cocktail parties, humor became the prime agent of social and political discourse. Children who misbehaved were teased, if necessary to tears, to show respect and adopt acceptable modes of conduct. Those persons who sought leadership were consistently reminded through rough humor that their positions of prominence rested solely on their ability to give wise counsel and lead effectually.

During the 1970s, I showed a documentary film about an urban Indian group organizing a powwow to my classes in Native American contemporary society. Students were invariably perplexed at one 10–12 minute sequence. It tracked the election of an Indian man-of-the-year who, after being informed of the honor is immediately subjected to verbal harassment by the selection committee. I had to explain to my students that Indian politics demand that individuals singled out for attention be reminded that they are of the people and only temporarily elevated above others.

Later in *Powwow Highway* Buddy confronts a Sioux friend and former fellow activist, Wolf Tooth, about leaving the Pine Ridge reservation to move to Denver, Colorado. He accuses Wolf Tooth of selling out to yuppie suburbia and abandoning the struggle for reservation political and economic autonomy. Wolf Tooth's wife interjects, defending the move, noting that the couple has been the victim of drive-by shootings, that the Pine Ridge water supply is contaminated, and that they are tired of poverty and strife. Buddy's caustic bitterness is expressed a third time in the movie when he chides Philbert for putting his faith in the wisdom of "the old ones," their Cheyenne ancestors who prevailed against hardships and tribulations through spiritual belief and ritual. Buddy suggests that the ancient wisdom cannot withstand the avarice of the white man, who "wants our coal and our uranium."

Powwow Highway effectively dispels romantic notions of reservations as rural havens for "traditional" Indians. The realities of tribal factionalism and the complexities of native struggles to balance economic, environmental, and cultural concerns with the need for natural resource development and Indian-directed capitalistic pursuits are graphically emphasized. Although the novel's explication of the problems inherent in intertribal cooperation and self-starting economic endeavors without preexisting local infrastructures is muted in the film, the moviegoer does gain a sense of the enormous odds facing individual Indians, tribes, and the national native community in U.S. society today.

Thunderheart is a slicker film that covers some of the same territory that *Powwow Highway* explores. Rather than an interior look at Native American life with two Cheyenne protagonists, it utilizes a putative non-Indian, FBI agent Ron Levoi, to acquaint audiences with tribal culture as he investigates a murder on a barely fictional South Dakota reservation, Bear Creek. During the ensuing drama, Levoi reluctantly becomes enthralled with the Sioux culture and empathetic with the radical-traditional coalition that opposes the Bureau of Indian Affairs-backed tribal government, which employs violence to suppress dissent. What separates this shopworn plot device used in *Broken Arrow, Little Big Man, A Man Called Horse,* and *Dances with Wolves* to bring non-Indians to an appreciation of native perspectives is the fact that Levoi is one-quarter Sioux, a heritage of which he was previously ashamed. Thus the film narrative becomes a personal journey of cultural self-discovery and identification. The audience has a seemingly white protagonist with which to identify, the moviemakers can cast a non-Indian in the pivotal lead role without fear of Indian community complaint, and the film can claim to be an improvement over *Mississippi Burning* (1988), which was heavily and accurately criticized for placing African Americans as secondary in the civil rights struggle directed by two white FBI agents.

The fictional counterpart to director Michael Apted's documentary, *Incident at Oglala: The Leonard Peltier Story* (1992), *Thunderheart* dramatizes the mid-1970s political happenings at Pine Ridge. Agent Levoi becomes a reluctant participant when his superiors assign him to the case on the basis of his partial Indian ancestry. He argues vainly that he remembers nothing of his Sioux father, who died when he was seven. Throughout the remainder of the film, Levoi recalls memories of his alcoholic father, and more disturbingly, witnesses apparitions of long-dead Sioux dancers and finally experiences a vivid mental reenactment of the 1893 Wounded Knee massacre in which he is among the Sioux fleeing from cavalry troopers. Apparently he is a descendant of Thunderheart, one of those slain in 1893, whose name is among those on a monument in the Wounded Knee cemetery.

Levoi teams with Walter Crow Horse, played by Graham Greene, a cynical motorcycle-riding tribal policeman, to solve a murder attributed to members of ARM (Aboriginal Rights Movement). He is disgusted with the poverty and disarray of the reservation, suggesting that the radicals "should clean up the front yards first" before worrying about tribal politics. The brutality of the tribal chairman's "goon squads," and suspicions that his fellow FBI agents are engaged in a cover-up, lead Levoi to the discovery of a conspiracy to conceal plans to sell uranium-rich reservation property to energy companies. Crow Horse and Levoi bond, the mixed blood "instant Indian" receives spiritual guidance from an elder, and the FBI's unholy intrigue with the tribal chairman and his henchmen is thwarted, at least for a time.

Despite the unfortunate decision to have an agent of the FBI as savior of a reservation, and some questionable plot turns and cultural nuances, *Thunderheart* does serve to illustrate some salient aspects of Native American travails with the majority culture's system of law. In showing how an agency of the federal government, the guarantor of Indian tribal sovereignty, could work at cross-purposes with the best interests of native people, the film makes a strong statement of outrage. If viewed in tandem with *Incident at Oglala,* the message is amplified and sharpened. Perhaps the most telling aspect of both movies involves the scenes of violence on an Indian reservation, a federally protected trust property. The American public needs to know that violence bred of poverty and despair occurs elsewhere than big city ghettos. Non-Indian viewers need to know that reservation resources are not an unmixed blessing, that their exploitation frequently leads to problems of pollution, fraud, and highly limited rewards for the tribespeoples who live on the lands.

Thunderheart's least satisfying moment is found in its conclusion: Levoi rides off with a new identity and the reservation is made safe for those who remain. This gives the impression that traditional law enforcement methods, exposing criminal conspiracies and crimes, can resolve complex legal, economic, and cultural quandaries. There is a passing comment by Crow Horse referring to the 1885 Major Crimes Act, the legislation that awarded jurisdiction on reservations to federal officers in cases of acts of murder, manslaughter, kidnapping, and so on. Beyond that brief commentary, *Thunderheart,* in common with every other Hollywood product of my research, fails to address the underlying realities that make up Indian America.

Indian polemicist Ward Churchill has suggested that a moviemaker who "would alter public perceptions of Native America in some meaningful way," must focus on the present and feature "the real struggles of living native people to liberate themselves from the oppression which has beset them in the contemporary era." He goes on to list the problems such as mineral expropriation, involuntary sterilization, and FBI repression of activists.[9] He might have mentioned the chief legal conundrum: Native American sovereignty. A condition that defies precise definition—witness the numerous and ongoing attempts by the U.S. Supreme Court to resolve the status of Indians in relation to the federal government—tribal sovereignty is a cruel, mocking legalism.

In essence sovereignty has to do with the ability of a people living in a specified area to exert control and authority over themselves and their property. As a simple, indisputable reality, native sovereignty disappeared when the various tribes could no longer militarily and politically resist the expansion of non-Indians into their territories. Once effectually encompassed by the United States, tribal sovereignty was defined and limited by the federal government and was rendered partial. If dependent upon a larger sovereignty for definition and "protection" then Indian sovereignty will necessarily be uncertain, changing, and subject to trends in lawmaking and interpretation that are themselves variable according to public opinion and understanding. Indian activists are among those who place an overweening and ultimately heartbreaking faith in partial sovereignty. *Incident at Oglala* illustrated this point dramatically. It traced the capture and trial of Sioux activist Leonard Peltier for the shooting of two FBI agents on the Pine Ridge reservation in 1975. The agents' presence at Pine Ridge for the purpose of monitoring AIM activities in relation to *internal* tribal politics substantiates the hollowness of Native American sovereignty.

Movies influence as well as reflect the public's mind. Churchill's emphases on a present-day focus and the struggle against colonialism are accurate and will likely not be addressed to his or my satisfaction in the near future. The legal issues, inextricably a part of political, cultural, and economic struggles, are too complex to render them easily accessible by filmmakers or their audiences. I have a foreboding that once the present spate of Indian topical movies, inspired by the success of *Dances with Wolves,* has run its course, Hollywood will revert to form and mostly ignore Indians as a continuing presence in American life. When

asked by students or others to name the film that I believe best epitomizes the film industry's views on Native Americans, I always reply,
High Noon. Those who have seen this classic 1952 western starring
Gary Cooper and Grace Kelly are consternated; they recall no Indians
in the movie. There are only two. Dressed in cowboy western clothing
except for distinguishing black reservation hats with feathers, they appear briefly outside the town saloon, following the progress of Cooper's
Sheriff Kane as he goes about the business of civilizing the community
by shooting the bad guys. Their time as serious obstacles to civilization
is past and they are now insignificant, nonthreatening onlookers, only
slightly picturesque as they fulfill the ultimate Indian role—background
local color.

Notes

1. *San Francisco Chronicle,* June 22, 1988. This information appeared in the
feature, "The Column of Lists," compiled by Irving Wallace, David Wallechin-
sky, and Amy Wallace.

2. Much has been published about the process of Euro-American land ac-
quisitions at the expense of native peoples. Among the better studies are Fran-
cis Jennings, *The Invasion of America: Indians, Colonialism, and the Cant of
Conquest* (Chapel Hill: University of North Carolina Press, 1975), Neal Salis-
bury, *Manitou and Providence, Indians, Europeans, and the Making of New
England, 1500–1643* (New York: Oxford University Press, 1982), Dorothy V.
Jones, *License for Empire: Colonialism by Treaty in Early America* (Chicago:
University of Chicago Press, 1982), and Wilbur R. Jacobs, *Dispossessing the
American Indian: Indians and Whites on the Colonial Frontier,* rev. ed. (Nor-
man: University of Oklahoma Press, 1985).

3. The essential text of the decision as well as those of the Cherokee Nation
cases with expert commentary can be found in David H. Getches and Charles
F. Wilkinson, *Cases and Materials on Federal Indian Law,* 2d ed. (St. Paul: West
Publishing, 1986), 37–40.

4. Ibid., 40–41.

5. Ibid., 46–47.

6. Among the book-length studies of federal Indian law and its effects on
Native Americans are Robert L. Williams Jr., *The American Indian in Western
Legal Thought: The Discourses of Conquest* (New York: Oxford University
Press, 1990), Charles Wilkinson, *American Indians, Time, and the Law: Native Societies in a Modern Constitutional Democracy* (New Haven: Yale University Press, 1986), Vine Deloria Jr. and Clifford M. Lytle, *The Nations Within: The Past and Future of American Indian Sovereignty* (New York: Pantheon,

1984), and Russel Lawrence Barsh and James Youngblood Henderson, *The Road: Indian Tribes and Political Liberty* (Berkeley: University of California Press, 1980).

7. This analysis and that found in succeeding paragraphs were informed and influenced by John E. O'Connor's incisive "A Reaffirmation of American Ideals: *Drums along the Mohawk (1939),*" in *American History/American Film: Interpreting the Hollywood Image,* ed. John E. O'Connor and Martin A. Jackson (New York: Unger Publishing, 1988), 97–119.

8. Edwin R. Sweeney, *Cochise, Chiricahua Apache Chief* (Norman: University of Oklahoma Press, 1991), 367–90.

9. Ward Churchill, *Fantasies of the Master Race: Literature, Cinema, and the Colonization of American Indians* (Monroe, Maine: Common Courage Press, 1992), 246.

ELEVEN

Pubic Execution

ANDREW J. MCKENNA

■

*The old saw that a homosexual is simply one variety of sick person,
like a pathological murderer, only commensurately less punishable,
is slowly dying a natural death, I believe, despite its being a reflex
habit of plots bent on apologizing for their own sensationalism.*

PARKER TYLER, *Screening the Sexes*

Sex, violence, and cinema go together as do no three other ingredients
that popular phraseology has ever produced. They are, among other
things, what the three recent Hollywood box office smash successes that
I want to consider in this essay, namely *Basic Instinct* (1992), *Silence
of the Lambs* (1990), and *Fatal Attraction* (1989), have in common. All
three have to do with murder, and the first two concentrate on a police
search for the killer. That is reason enough to consider their interest for
a discussion of law and film, but it is on the topic of sex that they exhibit a bizarre and, I think, ominous thematic unity.

In *Silence,* a transvestite serial killer who flays his victims is pursued
by a female FBI agent with the eerie and ambiguous assistance of a jailed
psychopath whose anomaly is to devour his victims. There is horror
here, but also symmetry, order, which is a key factor in explaining these
scenarios. In *Basic,* a detective is seduced by a brazen blonde bisexual
million-heiress whom he suspects is an ice-pick killer who lures her victims into bondage. Symmetry is provided as sexual rivalry by the detective's brunette police psychologist, who is also his mistress; she also
once dallied with the blonde and is also, as if on that account, suspected of being the killer. In *Fatal,* a married businessman finds himself and
his family being murderously pursued by a woman with whom he enjoyed a steamy weekend fling. Since this woman voices certain feminist

viewpoints when protesting her casual rejection, she resembles the villains in the other two films to the extent that her sexual freedom represents an alternative to institutionally standardized sexual roles. Her defeat is assured in a blood-curdling reaffirmation of family unity, and in preference to the original and more ambiguous ending, rejected by a focus group, in which the woman kills herself in a way that implicates the husband as her murderer.

In all three scenarios we are on the margins of the sexual arena and they are occupied by a maniacal but nonetheless methodical criminality that nourishes popular assumptions equating kinky with killing. My epigraph, expressing the renowned film critic Parker Tyler's optimism about the passing of this equation, dates from 1973. It seems that a more deeply rooted cultural constant is at issue here.

Sex, except when it is predatory, is for the most part thought to be a private, personal matter, but the control of violence, indeed its unquestioned monopoly, is the law's preeminent function. These films crown a variety of sexual themes with an invariant violence that is the single common denominator of all genre films. Classified by critics as westerns, police dramas, and horror and science fiction, these films are defined by a conventional array of characters whose interaction conforms to a predictable pattern of events, in which A harms B and is avenged by C, or A, for C is only a heroic representative of the socially accepted values represented by A, the victim in the scenario. As such, the scenarios of genre films continue the tradition of the revenge tragedy that dates from the early modern theater of the Renaissance. I have argued elsewhere that they gratify a popular demand for violent retribution that ordinary legal procedures do not display to the public.[1]

More specifically, the three films being discussed here conform to the conventions of the suspense thriller, in which sex and violence are, to say the least, intimately connected. What is, I shall argue, peculiar to these three specimens of the genre is the way the public's desire for law is variously teased and tested by laws of desire that are reproved in the form of an aberrant sexuality. As Fritz Lang and Alfred Hitchcock have fairly identified the genre with the genius of their own directorial persona, their greatest classics, M (1931) and Psycho (1962), will come into consideration for their paradigmatic significance, that is for their development of themes and techniques against which the social and legal significance of Basic, Fatal, and Silence can be assayed.

Some further generic considerations merit attention in order to circumscribe this topic further. It is in relation to the display and exercise of violence that the suspense thriller differs from the murder mystery on the one hand and from the adventure or action film on the other. In the latter, be it a western, science fiction, or a cops-and-robbers film, violence is typically on ubiquitous display. Its agency is frank and open—spectacular, in a word—rather than sinister and foreboding, and its exercise is neatly divided between villain(s) and hero(es), with the latter enjoying the decisive share of its efficacy and with whom therefore the viewers identify unequivocally throughout in their demand for violent redemption of the social order. The thriller is closer to the horror film in this respect, as its properly suspenseful dimension bears on the awaited outbreak of violence, its stressful deferral. Irony is the prevalent rhetoric or master trope of suspense. If we define irony as saying the opposite of what one means, it translates here as saying: you thought X, therefore it is P; you thought there, therefore it is here, you thought then, therefore now, and so on. Villainy is not in doubt—sooner or later there is a victim—but its agency frequently is and its deployment is experienced as a threat to the viewers subjected to the ironic twists of the plot.

In the typical murder mystery, the crime foregrounds the narrative, serving only as the pretext for the process of detecting the criminal. Violence is a kind of preface or prologue to its often peaceful investigation.[2] The classic who-done-it is an intellectual puzzle for the viewer to solve, and its distinct appeal relies on the dispassionate and external observation of clues that eventually combine to form a pattern susceptible to ineluctable detection. The spectator identifies exclusively with the pursuer, with a representative of the law and of the safety it promises. These narratives obey an ethos of disengagement from the lives of the people composing the pattern. The viewing public's detachment is that of the ideal jury in an ideal courtroom trial, which would lead to the criminal's self-confessed guilt to everyone's mental and moral satisfaction.

Just the opposite is the case with the suspense thriller, which engages the spectator in an emotional paroxysm. The viewer's identification is strategically confused between pursuer and pursued, between the subject and the object of the hunt, which is as essential to this genre as the gun duel is to the western.[3] The detective in *Basic* may be the next victim of the ice-pick killer; an eerie household stalking scene crowns the denouement of *Fatal* and *Silence,* whose gothic decor recalls the old-dark-house-with-mysteries-in-the-cellar motif of Hitchcock's *Psycho* by way of wedding sex and the sinister. The viewer shares in the fear of the victim, but also in the predatory glee of the hunter. One fears for the victim, with the victim, but from the perspective one enjoys with the predator. What is programmatically suspended is the spectators' identity, their role as observer as opposed to their role as participant; and the latter role bifurcates as they oscillate between cause and effect, victim and executor, subject and object of violence no less than of desire.

What essentially binds *Silence, Fatal,* and *Basic* in a common nexus of suspense is this juxtaposition of roles between hunter and hunted, stalker and prey. This ambiguity, tantamount to a loss of self, is exploitable in cinema as in no other media, as the viewer's perception is totally and rigorously subordinated to the camera, with which, as F. E. Sparshott makes clear, the viewer is constrained to identify.[4] In live drama, attention governs perception as our eye roams across the stage with relative freedom. In the movie house, attention follows perception, which is governed by the camera, which the French call an "objectif," as if insisting on its ontological control.

So even as we identify morally with the agent seeking the killer, that identity is compromised when the camera focuses on this agent, as is the case in *Silence* where this seeking is the object of the killer's eerie infrared vision, which we share. In *Fatal,* as in countless other thriller hunts, the murderer always emerges on camera where and when least expected, as if endowed with a magical, Protean ubiquity. The stealthy genius and commensurate threat that the huntress and her analogues demonstrate is superhuman; in fact it is an avatar of the sacred. For suspense draws its psychic resources from superstition, which Tobin Siebers reminds us "means to stand paralyzed with fear": "The superstitious person is the one who hesitates, . . . doubting of another's humanity, called the accusation of supernaturalism."[5] I will return to the role of the sacred when considering the social implications of these films.

Lang's *M* exercises this reversal of moral perspective ironically, as we identify perforce at times with the panic fear of the killer whom the united band of professional criminals is closing in on in their methodical search of an empty office building. The same mechanism is at work in *Psycho,* where Janet Leigh's sensual and moral pleasure in the shower (she feels good and clean as she plans to return the money she had stolen to unite with her lover) is interrupted by a perspective from which this pleasure is the object of a murderous approach. *No Way Out* (1987) is the name of another (spy) thriller that exploits this ambiguity, as we flee all over the Pentagon with an innocent murder suspect

In sex thrillers like *Basic Instinct,* provocative sexual "outsiders" like sexually liberated Catherine Tramel (Sharon Stone), shown fondling an ice pick, must be demonized and destroyed to reestablish middle-class moral values. (Courtesy of the Academy of Motion Picture Arts and Sciences.)

sought by a mob of government officials; *Jagged Edge* (1985), connoting, among other things, boundary collapse, skewed margins, names still another, in which a sex killer (rightly suspected, it turns out) seduces his defense lawyer—and we are party to the seduction. These titles can be seen as so many metaphors for this crucial juxtaposition of roles, the strategic ambiguity imposed by the camera. *Sea of Love* (1989), from which *Basic* borrows the motif of the detective seduced by his suspect, is another telling title, with the detective awash in desire and alcohol that dissolve differences and distinctions. In each case, the viewing subject oscillates between these identifications, and this oscillation is the essence of suspense. In other words, what is *automatically* prey to structural suspension in cinematic thrillers as in no other media and in no other genre is the viewer's identity, which is usurped, supplanted by the camera in a way that perversely compromises consumer autonomy.

I say perversely advisedly. Stanley Cavell's insightful comments on Hitchcock suggest that he has enshrined Gyges, who invisibly beholds others' pleasures, as the tutelary divinity of filmmaking: "Voyeurism is not merely one of his special subjects but a dominant mood of his narration as a whole. Voyeurism is a retracted edge of fantasy; its requirement of privacy shows its perversity. . . . Narrative voyeurism is Hitchcock's way of declaring the medium of film, a condition of which is that its subjects are viewed from an invisible state."[6] This illicit pleasure is thematized, emblematized, in Anthony Perkins's peep-hole view of Janet Leigh undressing, as well as in the opaque sunglasses of the highway patrolman whose invisible gaze she experiences as a knowing accusation of her theft. It is the archly self-referential motif of *Rear Window* as well, where a journalist, housebound by a broken leg, assembles the pieces of a murder puzzle as he observes his neighbor through binoculars.

Thus the price that viewers pay for their privileged perspective is a compromise of their moral integrity. In this regard, it is perhaps Hitchcock's vocation as filmmaker, rather than any neo-Catholic mythology as often averred, that explains his notorious cynicism, as he feels in a sense mechanically determined to involve his public in the essentially illicit act of seeing without being seen, of spying on the lives of strangers, and therefore as being structurally privy to the obscene. As Robin Wood observes, Hitchcock's suspense "always carries a sexual charge in ways sometimes obvious, sometimes esoteric; sexual relationships in his work are inevitably based on power, the obsession with power and dread of impotence being as central to his method as to his thematic."[7]

The power to see annuls the power to seize, an impotence with which Hitchcock delights in contaminating viewers. For Hitchcock, Wood continues, "repressed energies are evil and the surface world that represses them shallow and unfulfilling."[8] The camera that zooms in from the sky over Phoenix (a proper name that facilitates the *terror redivivus* theme) to the rear window of the hotel room where Janet Leigh lies undressed in bed advertises film's intrusive power to imaginatively penetrate surfaces that both society and its criminal adversaries require for their respective functioning. If "no heaven corresponds to Hitchcock's hell,"[9] it is perhaps because the camera's specialty is the underworld, the netherworld, which he, along with other makers of thrillers, never fails to expose in various layers of undress.

The phenomenology of the camera explains in part what we might call the fatal attraction of cinema to the representation of crime, which like sexual intimacy requires seclusion or occlusion for its realization. If film is in some sense voyeuristic in nature, as maximally, almost sardonically and self-parodically exploited by Hitchcock, the suspense thriller, even more than the western, goes to the essence of cinema, where we are typically witness to what by nature requires secrecy: sexual intimacy but also theft and murder, the two centrally imbricated themes of *Psycho*. Only the last two concern the law, which perhaps explains how suspense thrillers attract our interest: by linking sex, which everyone is encouraged to desire, with murder, which everyone is encouraged, by legal and spectacular agencies, to fear. Desire and fear, emotional attraction and repulsion, are thematic opposites. If they alternate in these scenarios, it is because of a fundamental ambivalence of desire itself that we need to interrogate further.

In distinguishing live theater from cinema, André Bazin insists that "eroticism is there on purpose and is a basic ingredient . . . a major, a specific, and even perhaps an essential one."[10] The theater permits any amount of sexual display but not intercourse, owing to the presence of a live audience before live actors and actresses. The stage separates spectacle from spectators, but within the same ontological reality. Bazin's example of the phenomenon of strip tease exemplifies by contrast the laws of desire at work in film: "[The actress] could not be undressed by a partner without provoking the jealousy of the entire male audience. In reality the strip tease is based on the polarization and stimulation of desire in the spectators, each one potentially possessing the woman who pretends to offer herself—but if anyone were to leap on the stage he would be lynched, because his desire would then be competing with, and in opposition to that of all others."[11] In *Psycho,* for instance, Janet Leigh's undress in alternately black and white lingerie offers itself only to the camera. It is a view the audience shares with her lover in an opening scene and in a later one with her killer, whose deed is explained at the end of the film by his incapacity to possess her owing to a maternal prohibition. This incapacity is also shared with the audience.

Here I would hazard the conjecture that the murder of alluring women in the movies is authorized by their inaccessibility, a condition that imaginatively simulates the prohibition affecting any object that is desired too intensely by rival subjects, by what Bazin describes as competing and therefore conflictual desires. Women are murdered because they cannot be possessed; they are punished for their unavailability but also as a surrogate for the violence of rival male desires, as a proxy victim of the lynching that would take place if possession were attemptable. In this sense a symbolic lynching does take place, in which the woman is sacrificed as a surrogate or repository for all the violence that desire for her excites. A frequent complaint among feminists applies to many a suspense thriller, namely that women are glorified as divinities in our culture and then punished for making themselves unavailable to male possession, which engages desire in the double bind of so prizing an object as to ensure its unattainability.[12] In *Fatal,* where a woman pursues a man, the gender roles of this jealousy motif are reversed, but it does not alter the program as the woman is metamorphosed into a hellcat. I would further conjecture that we divinize movie stars to keep the license we eagerly identify with their glamour at a distance from a domestic, family order that would be destroyed by it.

The notion of the surrogate victim is part of the anthropological vocabulary of sacrifice, whose dynamics are precisely what Bazin is describing in almost identical terms as René Girard in his theory of human behavior. Girard hypothesizes that the violent outcome of competing desires generates a notion of the sacred in which humans mask their own violence. Bazin's imaginary scenario depicts Girard's notion of mimetic desire, which imitates and identifies with other desires in the choice of its objects and which therefore is structurally destined to rivalry and violent conflict. "To imitate the desires of someone else is to turn this someone else into a rival as well as a model. From the convergence of two or more desires on the same object, conflict must necessarily arise."[13] In other words, the moment that I and my neighbor, imitating each other, reach for the same object, we become rival doubles and individual differences tend to disappear in the mounting frenzy of violent reciprocity. According to this theory, the conflict is resolved by a lynching, whose victim absorbs the violence of all.

It is the essential function of sacrifice to contain violence by investing it in a scapegoat whose expulsion unites a community in driving out one of its marginal members. This figure represents a violence that is common to all members of the group in their mimetically and therefore contagiously acquisitive rivalry; it is as common, in short, as the desires that divide them among themselves. Scapegoating is a substitution mechanism that effectively channels the conflict issuing from competing desires. When the violence of all against all in competition for the same object becomes the violence of all against one by the arbitrary selection of a single victim of unanimous fury, we move from conflict to concord, and a community is restored to its sense of order and identity, however fragile and momentary:

> The universal spread of "doubles," the complete effacement of differences, heightening antagonisms but also making them interchangeable, is the prerequisite for the establishment of violent unanimity. For order to be reborn, disorder must first triumph; for myths to achieve their complete integration, they must first suffer total disintegration.
>
> Where only shortly before a thousand individual conflicts had raged unchecked between a thousand enemy brothers, there now reappears a true community, united in its hatred for one alone of its number. All the rancors scattered at random among the divergent individuals, all the differing antagonisms now converge on a isolated and unique figure, the *surrogate victim*.[14]

The victim represents the group, but only in order for the group to misrepresent its own violence by blaming it on the victim with whose destruction violence ceases to blaze in its midst.

It is the fragility of this order, prior to the institution of laws stabilizing property and conjugal rights, that necessitates the repetition of the drama in ritual sacrifice, in which a marginal member of the community absorbs the violence of the whole. Ritual sacrifice is often accompanied by a recapitulation of the pathos of mimetic appropriation; just as in suspense thrillers, sexual license is encouraged, mock battles are staged. This disorder is requisite to the sacrificial resolution in the immolation of a scapegoat whose destruction unites the community. According to this view, the law is heir to sacrifice, consisting in an effort to rationalize revenge. It seeks to individuate and punish only the true cause of violence, but it nonetheless serves the same function as its ritual ancestor in preventing an endless series of vengeful reprisals that are destructive of the community. The law monopolizes revenge to prevent its spread.

In this regard the properly ritual character of the suspense thriller comes more easily into view. Defined as the formal repetition of prescribed words and gestures aiming at consensual confirmation of publicly acclaimed values,[15] ritual often requires a role for the disruption of the social order if its restoration is to be successfully, convincingly reenacted. As Victor Turner has shown, a suspension of rules governing behavior and identity is a frequent occurrence of the ritual imperative, for a representation of disorder is required for the reestablishment of a prescribed order.[16] A provisional loss of differences is but a prelude to their reconsolidation. For difference to be reborn, the representatives of indifference must be expelled, which is why, for instance, twins were sometimes regarded as intolerable monstrosities. In *Basic, Fatal,* and *Silence,* it is a role inherited by those who represent a challenge to sexual difference.

In the emotional ambivalence generated by the thriller's dissolution of viewer identity, there is a fundamental relation to the formal and substantial exigencies of religious ritual, as the latter is assigned the task of affectively involving the public in the reaffirmation of communal values, of collectively shared ideals and forms of behavior. The public participates in a veritable rite of passage composing stages of separation, transition, and reincorporation, and whose middle stage "is frequently marked by some form of social isolation and a condition of statuslessness."[17] In all such rites, certain differences are momentarily suspended for reasons having nothing to do with the impersonal operations of the law—justice, being blind, is not cinematic—and everything to do with the imposition of sanctions and the definition of boundaries that the law cannot exercise. In these three films sexual difference is at issue in a way that solicits or flatters public endorsement of established codes and roles.

One film critic has described ritual as "the celebration of temporarily resolved social and cultural conflicts, and the concealment of disturbing cultural conflicts behind the guise of entertainment, behind what Michael Wood terms the 'semitransparent mask of a contradiction.'"[18] The contradiction affecting a modern, libertarian society bears on the license freely extended to desire, even flagrantly advertised to it on the one hand, and, on the other, the public's well-founded apprehension of boundary collapse concordant with that license. For this conflict to be resolved, it must be displayed, represented, dramatized, and the trick is to involve the public in the conflict without ultimately compromising its values.[19] The public has to care about the conflict to want to see the film; and to be satisfied by its resolution, the public must be assured of its remoteness from its own personal lives. It is not enough to reaffirm sexual difference. Any challenge to it must assume monstrous proportions for its expulsion to be justified. This is what transpires in these three films, which is why they draw more on mythology than on legal methodology for the lethal sanctions they exact.

Rituals are essentially collective, as its scholars remind us; their evocative presentation, style, and staging "are intended to produce at least an attentive state of mind, and often an even greater commitment of some kind."[20] Thrillers heighten attention to the point of anxiety, though not especially as to the eventual outcome; we know that the villain will be defeated, but the moment of the tension's release is the object of nervous apprehension. So too in ritual, where one is "surprised by what is expected."[21] Violence is suspended over the public and its judicious—and in no wise juridical, procedural—release obeys the ritual imperative of the ordeal. The threat of violence must be experienced as real enough to warrant its unanimous expulsion and as formal, unsubstantial enough not to contaminate the community of observer-participants. In this regard, the camera's eye as predator satisfies the first of these conditions while its limitation to celluloid spectacle satisfies the second. To a certain extent, then, the suspense thriller fairly epitomizes film's role as social ritual.

This threat of violence is usually accomplished in one of two ways, affecting either the identity of the villain or the application of violence that suppresses him or her. In the first case, where elements of doubt, misgiving, or indecision are entertained about the identity of the villain, the latter is likely to be one nearest to the pursuer, and intimately bonded with him or her. This propinquity is the case with *Basic,* where the frantic detective sleeps with both suspects. But this proximity also presides with *Fatal,* where the known enemy is a former lover; and with *Silence,* in the weird sympathy between the imprisoned psychopath and the female FBI agent seeking his counsel. This too is an avatar of the sacred in the form of the uncanny, Freud's *Unheimlichkeit,* which he famously described as something at once strange and familiar, sinister and ordinary, homely (*heimlich*) and utterly alien.[22] In short, the viewer is encouraged to entertain a properly superstitious attitude, both physical and moral, toward violence; we are to fear it as the very worst, for it is at once unnatural and neighborly.

In sum, proximity to villainy, intimacy with violence, is a crucial dimension of suspense thrillers. Why? Because the director shares with the public a recognition of the potential for violence in all humans? That is how Fritz Lang has offered to explain the public's fascination with murder: "Gradually, and at times reluctantly, I have come to the conclusion that every human mind harbors a latent compulsion to murder."[23] But if that is the case, it is also this compulsion that is subject to radical expulsion in spectacular, that is, monstrous form, in the form of a monster from whom the public ardently dissociates its sensibilities. This, I submit, is the thematic role of sexual marginality, whose criminalization repolarizes gender indifference to coordinate with the universal and irreducible difference between victim and victimizer, between the social bond and those who threaten it. And exceptions prove the rule. In *Silence,* all males, save the agent's tightlipped, steel-rimmed glassy boss, play sinister or loser roles, but this is not out of veneration for the feminine: she, to the contrary, is defeminized, so that she is made to resemble the typical hero of westerns, "taciturn, tough, uncomplicated," as they are described in an essay on that topic.[24] The suspense thriller entertains our intimacy with violence, but only to reject it violently in the form of outlandish differences.

Fatal also shares with *Basic* and *Silence* the other variant of suspense, which concerns the moment of the final and definitive release of violence. Family integrity is restored in the last few minutes in what is literally a gorgeous splash of ferocity: the Medusa, with whom the husband had earlier shared some sex with the kitchen faucet, is drowned in a bathtub, but only to resurrect again to be shot by the wife in a more decisively cleansing gesture. In *Silence,* as in *Fatal,* there is no suspense as to who the monster is, but we are tantalized by its deferred destruction. This postponement is the occasion of the spatial or perspectival oscillation between pursuer and pursued, an ambiguity uniquely available to the technology of cinema. This structure is fairly thematized in *Silence,* at the end of which we view an eminently vulnerable and frightened FBI agent through the infrared goggles of her would be-killer, who alone can see in the dark. But he is not quite alone, for that is a solitude he enjoys with the viewing public as a whole. Procrastination enhances the sense of our nearness to violence, which must be entertained temporarily for its expulsion, its resolution, to be satisfactory to the public.

Here I would hazard another conjecture for future speculation. Whereas it seems normal and natural to conceive that the public approves what is licit and reproves what is illicit, the actual case may be more complicated and ultimately paradoxical, namely that it approves what is illicit and reproves that approval by punishing a surrogate in the form of a killer whose taking of a life is the ultimate act of possession, of consumer appropriation. This is a rather sardonic and Adorno-esque view of things, but it conforms to the ethic of "compensating values" adopted by Hollywood movies under conditions prescribed by the Hays office: virtue is to be rewarded, and sin punished. Cecil B. De Mille correctly interpreted this as the basic duality of audience: enjoy sin if you preserve your sense of righteous respectability in the process.[25] This preservation is accomplished by the expulsion of a surrogate for our desires, who becomes in turn a monstrous surrogate for our violence. In *Basic, Fatal,* and *Silence,* this surrogate takes the form of a deviant and/or self-indulgent sexuality—for that is how a certain representation of feminism is voiced in *Fatal*—that is eerily and monstrously criminalized.

It is the entertainment of sexual indifference that links these films in a compact with the public via the display of a killer who does not conform to clearly defined sexual roles. In *Silence,* the killer's confounding of sexual difference is such that we learn that his particular deviation consists in the delusion that he is a transvestite, a delusion he goes to the extremes of sustaining by flaying his victims to make himself a suit of their size fourteen flesh. In *Basic,* the blonde suspect is apparently as coolly indifferent to being investigated as she is to her choice of sexual partners, one of whom, her lesbian lover, tries to kill the detective. This vacillation is replicated in the detective's erotic involvement with both the police psychologist and the millionaire sybarite, the blonde and the dark Venuses who alternate for his and the public's conviction. That this rococo scenario should bear the title it does reflects an intention to convince the public of a foundational link between murder and sex, which it thereafter associates with such polymorphous luxuriance as to assure the average consumer's remoteness from it. There are three naked bedroom scenes and one in a living room, performed brutally from behind. That is a lot of action for one movie, connoting an elemental sacrifice of psychic substance to erotic titillation. Nothing is less basic than the decadent opulence of the absurdly wealthy suspect, or the trisexual disco palace that she frequents, where we see straights, male and female

gays, and rafts of coke and smoke amidst neon lights flashing over gothic arches, a decor whose emphatic role is to link sexual license with the
sacred.

Film is not the same as ritual but just what substitutes for it in a
modern, secular, and egalitarian society, which is therefore massively
deritualized, desacralized. It is an officially open society in which nothing by definition, indeed by disestablishment statute, is sacred, and in
which therefore nothing by implication is obscene. (A few seconds
cropped off the opening bondage murder in *Basic* changed its rating
from X to R, assuring its access to late adolescents.) It is a society in
which every and any difference is paradoxically legitimate and open to
question, and presumably to litigation. It would be foolish to deny that
unbridled sexual license is a threat to a social order, especially one that
continues to locate its moral center in the nuclear family—though on
the other hand a symptom of the latter's debility may be unwittingly
suggested by the violence deemed necessary to preserve it in a film like
Fatal. The (anti)feminist motif is not fortuitous, as it provides a determinate scapegoat whose expulsion ensures the restabilization of values
to the extent that the antagonist's sexual freedom is made to represent
her as a threat to social order. To flag this she-devil as feminist feeds
public apprehension about sexual equality. Gender rights, like gay
rights (in which *Fatal*'s square jawed Alex, with her masculine name—
why not Alice, or Suzie for that matter?—figures as well perhaps) are
still hotly at issue before the public and the courts, and until or unless
their claims are resolved legally and institutionally they are fair game
for a scapegoat role.

Viewed from the mainstream as sexual adventurers, gays and feminists
alike occupy the margins of sexually and socially differentiated roles. It
is a position that corresponds to the frontier in western movies, which is
where the difference between a wilderness of violent appropriation, of
wanton brutality, and a civilized society was mythically determined by
six guns. In these three films, the geographical frontier is resituated along
a libido staked out by Freud's pioneering vocabulary, but the sacrificial
dynamic remains unchanged, sex being a stand-in for whatever can be
shown as threatening the hierarchy of differences upon which social order is constructed and which thrives on spectacles of expulsion for its own
sense of cohesiveness and identity. The ritual is available to countless
repetitions and variations because it is not efficacious in a nontraditional society, in which roles are subject to constant change according to the
openness and mobility of a career, which modern culture has wrested

from the closure of preordained functions and status that typifies earlier social organization. Sex thriller scenarios reenact moments of a puberty rite enshrining sexual potency. Cinema is the apposite because endlessly repeatable rite of this passage for a culture whose desires are as elastic and expandable as the endlessly expanding market that addresses them so relentlessly; and adolescence is commensurately, indefinitely prolonged for the benefit of the market.[26]

A tragically delayed adolescence is the thematic core of *Psycho,* whose victim wants to marry her divorced lover, and whose killer is the jealous slayer of his mother and her lover. This theme is legible, too, in the puffy, effeminate child murderer played by Peter Lorre in Lang's *M.* But it is on the issue of public conviction that the pioneering genius of Lang's first talking film comes into view. Here the killer is sought by the police with such thoroughness that the underworld, disrupted by the dragnet, is roused to the same cause and succeeds in apprehending him and subjecting him to trial. He is a destroyer of difference between sexually available and unavailable objects of desire but also between the two orders, legal and illegal, upon which a society depends for its own self-understanding. In numerous scenes, Lang concentrates on the symmetry between these two orders, enabling us to ponder the sinister anomaly of the psychopathic killer, who is inaccessible to routine legal detection because he obeys no economic motive. In short he is outside the general economy that defines a society in terms of law and transgression, which, as the master criminal Shränker makes plain, are terms clearly understood on both sides of the law. The social world and the underworld compose together a coherent structure, with police assigned the role of apprehending criminals and criminals assigned the role of evading the police in pursuit of their illicit gains. The child killer represents a devastatingly destructuring element since he belongs to neither order. "Every person in the street could be the culprit," a fact born out by the businessman who is nearly lynched by the crowd because he gave a little girl the time of day, and again in a restaurant scene in which mutual suspicion nearly brings citizens dining together to blows. Total anarchy threatens a city whose rectangular arrangement alternates with motifs of circles and labyrinths suggesting the volatile alternation of order with chaos in modern urban life.

Originally entitled *Murderers among Us,* the plural noun thematizes a potentially ubiquitous violence, which the change of the title to *M* does nothing to attenuate. For the killer is represented as a cipher, a letter standing in for anyone, that is for a socially and economically unmotivated compulsion to murder.[27] Our psychologies are commissioned to unlock the mysteries and miseries of such compulsive behavior, and each of the films under discussion here offers a sketchy interpretation for their bizarre killers, either in the form of a repressed sexuality (in the case of *Psycho* and *Silence*) or its unbridled gratification (in the case of *Fatal* and *Basic*). These and other suspense thrillers exhibit the thesis that a frustrated sexuality can have the same murderous effects as its excessive indulgence. It is a thesis that rightly suspects the symbiosis of desire and violence, namely that the forces of desire may ultimately tell out as brute force; but the thesis plays out in a way that clouds the issue by isolating desire in the bizarreness of pathological subjects.

If *M* forgoes any rational explanation and even thematizes its absence—Lorre: "You petty criminals want to be what you are. I have no choice"—this does not reflect an effort to mythologize the killer, a desire to make a monster of him, but, quite to the contrary, to demystify violence. The film humanizes him, to the point of showing the momentary sympathy of the court of criminals who try him, by representing his compulsion as utterly beyond his rational or psychic control: "Ich muss! Ich will nicht! Ich kann nicht!" he screams. He is identified—though not initially apprehended—by police as a former mental patient, and he will presumably become one again, to the furious indignation of his criminal judges. As he is seized by the impersonal arm of the law just prior to being lynched, the film leaves this question open as a problem for an open, law-bound society. M contrasts sharply in this regard with the demonic Hannibal Lector in *Silence,* who glories in his cannibalism for which no explanation is offered and no apology on his part either. The demiurgic delight of this fiend in his literally all-consuming homicide is properly mythical, whereas M's compulsion is poised as an enigma, a human debility that burdens a human society to deal with it. It is not a mere puzzle, nor is it portrayed as a sacred *mysterium tremendum et fascinans,* but as a genuine social and legal dilemma.

Perhaps the film's most stunning originality is captured in the moment in which M faces his criminal accusers, who are arranged in ascending rows constituting the image of a jury, but also of a gallery of spectators, such as we find in a movie house. They return our gaze as we behold them in focused array on the accused, and we are seen seeing by a symmetry that installs us in their place. It is in this framework that the killer fleetingly captures the sympathy of his judges by his declaration of impotence against his compulsion—before the master criminal-prosecutor arouses them to furious shouts of "Kill the beast!" Lang's focus alternates between the killer and his accusers, while deftly staging the volatility of the mob, as of any public, as it is swayed, moved, *mob*ilized now by an appeal to its sympathy, now by a blinding appeal to its ire. This self-referential scene effectively demythologizes the suspense thriller, whose vengeful retribution often requires a threat of a properly mythic, monstrous character.

The film does not diagnose the killer because its focus is on systemic operations and alternations, including those governing film consumption. If it seeks neither to judge nor to excuse, to condemn nor exonerate the killer, but only to endorse his containment, it is because its properly critical focus is elsewhere. Like *Psycho*, the film stages the economy of legal and illegal dealings, of upper- and underworld, outside of which the suspense thriller constitutes its drastic appeal. More importantly in the dawning light of German fascism, the film sides clearly with the law against the mob, whose mounting and myth-prone violence contrasts starkly with the cinematically detached and thematically impersonal arm that seizes M's shoulder "in the name of the law." These are the very last words of the film, whose symbolic resonance is reinforced by the silent, blank screen that reads "Das Ende."[28] The film leaves the killer's fate unresolved, for it is not interested in punishing aberrancy or exploiting its connotations, but in marking—literally—the law's paradoxically benign because blind and principled indifference to any desires that are nobody's business, to any behavior, no matter how outlandish, that does not claim victims.

Notes

1. "'The Law's Delay': Cinema and Sacrifice," *Legal Studies Forum* 14:3 (1991): 199–214. For my understanding of genre, I am relying on the manifold discussions in *Film Genre Reader,* ed. Barry Keith Grant (Austin: University of Texas Press, 1986).

2. The most thorough analysis of this literary genre, as it concerns the dialectics of violence discussed here, is to be found in Jacques-Jude Lépine's "Agatha Christie: Maîtresse du soupçon," *Stanford French Review* 16:1 (1992): 95–110.

3. See Charles Derry, *The Suspense Thriller: Films in the Shadow of Alfred Hitchcock* (London: MacFarland, 1988), 9.

4. F. E. Sparshott, "Basic Film Esthetics," in *Film Theory and Criticism*, ed. Gerald Mast and Marshall Cohen (New York: Oxford University Press, 1974), 226–28.

5. Tobin Siebers, *The Romantic Fantastic* (Ithaca: Cornell University Press, 1984), 34.

6. Stanley Cavell, *The World Viewed: Reflections on the Ontology of Film* (Cambridge: Harvard University Press, 1979), 87.

7. Robin Wood, "Ideology, Genre, Auteur," in Grant, ed., *Film Genre Reader*, 71.

8. Ibid., 72.

9. Ibid.

10. André Bazin, *What Is Cinema?*, vol. 2., trans. Hugh Gray (Berkeley: University of California Press, 1971), 170.

11. Ibid., 173.

12. This is the objectionable core of sentimental romance. The simultaneous emergence of this genre and of the horror or gothic novel in the late eighteenth century is traced by Walter Kendrick in *The Thrill of Fear: 250 Years of Scary Entertainment* (New York: Grove, 1991), though without giving a clear sense of how they imply each other.

13. René Girard, *"To Double Business Bound": Essays on Literature, Myth, Mimesis, and Anthropology* (Baltimore: Johns Hopkins University Press, 1978), 140.

14. René Girard, *Violence and the Sacred*, trans. Patrick Gregory (Baltimore: Johns Hopkins University Press, 1978), 79.

15. See *Secular Ritual*, ed. Sally F. Moore and Barbara Meyerhoff (Amsterdam: VanGorcum, 1977), 3–6.

16. Victor Turner, *The Ritual Process: Structure and Anti-Structure* (Chicago: Aldine, 1969).

17. James C. Livingston, *Anatomy of the Sacred*, 2d ed. (New York: MacMillan, 1993), 112.

18. Thomas Schatz, "The Structualist Influence: New Directions in Film Genre Study," in Grant, ed., *Film Genre Reader*, 97.

19. This on the other hand is the trick of *The Crying Game* (1992), which scrupulously observes the conventions of the political thriller, centering on themes of kidnapping and brutal assassination, but only in order to systematically and somewhat sentimentally subvert the conventional expectations regarding the distribution of gender roles among heroes and villains.

20. Moore and Meyerhoff, eds., *Secular Ritual*, 7.

21. Ibid., 277.

22. Sigmund Freud, "The Uncanny," in *The Standard Edition of the Complete Psychological Works of Sigmund Freud*, ed. James Strachey et al., vol. 17 (London: Hogarth, 1953–74), 219–52.

23. See Lotte E. Eisner, *Fritz Lang* (New York: Oxford University Press, 1977), 111.

24. Edward Buscombe, "The Idea of Genre in the American Cinema," in Grant, ed., *Film Genre Reader,* 16.

25. See Arthur Knight, *The Liveliest Art: A Panoramic History of the Movies* (New York: Macmillan, 1957), 112–15.

26. For an anthropological analysis of this epochal difference between career and communal closure, see Eric Gans, *The Origin of Language: A Formal Theory of Representation* (Berkeley: University of California Press, 1981), chap. 7. The market-driven logic of prolonged adolescence is explained in his *"Madame Bovary": The End of Romance* (Boston: G. K. Hall, 1989), chap. 9, "Flaubert and the Market Place."

27. For Lang's rich involvement with letters, as in *Scarlet*[ter] *Street,* see Tom Conley, *Film Hieroglyphs: Ruptures in Classical Cinema* (Minneapolis: University of Minnesota Press, 1992), chap. 2, "The Law of the Letter."

28. Another print of the film ends with a discussion among mothers who conclude that, however the culprit is punished, they will not get their children back and that they should watch their children more carefully. I take this emphasis on parental vigilance rather than on social retribution as another demythologizing dimension of Lang's masterpiece.

Class Action

One View of Gender and Law in Popular Culture

MARK TUSHNET

∎

The opposition between law and justice is a persistent trope in discourse on law. As John Denvir shows, for example, Justice William Rehnquist's opinion in the DeShaney case assumes that law is—or at least ought to be—kept as removed from emotion as possible.[1] The compassion that might be an element of justice, while admirable, is not for Rehnquist part of the law. Almost equally persistently, law is associated with the Dominant, usually the white male, and justice with the Other. The Dominant is regulated by rules whose rigidity must be tempered from the outside, by mercy and a case-specific particularism associated with justice.

These associations create opportunities for dramatic tension, particularly when authors also associate anarchy with the Other. These opportunities arise because Western culture valorizes both law and justice. By linking justice with the Other, the "law versus justice" trope implicitly valorizes the subordinate Other as well. When the Other represents anarchy, the "law versus justice-and-anarchy" trope seems to valorize anarchy, a situation that demands adjustment. Even in the simple form, the "law versus justice" trope associating justice with the Other creates tension. Because popular culture finds it difficult to sustain a moral structure in which the subordinate is valued as much as the dominant, those who use this trope must somehow reconcile the implicit valorization of the Other with the valorization of the Dominant that domination entails.

Several dramatic story lines are common. In one the Dominant simply prevails over the Other: though justice is an important value, law somewhat regretfully displaces it, to eliminate the risk of anarchy with which justice is associated. The standard "good cop" movie ordinarily pursues this story line. Seeing how badly the so-called system of criminal justice works to achieve justice, the good cop is tempted—usually by one of his colleagues, the "bad cop"—to violate the law. In the end, however, the good cop decides to follow the law. The usual ending introduces an ambiguity, however: following the rules, the good cop attempts to arrest the wrongdoer, and engages in a perfectly lawful but quite violent confrontation in which the wrongdoer dies, thereby making it unnecessary for the good cop to bring the formal processes of the justice system into play.

In an alternative story line law and justice are reconciled: the Dominant and the Other each are affected by their confrontation, and their differences are transmuted into some mutual compromise. The story line may show how the initial opposition between law and justice was misconceived, that law and justice are quite compatible, and that the Dominant prevails because he embodies both law and justice. *Twelve Angry Men* (1957) offers an illuminating example of this story line. After hearing evidence in a trial of a young man for killing his father, the jury retires to decide his fate. Without discussion, the jurors take a preliminary vote. Only Henry Fonda votes against conviction. Throughout the remainder of the film, Fonda is reason's calm voice, seeking at first only a discussion of the facts and then quietly reminding his colleagues that the defendant "doesn't even have to open his mouth" to explain what happened. The script establishes the opposition between reason and emotion by saying that Fonda's "most powerful adversary . . . is [E. G. Marshall,] the man of logic, and a man without emotional attachment to this case."

Fonda's chief antagonist in the jury room, however, is Lee J. Cobb. Cobb says that he has "no personal feelings about this" and is "just as sentimental as the next fellow," but he insists that the defendant must "pay for what he did." He praises another juror for not letting "emotional appeals influence him." Although Fonda is reason's voice, Cobb understands him to be speaking emotionally. In the end, we understand that Cobb's insistence on the defendant's guilt reflects *his* emotional state—his estrangement from his own son, and his fear that at least metaphorically his son has killed him.

Gradually Cobb alienates the other jurors. What is significant, though, is the order in which the jurors come to agree with Fonda. The first to voice objections to Cobb is Joseph Sweeney, an old man, sometimes seeming befuddled during the discussions. His age sets him apart from the other jurors. Sweeney explains that he voted to acquit because "it's not easy [for Fonda] to stand alone against the ridicule of others." After another round of discussion, Jack Klugman changes his vote. Klugman sets himself apart from the others because he "lived in a slum all [his] life." Next comes George Voskovec, an immigrant who speaks with an accent. He changes his vote after correcting a statement by Cobb's staunchest ally that the defendant is "a common ignorant slob. He don't even speak good English." Then comes John Fielder, a slightly effeminate young man, and Edward Binns, a solid member of the working class.

Fonda, the reasonable man, first brings the jurors most obviously not of the Dominant into his camp: the old man, the man from the slums, the immigrant, the effeminate. Cobb calls the group "these old ladies." But, in the end, even Cobb comes around. Reason is vindicated by first aligning the Others with Fonda as representative of what is best about the Dominant, and then by demonstrating that the apparently most masculine representative of the Dominant's reason is actually driven by suppressed emotion. Richard Sherwin calls the opposition between reason and emotion that pervades *Twelve Angry Men* "modernist," and argues that in a postmodern era law's effort to associate itself with reason alone will come under pressure.[2] Yet, the modernist legal theory implicit in *Twelve Angry Men* does not associate law with "hyper-rationality," but with Fonda's simple reasonableness. Fonda not only does not need, but actually abjures, a "rhetoric of the emotions" as the road to justice.

Twelve Angry Men sustains its dramatic tension by establishing a conflict within the Dominant, as twelve men struggle to determine the defendant's fate. Fonda prevails by demonstrating that the compassion associated with the Other—the first jurors to come to his side—is actually part of the justice that law can achieve. In contrast, Cobb's hypermasculinity and lack of compassion turn out to be facades behind which the emotionalism of "old ladies" operates to break the connection between law and justice.

More subtle works using these story lines may introduce normative and dramatic ambiguities. So, for example, in *The Caine Mutiny* (1954) Lieutenant Greenwald (José Ferrer) provides an aggressive and successful defense of his client Lieutenant Maryk (Van Johnson). Maryk had seized control of the minesweeper U.S.S. *Caine* because, he had been led to believe, its captain Commander Queeg (Humphrey Bogart) had become mentally unstable. Greenwald's examination of Queeg at the court martial leads Queeg to break down on the stand, thereby demonstrating the "truth" of Maryk's judgment. Greenwald does not see this as a triumph of law and justice, however. For him, the mutiny was unjustifiable because Queeg may not have been unstable when it occurred, and because military necessity demands that subordinate officers resolve all ambiguities in favor of their commanding officers. Queeg, not Maryk, is "the real victim in this courtroom." The commander, whose formal role makes him the Dominant, becomes the Other in the courtroom.

The Other may be an indigenous person, a woman, a man who somehow has escaped the bonds of the Dominant, an immigrant or older person as in *Twelve Angry Men* or, as in *The Caine Mutiny,* a man who would ordinarily *be* the Dominant. As Perry Miller argued, in *The Leatherstocking Tales* Natty Bumppo is the Other, standing for justice, against the Dominant Judge Temple, standing for law.[3] Ordinarily the Other comes into the courtroom as a defendant, to illustrate the difficulty of vindicating justice in the face of the law. Occasionally, as in Theodore Dreiser's *American Tragedy,* the Other enters the courtroom as a victim. The Other cannot, however, easily become a subject actively constructing the law inside the courtroom precisely because he or she stands for justice and against the law.

Authors have the opportunity to bring the Other into the courtroom as a subject as readers become comfortable with women as lawyers. Because the law-against-justice trope is so familiar, and so frequently associated with the Dominant against the Other, sustaining dramatic interest becomes difficult: the woman lawyer stands for justice, the male lawyer for law, and some mediating compromise is worked out. But, because the woman is now in the courtroom as at least an ostensible representative of the law, the association between justice and anarchy is weakened. Law's victory, and the preservation of male dominance, becomes more ambiguous.

The remarkable *Adam's Rib* (1949) is a useful illustration of the dramatic possibilities. Adam (Spencer Tracy) and Amanda Bonner (Katherine Hepburn) are lawyers married to each other. Adam is an assistant district attorney in charge of prosecuting a woman who wounded her husband in his "love nest." Amanda, outraged by the prospect of a woman being convicted when a man in a similar situation would have gone free, decides to defend the woman. Amanda's strategy is to show that women are equal to men. She fills the courtroom with prospective women witnesses who she hopes will testify to their accomplishments. A chemist testifies about her scientific accomplishments. An acrobat demonstrates her athletic ability, at one point hoisting Adam aloft and subjecting him to newspaper ridicule.

As Adam says, this turns the courtroom into a "Punch and Judy" show, a circus like the one in which the acrobat appeared. The courtroom scene initially appears to confirm the association of the Other (Amanda), justice (her demand for equal application of the unwritten law), and anarchy (the circus-like atmosphere that the demand for justice creates). The scene is more complicated, however. Amanda's witnesses appear because the judge believes their testimony relevant; on seeing the courtroom filled with prospective witnesses, his only action is to ask that Amanda call only three to the witness stand. More dramatically, Amanda's closing argument to the jury is not an appeal that they disregard the law to do justice. A Yale-educated lawyer, she makes a classic legal realist argument that her client did not in fact violate the law because the law itself already incorporates the norm of equality. She is, in Stanley Cavell's words, "acting in the true spirit of the law."[4]

Almost without a misstep, *Adam's Rib* sustains the ambiguity created by its refusal to reproduce the hierarchy of law over justice and man over woman. To propel the action, Adam must be only partly feminist; he tells Amanda, for example, "You're cute when you get causy." But, for the time, the degree to which Adam acknowledges Amanda's equality is remarkable.

Even a scene that momentarily seems jarring ends up sustaining the theme of equality. Perhaps the only real error occurs when Adam finds a secondary character (David Wayne), rather clearly presented as homosexual,[5] flirting with Amanda. Adam apparently threatens to shoot him (with a gun that, it turns out, is made of licorice). Amanda invokes "the law" as an argument against Adam's threat, seemingly betraying her adherence to "justice" in the courtroom. The scene is complicated, however, by the fact that Adam earlier appears to acknowledge the flirt's homosexuality, and to communicate that acknowledgment to Amanda. As Cavell says, "We cannot imagine Adam to take Kip's attraction to Amanda seriously,"[6] which makes his indignation at the flirtation, and Amanda's fear at Adam's threat, somewhat ambiguous. The overt message, that allowing justice to determine every case would lead to violence, is undermined by the scene's unreality.

The scene is needed to ensure that both leading characters are placed on both sides of the law/justice divide. In this scene Amanda restates her commitment to law. Near the film's conclusion Adam shows that men can do just what women do, by producing on cue the tears that he and Amanda regard as "women's" weapons. The film ends restating the theme of gender equality. Adam announces that he has been asked to run as a Republican for a judgeship. After a pause Amanda asks whether the Democrats have named a candidate yet. Having stressed a somewhat different dimension of the public/private distinction than I have, Cavell points out that Amanda "has won the day, made her private point public, but [Adam] has won the night, made his public point private."[7] In my view, however, the film denies Adam a victory in the conventional sense. He has lost in the public forum of the trial, and he may lose in the public forum of the election. Although he has shown Amanda that "his" public norms of law occupy some of their private space, the effect is not to establish his dominance in the private forum of the home, but only a relation of equality with Amanda there.

Adam's Rib is a classic film about gender and the law precisely because it stands apart from the ordinary run in accepting gender and law/ justice ambiguities and refusing to acknowledge gender hierarchy. The recent film *Class Action* (1991) offers a more conventional variant on the opposition of law and justice, male and female, Dominant and Other. *Class Action* is an ordinary courtroom drama in which law stands against justice.[8] It pursues the second common story line, of reconciliation and mediation. It sustains dramatic tension, though, by initially displacing the association of law with the Dominant and justice with the Other. At the film's start, law is associated with the woman and justice with the man. The film's narrative is driven by the effort to realign these oppositions through a "reconciliation" in which the woman abandons law for justice, while the man synthesizes them.

As is typical, the reconciliation leaves the relations of dominance and subordination unchanged. But *Class Action* fails to work out the realignment of gender roles with complete success, leaving viewers unsatisfied with the flawed reconciliation of law and justice it offers. In the end, this makes *Class Action* an ordinary commercial film.

Class Action combines a courtroom drama with a family drama. Jedediah Tucker Ward (Gene Hackman) is a famous left-liberal lawyer who has represented protesters in criminal cases and, in his most celebrated case, a defense industry whistle-blower, Jack Tagalini. When the film opens, he is representing a defendant who drove his truck into a polluting chemical plant, forcing the plant to close down for a day at a cost to the plaintiff of $427,000. The film's main action involves a suit by a class of people injured in crashes involving a car called the Meridian. Over one hundred crashes involving the Meridian have occurred, under unusual circumstances. The class action has been pending for a while, and the original lawyers for the class have been unable to develop evidence that Argo, the Meridian's manufacturers, designed the car badly. Jed inherits the case and is convinced that something must have been wrong with the car's design. The courtroom drama centers around the discovery of the design defect.

Argo is represented by Maggie Ward, Jed's daughter (Mary Elizabeth Mastrantonio). She is an intense litigator for a major San Francisco law firm. Michael, her supervising partner and her lover, has handled the Argo account for years. The lawsuit against Meridian is particularly important because Argo is about to be taken over by a corporation deeply concerned to preserve its image as a good corporate citizen. This makes settling the class action out of the question.

Preparing for the trial, Maggie notices a reference to a report prepared by an engineer, Anton Pawel. She tracks down the report and Pawel himself. She learns that Pawel reported to his superiors that the Meridian's electrical system was designed in a way that made a gas tank explosion inevitable if the car was hit from behind while it was signaling for a left turn. These are exactly the circumstances of the cases in the class action. Further, she learns that the company's chief risk-assessment manager—called the "bean counter"—had calculated that the cost of retro-fitting the Meridian at the time managers learned of Pawel's analysis would exceed the cost of paying damages to victims of the explosions: the bean counter's calculations indicate that there would be 150 explosions if 175,000 cars were sold, almost exactly the real figure of 132 explosions for cars sold before the electrical system was redesigned. Finally, she learns that Michael failed to bring the design issue to the attention of his then-superiors because he was overworked, because he saw the Meridian account as the one that would make him partner (as it did), because raising questions about the Meridian would have impaired his career, and because, after all, Pawel's was "just another report."

Maggie tells Michael that they must provide the Pawel report through pretrial procedures allowing one side to obtain evidence from the other. He refuses, saying that it would ruin the corporate buy-out and his own career. They go to the firm's senior partner, who authorizes them to include the information about the existence of the Pawel report in a massive document production. This will be delivered so close to trial that Jed and his small group of associates will be unable to locate it. Michael goes further, though. First he tells Maggie that he will transpose the digits in the document index, to ensure that the report will not be found and yet give him "plausible deniability," in Maggie's words. Taking the next step, Michael deletes the references to the report from the document index entirely.

Maggie has been ambivalent about the aggressiveness of her representation of Meridian, at one point calling herself a "professional killer." She goes to her father's office, where, leafing through the document index, she discovers the deletion. She rushes to her office, only to find that someone has taken her copy of the Pawel report. She reports Michael's misconduct to the senior partner, who responds by saying that Michael's career with the firm is effectively over. He also promises Maggie that she will soon become the youngest partner in the law firm's history, but he refuses to disclose the deleted information to Jed.

Maggie devises a strategy to get around her supervisors' recalcitrance.[9] Just as her firm had buried the Pawel report in a huge document production, she presents Michael with a stack of discovery material for him to sign off on before sending it to Jed. Buried in the material is the name of the chief bean counter. When the class action goes to trial, Jed calls Pawel as a witness. Pawel does testify about his report, but Jed is unable to introduce the report itself. In an aggressive cross-examination of Pawel, Maggie shows him to be a confused old man unable to remember even his zip code or social security number. Jed then calls Michael to the stand. On direct examination Michael evades answering questions about whether he had ever seen the Pawel report. Maggie's cross-examination is simple: she asks for a straight answer to the questions, "Have you any knowledge of a report calling any version of the Meridian unsafe? Have you ever seen one, read one, or heard of one?" Believing that Maggie's questions have neutralized Jed's examination, Michael says no. Her senior partner, though, is visibly distressed at Michael's lie.

Jed then calls the chief bean counter to the stand. Maggie's senior partner knows that the bean counter will testify that he had done the cost-benefit calculation, which will devastate the defense. Before the bean counter can testify, the senior partner requests a conference with the judge. In chambers Jed turns down an apparently generous settlement offer. The jury then returns a huge verdict in favor of the class.[10]

This courtroom drama occurs in parallel with a family drama. The film opens on the day of an anniversary party for Jed and his wife Estelle. Jed

In the supposedly progressive courtroom thriller *Class Action,*
lawyer–daughter Maggie Ward (Mary Elizabeth Mastrantonio) stands
by and looks with awe as father Jedediah Ward (Gene Hackman)
struts his legal stuff. (Courtesy of the Museum of Modern Art.)

and Maggie meet in an elevator and address each other as if they were strangers; only Jed's reference to "your mother" suggests the family relation. Estelle argues with Jed after the party, saying that he is too self-righteous and that she feels as if she were caught "between two bickering children." Then Estelle meets with Maggie, who criticizes Estelle for staying with Jed after "all those women." Estelle says that Maggie "never understood" what was going on, and that she "got a lot more than I gave up by staying" with Jed.

Estelle accompanies Jed to the courthouse for a hearing. Jed engages in some trickery to persuade the judge to order Argo to produce a list of former employees' addresses: he shows how easy he had found it to get such an address when he pretended to be an Argo employee who needed it. After the hearing, Estelle has a stroke and dies. Jed and Maggie then have a series of confrontations. Maggie accuses Jed of having an affair with his law partner, Maggie's role model. She says that Jed stopped taking Tagalini's phone calls after winning Tagalini's case and getting his picture on the cover of *Newsweek,* as Tagalini sank into despair after losing his job and his friends (eventually Tagalini "blew his brains out"). Jed acknowledges the affair but says, "Young love was always your mother's line; I was busy trying to keep the planet in one piece," and that he "spent my life trying to help people." Tagalini's case "changed the law," Jed says. Maggie finds Jed "guilty as charged."

Maggie's work on the Meridian case makes her more sympathetic to her father. One of the lawyers who works with Jed tells her that people make mistakes but must go on. Although the reference is directly to Jed and his affairs, Maggie takes it to refer to her relation to Jed. Another lawyer tells Maggie that her "biggest aspiration is to be [Jed's] mirror image," but that she does not know what he is and therefore cannot succeed in that aspiration. Jed and Maggie do reconcile, beginning by recalling what Estelle meant to both. The film concludes at a victory party at the bar where the anniversary party took place, with Jed and Maggie dancing together for the first time.

On one level *Class Action* is simply a story about the vices of excess and the virtues of moderation. At the outset both Jed and Maggie are excessively devoted to their careers. Jed's excessive devotion leads him to hurt people he is close to (Estelle and Maggie especially, but also Tagalini); Maggie's leads her into a situation where she faces severe pressures to act unethically in her professional capacity. As the film develops, each learns that excess is harmful. Maggie helps her father win his case (although, it should be noted, at some risk to her professional commitment to her client); Jed comes to appreciate how hurtful his affairs were to Estelle and Maggie, which leads him to initiate the reconciliation with Maggie. Maggie's difficulty on this level is not that she wants to be a "mirror image" of her father, but that she is just like him.

On another level *Class Action* is a "father-son" film in a modern guise. The dramatic dynamic of such films is precisely the conflict between the controlling father and the son—now, child—who needs both to escape his control and yet come to acknowledge that, on all the essentials, the father was right. One of the finest recent examples is *The Great Santini,* but the genre is well-known. Modern conditions allow the "father-son" film to be transformed a bit into a "father-daughter" film like *Class Action,* but, on this view, the change in the younger character's gender does not change the psychological or dramatic dynamics.[11]

These views of the film capture part of its dramatic dynamic, but there is more. Two elements of the film provide a way into the subtler questions of gender and the law that the film deals with. First, Maggie and Jed are committed to excesses that differ significantly. Maggie's excess takes over her professional life, which cannot be distinguished from her private one, for her lover is her supervisor. In contrast, Jed's excessive commitment to his profession leads him to difficulties in his professional and personal lives, which are sharply separated. His treatment of Tagalini shows how his ambition distorted his professional life; his affairs show how it distorted his personal life. Indeed, Maggie rejects Jed's public interest career because of his affairs; otherwise she might have followed him and his partner, her role model, into such a career.

The two dramas in the film play themselves out consistent with this difference: Maggie changes in her professional life, while Jed confines his changes to his personal life (in relation to Maggie). Jed, the man, expresses the good public life, to which Maggie must become committed; the women—Estelle more than Maggie—express the good private life, to which Jed can retreat.

The second element indicating how important gender roles are appears in the film's opening scenes, which switch between two courtrooms. In one Maggie is arguing a motion to dismiss before a female judge, invoking the "black letter law" and asserting, "appeals to the contrary based on emotion have no place in a court of law." She continues, "The law, not charity, must dictate our course here today." Her corporate client, she says, is being victimized by a person of moderate means. The judge in the other courtroom is a man, to whom Jed says,

"This is not a court of law." The male judge's courtroom, according to Jed, is "wonderland." He appeals for the acquittal of his client based precisely on emotion. Deriding the corporation's concern about the cost of its shut-down, Jed asks, "How high a price is that to pay if he saved just one single life?" These scenes introduce the law/justice opposition and align Maggie with law and Jed with justice.

The gender dynamics of *Class Action* consist of realigning Maggie, so that she takes the appropriate gender role. The film establishes pathologies of reason and emotion, which are—in the view taken in popular culture—misaligned in gender terms. In addition to working to get reason and emotion down to acceptable levels, the film tries to adjust the gender alignments. Yet only Maggie's role is realigned, either because the writer and director did not fully work out the underlying gender dynamics, or because the only truly appropriate gender role that popular culture can readily accept has the man embodying both law and justice.

The bean counter's calculation of the relative costs of redesigning the Meridian and of the explosions that will occur makes Argo the film's example of the pathology of reason. Maggie, though, participates in that pathology through her careerism and representation of Argo. The film ratifies the association of law with reason when Maggie says, "Someone once told me an emotional lawyer is a bad lawyer. I've been a bad lawyer lately." Maggie introduces the language of the law in her first confrontation with Jed after Estelle's death, saying, "Case dismissed; you're guilty as charged." She conducts an aggressive examination at a deposition to demonstrate to the senior attorney that she will not pull her punches simply because her father is representing the plaintiffs. That is, she must show that she lacks what convention says women have, sympathy for victims and concern for family. After breaking down one of the class representatives to demonstrate how costly going to trial would be for him, the witness asks her, "Are you fucking human? I mean, do you even care, Miss Ward, about anybody?" Maggie's pathology is not as severe as Argo's because, as we know, she does care about her father and has misgivings about her work. Yet her commitment to law and calculating modes of reasoning is excessive.

The film takes longer to show how Jed's commitment to justice and emotion is similarly excessive. In contrast to Maggie's restrained gestures in the courtroom, Jed embraces his client. He says that you "just got to go with your gut, you know, the passion." At the anniversary party Jed's dancing is uninhibited; Maggie can barely be brought on to the dance floor. All this might seem desirable, and Maggie's estrangement from Jed merely an expression of her pathology. When we learn the reasons for Maggie's estrangement after Estelle's death, we also learn that, in its own way, Jed's passion was pathological, or at least excessive.

The film associates Maggie and Jed with another opposition. Maggie is a modern woman. Not only is she an independent professional woman; her offices are located in a modern skyscraper, bathed in light. Her affair with Michael shows that she will not disentangle the sexual from the other dimensions of her professional and private life. Jed's offices, located on the second floor of a charming old building, are dark and cluttered. He believes that his sexual infidelity, though it occurred with his partner and because he was away from Estelle too often, has no connection to his professional life. And, of course, he is committed to the "old-fashioned" notion that the legal system is a way of achieving justice. Yet Jed's infidelity has merely private consequences, for Maggie and Estelle, while Maggie's affair puts the public safety at risk because it makes it more difficult for her to reveal the Pawel report. The old-fashioned vice of adultery is presented as less troublesome than the modern regime of sexual liberation.

Figure 1, which diagrams the relations, suggests several possibilities for resolving the gender "problem." Jed and Maggie could switch sides, making Jed the representative of law and Maggie that of justice. The film hints at this but does not adopt it. Maggie's affiliation with justice becomes clear when she betrays her client by revealing the bean counter's name. Jed's affiliation with the law is less clearly suggested when he threatens Maggie's senior partner with physical violence if the partner does anything to impede Maggie's career. With some difficulty, this can be seen as enforcing the "change in the law" that Jed accomplished in the case of Jack Tagalini, the whistle-blower. But Jed's threat of violence places him outside the domain of law, closer to the anarchy associated with the Other, even as he utters the threat in a judge's chambers.

	Reason		Emotion	
	Law		Justice	
	Modern		Old-fashioned	
Pathology	Excess		Excess	Pathology
Meridian	Maggie		[Jed at trial]	[Jed during affairs]

Figure 1

Second, viewers might reject the initial alignment of Jed with justice and Maggie with law. Jed's self-absorption shows that he pursues justice only to satisfy his own ambition, not to "change the law," which is only a collateral benefit of his ambition. And viewers can hardly avoid noting the fact that Maggie is sleeping with Michael. She refuses to move in with Michael because, she says, "I don't want them saying I made partner for anything other than my work." Her associates, though, do tell offensive jokes about her sexuality behind her back. She fears that she can gain power in the office only by her sexuality and not, as she wishes, on her merits. She is right. From the start, Jed is an archetypal man and Maggie a woman. The inversion of gender alignments is too superficial to require any response.

A third possibility for resolution is to adopt some mediating strategy. Here the film is more obvious, by giving a prominent place to Estelle, a figure who embodies the mediating strategy. Though she dies relatively early in the film, Estelle nonetheless plays a crucial part in two ways. First, her death provokes the confrontation and then the reconciliation of Maggie and Jed. She is the nurturing wife and mother, seeking to mediate between her two "bickering children." Second, she has a public life as well. Jed first saw her when she was a spectator at the Army-McCarthy hearings, and observed her lips moving; he flew to Washington to meet her, and she told him that she had been mouthing, "McCarthy is a weasel." In addition to being a wife and mother, Estelle manages a day-care center, popular culture's perfect mediation of the public and the private, at least for a woman. In what is clearly a set-piece to establish Estelle's central position, after Estelle's death Maggie tells Jed a story: Maggie loved peanut butter and grape jelly sandwiches, but Estelle refused to support the grape industry by buying grape jelly during the farm workers'-sponsored boycott. Maggie agreed and tried to find a jelly made entirely of artificial ingredients. Estelle objected, though. She did not want her child to eat grapes, but she did not want her to eat toxic chemicals either. Estelle's solution was to introduce Maggie to marmalade.

Estelle, then, provides both the focus and the model for an acceptable mediation of law and justice, reason and emotion, the public and the private, and the modern and the old-fashioned. Maggie's movement toward the mediating position is clear enough. She learns to separate her professional life and her private one, as the model requires, when she uses Michael's technique of concealing information in a large mass of material to catch him. Her actions in the lawsuit produce a just outcome when the plaintiffs win. Although the film is less than clear on this, she may successfully reconcile law and justice by playing within the legal rules to promote a just outcome by providing the bean counter's name as the discovery request apparently requires, confident that her father will understand the significance of the appearance of a new name on the list he received. Whether she promotes justice by playing within the legal rules or by violating them in the name of the higher demands of justice, Maggie tempers her careerism and her legalistic orientation. It remains unclear at the end of the film whether Maggie will continue to work for a corporate law firm or will become a public-interest-oriented lawyer like her father.

In this sense, Maggie *becomes* her father, not his "mirror image." As Maggie says to Michael when he calls her a bitch for setting him up in the courtroom, "I guess it's in the genes." The context makes clear that the reference is essentially to Jed, not Estelle.

Although Maggie's trajectory from an extreme to a mediated position is clear and occurs along every dimension of the story, Jed's trajectory is less clear and is certainly less all-encompassing. He does reconcile with Maggie, but almost entirely on his terms. At the anniversary party, for example, Maggie gets annoyed when she sees her father "coming on" to one of his young female associates. We learn later that she believes that Jed continues to engage in the affairs that destroyed her trust in him. But it turns out that the associate is a lesbian. (As in *Adam's Rib,* confusion about the sexuality of a peripheral homosexual character serves to clarify the relations between the leading characters.)

Jed, therefore, need not *change* in his private life; he has already done so, and Maggie needs only to recognize it. It may be important, though, that the issue of change arises in connection with Jed's private life alone, whereas it arises in connection with Maggie's private and public lives. For, in the class action itself, Jed's commitment to justice is completely unalloyed and undergoes no changes as the drama unfolds.

In one sense *Class Action* might be more satisfying if both Jed and Maggie moved from the extreme to the mediating position. Instead, she simply comes over to his side. By the movie's conclusion, Estelle's earlier presence becomes somewhat puzzling. Because she had been offered to viewers as the embodiment of the mediating strategy, we were led to expect that Jed and Maggie would come together to reproduce the solution Estelle embodied. It may simply be an indication of its creators' limitations that they failed to exploit the dramatic possibilities of movement by both major characters, overlooking the way in which the movie's ending left Estelle's role unattached to her husband and daughter. Those limitations are expressed in other ways. For example, the film inconsistently deploys the opposition between light and dark, and, although there are moments when the film notices the possibility of mediating *that* opposition by working with earth tones, it does not develop that possibility systematically or, most notably, use Estelle or her day-care center as the vehicles for earth tones.[12]

Alternatively, the fact that Maggie changes comprehensively and Jed changes, if at all, only with respect to part of his private life may carry real ideological weight. This way of seeing the film makes it reinforce the distinction between public and private, a distinction ordinarily important in the construction of legality in our society. Probably more important, by having Maggie change and Jed stay largely the same, the film preserves the gender relations of dominance and subordination: Maggie, the Other, cannot escape from the Dominant. This point is driven home when the judge in the class action holds his in-chambers conference to discuss Jed's calling the bean counter: "Lead counsel only," the senior partner says, and Maggie stays outside while Jed defends her inside.

Notes

1. John Denvir, "Capra's Constitution," in this collection.

2. Richard K. Sherwin, "*Framed,*" in this collection.

3. Perry Miller, *The Life of the Mind in America: From the Revolution to the Civil War* (New York: Harcourt, Brace and World, 1965), 99–102.

4. Stanley Cavell, *Pursuits of Happiness: The Hollywood Comedy of Remarriage* (Cambridge: Harvard University Press, 1981), 195.

5. Cavell refers to the character's "mild show-biz homosexual tinge." *Pursuits of Happiness,* 214.

6. Ibid.

7. Ibid., 216.

8. Although *Class Action* is an ordinary film, it is not an artistic failure. Analyzing it may therefore shed some light on the notions of gender-linked concepts of law and justice prevalent in society. Michael Apted, whose other films have been well-received, directed the film, and he cast a significant older actor (Gene Hackman) and a rising younger actress (Mary Elizabeth Mastrantonio) in the film's major roles. This too suggests that the film captures something in the popular culture's views of law, justice, and gender.

9. It is unclear from the film whether she devises this strategy in consultation with her father.

10. This courtroom story raises some questions of legal ethics that can be explored in the classroom, although the film does not really grapple with the ethical issues. One might ask whether burying a damaging document in a massive disclosure violates the discovery rules, whether Maggie's personal decision to disclose the bean counter's name violates her obligation to her client, and what Maggie should have done on learning that her law firm would not respond—within the lawsuit—when it found out that her supervising attorney had concealed and destroyed material required to be produced on discovery.

11. I can imagine, of course, that the best versions of a modern "father-daughter" film—and, eventually, a truly modern "father-son" film—would introduce a specifically sexual tension between the father and the child. In the typical "father-son" film, however, the potential Oedipal element is rarely drawn on.

12. One might speculate about the reasons for differences between *Adam's Rib* and *Class Action*. (1) The strength of the former might result from the presence of extremely talented artists in every part of the film, from director to screenwriter to actors and actresses. (2) Production conditions in the late 1940s might have given those artists more room to express their personal visions than contemporary ones do. (3) In particular, the roles then available for stars like Katherine Hepburn may have allowed those stars to appear as equals of their male counterparts, in ways less common today.

THIRTEEN

Outlaw Women

Thelma and Louise

ELIZABETH V. SPELMAN AND MARTHA MINOW

∎

In the film *Adam's Rib* (1949), Katharine Hepburn plays an attorney defending a woman charged with attempting to murder her adulterous husband. In her closing argument, Hepburn urges the jury to imagine how they would sympathize with a man charged with attempting to murder his adulterous wife. As Hepburn describes each of the individuals—the defendant, the victim, the third parties—she reverses their genders and the film conjures up images of the male characters as female and the female as male. It does not really work. At least for many viewers, the attempt seems awkward and unbelievable. But can anyone elicit sympathy for women outlaws without invoking analogies to men admired or excused for breaking the law?

The noble "outlaw" is an oddly revered character, loosely associated in United States folklore with the West and with romantic ideas about personal development and freedom. The paradigmatic noble outlaw is a male whose lawbreaking can be understood as in some sense virtuous. It is therefore more unlikely that he will belong to any racial or ethnic group that has to fight the perception that their lawbreaking activities can only be the expression of "criminal proclivities." In short, the James Brothers could not have been Mexican American or African American and still become American heroes. Nor could they have been the James Sisters—certainly not if we imagine such women's "outlaw" behavior to involve rejecting the sexism they find in society, leaving their husbands, or defying social constraints. Unlike their male counterparts, whose "deviant" outlaw behavior heightens their manhood, such women risk appearing to be not just deviant citizens but deviant women.

There are, then, powerful constraints on the capacity of many United States observers to sympathize with lawbreakers who are not males of a certain description. But the movie *Thelma and Louise* (1991) attempts to make such understanding possible. Granted, *Thelma and Louise* is not a work of politics, law, or philosophy. It is a movie, and it offers no sustained argument. Nor does it pretend to document reality. Unlike many movies, *Thelma and Louise* provoked widespread and intense public debates. The film gives us an occasion to explore not only what it means in our society for women to be outlaws, but also: (1) how different kinds of viewers might perceive and judge outlaw women; (2) how class and race, along with gender, may influence viewer understandings of outlaw figures; and (3) what the world and moral reasoning might look like from the perspectives of the women characters cast as film outlaws.[1]

The Story and Its Viewers

Thelma and Louise combines the genres of buddy films and on-the-road stories; it is an outlaw film with the twist that the outlaws are two women. They are outlaws on their own; unlike male outlaws' "molls," they break the law without men. Susan Sarandon and Geena Davis play Louise, a waitress, and Thelma, a housewife, who leave a boyfriend and a husband for a weekend of fishing. But instead of fun, they meet crisis. Picked up at a dance-bar by a man who makes aggressive and ultimately violent sexual advances, Thelma is saved when Louise brandishes a gun. But when Harlan, the assaulter, is unrepentant, Louise shoots and kills him.

At that moment, Louise and Thelma become outlaws, and they hit the road. As state police and FBI agents search for them, Thelma and Louise head for Mexico, trying to deal with the men they left and the men they encounter. On their way, they encounter a truck driver who ogles them, and a hitchhiker who seduces Thelma and then steals Louise's money. Thelma sticks up a convenience store to make up for leaving the hitchhiker alone to steal Louise's money. A police officer stops them for speeding, but Thelma and Louise lock him in the trunk of his squad car. They make telephone contact with the detective who is tracking them and who seems to know about a prior experience with sexual assault Louise endured in Texas.

Reaching ever more spectacular southwestern vistas on their route to Mexico, Thelma and Louise speculate about their crimes, their pasts, their friendship, and their lives. They also undertake a kind of fantasy revenge against the trucker who has harassed them on the road. A chase scene complete with hordes of police and FBI agents includes moments of escape and moments that make capture seem inevitable. But at the close, the two women choose to drive off into the Grand Canyon rather than face death through a shoot out, or worse, capture and a criminal trial. The film does not leave the viewer with this suicide scene, however. Instead, it quickly returns to earlier images of hope, excitement, and pleasure on the faces of the two women.[2]

This is at least one version of the film's plot-line and structure. Yet, as Mary Joe Frug taught in her article, "Re-Reading Contracts,"[3] we can all understand a text better if we see how different readers read it differently. The mass media played up these differences, often framing them as male versus female reactions. For example, the *Boston Globe* ran under the heading "The Great Debate over 'Thelma and Louise,'" two opposing columns, one by a woman defending the film and one by a man attacking it.[4] The man, John Robinson, wrote: "Male bashing, once the sport of hairy women in denim jackets and combat boots, has flushed like toxic waste into the culture mainstream with the vengeance fantasy 'Thelma and Louise.'"[5] Reading the movie against a backdrop of feminist cultural and political activities, he found that "'Thelma and Louise' is the last straw."[6] He objected to the absence of enough sympathetic male characters who are strong but not obnoxious.[7] He acknowledged that more tyrants and abusers are found among men than among women,[8] yet he asserted, "'Thelma and Louise' would have the world believe that a good man is an exception, and that bad woman is an oxymoron." He also objected to the entrance into mainstream culture of the kinds of feminist messages that previously had been reserved for more elite artistic expression.[9]

The contrasting column by a woman reviewer, Diane White, argued that "there wasn't enough man-bashing in 'Thelma and Louise.'"[10] White wrote, "I wish they'd nailed that little weasel who ran off with all their money. And Thelma's toad-like yupster husband deserved more than just an emotional shock." Reversing the familiar comment that feminists take things too seriously and lack a sense of humor, White continued, "It's only a movie, and a comedy at that." Yet she herself reported on the strong positive reaction of women in her audience: "They cheered when

Louise plugged the roadhouse cowboy who was trying to rape Thelma. And when the two characters blew up the rig of a leering, tongue-waggling trucker, they cheered even louder." She concluded that "for some women 'Thelma and Louise' is a cathartic movie, a bit of wish fulfillment. . . . I know what it's like to be so brutalized and humiliated by a man that you'd like to murder him. But I didn't. Why? Because life isn't a movie. Besides, unlike Louise, I didn't have a gun handy."[11]

These reviews draw the differences in viewers strictly on gender lines, which may be somewhat simplistic. People who share genders may nonetheless respond differently to the film, perhaps because of differences of class, race, or other aspects of personal identity and experience. Similarly, conflicting viewer responses to the public drama enacted when Professor Anita Hill accused Supreme Court nominee Clarence Thomas of sexual harassment reflected not only gender, but also racial, class, and other differences in points of view. Nonetheless, an asserted gender difference or gender gap marked a striking dimension of the public debates over both the film and the nomination. It seemed to matter to many observers that more women than men would understand why a victim of sexual harassment would not complain, quit her job, or refuse to follow the harassing boss to an improved career opportunity; it seemed to matter to many observers that many women viewers could identify with and feel empowered by Thelma and Louise, while male viewers might feel threatened by their actions.[12]

Yet the risk in typing viewers according to sociological characteristics is to replicate the pigeonholes that the movie itself critiques. One reviewer optimistically argued that the movie grants empowerment to two women in the midst of the worst trouble of their lives, and "we all gain a realization not only of the different needs of the sexes, but also of how deeply society pigeonholes men and women, and what it takes to even attempt to get out."[13] "We all gain" is the hopeful statement that any viewer, regardless of status identity, can identify with the characters in the movie. The gendered reaction to the film portrayed or manufactured by some reviews neglects this possibility of identification across differences. Actress Geena Davis, who plays Thelma, argued "'Men who feel threatened by this movie are identifying with the wrong characters. It's not a movie to set the record straight. This is a movie about people claiming responsibility for their own lives. This is a film about freedom. Anyone should be able to identify with it.'"[14] Similarly, screenplay author Callie Khouri maintained that the movie is not hostile toward men: "'I think it is hostile toward idiots.'"[15]

Yet even these comments imply that the only differences that matter are gender differences. We think it's more complicated than that. A closer look at "outlaw" status may help.

The Canon of the Gun: On Outlaw Pedigrees

Are Thelma and Louise noble outlaws, or is some other description of their lawbreaking more apt? Insofar as "outlaw" suggests someone who self-consciously and consistently breaks the law, Thelma and Louise qualify as outlaws: they knowingly break a number of laws; they come to take pleasure in breaking them, especially as they become more skilled and capable of a kind of fastidiousness in doing so. Escaping the long arm of the law becomes central to their lives and indeed to their deaths. Law's centrality does not mean its utility; Thelma and Louise never feel that they can try to use the law to accomplish their ends such as they emerge.

North American history and literature are filled with examples of daring figures who are presented as having to break the law in order to bring about a kind of justice the law or its agents cannot effect. One late twentieth-century version of this type not surprisingly rode the subway instead of a horse: in a much publicized case, New York City dweller Bernhard Goetz, fed up with being harassed on public transportation, shot at four young men trying to exact money from him on the subway.[16] One of the young men was seriously injured.[17] According to the jury in *People v. Goetz,* the only illegal thing Goetz did was to carry an unlicensed handgun.[18]

Whether or not the facts in the case were sufficient to establish that Goetz acted in self-defense, Goetz became a hero, at least in some communities. His status as a hero reveals the public's admiration for one who dares to do something not permitted by law, and especially for one who enacts common fantasies of unlawful but just revenge.[19]

Flouting the law may be necessary, but it is by no means a sufficient condition for being considered a *noble* outlaw. Those who hailed Goetz as a hero did not admire the young would-be robbers for *their* lawbreaking. Goetz could not have been treated as a noble lawbreaker—a hero—unless those on whom he exacted revenge were seen as ignoble lawbreakers, indeed as criminal scum.

Goetz was frequently referred to as the "Subway Vigilante." "Vigilante" is one of many terms for lawbreakers. Vigilante, outlaw, avenger, bandit, fugitive, criminal, deviant, scofflaw, and thug all have different if not fully determinate meanings, and each suggests a variety of evaluations. When the adjective "noble" is added, the elevated status of public appeal transforms the lawbreaker into a hero.

But as reflections on the *Goetz* case suggest, the gratitude and admiration we feel toward lawbreakers depends on the observer's sense of the justice or fairness of the vision that motivates or is used to defend the lawbreaking activities. This, in turn, depends largely on whether the observer believes the victims of such actions deserve what happens to them. The observer's conclusions are likely to rest not only on what the purported noble outlaws believe but on who they are. Suppose Goetz had been a black man, and the young men he shot at, white?[20] Or suppose that Goetz, the white man, had shot at other whites—say, fraternity boys out on a little spree?[21]

Viewers of *Thelma and Louise* who are ready to regard the two women as noble outlaws have to be able to think about both the women and those affected by their actions in fairly specific ways. Thelma and Louise have to be seen as acting, preferably self-consciously, in accordance with a just principle or concern. The would-be rapist, Harlan, and others directly affected by the women's actions have to be seen as in some sense deserving what they got, whether or not the law prohibits their being treated that way.

There is, then, much that complicates the answer to the question of whether Thelma and Louise are noble outlaws. It does seem fairly clear that some viewers who love the film greatly admire the outlaw qualities of Thelma and Louise, while many viewers upset by the film are worried that it glorifies an ignoble kind of lawlessness. As Callie Khouri has suggested, perhaps both reactions mistake the film for a political treatise.[22] But even if the film is not such a treatise, it is naive or disingenuous to think about it and the reaction to it in isolation from a volatile political climate in which those clamoring for "law and order" rarely join protests against the everyday forms of the abuse of women on exhibition in the film.

The law has done little to protect women from the violence of rape and other forms of sexual abuse. In such a context, Thelma and Louise's resistance to Harlan's sense of entitlement, and to his assumption of immunity, invite sympathetic viewers to see the women as heroines. It is of course one thing to fight back as Thelma does, and another to shoot Harlan dead as Louise does. But sympathetic viewers' high regard for Thelma's acts of self-defense—acts sanctioned by law—could flow easily into enthusiastic admiration for Louise's murder of Harlan. The movie itself offers an explanation for that murder, but not thereby a justification.[23] Such admiration arises, when it does, despite the fact— or maybe in part because of it—that the canonical list of noble outlaws (such as Robin Hood, Jesse James, and Bernhard Goetz) includes very few women. Such admiration arises, when it does, despite the fact that everyday violence against women has not been among the canonical evils to which outlaw behavior has been regarded as an appropriate response. Young black men who seem threatening to a white man on the subway are one thing; an inebriated white fellow who has earned his right to sleep with a flirtatious, sexy, and inebriated lady acquaintance is another. In short, the history of noble outlaws makes it difficult for women to qualify for inclusion, especially if what motivates them is something as apparently banal as everyday violence against "cock-teasing" women.

If, as women, Thelma and Louise are unlikely candidates for outlaw status, the fact that they are working-class women makes the possibility of their becoming outlaws more probable. Their class status may also make their outlaw behavior more palatable to the middle-class audiences to whom the film is directed than if the heroines were solidly middle- or upper-middle class.

Compare *Thelma and Louise* with the earlier film classic exhibiting feminist consciousness. In *Adam's Rib,* a female lawyer successfully defends a working-class woman charged with attempting to murder her husband. It would have been quite a different movie altogether if the lawyer had had to defend herself against the charge that she had tried to murder her lawyer husband. The film then would not have provided the cozy though necessarily tacit lesson that middle- or upper-middle-class professional heterosexual couples work out their gender problems in the much more "civilized" way of talk, compared with working-class couples, who are depicted as violent (prosecutor Spencer Tracy elicits the fact that defendant Judy Holliday had on occasion hit her husband just as he hit her).

Thelma and Louise are working-class women; Harlan, the hitchhiker, and the truck driver are portrayed in ways that seem to signal to viewers that they are working-class.[24] The middle-class viewers who are tempted to describe themselves as identifying with Thelma or Louise might ask themselves how far the identification really goes. After all, the neat thing about admiring outlaws from a class you perceive as lower than your own is that you can have your cake and eat it too: a middle-class woman's partial identification with a working-class female outlaw could enable her to imagine taking unlawful revenge against a man while not having to endure the thought that she is really an outlaw type, or confront the strong possibility that there really are no legal resources on which she could draw. A middle-class woman's admiration for a working-class woman who breaks the law may be easy, as long as the middle-class woman remains confident that she will not be seen and treated as a working-class woman.

This is not to suggest that middle-class women have an easy time using the law to defend themselves against rape and other forms of sexual violence and abuse. But it is to suggest that in the United States in the 1990s, there are sharp differences, partly summarized by class, between women with access to the law and to the chance of pushing it to its limits in order to defend themselves, and someone like Louise who knows the terror of seeing no source of support within the system, no possible legal leeway, and no hope of positive publicity that would mitigate the effects of her avenging act.

One of the privileges of class dominance is to be able to admire what one sees as a courageous act without having to worry about the likely consequences of that act for the agent. In this connection, the film poses a very serious question: Are feminists who enthusiastically embrace the film's depiction of direct and violent confrontation with violent and abusive men prepared to give concrete support to women who are confrontative in just those ways? What if those confrontative women are unlikely to have access to the legal and extra-legal resources that might somewhat cushion the blow of such confrontation?

What seems a plausible form of liberation has a great deal to do with the predicted consequences that acts of such liberation are likely to entail. The lack of rebellion by some slaves and Holocaust victims does not inspire blame (although their rebellion would have been courageous, laudable, and inspiring) because rebellion could have cost them or their co-sufferers their lives. *Thelma and Louise* contains—even if it does not explicitly articulate—a very closely related caution: perhaps we ought to be careful about facile praise for people for acting in ways that are audacious, courageous, and inspiring, when we are more likely to be protected from the consequences of such acts than they are. We who differ from them may experience, partially, their world. But, partial vicariousness can be very cruel. It is partial if the viewers hope the characters have an experience that we would like to have too, although the characters have to bear the consequences of it in a way that we would not. And it is partial if the viewer neglects the moral dilemmas and distress experienced by the character herself.[25]

If class difference may make it safe for many viewers to like Thelma and Louise, one might ask whether Harlan and the truck driver seem to deserve what they get because they are presented as working-class men. The notions of appropriate revenge that surface even in our fantasies—perhaps especially in our fantasies—are likely to be class coded. In *Adam's Rib,* the female lawyer gets back at her husband by outdoing him in court,[26] but the working-class female defendant gets her revenge by shooting at her husband. While admiration of outlaws depends on a view of their victims as, in some sense, and perhaps with some regret, expendable, the possibilities of expendability are likely to be closely tied to some of the more invidious aspects of class distinctions. It is worth asking whether the working-class status of Harlan and the truck driver makes it easier for middle-class women to think of them as unregenerate creeps who fully and unquestionably deserve everything Thelma and Louise dish out to them. No doubt their being working-class men makes it easier for middle-class men to deny that they are like these guys and thus to insist that they surely do not deserve to be treated like Harlan and the truck driver.

There is a sense in which Thelma and Louise have questionable status as outlaws: unlike many of their kind, they stumble into this always hazardous and sometimes noble career. These two women who plot a secret get-away weekend from the men in their lives are not portrayed as potential heroines whose visions of justice or creative needs or deep yearnings for freedom require standing outside the law. They are not portrayed, at least early on, as having a criminal or outlaw "mentality" (hence Thelma's husband Darryl's incredulousness while watching a security videotape of Thelma holding up the convenience store). On the contrary, Thelma and Louise initially have nothing more in mind than a brief bout of naughtiness. It is a measure of their relative lack of freedom and power that what begins as their naughtiness spirals so quickly and so inexorably into their becoming, to their initial horror, continuing surprise, and emerging delight, fugitives from the law. Unlike many noble outlaws, it is not at all as if their visions of the shortcomings of the law and of the society that produces it lead them to put themselves outside it. On the contrary, for Thelma at least, learning that "law is some tricky shit" comes as a result of her becoming an outlaw.

The Outlaws Look at Law and Morality

Thelma and Louise had no lawyers to consult or to guide them through the law's response to their actions. Nonetheless, like many outlaws and many who seem marginal to the law's operations, Thelma and Louise had complex understandings of the legal system and how it would treat them. Although the law put them beyond its ken and beyond its protection, Thelma and Louise engaged in a continual discussion about blame and guilt, and about responsibility and obedience. In their own actions and judgments, they confronted and addressed punishment and proportionality of punishment to offense. Placing at the center these *outlaws'* views of law and morality displaces societal images of the outlaw as amoral. Their own moral judgments afford a critical perspective on law and conventional morality.

To Thelma and Louise, "law is some tricky shit." Louise knows and Thelma comes to realize that the official legal system will not take seriously a charge of rape or attempted rape by a woman who publicly danced, drank, and flirted with a man who picked her up at a raucous bar. Thelma asks, "shouldn't we go to the cops?" and Louise replies, "who's going to believe" us? Louise starts crying, "we don't live in that kind of world."[27]

Detectives and police officers are to be avoided and diverted; they will not understand women who fight back against violent men. Louise does engage in repeated phone conversations with one detective who claims to understand, but she does not trust him either. She knows that he is trying to keep her on the phone long enough to trace the phone call's source.

Even Thelma, portrayed for the first half of the film as naive and gullible,[28] knows that it could only be the tricky law or its offices that prompted her husband Darryl[29] to be sweet to her on the phone; his very sweetness tells her that police are there with him, so she hangs up the phone. Curiously, Darryl believed the FBI agent who urged him to sweet-talk his wife because "women love that shit." Maybe they do, maybe they don't, but this advice could only stem from total disinterest in the particularities of the actual relationship between this man and this woman. If its own agents do not care about those actual details, it is no wonder that the law itself seems remote and uncomprehending to the two women it outlaws.

Between themselves,[30] however, the two women constantly discuss issues of moral boundaries, duties, and responsibilities.[31] Shortly after

Louise shoots Harlan, she starts to blame Thelma: "If you weren't so concerned about having fun. . . ." But she stops short as Thelma interjects: "So this is all my fault, is it?" Louise and Thelma both hear and reject the echo of societal conversations blaming women who get raped because "they asked for it." Yet both women wrestle with the question of fault and responsibility. Much later, after more time on the road, Thelma says, "I know this whole thing was my fault." But this time Louise says, "This wasn't your fault." And Thelma with appreciation and forgiveness on her own part replies, "I'm glad I came with you." Not only does she affirm their friendship, she also affirms their journey, their jeopardy, and their sacrifice.

Days later, still on the road, Louise says "I think I fucked up. I think I got us in a situation where we both could get killed." Thelma then reveals how much she has been replaying the options, and reevaluating who is to blame and who is responsible. She observes that if they had sought to prosecute the rapist, no one would have believed them, "probably nothing would have happened to him . . . [and] my life would have been ruined a whole lot worse than it is now. I'm not sorry that son of a bitch is dead." But she is sorry about something—that it was Louise who killed him rather than herself. Given a world without a comprehending legal system, working outside the law is essential. And the best remedies are by the self.[32]

Less intense, but no less expressive of normative concerns, is Louise's warning to Thelma as she starts to throw an empty liquor bottle out of the convertible: "Thelma, don't you litter." Her tone is stern and commanding. Perhaps it reflects a sense of pride in the fantastic scenery, or simply a concern with obeying the rules. The comment certainly occasions laughter from an audience watching the outlaws flee from the law. But more than incongruity is at work here. The comment is true to Louise's continuing respect for norms, her knowledge of the price of disobedience, and perhaps her sense of right and wrong.

But are they engaged in moral argument or judgment when they commit their own acts of violence? Their concern for one another is at the center of the violence they encounter and the violence they commit. In the disturbing scene when Thelma is sexually assaulted by Harlan, who picked her up at the Silver Bullet bar, the violence escalates when Thelma tries to halt Harlan's aggression by telling him that Louise will wonder where she is. Harlan responds, "Fuck Louise." Thelma slaps him. He whacks her and roughly pins her against a car and starts to rape her. Louise shows up and pulls out the gun. Harlan tells her, "Calm down, we're just having a little fun." Louise says, "Looks like you have a real fucked up idea about fun. . . . In the future, when a woman is crying like that, she isn't havin' any fun." Harlan says quietly, "Bitch. I should have gone ahead and fucked her," to which Louise demands, "What did you say?" Harlan turns defiantly and answers, "I said suck my cock." Louise shoots him dead and then, after telling Thelma to get in the car, whispers, "You watch your mouth, buddy." Louise did not shoot when Harlan was attacking Thelma; pointing the gun was enough to interrupt him. She shoots when he demonstrates he is undeterred and unrepentant, and verbally repeating the sexual assault. She shoots in judgment; she has judged that he will not stop this behavior and that even if Thelma gets away, other women will be victimized.

Although she clearly makes a judgment here, Louise becomes at this moment an outlaw, not a judge or jury. Indeed, in strictly legal terms, this judgment makes her conduct intentional and thus, in the eyes of the law, more culpable than one committed instinctively or in the heat of passion. Moreover, since Harlan was unarmed and because he stopped his assault at least temporarily at the sight of the gun, it would be difficult to fit this scene into the legal framework of self-defense. That framework uses the archetype of intense hand-to-hand combat between two men.[33] It does not justify or excuse the use of a gun against a verbal assault. Yet, precisely because it is so deliberate, Louise's act of violence does serve as a judgment, a sentence for the audience to reckon with as well as a moment that changes her own life. She becomes a judge of the proper response to the crime when she later chastises Thelma for laughing at the thought of the look on Harlan's face when he was shot. Thelma says, between laughs, "He sure wasn't expecting that." Louise says sharply, "It's not funny." Thelma sobers up: "I know."

Thelma herself becomes an outlaw when she robs a convenience store after failing to guard Louise's life savings from a hitchhiker.[34] Louise is horrified by Thelma's crime. Thelma argues back: "It's not like I killed anybody." Intended or not as a comparison with Louise's crime, Thelma's statement raises the moral question: Which act is more serious, which deliberate violation of the law is more excusable or justifiable— the shooting of an unrepentant rapist or the burglary of a store for cash and liquor?[35] Louise mulls over this implicit question. Later, she tells Thelma her conclusion: there is "no such thing as justifiable robbery."[36]

Louise and Thelma engage in what they perceive to be justifiable action when they teach a lesson to the truck driver who several times leers, ogles, and harasses them with sexual remarks and gestures when they pass him on the road. It is a fantasy revenge scene, but it is as remarkable for the women's restraint as it is for their revenge. They operate with calculated judgment and a sense of proportionality rather than the boundless fury that revenge so often unleashes. They first lure him off the road with the suggestion that they accept his overtures. The camera shows him take off his wedding ring, spray some breath freshener in his mouth, and hop out of the enormous oil rig, ready for action. But to his initial surprise and disbelief, he encounters not a sexual opportunity but a lecture and an invitation to apologize. "We think you have really bad manners. Where do you get off" behaving so obnoxiously? Thelma and Louise try to instruct him: What if some man did this to your mother or your sister or your wife? They invite him to grow, to learn. He does not get it. They ask why he ogles women by flapping his tongue repeatedly; they try to communicate how disgusting that is from their point of view. He still does not get it, and indelicately responds: "You women are crazy. I ain't apologizing for shit." They ask him to say he's sorry. "Fuck that" is his answer. And then the fantasy of revenge takes off.

They shoot the tires on his truck; it marvelously sinks into the ground. "God damn, you bitch" is his comment. Thelma tells Louise, "I don't think he's gonna apologize." They shoot the truck again, and it explodes, beautifully, dramatically, clouds billowing against the desert's expanse. Riding toward him in their car, they grab his hat as a souvenir, encircle him with the car and ride off. The difficulties he will encounter getting help and explaining what happened are suggested by the camera shots of his isolation with the burning truck; the women's satisfaction with their act is contagious. But the revenge *was* restrained. He was unharmed physically, though humiliated and left powerless. The punishment thus fit the crime, giving the perpetrator some of his own medicine. It is as if Thelma and Louise are saying, now you know how women feel when you humiliate them and leave them helpless.[37]

Does the movie make its own moral judgment about Thelma and Louise? It gives them no way out, underscoring how there is no place in this world for women who resist with violence. It offers them only the dignity and transcendence of chosen, joint, sisterly suicide.[38] Yet the film itself is forgiving and even adoring of Thelma and Louise. Pursued by a horde of police cars and helicopters, they leap in the car into the Grand Canyon, and immediately the film cuts back to prior, vibrant images of the women, replacing their death with their lives. The closing moments, then, are snippets of the high points of the film; the audience is left with their

In *Thelma and Louise,* female "outlaw" Thelma (Geena Davis)
terrorizes a sexist state trooper. (Courtesy of the Museum of Modern Art.)

smiles, their excitement about their weekend away, their hair waving in the wind and the open space of the T-bird.[39] Different viewers, of course, may have different reactions.

Conclusion: At the Brink of the Canyon

As we suggested in our introduction, there is a sense in which *Thelma and Louise* picks up where *Adam's Rib* left off. There are important differences in structure and outcome between the two films. The Katherine Hepburn figure won her case—suggesting that the jury in the film found the sex-change fantasy of her closing argument believable, even if as viewers we cannot imagine how it could have been convincing. The avenging wife, played by Judy Holliday, broke the law. Perhaps she nevertheless was not an outlaw. Surely she was not the film's heroine. That status clearly belongs to the female lawyer, who, at apparent risk and deliberate challenge to her relationship with her prosecutor husband (Spencer Tracy), initiated contact with the accused, then cleverly used every legal and extra-legal device she could to get her client acquitted.

In contrast, no lawyer appears in *Thelma and Louise*. Thelma and Louise neither seek nor are sought out by legal counsel. This helps delineate their status as outlaws in two distinct and important senses. They do not turn to the law to effect the justice they envision. Nor are they under the protection of the law, inasmuch as they neither consult nor even imagine anyone who knows its tricky ways to be their witness or their defender. *Thelma and Louise* underscores yet a third sense in which the story of these two women is an outlaw story. Suppose they had, like Judy Holliday's character, the defendant in *Adam's Rib,* come to have the law used in their defense. Most of what we learned about them on the road would be irrelevant or at best damaging in a courtroom. It is of no interest to the law or its agents what the accused think about the law and its failure to fit with their lives. The law has its own rules about what are the relevant and irrelevant facts about people's lives. The price of being protected by the law in court is to surrender control over the telling of your story. Its rich, complicated, and confusing textures are not digestible by the legal record. People's real stories are outside the law. Had Thelma and Louise turned themselves over to the law—whether to the sheriff or to an attorney—they would have become subject to constraints much like those from which they found themselves fleeing, constraints that among other things make their versions of themselves and of the world irrelevant.

Screen author Calli Khouri thus might be said to have this to say to observers of law: We have as much to learn about the law from those who find themselves (in both senses of that phrase) outside it as those who enforce it, wield it, or study it.

Notes

Many thanks to Joe Singer, Betsy Bartholet, Larry Blum, Juliet Brody, Karen Engle, Jody Freeman, Mary Ann Glendon, Judi Greenberg, Duncan Kennedy, Lisa Krakow, and Judy Smith. An earlier version of this essay appeared in 26 *New England Law Review* 1281 (1992). © Copyright New England School of Law 1991. All rights reserved. Reprinted by permission.

1. This essay was originally written as a tribute to Mary Joe Frug, whose work addressed women most terrorized by others and ruled out by law.

2. Nonetheless, some viewers perceive the ending of the movie as a statement that the world holds no place for women who rebel. See, for example, Claire Reinelt, "Letters to the Editor," *Boston Globe,* June 21, 1991, p. 14. Thelma and Louise "would rather die of their own choice than be subjected to male authority. . . . There was no other alternative for them, and that is a sad commentary on the fate of women who refuse to play by men's rules."

3. Mary Joe Frug, "Re-Reading Contracts: A Feminist Analysis of a Contracts Casebook," 34 *American University Law Review* 1065 (1985). The article identifies eight fictional readers who "resemble students and colleagues"—the Feminist, the Woman-Centered Reader, the Reader with a Chip on the Shoulder, the Innocent Gentleman, the Reader Who is Undressed for Success, the Individualist, the Civil Libertarian, and the Undeserving Male or Female Reader. We rely here on public comments about the movie *Thelma and Louise* to illustrate different kinds of viewers.

4. Diane White, "The Great Debate over 'Thelma and Louise,'" *Boston Globe,* June 14, 1991, p. 29; John Robinson, "The Great Debate over 'Thelma and Louise,'" *Boston Globe,* June 14, 1991, p. 29.

5. Robinson, "Great Debate," p. 29.

6. Ibid., p. 36.

7. Ibid.

8. "Men know that for every Pam Smart there are legions of wife abusers. For every Inquisition-minded Queen Isabella there are a dozen Stalins and Hitlers. For every Witch of Wall Street there are armies of Donald Trumps and Henry Kravises and Ivan Boeskys." Ibid.

9. Ibid.

10. White, "Great Debate," p. 29.

11. Ibid., p. 36. Elsewhere, Terrence Rafferty expressed a different reaction: "In the end, *Thelma and Louise* seems less a feminist parable than an airy, lyrical joke about a couple of women who go off in search of a little personal space and discover that they have to keep going and going and going to find a space that's big enough." Terrence Rafferty, "The Current Cinema: Outlaw Princesses," *New Yorker,* June 3, 1991, p. 87.

12. Compare Larry Rohter, "The Third Woman of *Thelma and Louise,*" *New York Times,* June 5, 1991, p. C21—Callie Khouri, who wrote the screenplay, describes "the controversial scene in which Louise kills Thelma's assailant" as "'a very cathartic one for women'"—with Peter Keough, "Who's Bashing Who?" *Boston Phoenix,* May 24, 1991, p. 6: "Audiences are used to seeing men pull triggers on malefactors, but the sight of a woman offing a man in defense of a member of her own sex touches off some fundamental anxieties."

13. Kenneth Turan, "Smooth Ride for *Thelma and Louise,*" *L.A. Times,* May 24, 1991, p. F1.

14. Keough, "Who's Bashing Who?" p. 6 (quoting Geena Davis).

15. Rohter, "Third Woman," p. C21 (quoting Callie Khouri).

16. *People v. Goetz,* 497 N.E.2d 41, 43 (N.Y. 1986).

17. Ibid. at 44.

18. *People v. Goetz,* 520 N.Y.S.2d 919 (N.Y. Sup. Ct. 1987), *aff'd,* 529 N.Y.S. 2d 782 (N.Y. App. Div.), *aff'd,* 532 N.E.2d 1273 (N.Y. 1988). Goetz was convicted of one count of criminal possession of a weapon in the third degree.

19. See Martha C. Duncan, "'A Strange Liking': Our Admiration for Criminals," 19 *University of Illinois Law Review* 1 (1991).

20. Patricia J. Williams, *The Alchemy of Race and Rights* (Cambridge: Harvard University Press, 1991).

21. Are young black men in New York ever described as being "out on a little spree," and allowed the impunity of "boys will be boys"?

22. In Rohter, "Third Woman, p. C21.

23. See the discussion below concerning the separation of Louise's pointing the gun from her shooting.

24. What about Thelma's husband, Darryl? Some may describe him as yuppified; he's a car salesman/manager.

25. See the discussion below concerning Thelma and Louise's reflections on moral responsibility.

26. But Spencer Tracy says she has crossed the bounds and shows no respect for law *inside* this very civilized courtroom fight. Still, they are *in it* together enough to have words instead of guns (until Spencer fakes an entrance with a gun—that turns out to be licorice).

27. Louise also knows something from a prior, veiled, and terrible experi-

ence in Texas. She asks Thelma to find a route on the map to Mexico without going through Texas; Thelma says, "We're running for our lives. . . . Can't you make an exception?" Louise finally answers, "You shoot off a guy's head with his pants down and Texas is not the place you want to get caught."

28. In many ways, the film is about Thelma's coming of consciousness as a woman, as an adult, and as a critic of male dominance. She says toward the end of the film, "I feel awake. . . . Wide awake. I don't remember ever feeling this awake. . . . Everything looks different. You feel like that, too—like you got something to look forward to?" This is when they are quite desperately racing from the police and hoping to reach Mexico. Still later, and somewhat more lightly, she says that she feels a little crazy; Louise responds, "You've always been crazy. This is just the first chance you've ever really had to express yourself."

29. Manager of a car dealership, Darryl has a license plate on his car that reads: "THE 1."

30. It is not the case, though, that they can discuss anything with each other. Thelma says to Louise, "It happened to you, didn't it[?] . . . You was raped." Louise stops the car. "I'm warning you—just drop it. . . . I'm not talking about it."

31. It is not a verbal comment, but Louise throws up soon after she shoots Harlan—not a typical reaction in movie depictions of shootings, yet one that says something about sensibilities and visceral judgment.

32. Perhaps Thelma is thinking that it is better for the victim herself to fight back rather than to be aided by a friend, and that it is better to keep a friend out of it and to find one's own strength to fight back.

33. Consider the efforts to fit the conduct of battered women who kill their batterers in their sleep into the self-defense framework.

34. Thelma and J.D. engage in mutual seduction. This underscoring of the film's morality does not reject sexuality and sensuality, but does reject violent and nonconsensual sex.

35. Watching a video of the robbery, Thelma's husband, the FBI agents, and a police detective each intone the divinity: "Jesus Christ," "Good God," and "My Lord," as if only the highest judge could understand what had happened.

36. Detective Slocum actually implies a kind of excuse for the robbery when he interrogates J.D., the hitchhiker, about his role in what happened. Slocum inquires of J.D. whether he thinks that Thelma would have committed armed robbery if he "hadn't taken all their money. . . . There's two girls out there . . . they had a chance . . . and now they're in some serious trouble. . . . I'm gonna hold you personally responsible."

37. Proportionality also characterizes their treatment of a lone police officer who stops them for speeding. Knowing that a radio check would alert the officer to the FBI search for them, Thelma points the gun at him, shoots air holes in the trunk, directs the officer into it, and throws the trunk keys a few

yards away. No greater restraint is used than is needed to let the outlaws get away, and solicitation for the officer's needs is shown. The officer begs for mercy because he has a wife and children, and Thelma treats this as an occasion for a moral lesson. "You're lucky. You be sweet to 'em. Especially your wife. My husband wasn't sweet with me—look how I turned out."

In a strange follow-up scene, a Rastafarian bicyclist comes across the apparently abandoned squad car and hears the officer banging from inside the truck and asking for help. The bicyclist responds by blowing reefer smoke through the air holes in the trunk.

38. See also Yigael Yadin, *Masada: Herod's Fortress and the Zealots' Last Stand* (New York: Random House, 1975), 11–13.

39. Displayed like snapshots are pictures of the two women waving at the camera and smiling in the wind. The last song on the soundtrack uses the lyric: "you're a part of me, I'm a part of you"—perhaps playing on the viewers' capacities to identify with the characters.

FOURTEEN

Law Noir

NORMAN ROSENBERG

■

In order to highlight the rhetorical and discursive dimensions of legal writing, students of law are increasingly considering *how,* as well as *what,* legal texts might mean.[1] Similarly, recent film scholarship also foregrounds "how" questions, emphasizing *how* the films from the era of Classical Hollywood (roughly 1930 to the mid-1960s) can work to conceal the process of filmic re-presentation and highlighting *how* every cinematic shot constructs a complex set of multilayered images on the screen.[2] Despite the tendency of dominant Hollywood cinema to conceal questions of choice,[3] there is no "inevitable" or "natural" way of representing a particular film story. Consequently, any "legal reelist" movement might profitably draw upon film scholarship in order to take account of the unique "grammars" found in cinema.

In a related vein, legal reelism might emulate other forms of recent scholarship, in both film and law, by foregrounding issues of representation and narrative construction. The particular ways in which any legal narrative, including those represented through film, gets articulated invariably exclude alternative means of telling the same story. Similarly, the politics of storytelling, whether in a legal document or in a Hollywood film, bear important connections to how stories are "translated"—into legal or cinematic discourse—and how they become inscribed within authoritative, and persuasive, "legal" texts.[4] In order to highlight some of the ways in which legal reelism works, this essay will look intensively at two films from the 1940s, *Call Northside 777* (1948) and *Knock on Any Door* (1949), and suggest how the Hollywood production system constructs these two related, yet ultimately very different, legal texts.

In addition, this essay seeks to examine how these two motion pictures negotiate two related questions that can be found in many of Hollywood's legal films. First, how effectively can *public* authorities resolve the legal problems posed in the narrative? And, second, when must a successful resolution depend upon intervention by some resourceful, *private* hero? *Call Northside 777*, I will argue, resembles Hollywood's westerns (and "disguised westerns" such as *Casablanca*): Only extra-legal heroics, from people such as the archetypal gunfighter from a film like *Shane,* can resolve narrative complications. The legal system appears relatively ineffectual in achieving narrative closure, let alone in producing a result that might confidently be considered "just." In contrast, *Knock on Any Door* features significantly different, more affirming representations of legal power.

Finally, *Call Northside 777* and *Knock on Any Door* are part of an important cycle of films, the fabled *film noir.* Film noir, critics have come to emphasize, constructs a cinematic world in which nearly every social practice and institution—from gender roles to the Hollywood production system itself—come under scrutiny. Few things seem settled or even potentially amenable to settlement. As film scholar J. P. Telotte suggests, film noir explores "why *all* of our traditional formulations—and cinematic formulas—seemed to have lost so much of their substance and authority."[5]

Not surprisingly, then, film noir opens novel, critical spaces within the dominant, often apologetic, Hollywood paradigm for representing "things legal."[6] Film scholar Michael Walker notes that although many different types of Hollywood films criticized the law, film noirs were able "to go further than the norm."[7] Moreover, within the larger body of noir films, it is possible to identify a coherent subcycle of movies that I call *"law noir."*[8] In these films, attorneys, courts, policing institutions—and, ultimately, that "shadowy" force called "the law"—assume central narrative and symbolic importance.

Although some historians see noir simply reflecting World War II and postwar tensions,[9] many of the thematic and stylistic markers of film noir, and of *law noir* as well, are already discernible during the 1930s.[10] Thus, for students of mid-twentieth-century legal culture, *law noirs* provide rich texts by which to map the contested cultural terrain from which popular representations of law emerged between the mid-1930s and the late 1950s.

Law Noir before World War II

Just as court opinions cite earlier judicial literature, Hollywood films also "cite" previous cinematic texts. Thus, *Call Northside 777* and *Knock on Any Door* build upon *law noirs* of the 1930s, including *Fury* (1936), *Marked Woman* (1937), and *Stranger on the Third Floor* (1940). In turn, these three motion pictures recall earlier gangster and crime films, such as *I Am a Fugitive from a Chain Gang* (1932), which preceded Hollywood's stricter Production Code of 1934.[11] All of these films portray people, some entirely innocent and others not-so-innocent, trapped in a highly fallible legal system, and develop images of a dangerous and crime-filled world. Similarly, the baleful view of lawyers, inscribed within many *law noirs,* may be seen in the pre-Code "shyster" films, such as *Mouthpiece* (1932).[12]

Warner Brothers, for example, planned *Marked Woman* within the familiar "mouthpiece" frame; as the production process went along, however, it became a very different, much more complex text in which shyster lawyers fade into the background. The final product anticipates postwar *law noirs*—such as *Force of Evil* (1948)—by representing the legal system as the site for generating powerful discourses and social practices that, in the end, offer relatively little to ordinary people who turn to the law in order to find "justice."[13]

In contrast to shyster films from the early 1930s, however, the *law noir* cycle draws from cinematic devices used in German cinema of the 1920s. Tilted camera angles, flashbacks, voice-overs, unconventional lighting patterns, and a variety of other practices help to represent a legal order that can easily spin out of control.[14]

In *Stranger on the Third Floor,* sometimes hailed as the first "true" noir,[15] Mike Ward (John McGuire), a young reporter, becomes ensnared in a legal nightmare. The star witness in a murder trial, Mike testifies that he saw Joe Briggs (Elisha Cook Jr.) standing over the body of a slain coffee shop owner, and this eyewitness evidence helps seal a murder conviction and death sentence against the defendant.

Mike's public performance soon brings private anguish. As other reporters and even his fiancé Jane (Margaret Tallichet) question the relevance of his testimony, Mike begins to doubt the meaning of what he has seen. While dreaming, he imagines his own conviction, on the basis of testimony similar to the kind he himself had given against Joe Briggs, for murdering a meddlesome neighbor. Mike envisions a trial, depicted through a variety of expressionist filmic devices, in which everything seems (literally) tilted against him. Even Jane's testimony, about threats toward the neighbor, ironically parallels Mike's own statements on the witness stand during the Briggs case. "I'm sorry Michael," Jane tells him. "I had to tell the truth."

Mike's noirish dream proves prophetic. After awakening in panic, he discovers the neighbor has been killed in the same manner as the victim in the Briggs case. Citing evidence of past quarrels between Mike and his neighbor, police discount Mike's story about seeing a mysterious stranger and arrest him on suspicion of murder. While he is trying to tell his story—one that film spectators share—the politically ambitious DA stares into a mirror; he goes about an elaborate shaving ritual that seems as far removed from justice as the courtroom rituals in other parts of the film. In representing both Mike's dream about and his real-life nightmare with the law, *Stranger on the Third Floor* highlights inept legal officials and flawed procedures. And by aligning Mike's vision, including his view of the DA, with that of film spectators, *Stranger on the Third Floor* tries to make his fears of the law our own.

Left alone, Jane must find a *private* solution to what are represented as fundamental *public* problems with legal and courtroom discourses.[16] With legal authorities disinterested, she locates Mike's elusive stranger, an escaped mental patient (Peter Lorre). Chasing Jane into the street, he is run over by a truck but lives long enough to confess the killings wrongly attributed to Briggs and Mike. In these sequences, legal officials remain ineffectual; they are merely mute observers, passively listening to the murderer's confession.

Fury, a more complex and ambitious film, also imagines a private, rather than a public, resolution to difficulties attributed to a faulty legal system. Enraged that he had been wrongly arrested as a kidnapper and then nearly murdered when an angry lynch mob burned down the jail in which he was unjustly being detained, Joe Wilson (Spencer Tracy) vows to use the legal system as an instrument of private revenge. Rebuffing suggestions that he hire a lawyer and pursue traditional legal remedies, Joe concocts an elaborate scenario premised upon the flawed nature of the legal system. Concealing his miraculous escape, Joe allows an unsuspecting District Attorney to prosecute twenty-two of his attackers for murder.[17] Even his fiancé Catherine—indeed, everyone but his two brothers—believes Joe to be dead.

Working secretly behind the scenes, Joe assists the unsuspecting prosecutor. At a crucial point in the case, for example, when defense attorneys demand evidence that Wilson actually perished in the fire, Joe himself, the murder "victim," sends the presiding judge a fire-singed ring. This ploy seals guilty verdicts against most of the defendants and allows Joe, in effect, to script the trial's conclusion. Applauding his production, Joe insists that the legal system has unknowingly given him "justice." Eventually, Catherine realizes that Joe must still be alive, locates his hiding place, and urges him to halt the trial before it ends in tragedy. Joe remains unmoved. "They could stand seeing me burned to death, but they can't stand an *honest* trial." But a few hours by himself, trying to celebrate his courtroom triumph, convinces Joe he cannot live without Catherine. "Don't leave me alone!" he cries out.

Joe's subsequent decision to stop the trial judge from sentencing any of the defendants to death owes little to concerns about law or justice. Skillfully integrating dialogue with camera shots, which alternate between Joe and Catherine, *Fury* portrays Joe's judgment to be motivated by purely private desires. Although he once cared deeply about law and justice, the jailhouse fire had burned those "silly things" out of him. "I came here today for my own sake," he tells the crowded courtroom. By scheming to punish the would-be lynchers, Joe has also been devouring *his* own very being. More important, he cannot stand the thought of losing Catherine and sleep-walking through a harsh world in which neither law nor other institutions seem to play even ameliorative roles.[18]

Thus Joe—and his personal relationship with Catherine, and not the judge and his relationships with law—dominates the final sequences. Until the very brief final shot, when Joe and Catherine embrace at the foot of the judge's bench, the camera (except for a quick pan down the front row of defendants) alternates only between shots of Joe and Catherine. Joe may accept the brute force of law, for *Fury* underscores how legal discourse carries the power to inflict pain and even death,[19] but he disdains any moral obligation to revere law or to accept its legitimacy.[20] His former reverence for the legal system was consumed in the jailhouse flames, and nothing, it seems, can rekindle his old faith.

Call Northside 777 and Postwar *Law Noir*

Although a number of *law noirs* of the 1940s and 1950s adapt themes and visual styles from pre-war pictures, the semi-documentary *Call*

Northside 777 is a particularly powerful example. It employs a brief, documentary-style history of Chicago as a general prologue to an equally brief chronicle of the 1932 murder of a police officer in a grocery store. With a stentorian voice-over continuing to add a documentary aura,[21] film spectators see the officer's murder (but not the identities of his killers) and the apprehension of two suspects, Tomak Zaleski and Frank Wiecek (Richard Conte).

From the outset, *Call Northside 777* paints a critical view of the law. By focusing on the transcript of a police interrogation, the camera, for instance, subtly underscores how much of the legal case against the two suspects depends on insignificant inconsistencies in their alibis. Similarly, an abrupt fade-dissolve shot, followed by an unusual camera technique (involving a pan followed by a tracking shot), unexpectedly transports viewers from Zaleski's police-station interrogation to a very brief courtroom sequence. It takes less than a minute of film time for the grocery store owner, Wanda Skutnik, to identify Zaleski and Wiecek as the murderers and for the film's voice-over to announce their convictions and sentences of ninety-nine years in prison. Mug shots of the pair suggest that their cases have been closed and filed away as a part of history.

As in the pre-war *law noirs,* then, filmic style, and not simply dialogue among the characters, constructs *Call Northside*'s perspectives of law. Initially, for example, the cinematic imagery works either to alienate or separate viewers from the operation of the quickly moving legal process. Generally photographed in long shots, which highlight their anonymity, legal officers seem cold and distant; their views of the murder case are rarely aligned with that of the film audience.

In contrast, when *Call Northside* suddenly jumps ahead eleven years in time, and switches its attention from the legal to the newspaper industry, the film's cinematic focus also changes. In the initial sequences that represent 1944, the camera is located over the shoulder of a newspaper editor (Lee J. Cobb). Spectators are thus encouraged to adopt his gaze as theirs and to join him in spotting a newspaper ad, offering $5000 to anyone with information about the Wiecek murder case. McNeal (Jimmy Stewart), one of the paper's best reporters, is assigned to write the story and quickly locates Tillie Wiecek, who is trying to "buy" justice for her son Frank. An earlier offer of $3000 for information had produced nothing, she tells McNeal; if a "bid" of $5000 cannot clear her son, she is willing to pay $10,000 (or another eleven years working at scrubbing floors) in order to establish his innocence.

Although willing to placate his editor and pursue the story of the $5000 offer, McNeal harbors no romantic illusions about the innocence of Tillie Wiecek's son. After all, Frank Wiecek had a police record; a jury found him guilty; a judge sentenced him to prison; and the Supreme Court of Illinois reviewed the entire trial record. Besides, McNeal himself examined all "the file's on the case." There can be no doubt, this reporter-investigator tells everyone, about the guilt of "that scrub woman's boy."

Yet, as the film carefully reconstructs the law's initial construction of the case, doubts begin to emerge—in the mind of McNeal and, presumably, in those of film viewers as well—about what Frank Wiecek calls the "true facts" of his ordeal. The rest of the film, set in 1944 (with only a single flashback), slowly deconstructs the 1932–33 murder case. A single, teenage shoplifting charge, it seems, comprised Wiecek's prior criminal "record." The judge, who died soon after the trial, had privately criticized the jury's verdict and had promised help in overturning it, Frank claims. Moreover, Frank's lawyer, now disbarred, had been drunk during the trial proceedings. And, most important, Wanda Skutnik had twice failed to recognize Wiecek and identified him only *after* having been dragged from police station to police station in his company.

As he follows Wiecek's story, the reporter-investigator's world turns inside out. McNeal comes to believe that Wiecek is innocent of murder and that the legal system is guilty of having carried out, and now of covering up, a terrible injustice. Because his personal belief cannot effect remedial action, McNeal confronts a dilemma common to so many *law noir* protagonists: What can a person do to convince others of the validity of their personal vision? Here, McNeal's dilemma anticipates what would become the title of another, very powerful *law noir, They Won't Believe Me* (1951). In McNeal's case, "they" comprise a hostile legal establishment—which includes the Chicago police, the State's Attorney's Office, the State's Board of Pardons, and his own newspaper's corporate counsel—that must be persuaded to adopt his viewpoint on the Wiecek case.

Even the emergence of clear lines of dispute helps little. McNeal's belief in justice and faith in technology—especially anything involving photography—appear to be no match for the law's commitment to process and its trust in time-tested legal procedures. Employing several lengthy, carefully composed, and documentary-like sequences, *Call Northside 777* reveals Wiecek taking a lie detector test. Then, close-ups show two other pieces of technology, McNeal's typewriter and the newspaper's linotype machine, tapping out the lie detector's verdict: "Frank Wiecek is innocent of the murder of Policeman Bundy." But informational machinery cannot easily move legal machinery. The newspaper's lie detector stunt may sway readers, various lawyers remind McNeal, but it means nothing in any legal tribunal.

Meanwhile, film viewers join McNeal as he locates other evidence. Employing various deceptions, he unearths Wiecek's old arrest records, which the police are trying to withhold, and secretly photographs them with a pocket camera. In this sequence, the cinematic camera aligns the vision of film spectators with the lens of McNeal's still-camera. Here, as elsewhere, *Call Northside 777* suggests the superiority of the media's gaze—and its ways of knowing and re-presenting "reality"—over the gazes, and the ways of seeing and knowing, traditionally employed by the legal system. Close-ups of McNeal's camera reproducing the police records allow film viewers to see what the reporter is seeing, that more than a day apparently elapsed between the time Wanda first encountered Frank Wiecek at a police station and the time she identified him as one of the police officer's killers. Similarly, viewers are encouraged to share McNeal's suspicion that Wanda Skutnik was lying when she claimed to have seen Frank only three times: the day of the killing, the day she testified in court, and the day on which she identified him from a police lineup, December 23, 1932. As noted earlier, no analogous shots try to align film viewers with the perspective of police or legal officials.

The film's privileging of mediated, visual "evidence" over legal "proof" extends to McNeal's discovery of a photograph, from the archives of a defunct Chicago tabloid, that shows Wanda and Frank entering a police station together. This picture appears to confirm Frank's story about the police having hauled Wanda and him "around the horn" together until she finally "fingered" him. At this point, McNeal's publisher agrees to support an official appeal, on Frank Wiecek's behalf, to the Illinois Board of Pardons.

But two crucial confrontations with the newspaper's attorney, Martin Burns (Paul Harvey), crush McNeal's legal theories.[22] The initial exchange between Burns and McNeal underscores the two men's conflicting views of the Wiecek case: Burns, the lawyer, maps the case through the rules of evidence and of legal process while McNeal, the lay investigator, calls upon evidence largely obtained through visual sources on behalf of the cause of "justice."

Initially, Burns emerges victorious. The lawyer demolishes the reporter's "case" by emphasizing the lack of any "real" proof; none of McNeal's "evidence" would be "admissible" in any legal tribunal. McNeal cannot prove, for instance, that the tabloid picture had been taken *before,* and not *after,* Wanda's identification of Frank. McNeal's newly found passion for Wiecek's innocence has unwisely overridden his previous skepticism. The old lawyer, though, gives the young reporter one piece of advice: If he wants a positive decision from the Board of Pardons, McNeal must do all he can, in the very short time available, to find and then discredit the state's eyewitness, Wanda Skutnik.

This advice eventually leads to a second Burns-McNeal confrontation. In several brilliantly filmed noir sequences, which highlight the sociocultural gulf between McNeal's and Wanda's worlds, the reporter combs Chicago's fabled "Back of the Yards," working every neighborhood bar in hopes of locating the missing witness. After plying an old woman with rye, McNeal finally finds Wanda, but she refuses to change her story, even for Mrs. Wiecek's $5000. Frustrated, McNeal lashes out at Wanda in a newspaper story, a libelous piece that convinces Burns that the paper must back down. He will withdraw the paper's appeal of Wiecek's conviction, and the publisher must order McNeal to write a "finish story" about Wanda, in order to "get the paper off the hook." At this point, both the diegetic newspaper series about Frank Wiecek and *Call Northside*'s own story about the search for justice face a narrative problem: "How do you end it," McNeal asks?[23]

The public legal structure, it seems, looms as an imposing impediment to achieving justice for Frank Wiecek. When McNeal talks to Frank's mother, seeking a journalistic hook upon which to hang his final story, she berates his paper for abandoning her son. When he tells her that an appeal to the Pardons Board stands "no chance," Mrs. Wiecek remains defiant. "You've got lawyers. . . . the best." When McNeal tells her that they, too, have no new evidence that is legally admissible, she replies, "Evidence? What is this evidence?" She has been a "big fool," she believes, to have ever trusted McNeal; he has caved into the same legal machinery that had, eleven years earlier, taken away her son.

But if legal processes cannot save the day, technological wizardry can; it can even convert hostile police officers and skeptical attorneys. After leaving Mrs. Wiecek's house and heading back to his office, McNeal sees a newspaper story about a new photo enlargement process.[24] By "blowing up" a small portion of a photograph many times, small details can be revealed. Quickly heading for the police lab, McNeal convinces a skeptical technician to work on the tabloid photograph that shows Wanda and Frank outside a police station. Martin Burns also undergoes a magical conversion; a single call from McNeal, informing him of the impending photo blowup, suddenly transforms the newspaper's lawyer into a true believer in McNeal's cause. He skillfully stalls the Pardons Board until McNeal arrives and alerts the board to the new evidence that will soon arrive over the AP's press wires.

While the Pardons Board awaits the photo's transmission, *Call Northside 777* continues to highlight the limits of the legal vision. He understands that legal authorities need "evidence," McNeal tells the board. "But sometimes the weight of evidence, just because it is in the [legal] record is heavy enough to crush the truth." In a beautifully composed sequence, the camera then focuses upon a statue of "Blind Justice," with a sword in her hand, as McNeal sardonically notes that her two-edged blade seems to have cut the ground out from under Frank Wiecek while leaving Wanda's position intact.

When the photo arrives and is developed, it does what the law and "Blind Justice" have been unable to do: slash Wanda's testimony to ribbons and vindicate Frank's story. Greatly magnified, the photograph enhances a small portion of the original picture and reveals a newspaper date that "proves" Wanda had, as Frank claimed, been with him on December 22, 1932, the day *before* she finally identified him as a "cop-killer." Although, for eleven years, legal authorities had accepted Wanda's testimony, that she had seen him only once before the crucial lineup, a single photograph instantly reveals her perjury. The film concludes with Frank's release.

Call Northside 777 does relatively little to soften or contain its critical representations of the law. As Frank stands outside the prison, reunited with his son and former wife (who, at his urging, had long ago remarried), the film briefly genuflects to Hollywood's Production Code as McNeal tells Wiecek that "it's a big thing when a sovereign state admits an error. And remember this: There aren't many governments in the world that would do it."

Yet the film's final images—in line with its larger cinematic structure—continues a much more bitter critique. In the last shot, for example, no legal officials are present, only McNeal and Frank's family. Framed before a massive prison, the only visible symbol of legal authority (whose terrifying rows of "cages" have been featured in several earlier sequences), private citizens stand as the narrative's heroic figures. The film's authoritative voice-over plays upon Frank Wiecek's comment that "It's a good world, outside." "Yes it is a good world," the voice-over replies. The law, however, appears to have had little to do with this goodness. Instead, Frank owes his freedom to "a mother's faith, the courage of a great newspaper, and one reporter's refusal to accept defeat."

In this sense, *Call Northside 777* underscores a position articulated in other *law noirs:* justice primarily depends upon those who stand *outside* the law. Here, Frank's remark that "It's a good world, outside," might signify the wish for a world in which people are free from the routines, politics, and pressures of "the law" itself. In contrast to westerns, or even a screwball legal comedy such as *Talk of the Town* (1942),[25] it is not the person with a gun who corrects the failures of the law; rather, it is the person who wields the technologies of visual reproduction. *Call Northside 777*, in some ways, thus balances its critique of one postwar icon, the law, with its celebration of another, the institution of a "free" press.

Knock on Any Door (1949)

In contrast to *Call Northside 777*, with its story of an innocent person ensnared in a fallible legal system, most of the other *law noirs* from the postwar era feature "flawed heroes" who desire, for one reason or another, to challenge or distort the law. This theme becomes especially interesting in noirs with attorneys as their protagonists. In *Force of Evil* (1948), for instance, Joe Morse (John Garfield) uses his legal expertise to assist a gangster-client's plan to take over New York City's illegal numbers racket and convert it into another "legitimate" business. In the end, legal authorities play only a minor role in halting Joe's legal machinations.[26] Instead, it is internecine warfare among the mobsters themselves and the resultant death of his brother that halt Joe's schemes and lead him, in an unconvincing final scene, to pledge future cooperation with the film's never-seen District Attorney—a shadowy, wire-tapping figure known only as "Hall."[27]

The File on Thelma Jordan (1950) offers a similar scenario. In this important *law noir,* an assistant DA (Wendell Cory) successfully employs an insider's knowledge and expertise to secure an acquittal for his lover Thelma (Barbara Stanwyck) in a murder trial he is charged with prosecuting. Structured in a way that encourages film spectators to identify with the DA's efforts, the narrative suddenly reveals Thelma's complicity in the killing of her aged aunt, a post-trial turn that leads to extra-legal punishment for her crime. Thus, this film, like *Force of Evil,* denies any effective power to the legal system. Instead, it is Thelma Jordan herself, overcome with remorse while fleeing with her accomplice, who deliberately crashes the get-away car. Her deathbed confession, rather than any legal proceeding, closes the "case" and reveals the DA's criminal behavior.[28]

Similarly, *Knock on Any Door* imaginatively reworks themes and images from other *law noirs.* While eschewing *Call Northside*'s documentary style, it also begins with the killing of a police officer by a gunman whose identity is concealed from the camera's eye. The police quickly arrest Nick Romano (John Derek), a dashing young punk with a long criminal record. ("Live fast, die young, and have a good-looking corpse," Nick advises a friend.) Recalling *Fury,* the ensuing murder trial becomes a media event. The tabloids feature stories about "Pretty Boy" Romano, while the DA (George Macready) openly seeks the governor's chair.

In contrast to the ambitious DA, Andy Morton (Humphrey Bogart) throws away a lucrative law-firm partnership to defend Nick. Once a tough street-kid himself, Morton convinces himself that Nick could not have committed a cold-blooded murder. In part, Andy's faith in Nick stems from personal remorse about his earlier failure, when he was a struggling attorney fresh out of night law school, adequately to represent Nick's father in a petty assault case; while in prison, Mr. Romano suffered a fatal heart attack. His prison-induced death, Morton argues to the jury, drops the Romano family into poverty, inflicts great psychological damage on young Nick, and ultimately buries him in an admittedly "deplorable and anti-social" life of crime. Interspersing numerous flashbacks with courtroom sequences, *Knock on Any Door* traces Nick from petty thief to accused murderer.

The film portrays a legal trial as a contest between two conflicting narratives. Jurors—and film viewers themselves—must decide between Morton's story about "a boy who is being railroaded" and the DA's tale about a vicious "hoodlum killer." The flashback sequences highlight Nick's unhappy life, which includes the suicide of his loyal wife Edna. Both attorneys exploit every possible advantage, and Judge Drake (Barry Kelley) struggles to keep them in line.

Thus, *Knock on Any Door* portrays the judge as fair, neutral, and hard-working; although elevated above the courtroom proceedings, he also seems an idealized "everyman" who has naturally ascended to a judicial chair. Following a particularly harsh exchange, for example, the judge calls the squabbling lawyers into his chambers to cool off. With the camera positioned within an imaginary wash-closet, film viewers see the judge washing his face and changing his sweat-soaked shirt. Later, during the questioning of key witnesses, the judge is often positioned in the arbiter's position, conspicuously tucked between the lawyers and the witnesses. And when the trial is finished, a close-up shot reveals a large, damp circle on the back of the hard-working judge's chair.

Despite its affirmative images of Morton's passion and of the judge's fairness, *Knock on Any Door* still invokes pre-war noirs by portraying the defendant as the victim of an uncaring system. Morton's courtroom sallies undermine the shaky stories offered by prosecution witnesses, a mixed group of callow opportunists and frightened victims. The prosecution, it seems, has either treated them with gifts or threatened them with retribution. Disfigured by a prominent scar across his cheek, the DA seems the perfect villain, especially when he savagely cross-examines Nick, whom he derisively calls "the pretty boy."

Then, suddenly, Andy Morton's story about a boy who is being falsely accused collapses. Just when it seems that the DA will gain nothing from his ruthless cross-examination of Nick, he suddenly focuses upon Nick's alleged responsibility for his wife's suicide; this turn in the DA's story cracks Nick's volatile and fragile psyche and prompts a melodramatic, witness-stand confession. The DA's cruel probing of Nick's personal life, the film argues, is justified by its results. Law work can be a tough, nasty, even brutal business.[29] "Sorry, I had to do it the hard way," the DA tells Andy Morton—and the film audience. A violence-prone punk, Nick Romano had been coddled far too long, and only an equally hardened lawyer could break through his well-practiced pose of innocence and self-confidence.

At the sentencing hearing, Morton apologizes for his earlier failure to see through Nick's façade, but he still pleads for his client's life. Can Andy Morton do what Joe Wilson accomplished in *Fury* and seize control of the legal narrative and the dominant cinematic gaze? He had naively been taken in by Nick's lies, Morton admits, because "I wanted to believe" that the young man's difficult past had not produced a killer.

Still, Nick's culpability must be put in a larger, social context. "Nick Romano is guilty," Morton admits, "but so are we, and so is that precious thing called society. . . . Knock on any door and you may find Nick

Romano." Can the pain of Nick's life and the public's toleration of the inhuman social conditions that caused his pain be translated into a legal discourse? "We good people . . . labeled and brutalized" Nick years ago. If he dies, "we killed him."

Morton's plea for mercy, and for leavening law with social understanding, fails to move the judge. Consistently represented as a hardworking paragon of fairness and rectitude, he sentences Nick to be executed. In the film's final scene, with the top of his luxuriant head of hair conspicuously shaved (thus denying him the "good-looking corpse"), Nicks shuffles toward the electric chair.

In appreciating *how* effectively the film articulates this narrative resolution, it is important to look closely at cinematic style. If one focuses only on dialogue, the judge rather curtly rejects Morton's appeal and hands down the death sentence. Read only as a contest of rhetorical eloquence, the final sequence even can appear to mark Morton as the clear winner. On the other hand, *Knock on Any Door* employs several different cinematic techniques—ones that might profitably be compared to those used in *Fury*—that can work to align the film's audience with Judge Drake rather than with Andy Morton.

The film's final sequences, for example, deny Morton (and, therefore, even Humphrey Bogart, the film's "star") the kind of cinematic positioning granted Joe Wilson in *Fury*. In that film, the camera frames Wilson (and, therefore, Spencer Tracy) so that he directly addresses the filmic audience, a technique that suggests cinematic spectators' possible complicity in tolerating the kind of injustices that had been done to Joe. Joe's problem becomes "ours." Moreover, the disappearance of the courtroom spectators (who were visible in the sequence's establishing shot) underscores members of the film audience as the "real" objects of Joe's—and the film's—address.

Equally important, *Fury* ascribes scant "potency" to the presiding judge. Indeed, the sequence in which Joe sends his fire-charred ring to the judge marks the beginning of the jurist's decline. First, it strips away the judge's "neutrality," a fact visually highlighted when, for the first time, he is photographed away from his judicial pedestal. By stepping down from the bench to become a mere witness, testifying to the fact of the ring's arrival, the judge becomes ensnared in Joe Wilson's prescripted revenge drama. And when Joe enters the courtroom, to argue that purely legal considerations cannot resolve the film's dilemmas, *Fury*'s representational practices deny the judge any effective narrative

Top: In *Call Northside 777,* the camera "shadows" a suspect who will later be found to be falsely accused. *Bottom:* In *Knock on Any Door,* the camera "spotlights" a suspect who will later be shown to be guilty. (Courtesy of the Museum of Modern Art.)

role or even any diegetic "voice." Striding into the courtroom with the gait of a western gunfighter, Joe speaks the film's final lines; the judge, officially the symbol of legal power, remains entirely silent!

The final courtroom sequences in *Knock on Any Door,* in contrast, generally capture Andy Morton as he is talking to a diegetic audience within the film, the publicity-starved voyeurs who breathlessly await the conclusion of the "'Pretty Boy' Romano story." (During the few close-ups in these sequences, Morton looks toward the courtroom audience, not straight out to the film's spectators.) More important, as Morton's speech concludes, the camera peers down on him from an extremely high angle, a shot taken from the position of the judge. This noirish technique makes Morton suddenly look very small, almost dwarf-like. As Nick Romano joins him, the camera moves even higher, emphasizing the majesty of Judge Drake's perspective, especially when compared to that of Morton and his client.

Equally important, the judge's elevated, cinematic viewpoint also becomes that of the film spectator. Like the judge, who is never shown during this final sequence, film viewers are placed in the position of enjoying the power that comes with official legal discourse. The judge's disembodied voice, it might be argued, metaphorically becomes the film audiences' collective voice. In contrast to a film such as *Fury,* then, the symbol of legal authority never loses—but, in fact, actually gains—cinematic authority in *Knock on Any Door.* Morton's attempt to re-frame Romano's trial, by making the question of his legal guilt or innocence on the charge of murder irrelevant, fails. Unlike the situation in *Fury,* where the judge is given an image and denied a voice, Judge Drake remains faceless, yet his final words are both authoritative and, for Nick Romano, lethal. Andrew Morton, unlike Joe Wilson, cannot displace the ultimate power of the law.

The Politics of *Law Noir*

Call Northside 777 and *Knock on Any Door* display important elements of the broader *law noir* cycle. Drawing upon earlier noirs of the 1930s, the first film articulates complex, critical discourses about law, while *Knock on Any Door* exemplifies those postwar noirs that feature attractive, yet ultimately dangerous, protagonists whose challenge to law is contained by law enforcers themselves.

Call Northside 777, especially with its semi-documentary filmic approach, points toward paths not taken in most other postwar *law noirs.* The film's power, in large part, comes from its almost utopian promise that visual imagery, the photos within the diegesis and its own cinematic apparatus, can reveal "truths" that other cultural forms, including law, cannot see. As J. P. Telotte suggests, the film's own "technical prowess" asserts that cinema "can provide the images we *need* to see, those that might hold a key to our own truth or that might, after a fashion, free us, as they do Frank Wiecek, from imprisonment to and within a fictional world."[30]

Yet the apparent triumph of informational technology—and the related critique of law—ultimately falter. McNeal's victory, though important to the Wiecek family, seems only partial. As the film ends, Wiecek's friend stays in jail; Wanda's perjury remains unpunished; and the identity of the "real" killers remains a mystery. Confronted by clear evidence of a mistake, the legal bureaucracy backs down, but its power, symbolized again by the vast prison, persists. Ironically, the great modernist institution celebrated in *Call Northside 777,* the Chicago *Times,* had already faded from the journalistic scene by the time the film appeared in 1948.[31] Moreover, visual images themselves do not always reveal hidden "truths," a point brilliantly explored in one of the final entries in the postwar *law noir* subcycle, *Beyond a Reasonable Doubt* (1956).[32]

More subtly, *Call Northside 777*'s own noir style can even suggest the need for the kind of overwhelming legal power represented by the final image of the prison. As McNeal moves through the dark, sinister world of Wanda and her gun-brandishing friends, for instance, the film itself constructs noirish images that, in other postwar motion pictures, call forth discourses about the need for strong, even ruthless legal containment.[33]

In this sense, *Knock on Any Door,* with its more complex representations of law, suggests a trajectory found in the majority of postwar *law noirs.* Most obvious, of course, Nick Romano, unlike *Fury*'s Joe Wilson or even *They Won't Believe Me*'s Larry Ballentine (Robert Young in the unusual role of an amoral cad), is guilty of the crime of which he is accused. Equally as important, the filmic apparatus decisively shifts its gaze so that the camera aligns viewers with the vantage point of the law enforcer, Judge Drake. The judge's decision to sentence Nick to die in the electric chair flows every bit as smoothly from the flashback sequences, which portray the noirish world of big-city crime, as does Andy Morton's plea for mercy. Only a strong, sometimes even harsh, legal order can control the kind of dark criminal elements represented in most noirs.

Knock on Any Door punctuates this point in its final sequence. As Nick Romano begins to move toward the electric chair, the familiar words, "THE END," appear on the screen but not in the formulaic way. They remain on the screen for an inordinately long time, about thirty seconds (or almost as long as it took *Call Northside 777* to represent Frank Wiecek's trial). Although the words certainly underscore, from Andrew Morton's perspective, the tragedy of Nick's impending death, they also, from the absent Judge Drake's vantage point, remind viewers of the power of legal discourse.

In this sense, the themes and style of *Knock on Any Door*—with their emphasis on the force, as opposed to the fallibility, of law—become powerfully inscribed within the postwar *law noir* subcycle. Themes that appear most strongly at the end of *Knock on Any Door* run throughout a number of other *law noirs*, especially those that, ironically borrowing from *Call Northside 777*'s documentary approach, focus upon the routines and processes of law enforcement.[34]

Law noirs rarely represent the law as a benevolent, progressive social force. In this sense, *Call Northside 777* and *Knock on Any Door* offer complementary representations. But as *Knock on Any Door* suggests, *law noirs* increasingly come to represent the legal system as an essential, if flawed, bulwark against the social and cultural disorder that dominates the larger body of noir films. Indeed, the very fact that popular discourses seem unable to acclaim the legal process may ironically suggest the necessity, especially in the dark and dangerous world that noir itself constructs, for a legal order that, if nothing else, operates with brute power and ruthless efficiency.[35]

Notes

A number of people have responded, most helpfully, to earlier versions of this essay: participants in the Legal Culture Section of the American Culture Association, particularly David Papke, John Denvir, Paul Hayden, and Chris Rideout; my colleagues at Macalester, particularly Leslie Vaughan, Linda Schulte-Sasse, Clay Steinman, and Emily Rosenberg; Lary May of the University of Minnesota; and two anonymous reviewers for the University of Illinois Press.

1. Even two writers who seem to disagree about almost everything else, for example, seem to concur in the importance of focusing upon *how* legal discourses are constructed. See the "Colloquy" in *Georgetown Law Review* (1992): 251–350, which includes Mark Tushnet, "The Degradation of Constitutional Discourse," Gary Peller, "The Discourse of Constitutional Degradation," and Tushnet, "Reply."

2. As David Bordwell notes, it is almost unthinkable for a contemporary piece of film scholarship to ignore issues of "film language." David Bordwell, *Making Meaning: Inference and Rhetoric in the Interpretation of Cinema* (Cambridge: Harvard University Press, 1989), 107. See also David Bordwell and Kristin Thompson, *Film Art: An Introduction,* 4th ed. (New York: McGraw-Hill, 1993), passim.

3. Robert Ray, *A Certain Tendency in the Hollywood Cinema, 1930–1980* (Princeton: Princeton University Press, 1985), passim.

4. For treatments of these issues in film scholarship, see Edward Branigan, *Narrative Comprehension and Film* (New York: Routledge, 1992), and Robert Stam, Robert Burgoyne, and Sandy Flitterman-Lewis, *New Vocabularies in Film Semiotics* (New York: Routledge, 1992). Although there are many recent explorations of the role of narrative in legal texts, Clark Cunningham, "The Lawyer as Translator, Representation as Text: Towards an Ethnography of Legal Discourse," *Cornell Law Review* 77 (1992): 1298–1387, provides an excellent, critical perspective. See also Peter Charles Hoffer, "Text, Translation, Context, Conversation, Preliminary Notes for Decoding the Deliberations of the Advisory Committee that Wrote the Federal Rules of Procedure," *American Journal of Legal History* 37 (1993): 409–39.

5. J. P. Telotte, "Book Review," *Film Quarterly* 46 (1992): 39–40, 40.

6. After 1934, Hollywood films that dealt with legal themes had to negotiate the industry's Production Code. One of the Code's three "General Principles" decreed that "Law, natural or human, shall not be ridiculed, nor shall sympathy be created for its violation." "Appendix" to Ruth A. Inglis, *Freedom of the Movies: A Report on Self-Regulation from the Commission on Freedom of the Press* (Chicago: University of Chicago Press, 1947), 205. For an important set of revisionist essays on the operation of the Production Code see the symposium entitled "Hollywood, Censorship, and American Culture," *American Quarterly* 44 (1992): 509–649. The wonderful phrase "things legal" comes from Karl Llewellyn, "Some Realism about Realism—Responding to Dean Pound," *Harvard Law Review* 44 (1931): 1222–56, 1222.

7. Michael Walker, "Robert Siodmak," in *The Book of Film Noir,* ed. Ian Cameron (New York: Continuum, 1993), 148.

8. In breaking down the larger film noir cycle into various subcycles, I follow, among others, Frank Krutnik, *In a Lonely Street: Film Noir, Genre, Masculinity* (New York: Routledge, 1992), and J. P. Telotte, *Voices in the Dark: The Narrative Patterns of Film Noir* (Urbana: University of Illinois Press, 1989).

9. See, for example, Warren Susman, with the assistance of Edward Griffin, "Did Success Spoil the United States? Dual Representations in Postwar America," in *Recasting America: Culture and Politics in the Age of the Cold War,* ed. Lary May (Chicago: University of Chicago Press, 1989), 29–30.

10. There is a vast literature on film noir but very little agreement on how even to map, let alone to interpret, this group of films. Some students of noir take a very narrow approach, including only films produced between 1941 (beginning with *The Maltese Falcon*) and 1958 (ending with *Touch of Evil*). Michael Walker, "Film Noir: Introduction," in *The Book of Film Noir,* ed. Ian Cameron (New York: Continuum, 1993), 8. Although the two *law noirs* highlighted in this essay fall within the traditional periodization, I prefer to take a broader view by including films made during the 1930s within the territory marked by the term *noir.* See Marc Vernet, *"Film Noir* on the Edge of Doom," in *Shades of Noir,* ed. Joan Copjec (London: Verso, 1993), 2–4. See also Norman Rosenberg, "Hollywood on Trials," *Law and History Review* 12 (1994): 341–67.

11. The gangster genre has long provided important representations of both lawlessness and the legal system. See, for example, David Ray Papke, "Myth and Meaning: Francis Ford Coppola and Popular Response to the Godfather Trilogy," in this volume.

12. On *Mouthpiece* and the larger "shyster" genre, see Andrew Bergman, *We're in the Money: Depression America and Its Films* (New York: Harper & Row, 1971), 23–29, and Roger Dooley, *From Scarface to Scarlett: American Films in the 1930s* (New York: Harcourt, Brace, Jovanovich, 1981), 310–27.

13. Brian Neve, *Film and Politics in America: A Social Tradition* (New York: Routledge, 1992), 18–20, 133–36; Charles W. Eckert, "The Anatomy of a Proletarian Film: Warner's *Marked Woman,"* in *Imitations of Life: A Reader on Film and Television Melodrama,* ed. Marcia Landy (Detroit: Wayne State University Press, 1991), 205–26; and Mary Beth Haralovich, "The Proletarian Woman's Film of the 1930s: Contending with Censorship and Entertainment," *Screen* 31 (1990): 172–87.

14. *Stranger on the Third Floor* and *Fury* were directed by filmmakers Boris Ingster and Fritz Lang, who had worked in Germany and fled Nazism for the United States. If one were to focus more intensively upon the directors of these films, it might be possible to link the representations about law and "mob behavior" to anti-fascist discourses of the late 1920s and 1930s. See generally Norman L. Rosenberg, "Another History of Free Speech: The 1930s and the 1940s," *Law and Inequality* 7 (1989): 333–66.

15. Walker, "Film Noir," 8, 27.

16. In this sense, *Stranger* is one of the noirs in which a woman assumes the role usually reserved for men, "the position of the investigator who 'seeks to restore order.'" See Elizabeth Cowie, *"Film Noir* and Women," in *Shade of Noir,* ed. Copjec, 133–34.

17. Although I can agree with Francis Nevins's point, that lawyers "admitted to the bar of Cloud Cuckoo Land" seem to have advised the studio on legal matters, I reject the suggestion that faithfulness to "proper" procedures—or any other measure of verisimilitude—is the only relevant standard for the use of films in legal writing. See Francis M. Nevins, "Through the Great Depression on Horseback: Legal Themes in Western Films of the 1930s," in this volume. I offer an extended analysis of *Fury* in "Hollywood on Trials."

18. In this sense, both *Fury* and *Stranger on the Third Floor* fit the dominant Hollywood pattern in which the creation of a heterosexual couple is either the main or a secondary plot. See Virginia Wright Wexman, *Creating the Couple: Love, Marriage, and Hollywood Performance* (Princeton: Princeton University Press, 1993), 3.

19. Robert Cover, "Violence and the Word," *Yale Law Journal* 95 (1986): 1601–29.

20. On this point, see Milner S. Ball, "Obligation: Not to the Law but to the Neighbor," *Georgia Law Review* 18 (1984): 911, esp. 925–27.

21. Michael Walker argues that this "authoritative 'voice of God'" narration means that *Call Northside* represents a "shift away from the radicalism of *film noir*" to the semi-documentary style introduced by Louis de Rochemonent, who had earlier produced newsreels for *The March of Time*. Walker, "Film Noir," 37. In contrast to Walker, I not only follow other students of noir, such as J. P. Telotte (*Voices in the Dark,* 145–52, passim), in locating *Call Northside* within the domain of noir but also argue that the film offers a more "radical" view of law than a later film, firmly within the noir canon, *Knock on Any Door.* Indeed, Walker himself acknowledges that *Call Northside* may been see as "a hybrid," with a number of themes and cinematic sequences strongly identified with noir ("Film Noir," 37–38).

22. Both of these filmic sequences articulate the view, elaborated in the recent "law and society" literature, that "legal" positions are constituted in a variety of non-official settings, such as a lawyer's office, and not just before official tribunals. See, for example, Austin Sarat and William L. F. Felstiner, "Law and Strategy in the Divorce Lawyer's Office," *Law and Society Review* 20 (1986): 93–134.

23. On the difficulty of achieving narrative closure in other films of the 1940s, see Dana Polan, *Power and Paranoia: History, Narrative, and the American Cinema, 1940–1950* (New York: Columbia University Press, 1986), 21–43.

24. This sequence carries out the basic noir idea about the role of fate and chance, for McNeal learns of the newspaper story when his cab driver casually hands him that morning's paper. In addition, of course, this device further underscores the crucial role of private, as opposed public, legal actors in the Wiecek case.

25. For a perceptive analysis of *Talk of the Town,* see Robert Post, "On the Popular Image of the Lawyer: Reflections in a Dark Glass," *California Law Review* 75 (1987): 379–89.

26. Initially, the film was to be framed by courtroom sequences, in which Morse was to testify about the corruption spreading through law and politics in New York City. After at least several scenes were shot, this framing device was dropped, a decision that made the possibility for legal redress seem very remote.

27. Although Alain Silver and Elizabeth Ward's encyclopedic *Film Noir,* rev. ed. (Woodstock, N.Y.: Overlook Press, 1988), 105, credits Arthur O'Connell with playing "Link Hall," any scenes with the DA were cut from the final print. As a result, this symbol of lawful authority becomes an almost menacing figure, perhaps even a stand-in for the headline-hunting red-baiters who were soon to ensnare Polonsky, Garfield, and other Hollywood "progressives." See, for example, the director Abraham Polonsky's own reading in *The Director's Event: Interviews with Five American Film-Makers,* ed. Eric Sherman and Martin Rubin (New York: Signet, 1972), 11–45, esp. 21.

28. See Norman L. Rosenberg, "The 'Popular First Amendment' and Classical Hollywood, 1930–1960: *Film Noir* and 'Speech Theory for the Millions,'" in *Freeing the First Amendment: Critical Perspectives on Freedom of Expression,* ed. David S. Allen and Robert Jensen (New York: New York University Press, 1995), 143–68. My estimation of the importance of *The File of Thelma Jordan* is bolstered by Michael Walker's recent essay, "Robert Siodmak," in *The Book of Film Noir,* 145–51.

29. The same point is made in the more recent courtroom drama, *A Few Good Men* (1993).

30. Telotte, *Voices in the Dark,* 149.

31. In 1947 the *Times* was merged into the present-day Chicago *Sun-Times.* And, at a more metaphorical level, the majesty of the gunfighter hero, to which McNeal's reporter-hero is indebted, will slowly fade away as well. See, for example, Ray, *A Certain Tendency,* 215–43.

32. This theme—the ambiguity of visual imagery as an accurate re-presentation of "reality"—becomes a staple of many films from the 1960s and 1970s, especially *Blow-Up* (1968) and the fascinating neo-noir, *Night Moves* (1975). For a suggestive reading of *Beyond a Reasonable Doubt,* see Douglas Pye, "Film Noir and Suppressive Narrative: *Beyond a Reasonable Doubt,*" in *The Book of Film Noir,* ed. Walker, 98–109.

33. See, for example, Republic's infamous (and unintentionally) hilarious paean to red-baiting, *Red Menace* (1949).

34. *He Walked by Night* (1949), for example, blends the approaches of *Call Northside 777* and *Knock on Any Door* in order to lionize an almost faceless law enforcement bureaucracy as it pursues a brilliant, charismatic, but de-

ranged cop-killer through the noirishly realized backdrop of postwar Los Angeles. Although the film ascribes greater emotional depth and (flawed) humanity to the killer than to his police pursuers, the cinematic apparatus lines up fully behind the law. Much like *Knock on Any Door* seeks to align its audience with Judge Drake, *He Walked By Night* tries to join spectators to the harsh, yet very necessary, search for a dangerous lawbreaker. For another good example, see *White Heat* (1949).

35. Again, this is the way I read films such as *He Walked by Night*.

Contributors

ANTHONY CHASE is a professor at the Nova University Law Center. Before entering academia, he worked as a journalist, art dealer, and bookseller. He has written several important articles on the relationship between law and popular culture, including "Towards a Legal Theory of Popular Culture" in the *Wisconsin Law Review.*

TOM CONLEY is a professor of Romance languages at Harvard University, where he teaches film and literary studies. He has written *Film Hieroglyphs* (1991) and *The Graphic Unconscious in Early Modern French Writing* (1992) and has translated Michel de Certau, *The Writing of History* (1992) and Gilles Deleuze, *The Fold: Liebniz and the Baroque* (1993). He is completing a study of cartographical writing in the French Renaissance.

JOHN DENVIR is a professor at the University of San Francisco School of Law. He has written several articles on the relationship between constitutional theory and the study of literature, including "William Shakespeare and the Jurisprudence of Comedy" in the *Stanford Law Review.* He also was the guest editor of a special issue of *Legal Studies Forum* on the interaction between legal theory and film, which included his essay "Frank Capra's First Amendment."

JUDITH GRANT is an associate professor in the Department of Political Science at the University of Southern California. She has written extensively on the relationship between gender and political theory. She also has written pioneering work on the depiction of politically charged issues in the popular media, including "Prime Time Crime: Television Portrayals of Law Enforcement" in the *Journal of Popular Culture.*

ANDREW J. MCKENNA is a professor in the Department of Modern Languages and Literatures at Loyola University in Chicago. He is author of *Violence and Difference: Girard, Derrida, and Reconstruction* (1992). He also contributed an essay to the *Legal Studies Forum* special issue on law and film.

MARTHA MINOW is a professor at Harvard Law School. She is the author of, among other works, *Making All the Difference: Inclusion, Exclusion, and American Law* (1990).

FRANCIS M. NEVINS is a professor at the St. Louis University Law School. Besides his work as a law professor, he has published several mystery novels and anthologies, and nonfiction works on mystery writing; he has received two Edgars from the Mystery Writers of America. He also has authored *The Films of Hopalong Cassidy* (1988).

DAVID RAY PAPKE is a professor at the University of Indiana Law School. He is the author of *Framing the Criminal: Crime, Cultural Work, and the Loss of Critical Perspective, 1830-1990* (1987) and editor of *Narrative and the Legal Discourse: A Reader in Storytelling and the Law* (1991). He is also editor of the *Legal Studies Forum*.

NORMAN ROSENBERG is DeWitt Wallace Professor of History at Macalester College. He is the author of *Protecting the "Best Men": An Interpretive History of the Law of Libel* (1986, 1990) and coauthor of *In Our Times* (5th ed., 1995). He also contributed the essay "*Young Mr. Lincoln*: The Lawyer as Super-Hero" to the *Legal Studies Forum* special issue on law and film.

MARGARET M. RUSSELL is associate professor of law at the Santa Clara University Law School. She has written extensively on law and racism, including "Entering Great America: Reflections on Race and the Convergence of Progressive Theory and Practice" in the *Hastings Law Review,* and also on racism in film in "Race and the Dominant Gaze: Narratives of Law and Inequality in Popular Film" in the *Legal Studies Forum* special issue on law and film.

CHEYNEY RYAN is a professor in the Department of Philosophy at the University of Oregon. He is the author of *The Possibility of Social Theory* (1990) and also has authored several plays. He was also nominated for an Obie award as contributing lyricist to "Best Foot Forward."

RICHARD K. SHERWIN is professor at New York Law School. He is a leader in the emerging "lawyering theory" movement and has published numerous articles in the fields of criminal procedure, jurisprudence, and the rhetoric of law, including "A Matter of Voice and Plot: Belief and Suspicion in Legal Storytelling" in the *Michigan Law Review.*

ELIZABETH V. SPELMAN is a professor in the philosophy department at Smith College. She is the author of *Inessential Woman: Problems of Exclusion in Feminist Thought* (1988).

MARK TUSHNET is associate dean and professor at the Georgetown University Law Center. One of the most influential writers in the Critical Legal Studies Movement (CLS), he is the author of several books, including *Red, White, and Blue: A Critical Analysis of Constitutional Law* (1988) and coauthor of the casebook on constitutional law most widely used in American law schools.

TERRY WILSON was formerly professor of Native American studies and ethnic studies at the University of California at Berkeley. He teaches courses in American Indian history as well as film classes dealing with images of race, gender, and ethnicity. He has received Berkeley's Distinguished Teaching Award. His publications include *The Underground Reservation: Osage Oil* (1985), *The Osage* (1988), and *Teaching American Indian History* (1993).

Index